Egon R[illegible]y's Guide 1996

Paris

BOOKMAN

Egon Ronay's Guides
35 Tadema Road
London SW10 0PZ

Editorial Director **Andrew Eliel**
Publishing Director **Angela Nicholson**
Listings Editor **Peter Long**

Chairman **Roy Ackerman**
Leading Guides Ltd
Part of the Richbell Group of Companies

The contents of this book are believed correct at the time of printing. Nevertheless, the publisher can accept no responsibility for errors or omissions or changes in the details given.

ISBN 1 898718 06 7

Designed and typeset in Great Britain by Paul Fry, Bookman Projects Ltd.
Printed in Italy.

First published 1996 by Bookman Projects Ltd.
Floor 22
1 Canada Square
Canary Wharf
London E14 5AP

Establishments are independently researched or inspected. Inspections are anonymous and carried out by Egon Ronay's Guides team of professional inspectors. They may reveal their identities at hotels in order to check all the rooms and other facilities. The Guide is independent in its editorial selection and does not accept advertising, payment or hospitality from listed establishments.

Egon Ronay's Guides Awards

This year's award winners are presented here. Full details of the recipients can be found on the pages indicated.

10 Hotel Bristol
Hotel of the Year

12 Carré des Feuillants
Restaurant of the Year

A Jug of
Fresh

Water

Your body loses around 1.5 litres of water every day.

Drinking 2 litres of fresh water each day not only replenishes this loss, but also helps keep the body in good health.

For a source of fresh drinking water with the highest standards of purity and good taste, look no further than the tap. Served chilled, tap water is a refreshing and re-vitalising drink. It is perfect for drinking at home, at work, and also when eating out.

Our drinking water is world class.

To ensure it is the best, our water is quality tested and analysed millions of times each year.

So next time you are eating out, ask for and enjoy a jug of fresh water - a perfect accompaniment to any meal.

WATER SERVICES ASSOCIATION

Introduction
by Andrew Eliel

Paris has recently had to exercise all her considerable charms in order to attract visitors, especially from the UK. The main culprit has been the miserable exchange rate, which, along with the increase in French VAT, has made eating out in Paris a much more expensive proposition.

Other negative factors – slower and slower traffic, faster and faster food, the spate of terrorist attacks – have been at work, and the search for the good things has had to be intensified. But those good things are still there in abundance – the colourful street markets, the vibrancy of the night life, the museums and galleries, the imposing churches, the handsome old buildings and the often startling new, the elegant shops, the beguiling cafés and, of course, the restaurants. The range and quality of serious eating in Paris is perhaps not now at its most impressive, and value for money is certainly harder to find than in provincial France, but there's still plenty to suit most pockets and tastes.

This Guide spans the possibilities in its 380+ restaurant entries. Read, and eat well.

EGON RONAY'S GUIDES 1996

How to use this Guide

Hotels (H) and Restaurants (R) are listed in alphabetical order within their arrondissements.

Hotel room prices are quoted per night for a double room with private facilities; prices will often vary considerably according to the season and the length of stay. Breakfast is not usually included in the price.

Restaurant meal prices are for two people - three courses à la carte, a modest bottle of wine, and coffee. We do not quote a meal price for a few, generally informal establishments such as wine bars. Prices on French menus are always inclusive of all taxes and service. Opening times and closures are liable to alteration, and it's always best to book.

The nearest Metro station (M^{O}) is shown for each hotel/restaurant.

Bear in mind that many restaurants are closed during August, when most Parisians take their holidays. Those open during August can be identified from the summary at the back of the book, as can restaurants with weekend opening and late opening. That summary also shows stars, meal prices and room rates.

A map of all Paris appears on pages 18-19, and general information plus major tourist attractions on the two pages before the map. Each arrondissement is preceded by a map of that arrondissement, with hotel and restaurant entries plotted by number. The map reference and number will be found by each entry. Opposite each map are listed major local places of interest with phone numbers and nearest Metros.

We award one, two or three stars for excellence of cooking. One star represents cooking much above average, two outstanding cooking, and three the best in Paris. A list of starred restaurants is on the next page.

The symbol denotes our particular favourite restaurants. These do not necessarily serve the best food, but they are certainly places we can thoroughly recommend as providing a real atmosphere and taste of Paris, whether a humble bistro or one of the grands tables. See list on page 9.

All establishments (239 hotels, 387 restaurants) are listed alphabetically in the index at the back of the book. A glossary of French menu terms starts on page 274.

To call Paris from the UK dial 00 33 1 then the 8-digit number printed. To call Paris from elsewhere in France, dial 16 1, then the 8-digit number (from 18 October 1996, 01 will replace 16 1).

Starred Restaurants

1st Arr

★★ Carré des Feuillants
★★ Gérard Besson
★★ Le Grand Véfour
★ Goumard-Prunier
★ Mercure Galant
★ Le Meurice
★ Ritz, L'Espadon

2nd Arr

★★ Drouant
★ Pile ou Face

4th Arr

★★ L'Ambroisie
★ Benoit
★ Le Bistrot du Dome

5th Arr

★★★ La Tour d'Argent
★ La Timonerie

6th Arr

★ Les Bookinistes
★ Le Chat Grippé
★ L'Epi Dupin
★ Hotel Lutétia, Le Paris
★ Relais Louis XIII

7th Arr

★★ Le Divellec
★★ Duquesnoy
★ L'Arpège
★ Le Bellecour
★ La Bourdonnais, La Cantine des Gourmets
★ La Ferme Saint-Simon
★ Jules Verne
★ Le Récamier

8th Arr

★★★ Taillevent
★★ Hotel de Crillon, Les Ambassadeurs
★ Lasserre
★ Laurent
★ Ledoyen
★ Le Bristol
★ Chiberta
★ George V, Les Princes Restaurant
★ Lucas Carton
★ La Marée
★ Vancouver
★ Hotel Vernet, Les Elysées du Vernet

9th Arr

★ La Table d'Anvers

11th Arr

★ A Sousceyrac

12th Arr

★ L'Oulette
★ Au Pressoir
★ La Sologne
★ Au Trou Gascon

14th Arr

★ La Cagouille

15th Arr

★ Morot-Gaudry
★ Le Relais de Sèvres

16th Arr

★★★ Faugeron
★★ Le Pré Catelan
★ La Butte Chaillot
★ Conti
★ Le Parc, Le Relais du Parc
★ La Petite Tour
★ Relais d'Auteuil
★ Le Toit de Passy
Vivarois

17th Arr

★★★ Guy Savoy
★★ Apicius
★★ Michel Rostang
★ Amphyclès
★ Faucher
★ Le Manoir de Paris
★ Le Méridien Etoile,
★ Le Clos Longchamp
★ Le Petit Colombier
★ Sormani

20th Arr

★ Les Allobroges

Around Paris

★ Trianon Palace, Les Trois Marches

Champagne List

Our personal favourites

1st Arr
L'Ami Léon
Carré des Feuillants
Gaya Rive Droite
Juveniles
Paolo Petrini
Pharamond

2nd Arr
Chez Georges
Les Noces de Jeanette
La Rotisserie Monsigny

3rd Arr
Bar à Huitres

4th Arr
Le Bistrot du Dome
A L'Impasse (Chez Robert)
Jo Goldenberg

5th Arr
Bar à Huitres

6th Arr
Les Bookinistes
Le Chat Grippé
L'Epi Dupin
Brasserie Lipp
Mariage Frères

7th Arr
Chez Françoise
Duquesnoy
Le Récamier

8th Arr
Ledoyen
Taillevent

9th Arr
Chartier
Le Royal Vignon

10th Arr
Aux Deux Canards
La Petite Tonkinoise
Terminus Nord

11th Arr
Astier
Le Villaret

12th Arr
L'Oulette
La Sologne

13th Arr
Le Petit Marguery

14th Arr
Bar à Huitres
Le Bistrot du Dome
La Coupole

15th Arr
La Farigoule
Le Gastroquet

16th Arr
La Butte Chaillot
Faugeron
Le Parc: Le Relais du Parc
Paul Chene
La Petite Tour
Brasserie de la Poste
Relais d'Auteuil
Brasserie Stella

17th Arr
Le Bistrot d'à Coté
Le Bistrot de l'Etoile
Chez Georges
Le Congrès Maillot
Goldenberg
Le Petit Colombier
Pétrus
Le Relais de Venise (L'Entrecote)
La Rotisserie d'Armaillé

18th Arr
La Galerie

20th Arr
Les Allobroges

Egon Ronay's Guides Paris Hotel of the Year

Le Bristol

112 rue du Faubourg St-Honoré 75008

Set among the exclusive shops of Rue du Faubourg St-Honoré, Le Bristol has been a haven of peace and tranquillity since the 1920s. Elegant public areas with Oriental rug-strewn marble floors and glittering chandeliers are matched by bedrooms that combine traditional furnishings and style with such modern comforts as air-conditioning and splendid white marble bathrooms. Levels of service appropriate to the luxurious surroundings add the finishing touch to a fine hotel.

EGON RONAY'S GUIDES 1996

Awards

PAST WINNER	
1995	**Ritz** 75001

Egon Ronay's Guides congratulate the

Paris Hotel of the Year 1996

LE BRISTOL

Egon Ronay's Guides Paris Restaurant of the Year

Carré des Feuillants

14 rue de Castiglione 75001

Firmly rooted in his native Gascony, Alain Dutournier's highly accomplished cooking has a real sense of place and enormous appeal that combines sophistication with a welcome lack of pretension. The setting is equally delightful, with three pearwood-panelled dining-rooms sporting specially commissioned foody pictures and Venetian glass chandeliers, off a glass-covered courtyard/reception lobby from which one can see in to the kitchen. Add smooth, professional service and an outstanding cellar (the actual cellars under the restaurant have just been opened up and now include a wine shop), and the result is a satisfyingly complete restaurant.

EGON RONAY'S GUIDES 1996

Awards

Past Winner	
1995	**Faugeron** 75116

Egon Ronay's Guides congratulate the

Paris Restaurant of the Year 1996

Carré des Feuillants

French Wines

by John Hoskins MW

Winner, Cellar(s) of the Year Award, Egon Ronay's Cellnet Guide 1996 Hotels & Restaurants

From a British angle, wines of the New World seem to have taken over. Of course, container-loads of French plonk are still consumed at every event where the label is not on view. And those with the cash will still drink the finest of the fine. But in the interesting middle ground, France seems to have had its day. Or so the journalists tell us.

In truth French wine is already making its come-back. Firstly because of the revolution in the Languedoc – an area previously famous only for its generous contribution to the EEC wine lake. In the last five years there has been a harnessing of the very technology and know-how that had earlier released the potential of sun-drenched areas elsewhere in the world. With a certain amount of New World marketing thrown in (chiefly in terms of labelling by grape variety) the Languedoc now finds itself able to compete hard in terms of both quality and value.

The French also like to reiterate the controversial argument that maturing palates eventually tire of sun-drenched flavours and seek instead a greater subtlety and discretion. Statistical evidence is not yet bearing this out, but it is a theme one often hears raised by the small but significant band of British wine buffs, the very readers of the journalism that is still so New World in spirit.

In France itself such arguments are of no relevance to anyone. Every pretentious restaurant does of course now have a token list of wines from around the world. There is even the odd serious city bar or bistro with a truly international selection. But these are the exceptions that prove the rule. Most French restaurants adhere strictly to the local diet. And what's wrong with that – when in Burgundy you probably want to eat Boeuf Bourguignon, and it's only natural to wash it down with Bourgogne Rouge.

Paris, while not being in the midst of a wine region, shows in its restaurants perhaps the most conservative taste of all. Grand addresses are chock full of expensive Burgundy and Claret. The lively brasseries, the heart of Parisian eating, remain firmly behind the Loire, Alsace and the Rhone.

Outside of Nantes and the north-western fishing towns, Muscadet sales have taken a world-wide dive. The thin, tart flavours that used to be the first choice for a palate attempting to sophisticate itself now represent the polar opposite of the easy-going, fruit-driven wine styles so beloved of a new generation of imbibers. Except in Paris. There you eat crustacea and drink Muscadet. And, on a summer lunchtime, the likely selection is a high-acid red Loire (a Gamay de Touraine or perhaps a Saumur Champigny) – the sort of wine the wine trade calls "difficult to understand".
And yet in Paris nobody's complaining. This is not only because the city's waiters are the world's most ferocious, but also because the very austerity of such wines is the right medicine for a stuffy city and a robust cuisine. Thirsts need instant quenching but after lunch you have to stagger out into the afternoon without blinking.

The Parisian introduction to these out-of-favour wines for a good number of the world's business leaders, and many of the world's tourists, will (with luck) help wine's fashion cycle to turn.

My own experience says that France in general, and Paris in particular, is not the place for the discovery of exciting new tastes. But for the re-discovery of forgotten classics, France remains inspirational.

Paris: General Information

Useful Telephone Numbers

To call Paris from the UK dial **00 33 1** then the 8-digit number. To call Paris from elsewhere in France dial 16 1 then the 8-digit number (from 18 October 1996 01 will replace 16 1). To call the UK from Paris, dial 19 44 then the number, ignoring the initial 0.

Central Tourist Information
127 ave des Champs Elysées 75008, **49 52 53 54**, M^{O} Etoile

France Information in the UK
0891 244123 (Mon-Fri 8.30am-9.30pm, Sat 9-5)

British Consulate
9 ave Hoche 75008, **42 66 38 10**

British Embassy, Commercial Section
35 rue du Faubourg St Honoré 75008, **42 66 91 42**

In An Emergency

Fire Brigade **18**
Police **17**
Ambulance **15**
Dental emergency **43 37 51 00**
24hr pharmacy, 84 ave des Champs Elysées, **45 62 02 41**
Anti-poison centre, **40 37 04 04**

Flight Information

Charles de Gaulle/Roissy **48 62 22 80**
Orly **49 75 15 15**
City Air Terminals information **44 08 24 24**

Rail Travel

Eurostar booking in UK **01233 617575**
French Railways Ltd, 179 Piccadilly, London W1 **0171-803 3030**
RATP information **43 46 14 14**
SNCF information **45 82 50 50**

Public Holidays

New Year's Day, Easter Monday, 1 & 8 May, Ascension Day, Whit Monday, 14 July, 15 August, 1 & 11 November, Christmas

Popular Annual Events 1996

SMT (Tourism & Travel Show) Paris – Porte de Versailles: 27 March-1 April
Paris Marathon 21 April
Foire de Paris 16 April-8 May
Tennis – French Open 27 May-9 June
Tour de France 6-28 July
Fair of Contemporary Art 1st two weeks July
Paris "Halle that Jazz" festival at La Villette 1st two weeks July
Bastille Day celebrated throughout France 14 July
Prix de l'Arc de Triomphe 6 October
International Boat Show 29 November-9 December

Paris: Major Locations

Listed by arrondissement

1	Tuileries, Louvre, Chatelet, Halles
2	Théatre des Variétés, Bibliothèque Nationale, Bourse, Sentier, Réaumur-Sébastopol
3	Temple, Arts et Métiers, Le Marais
4	Hotel de Ville, Centre Georges Pompidou, St-Paul, Place des Vosges, Bastille
5	Panthéon, Bd St Germain, Bd St-Michel, Jardin des Plantes
6	St-Germain-des-Prés, Odéon, Luxembourg, St-Michel
7	Invalides, Ecole Militaire, Sèvres-Babylone, Tour Eiffel, Champ de Mars
8	Etoile, Parc Monceau, Champs Elysées, Concorde, Madeleine, Gare St-Lazare
9	Pigalle, Opéra, Bd Haussmann
10	Gare du Nord, Gare de l'Est, Bd de Magenta
11	République, Bd Voltaire
12	Reuilly, Daumesnil, Gare de Lyon
13	Gare d'Austerlitz, Gobelins, Place d'Italie, Porte d'Ivry
14	Montparnasse, Raspail, Denfert Rochereau, Porte d'Orléans, Porte de Vanves
15	Gare Montparnasse, Bienvenue, Pasteur, Grenelle, Porte de Versailles, Convention, La Motte Picquet
16	Passy, Victor Hugo, Trocadéro, Auteuil, Porte de St-Cloud
17	Wagram, Ternes, Péreire, Ave de Villiers, Palais des Congrès, Porte de Clichy
18	Montmartre, Sacré Coeur, Porte de Clignancourt
19	Belleville, La Villette, Buttes-Chaumont
20	Père Lachaise Cemetery, Gambetta, Ménilmontant

Jump the queue

See the title page of each arrondissement for local places of interest. The best way to visit museums is with a *Carte Musée*, valid for 1, 3 or 5 days. Buy them at a museum or major metro station and jump the queue at 65 museums in and around Paris.

Books of tickets

For travelling in Paris by bus or train, you should equip yourself with a *carnet* of tickets, available from any Metro station (10 tickets for 44F).

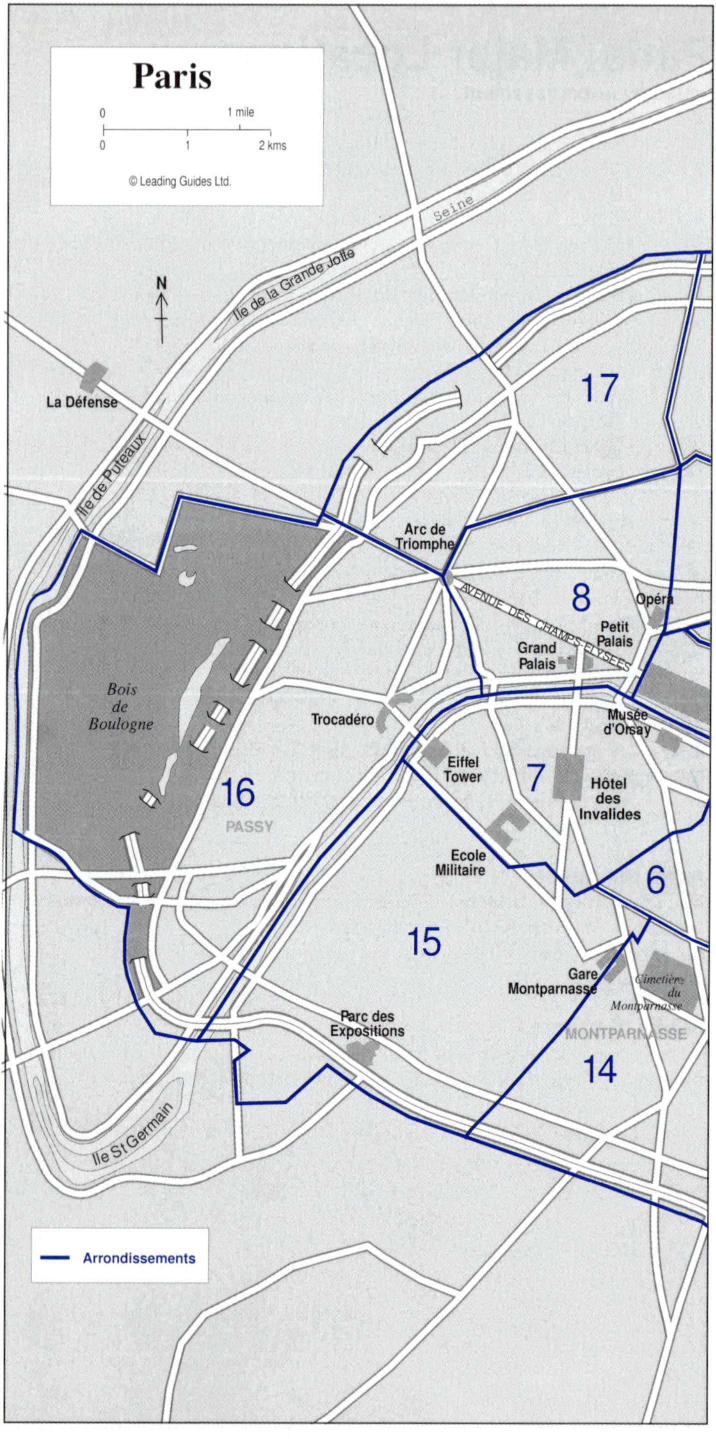
Paris
0
1 mile
0
1
2 kms
© Leading Guides Ltd.
Seine
Ile de la Grande Jatte
N
La Défense
Ile de Puteaux
17
Arc de Triomphe
8
Opéra
AVENUE DES CHAMPS-ELYSEES
Petit Palais
Grand Palais
Bois de Boulogne
Trocadéro
Musée d'Orsay
Eiffel Tower
7
Hôtel des Invalides
16
PASSY
Ecole Militaire
6
15
Gare Montparnasse
Cimetière du Montparnasse
Parc des Expositions
MONTPARNASSE
14
Ile St Germain
Arrondissements

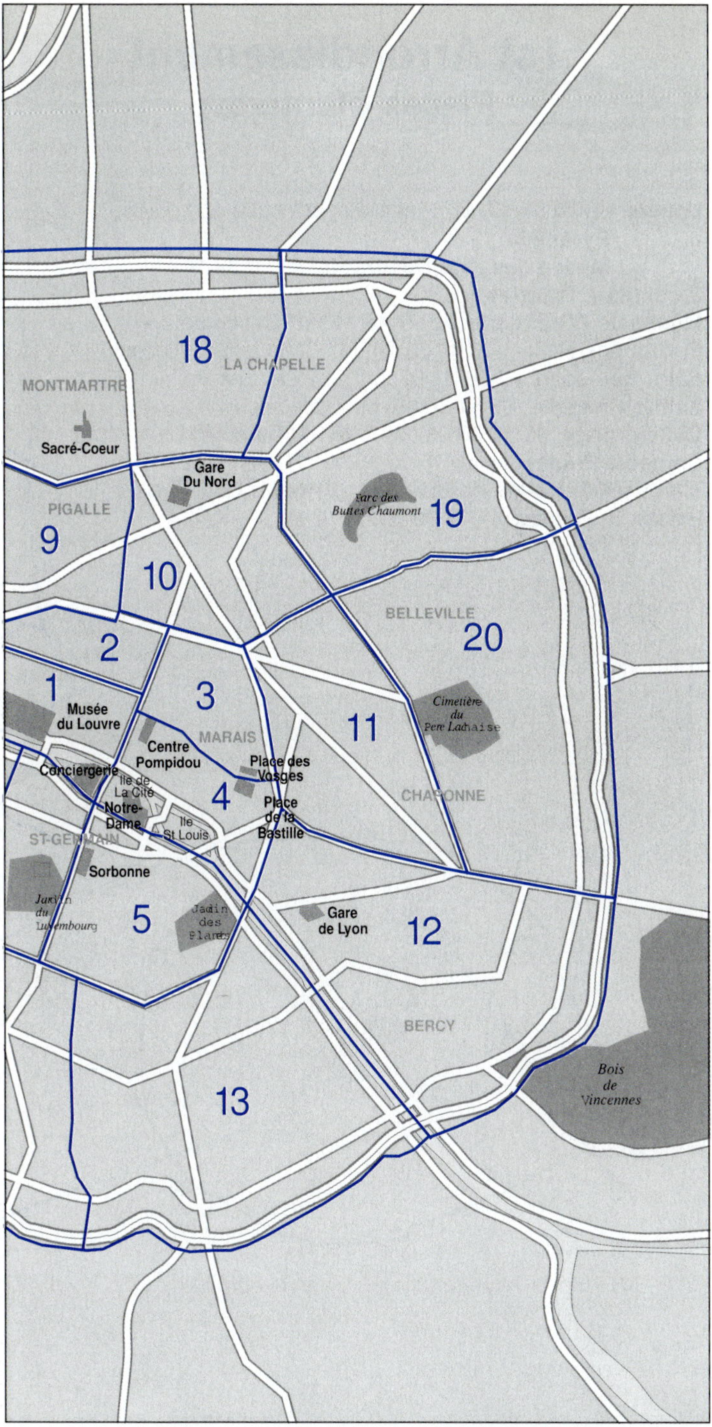
18
LA CHAPELLE
MONTMARTRE
Sacré-Coeur
Gare
Du Nord
Parc des
Buttes Chaumont
19
PIGALLE
9
10
BELLEVILLE
20
2
1
Musée
du Louvre
3
MARAIS
11
Cimetière
du
Pere Lachaise
Centre
Pompidou
Place des
Vosges
Conciergerie
Ile de
La Cité
4
CHARONNE
Notre-
Dame
Ile
St Louis
Place
de la
Bastille
ST-GERMAIN
Sorbonne
Jardin
du
Luxembourg
5
Jadin
des
Plantes
Gare
de Lyon
12
BERCY
Bois
de
Vincennes
13

1st Arrondissement

Places of Interest

Louvre, 40 20 53 17, M° Palais-Royal/Musée du Louvre
Pyramide
Musée des Arts Décoratifs, 42 60 32 14
Jardin des Tuileries
Musée de l'Orangerie, 42 97 48 16, M° Concorde
Forum des Halles, 40 39 38 74, M° Chatelet/Les Halles
Saint-Eustache, 42 36 31 05, M° Chatelet/Les Halles
Sainte-Chapelle, 43 54 30 09, M° Cité
Conciergerie, 43 54 30 06, M° Cité/St-Michel
Comédie Française, 40 15 00 15, M° Palais-Royal
Théatre Musical de Paris, 40 28 28 40, M° Chatelet
Palais de Justice, 44 32 50 00, M° Cité

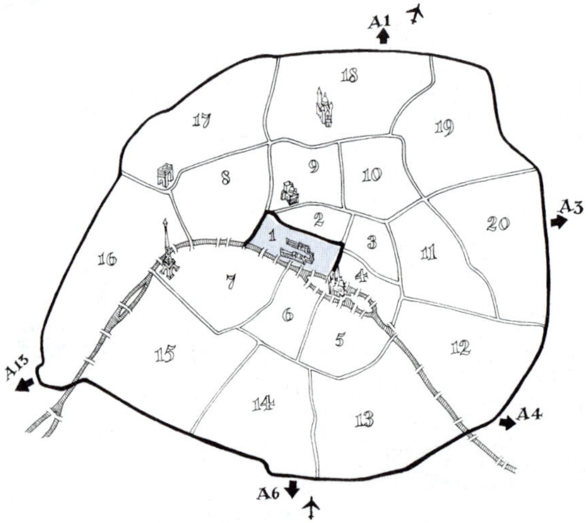

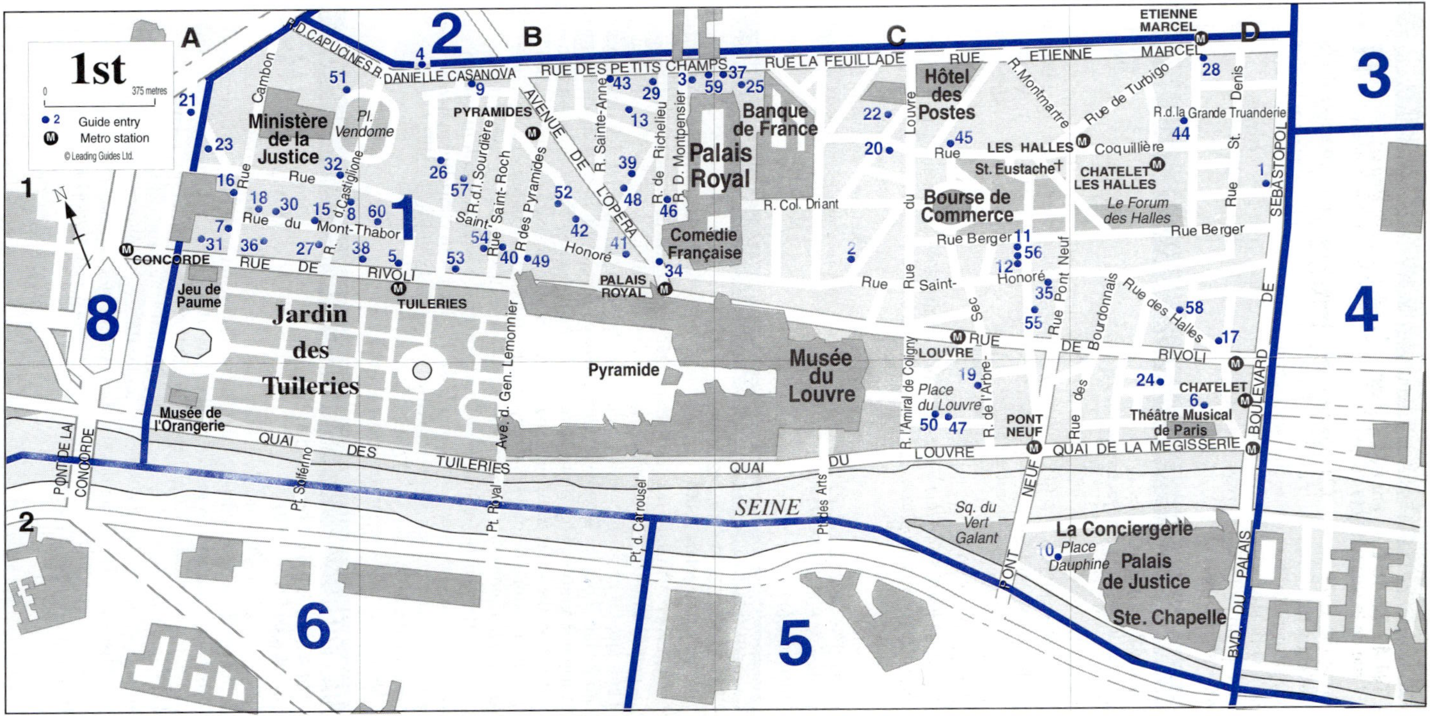
1st
0 375 metres
2 Guide entry
Metro station
© Leading Guides Ltd.
A
B
C
D
1
2
3
4
5
6
8
Ministère de la Justice
Pl. Vendome
Palais Royal
Banque de France
Comédie Française
Hôtel des Postes
Bourse de Commerce
St. Eustache
Le Forum des Halles
Jardin des Tuileries
Jeu de Paume
Musée de l'Orangerie
Pyramide
Musée du Louvre
Place du Louvre
Sq. du Vert Galant
La Conciergerie
Place Dauphine
Palais de Justice
Ste. Chapelle
Théâtre Musical de Paris
SEINE
CONCORDE
TUILERIES
PYRAMIDES
PALAIS ROYAL
LOUVRE
PONT NEUF
CHATELET
CHATELET LES HALLES
LES HALLES
ETIENNE MARCEL
BD.CAPUCINES
R. DANIELLE CASANOVA
RUE DES PETITS CHAMPS
RUE LA FEUILLADE
RUE ETIENNE MARCEL
RUE DE RIVOLI
AVENUE DE L'OPERA
Rue Cambon
Rue du Mont-Thabor
R. d. Castiglione
R.d.l.Sourdière
Rue Saint-Roch
R des Pyramides
R. Sainte-Anne
R. de Richelieu
R. D. Montpensier
R. Col. Driant
Rue du Louvre
R.Montmartre
Rue de Turbigo
Coquillière
R.d.la Grande Truanderie
Rue St. Denis
Rue Berger
Rue Saint-Honoré
Rue Pont Neuf
Rue des Bourdonnais
Rue des Halles
Rue Sec
R. de l'Arbre-Sec
R. l'Amiral de Coligny
Rue des
Ave. d. Gen. Lemonnier
QUAI DES TUILERIES
QUAI DU LOUVRE
QUAI DE LA MEGISSERIE
BOULEVARD DE SEBASTOPOL
BVD. DU PALAIS
PONT DE LA CONCORDE
Pt. Solférino
Pt. Royal
Pt. d. Carrousel
Pt des Arts
PONT NEUF

AGORA 500F

Tel 42 33 46 02 **Fax 42 33 80 99**
7 rue de la Cossonnerie 75001
Map D1.1
M° Les Halles
H

From the 1900 facade steps lead up to reception, where a welcome awaits from smiling staff. Bedrooms, mostly with shower and WC only (there's a 105F supplement for the five rooms with a bathtub), extend over five floors (there's a lift), with rooms on the top floor having the charm of sloping ceilings. Reception and room service operate 24 hours a day. ***Rooms*** *29. Amex, Mastercard, Visa.*

L'AMI LÉON 350F

Tel 42 33 06 20
11 rue Jean-Jacques Rousseau 75001
Map C1.2
M° Louvre
R

Tiny, old-fashioned restaurant with just half a dozen tables hidden away behind its heavy lace curtains. The eponymous Léon works single-handed in the kitchen while Madame does everything front of house. A short carte that changes with the seasons might include a duo of salmon *en rillettes*, parfait of chicken livers, pancake of red mullet with basil, half a pigeon stuffed with herbs and pine nuts, fillet of veal with a thyme crust and rump steak with paprika and tarragon. For afters there's *nougat glacé,* charlotte, gratinated fruit and a seasonal fruit tart. The *prix-fixe*, with three choices at each stage, is excellent value for money. Short selection of French bottles plus a Cote de Ventoux by the 25cl *pichet*. Set menu 97F. ***Seats*** *20. L 12-2 D 8-10.* ***Closed*** *L Sat, all Sun, 1 week May, 14 Jul-15 Aug & Public Holidays.*
Mastercard, Visa.

ARMAND AU PALAIS-ROYAL 700F

Tel 42 60 05 11 **Fax 42 96 16 24**
6 rue de Beaujolais 75001
Map B1.3
M° Palais-Royal
R

Named after Armand's Jean du Plessis, Duc de Richelieu, the restaurant is located in an old stone-faced building looking at the back of the Palais-Royal. The setting is romantic, with candle-light, beamed ceilings and rich upholstery, and Bruno Roupie's intelligent, innovative cooking combines classic and modern in happy harmony. He admits to no speciality dishes but there is an emphasis on seafood on the short fixed-price menu: red mullet provençale, salmon grilled *unilatéral* (skin-side only) and served with two butters, ragout of langoustine and sole, *sauté d'agneau printanier au pistou*, roast Bresse chicken with a devilled sauce. Starters might include *crepe monsieur* (filled with foie gras in a sherry vinegar cream sauce) and a tartare of salmon. Delicious chocolate desserts. French wines span the regions and the price range. Set L 180F Set D 250F. No à la carte. ***Seats*** *40. L 12-2 D 8-11.30.*
Closed *L Sat, all Sun. Amex, Mastercard, Visa.*

BRIGHTON 600F

Tel 47 03 61 61 **Fax 42 60 41 78**
218 rue de Rivoli 75001
Map B1.5
M° Tuileries
H

Japanese-owned hotel in a 19th-century building with a prestigious position facing the Tuileries. Bedrooms are on five floors and both size and decor vary considerably. Largest rooms overlooking the Rivoli Gardens are on a grand scale, with lofty moulded ceilings, brass beds and handsome period furnishings. A couple of bathrooms boast spectacular mosaics – much in demand for magazine 'shoots'. At the top of the building, under the eaves, rooms are small but very charming. The Salon de Thé is a relaxing spot for a light snack. Room service till 7.30pm. Friendly, professional staff. ***Rooms*** *70. Amex, Diners, Mastercard, Visa.*

BRITANNIQUE 720F

Tel 42 33 74 59 **Fax 42 33 82 65** Map D2.6 **H**
20 ave Victoria 75001 Mº Chatelet/Les Halles

In a side street between Rue de Rivoli and the Seine, the Britannique is handily placed for tourists, being just a short walk from both the Ile de la Cité and the Louvre. Bedrooms are all of a similar standard, with direct-dial phones, mini-bars, safes, soundproofing and 10-channel TV. All have private bathrooms (a few with shower and WC only). Reading room and TV lounge but no restaurant other than the breakfast room. ***Rooms** 40. Amex, Diners, Mastercard, Visa.*

CAMBON 1480F

Tel 42 60 38 09 **Fax 42 60 30 59** Map A1.7 **H**
3 rue Cambon 75001 Mº Concorde

Concorde, the Tuileries Gardens, Madeleine and the Champs Elysées are all moments away from the Cambon, a privately owned hotel whose bedrooms all have double beds (the rate for single occupancy is 1080F) and a range of modern comforts from air-conditioning and mini-bar to room safe and cable TV. Bathrooms all have both tub and shower. No restaurant. ***Rooms** 42. Amex, Diners, Mastercard, Visa.*

CARRÉ DES FEUILLANTS ★★ 1300F

Tel 42 86 82 82 **Fax 42 86 07 71** Map A1.8 **R**
14 rue de Castiglione 75001 Mº Tuileries

The site of Alain Dutournier's restaurant, with its entrance hidden away under an arcade just off Rue de Rivoli, has a rich history - Marie de Médicis and Anne of Austria prayed here to be given sons and it was the setting for some of Robespierre's and Danton's revolutionary speeches. Today the little (now glass-covered) courtyard with its old stone trough has gained a wrought-iron vine canopy with lights in the form of bunches of grapes (not nearly as naff as it sounds), and windows into the kitchen; it now acts as the reception area for three charming dining-rooms that feature pearwood panelling, specially commissioned foody pictures and splendid Venetian glass chandeliers. Green is the predominant colour, a deep hue for the carpet, paler for the waiters' jackets and also picked up in the pictures and on the china as it reminds Alain of his verdant and much-beloved South-West of France. It is Gascony that provides the inspiration for his cooking, too, in dishes that are sophisticated, but never 'precious', and always full of flavour. From a recent autumnal, six-course "Idées de la Saison" menu (the *dégustation* that for an extra 190F comes with four different glasses of wine to harmonise with the dishes) came a wonderfully moreish cream of hen pheasant and chestnut soup garnished with a sausage-like mousse of the breast, a warm cep paté with parsley sauce, *lievre à la royale, façon aquitaine* and a pistachio cream cake typical of the South-West. The à la carte, meanwhile, included a simple dish of crispy eel with seasonal herbs and a nougatine of sweet garlic and pepper, a fresh shellfish soup with special Gascony beans, roast red mullet with potatoes and an oyster dressing, sautéed Chalosse chicken with fresh foie gras and truffles, and a traditional stew from the South-West made with preserved goose, sausage, cabbage and white haricot beans from Tarbes. Cheeses are chosen, as is the whole menu, with a strong awareness of the season and there are desserts such as pear with spices and rosemary, chocolate leaves with bitter cherries, a crispy strudel with figs and nougat ice cream, and French toast with seasonal fruits macerated in old armagnac. The wine list is highly impressive, mostly French but with a few token offerings from elsewhere in the world, with all the great names present, often with several vintages to choose from. Prices are quite high but not unreasonable. There is also a short list of unusual wines – *"curiosités"* – served by the glass. As we went to press a multi-million-franc investment, which had enlarged the kitchen among other things, was nearing completion with the

See over

opening-up of the stone-vaulted cellar to create a wine shop by day and a venue for wine tastings and the taking of digestifs at night. Our Paris Restaurant of the Year for 1996. Set L 285F Set L&D 600F *(dégustation).* ***Seats*** *70. L 12-2.30 D 7.30-10.30.* ***Closed*** *L Sat, all Sun & Aug. Amex, Diners, Mastercard, Visa.*

LES CARTES POSTALES — 750F

Tel 42 61 02 93 Map B1.9 **R**
7 rue Gomboust 75001 Mº Pyramides

A changing collection of framed art-postcards down one wall explains the name of this little restaurant where the cooking is rather more ambitious than the decor. Yoshimasa Watanabe's menu includes dishes with an Oriental influence – marinated mackerel with Chinese herbs, brill half-cooked and half-raw in the Japanese fashion – along with the likes of croustade of pheasant and foie gras, red mullet fried in Provençal herbs with green peppercorn vinaigrette, and veal sweetbreads braised with wild mushrooms. Look out for a classic chocolate gateau among the desserts. Wines are exclusively French. Set L 135F Set L& D 285F & 350F. ***Seats*** *30. L 12-2 D 6.30-10.30.* ***Closed*** *L Sat, all Sun. Mastercard, Visa.*

LE CAVEAU DU PALAIS — 500F

Tel 43 26 04 28 **Fax 43 26 81 84** Map C2.10 **R**
17-19 place Dauphine 75001 Mº Pont-Neuf

On one of the prettiest squares in Paris, the house was built in 1604, and much of the original fabric remains. Cooking is traditional and competent: *moëlle de boeuf, salade de cervelle, blanquette de veau, coquilles St Jacques aux pates fraiches* – individual dishes vary according to the season. The owner has been here since 1972, and her son owns the next-door wine bar, where wines by the glass accompany sandwiches and snacks. Set menu 160F. ***Seats*** *60 (+ 30 outside). L 12.15-2.30 D 7.15-10.30.* ***Closed*** *Sat (Oct-May), Sun & 21 Dec-1 Jan. Amex, Mastercard, Visa.*

CHEZ CLOVIS — 450F

Tel & Fax 42 33 97 07 Map C1.11 **R**
33 rue Berger 75001 Mº Les Halles

Famous, traditional bistro by Les Halles, personally run by the same family for over 50 years. The unspoilt interior is full of black and white photographs of Les Halles in the old days when it was the main food market for Paris. The menu, which they describe as 'cuisine à l'ancienne', is full of specialities such as stuffed neck of duck, *blanquette de veau à l'ancienne*, foie gras of duck in aspic, *tete de veau sauce gribiche* and hot Lyonnais sausage with lentils. Unusually for a Parisian restaurant there are some 20 wines available by the glass (small or large). Set menu 89F. ***Seats*** *100 (+ 50 outside). L 12-3 D 7-12 (Fri & Sat till 1am).* ***Closed*** *Sun & 25 Dec. Amex, Mastercard, Visa.*

CHEZ ELLE — 450F

Tel 45 08 04 10 Map C1.12 **R**
7 rue des Prouvaires 75001 Mo Chatelet/Les Halles

Turn-of-the-century, black-and-white photographs of female nudes bedeck the walls of this unpretentious restaurant near Les Halles. The traditional menu does not change much, with *moules marinière* or *à la crème, escargots de Bourgogne* and *oeufs en meurette* among the starters, salmon *en papillote*, sole meunière, grilled fillet of beef, *magret* of duck and veal kidneys *grandmère* typifying the main dishes and familiar desserts such as crème brulée, chocolate mousse, floating islands and the tart of the day. One of the tables can accommodate up to 12 diners. Set D 95F. ***Seats*** *50 (+ 18 outside). L 12-2.30 D 7.30-11 (occasionally till midnight Thu & Fri).* ***Closed*** *L Sat, all Sun & Public Holidays. Amex, Visa.*

CHEZ PAULINE 840F

Tel 42 96 20 70 **Fax 49 27 99 89** Map B1.13 **R**
5 rue Villedo 75001 Mº Pyramides

Archetypal Parisian bistro – zinc bar, red banquettes, mirrored walls, moulded ceiling – on two floors with air-conditioning to the upstairs room. *Ris de veau en croute*, a warm salad of *tete de veau* with *sauce gribiche*, *jambon persillé*, roast Bresse chicken (for two) – the wings served with *gratin dauphinois* and the legs with salad – and *boeuf bourguignon* served with tagliatelle are all fixtures on chef-patron André Genin's carte, with other dishes changing fortnightly. Game is a speciality in season with *compote de lièvre royale* a particular favourite. Desserts include a dark chocolate gateau with *crème anglaise* and vanilla ice cream, *l'assiette pomme, pomme, pomme* (a selection of apple desserts) and crème brulée. Bordeaux and Beaujolais are the best represented regions on a mainly French wine list. Set menu 220F. ***Seats** 80. L 12.15-2.30 D 7.15-10.30. **Closed** Sat (except D Oct-Feb) & Sun. Amex, Diners, Mastercard, Visa.*

CHEZ ROSINE 400F

Tel 49 27 09 23 Map B1.60 **R**
12 rue de Mont-Thabor 75001 Mº Concorde/Tuileries

Rosine Ek has moved from Rue St Maur in the 11th to a new address, just up from Rue de Rivoli. The location has changed, but not the splendid cooking, using in the main traditional Cambodian recipes for fragrant soups, grilled seafood using rare roots and spices, and a *gateau maison* using jackfruit, coconut milk and palm fruit. Set menus 108F (L only), 148F & 198F. ***Seats** 45. L 12-2.30 D 7.30-11. **Closed** L Mon, all Sun, 1 May & 25 Dec. Amex, Mastercard, Visa.*

HOTEL DU CONTINENT 602F

Tel 42 60 75 32 **Fax 42 61 52 22** Map A1.15 **H**
30 rue du Mont-Thabor 75001 Mº Concorde

In the same group and offering basically the same facilities as the *Louvre St-Honoré* and the *Saint-Romain (qqv)*. This one is equally well situated, moments from the Tuileries and round the corner from Place Vendome, and offers similarly well-equipped bedrooms. There is a 60F supplement for the 16 rooms that have bathtubs in addition to the shower. No restaurant. ***Rooms** 28. Amex, Diners, Mastercard, Visa.*

DEMEURE HOTEL CASTILLE 1990F

Tel 44 58 44 58 **Fax 44 58 44 00** Map A1.16 **H**
37 rue Cambon 75001 Mº Madeleine

Rubbing shoulders with Chanel and the Ritz, the Castille is itself certainly not lacking in either style or luxury. Italian Renaissance-style decor features in the day rooms – 18th-century paintings, old engravings, rich damask fabrics, imported marble – and in most of the bedrooms, although 24 new rooms (they have just taken over the building next door) have a more traditionally French feel. All come with air-conditioning, three telephones per room, multi-channel TV and marble bathrooms that boast towelling robes, high-quality toiletries and separate WCs. A central courtyard, complete with fountain and murals, is overlooked by many of the bedrooms. 24-hour room service. Parking for ten cars. ***Rooms** 111. Amex, Diners, Mastercard, Visa.*

HOTEL DES DUCS D'ANJOU 592F

Tel 42 36 92 24 **Fax 42 36 16 63** Map D1.17 **H**
1 rue Ste-Opportune 75001 Mº Chatelet

Comfortable accommodation in a central location. Rooms are generally not all that large, the best pair being two on the top floor with mansard ceilings. Three cheaper rooms have shower only, with a shared WC along the corridor; the rest

See over

have either bath tub or shower (both with WC) but not both. A few rooms have mini-bars. No restaurant but the basement breakfast room is now air-conditioned. ***Rooms*** *38. Amex, Diners, Mastercard, Visa.*

DUMINY-VENDOME 870F

Tel 42 60 32 80 **Fax 42 96 07 83** Map A1.18 **H**
3 rue du Mont-Thabor 75001 Mº Tuileries

Built on the site of a convent, this is a hotel of charm just 5 minutes from the Louvre. Bedrooms are furnished variously with old pieces and modern, but all have marble bathrooms (just a few have shower and WC only) and the usual amenities. Next door to the hotel is the house where the poet Alfred de Musset lived. Breakfast is included in the room price. No restaurant. ***Rooms*** *79. Amex, Diners, Mastercard, Visa.*

FELLINI 550F

Tel 42 60 90 66 Map C2.19 **R**
47 rue de l'Arbre-Sec 75001 Mº Louvre

With exposed stone walls this is the more attractive of the two Fellinis (the other is in the 15th) and has an atmospheric stone-vaulted cellar for private parties of up to 25. Described as 'creative Italian cuisine', the menu nevertheless offers plenty of familiar-sounding dishes – *spaghetti alle vongole*, bruschetta with Parma ham and mozzarella, *scampi al forno*, tiramisu, zabaglione – along with the likes of carpaccio of tuna with olive oil and fennel, smoked bresaola on a bed of rocket, veal with pistachio, sea bass with herbs and giant prawns sautéed with artichokes. Classy Italian wine list with bottles from about 100F upwards. Set L 110F. ***Seats*** *40. L 12-3 D 7-11.30. Mastercard, Visa.*

LA FERMETTE DU SUD-OUEST 440F

Tel 42 36 73 55 Map C1.20 **R**
31 rue Coquillière 75001 Mº Palais-Royal/Louvre

Dating back to the 16th century, this unpretentious, welcoming restaurant features rough stone walls, old beams and the cooking of South-West France. Home-made *boudins* and terrines, *cochonailles, confit de canard* with ceps, cassoulet, *feuilleté à l'orange* and *tarte tatin* are all big on flavour and satisfaction level. A choice of just six wines – one each from Cahors, Buzet and Madiran plus three from Bordeaux – all served on a pay-for-what-you-drink basis. Set L 145F. ***Seats*** *35. L 12-2.30 D 7.30-10.30.* ***Closed*** *Sun & 1 week mid-Aug. Mastercard, Visa.*

GAYA RIVE DROITE 600F

Tel 42 60 43 03 **Fax 42 60 04 54** Map A1.21 **R**
17 rue Duphot 75001 Mº Madeleine

Sister restaurant to *Gaya Rive Gauche (qv)* on the Left Bank, and both are scions of *Goumard-Prunier (qv)* just down the street from this address. Describing itself as a 'Bistrot de la Mer', it has a menu which changes daily according to the market, offering wonderfully fresh, simply prepared fish dishes like fried monkfish with tartare sauce, grilled John Dory with tarragon and a peppery fish soup, all swiftly served by waiters in blue-bibbed aprons. On two bustling floors the decor features some fine ornamental blue and white tiling that dates from the turn of the century when this was a Portuguese bar – apparently serving only port wine. ***Seats*** *85. L 12-2.30 D 7-10.30.* ***Closed*** *Sun & 2 weeks Aug. Amex, Mastercard, Visa.*

The best way to get around Paris is by bus or metro –
buy a book (carnet) of tickets at any metro station and save money

Gérard Besson ★★ 1200F

Tel 42 33 14 74 **Fax 42 33 85 71** Map C1.22
5 rue Coq-Héron 75001 M° Les Halles/Palais-Royal **R**

Silver carafes in display cases, old paintings and immaculate settings at well-spaced tables are all part of the elegant scenery, but it's Gérard Besson's superb cooking which takes centre stage at this outstanding restaurant in the old Les Halles area. The marriage of traditional cuisine with innovative flair delights in dishes like hot foie gras tartlet with a truffle coulis; Brittany lobster on a bed of artichoke, mushroom and fennel; roast zander with turnip and anchovy confits; veal sweetbreads meunière with champagne sauce, and Bresse chicken cooked with a gratin of macaroni and foie gras and a classical *sauce albuféra.* Desserts are equally tempting with such creations as a white-cheese bavarois with melon balls and crushed black peppercorns, and a fresh fruit cocktail with almond milk and zest of lime. Classy French wine list with just a handful of foreign interlopers. Set L 260F Set L&D 480F & 780F (*dégustation*) ***Seats*** *40. L 12-2.30 D 7.15-10.30.* ***Closed*** *L Sat, all Sun. Amex, Diners, Mastercard, Visa.*

Goumard-Prunier ★ 1350F

Tel 42 60 36 07 **Fax 42 60 04 54** Map A1.23
9 rue Duphot 75001 M° Madeleine **R**

For well over 100 years the name of this most famous of seafood restaurants was simply 'Prunier'. The prefix arrived in 1992 along with Jean-Claude Goumard, who effectively saved the restaurant and who, with chef Georges Landriot, continues to enhance its reputation. Jean-Claude's early-morning trips to Rungis market ensure that only the best and freshest of seafood arrives in the kitchen, where George's light, modern touch makes the very best of it. Specialities inlcude fish and saffron soup, *craquants de langoustines et salade d'herbes,* fricassee of mussels with girolles, *rougets de roche en bécasse* and line-caught bass grilled with artichokes and Indian peppers. ***Seats*** *100. L 12-2.30 D 7-10.30.* ***Closed*** *Sun (except Oct-Mar) & Mon. Amex, Diners, Mastercard, Visa.*

Grand Hotel de Champagne 640F

Tel 42 36 60 00 **Fax 45 08 43 33** Map D2.24
17 rue Jean-Lantier 75001 M° Chatelet/Les Halles **H**

The facade is simple enough, but inside, the hotel has been kept in 'Old Paris' style, with beams and exposed stonework in most bedrooms. Refurbished since last year, each room is different in detail and four have balconies where guests can enjoy one of the hotel's selling points – a gourmet breakfast buffet (55F) including charcuterie, cheese, patisserie, cereals, fruit tarts, fruit salad, etc. Prices range up to 800F for the largest rooms. No restaurant. ***Rooms*** *43. Amex, Diners, Mastercard, Visa.*

Le Grand Véfour ★★ 1400F

Tel 42 96 56 27 **Fax 42 86 80 71** Map C1.25
17 rue de Beaujolais 75001 M° Bourse **R**

The origins of this historic restaurant stretch back to 1784 when a café opened in a wing of the (then new) Palais Royal. The current owners, Taittinger, restored the ornate interior a few years ago and chef Guy Martin has established a top-class kitchen, producing classic gourmet cuisine. Frogs' legs with garlic, foie gras ravioli with creamed truffles and egg in a jelly of pepper, Sichuan pepper and caviar are typical summer starters on his seasonal carte. Main dishes are also stunning yet relatively simple: *rouget barbet cuit entier, jus avec son foie* (whole red mullet served with a jus of its own liver), *parmentier* of oxtail with truffles, and *cote de veau de lait poelée aux cèpes* (milk-fed veal chops, pan-fried with ceps mushrooms). Chocolate is a feature of the dessert menu, as in the enigmatic-sounding *evanescence en noir et blanc* and the extraordinary *déclinaison sur la thème du chocolat au thé vert 'Fuji-Yama', au café d'Ethiopie, à la bière 'pur malt'*. If you have trouble making up your mind, the

See over

chef's choice of the day, the *menu plaisir*, can be sampled by your whole table. Set L 305F. ***Seats** 60. L 12.30-2.15 D 7.30-10.15. **Closed** Sat, Sun & Aug. Amex, Diners, Mastercard, Visa.*

A LA GRILLE SAINT-HONORÉ 550F

Tel 42 61 00 93 **Fax 47 03 31 64** Map B1.26 **R**
15 place du Marché St-Honoré 75001 Mº Tuileries

Chef-patron Jean Speyer is down at the markets each morning choosing only the best and freshest of produce for what is essentially a *cuisine d'auteur* at his intimate restaurant on the corner of the Place du Marché. There are both English and Japanese versions of the sensible-length *carte* that might include cassolette of lobster, prawns and asparagus tips; duck sausage with fresh figs; and *terrine de foie gras frais landais* among the starters and fricassee of lobster and langoustine with truffle juice, wild duck with honey and lime, and roast saddle of rabbit with girolles among the mains. Game is the speciality in season. Desserts range from *croquant de poire glace caramel* to thin slices of peach with its sorbet and *charlotte au chocolat crème anglaise.* Wine list majors on Bordeaux. Set menu 180F. ***Seats** 60 (+ 25 outside). L 12-2.30 D 7-10.30. **Closed** Sun, also Mon (except Oct-Dec) & 1st 3 weeks Aug. Amex, Diners, Mastercard, Visa.*

HOTEL INTER-CONTINENTAL 2900F

Tel 44 77 11 11 **Fax 44 77 14 60** Map A1.27 **HR**
3 rue Castiglione 75001 Mº Concorde/Tuileries

Situated off Place Vendome and facing the landscaped Tuileries Gardens, this extremely elegant hotel is a listed historic monument. Of the 450 air-conditioned rooms, 70 are spacious suites, and all offer the highest standards of luxurious accommodation. Eleven function rooms (max 900 for a banquet, 1200 for a theatre-style conference) – two with elaborate mouldings and painted ceilings, chandeliers and columns. ***Rooms** 450. Amex, Diners, Mastercard, Visa.*

Terrasse Fleurie 1200F

Tel 44 77 10 44

A stylish and attractive restaurant whose best feature is the glass-ceilinged and columned central courtyard which has been designed with a winter garden theme. Chef Raoul Gaïga serves modern French cuisine with dishes such as fillet of young mackerel served with a refreshing minty tabbouleh, finely sliced duck breast served with a pea salad, garlic broth and snail-filled ravioli and sole goujons prepared with grilled noodles as starters, followed by millefeuille of calf's sweetbreads with artichoke, beef casserole with chanterelles and onions or free-range cockerel in red wine. In the mornings they serve a splendid breakfast. Set menu 310F. ***Seats** 40 (+ 90 outside). L 12-2.30 D 7-10. **Closed** 25 Dec-1 Jan.*

JOE ALLEN 420F

Tel 42 36 70 13 **Fax 40 28 06 94** Map D1.28 **R**
30 rue Pierre Lescot 75001 Mº Etienne Marcel

Modelled on the New York original (there's another in London), the decor of exposed brick walls, bare-board floor and check table-cloths goes along with a brash, informal atmosphere. The menu, written in American with French sub-titles, ranges from Buffalo chicken wings with blue cheese dressing and fried eggplant with mozzarella cheese in tomato and basil sauce to T-bone steak, BBQ spare ribs with corn on the cob and baked potato, and tuna burger. Puds are as American as brownies and Nancy's apple pie. About a dozen different wines by the glass and even more beers. On Saturdays, Sundays and Public Holidays there is a special brunch menu in addition to the regular carte. ***Seats** 115 (+ 32 outside). **Meals** noon-1am. Amex, Mastercard, Visa.*

JUVENILES

Tel 42 97 46 49 **Fax 47 03 36 93**
47 rue de Richelieu 75001

Map B2.29
M° Palais-Royal/Bourse

R

Englishman Tim Johnston is a wine merchant, and sometime *vigneron*, rather than a restaurateur, but his cheerfully informal tapas bar gives customers an excellent excuse to sample his wines whilst enjoying a flavoursome nibble. The tapas range from grilled squid and Spanish tortilla with salsa verde to tapénade of aubergine, anchovy croutons and succulent roast quail. There are also *plats* such as steamed salmon with fennel and saffron, and grilled steak with tomatoes *provençale*. Cheeses include Montgomery Cheddar and Colston Basset Stilton or go for one of the puds: chocolate cake, apple crumble with vanilla ice cream, tiramisu. Wines, of which some 14 or so are available by the glass, major on Cotes du Rhone; sherry is also a speciality. Set menu (tapas for two) 138F (220F with wine). Willi's Wine Bar (*qv*) is in the same ownership. ***Open** 12-11 (12-3 & 7-11 Mon & Sat). **Closed** Sun. Mastercard, Visa.*

KINUGAWA 800F

Tel 42 60 65 07 **Fax 42 60 45 21**
9 rue Mont-Thabor 75001

Map A1.30
M° Tuileries

R

Bright Japanese restaurant with a menu that's strong on seafood: salmon eggs and sea urchins, steamed seafood flavoured with saké, a dozen varieties of sashimi including sea bream, tuna, squid and ormers as well as grilled shrimps and the day's choice grilled with a teriyaki sauce or prawn fritters. Meat-eaters weigh in with sliced beef and ginger, roast beef with ponzou sauce, cold roast duck, quail teriyaki and a sustaining pot-au-feu (shabu shabu). For special occasions try the Kaiseki (chef's recommendation) menus (510F, 560F, 580F & 700F). There's a sister restaurant of the same name in the 8th (4 rue Saint Philippe Tel 45 63 08 07) with the same hours and closures. Set L 245F. ***Seats** 80. L 12-2.30 D 7-10. **Closed** Sun & 2 weeks Christmas-New Year. Amex, Diners, Mastercard, Visa.*

LESCURE 300F

Tel 42 60 18 91 **Fax 40 15 91 27**
7 rue de Mondovi 75001

Map A1.31
M° Concorde

R

Traditional home cooking at very kind prices in a rustic, convivial restaurant that's been in the same family since 1919. The three-course *prix-fixe* (which includes wine or beer) never changes: chicken liver paté, mackerel fillets marinated in white wine, *boeuf bourguignon,* poached haddock, *poulet basquaise*, chicken croquettes provençale, crème caramel, peach compote. The carte changes every two weeks and might include cassoulet, seasonal game, poached turbot with a velouté sauce, wild boar in white wine, *sauté d'agneau, magret de canard* and vacherin of raspberries or strawberries. Speciality Cahors and Macon wines – you only pay for what you drink. No bookings. Set L & D 100F (inc wine). ***Seats** 40 (+ 28 outside). L 12-2.15 D 7-10.15. **Closed** D Sat, all Sun & Aug. Mastercard, Visa.*

LOTTI 2200F

Tel 42 60 37 34 **Fax 40 15 93 56**
7 rue Castiglione 75001

Map A1.32
M° Opéra/Tuileries/Concorde

H

Built around 1900 and opened as a hotel ten years later, the Lotti is now run by the Italian chain Jolly Hotels. Peace and comfort are keynotes, from the elegant reception area to bedrooms decorated in Louis XIV, XV and Empire styles. Top-floor rooms, with sloping ceilings, are reserved for non-smokers. All rooms feature multi-channel TV, radio, direct-dial phone, mini-bar, safe, air-conditioning and soundproofing. Valet parking. ***Rooms** 133. Amex, Diners, Mastercard, Visa.*

HOTEL DU LOUVRE 1350F

Tel 44 58 38 38 Fax 44 58 38 01 Map B1.34 **H**
place André Malraux 75001 Mº Palais-Royal

Between the Louvre and the Palais-Royal stands this handsome hotel whose accommodation, extending over 5 floors, includes 16 junior suites and 4 full suites. Bedroom size and decor vary – some art deco, some in quiet pastels – but all are well appointed with multi-channel TV and individual air-conditioning to keep things comfortable. Service extends to 24-hour room service and an efficient concierge. ***Rooms** 200. Amex, Diners, Mastercard, Visa.*

LOUVRE SAINT-HONORÉ 762F

Tel 42 96 23 23 Fax 42 96 21 61 Map C1.35 **H**
141 rue St-Honoré 75001 Mº Louvre

Two period buildings, one of eight storeys, the other of seven, are divided by a glass pyramid covering a courtyard – the setting for a relaxed breakfast. Some of the modern bedrooms overlook this courtyard, others the road; all come with mini-bar, safe, cable TV and hairdryer and it was planned to install tea and coffee-making facilities by the end of 1995. There are some larger rooms at 862F. The hotel, just a few steps from the Louvre, is part of Hotels les Beaux Logis de Paris, also responsible for *l'Hotel du Continent* and *Hotel St-Romain* (see entries). No restaurant. ***Rooms** 40. Amex, Diners, Mastercard, Visa.*

MAYFAIR 1100F

Tel 42 60 38 14 Fax 40 15 04 78 Map A1.36 **H**
3 rue Rouget-de-Lisle 75001 Mº Concorde

Just off Rue de Rivoli (and, like that renowned thoroughfare, dating from 1880), there's an elegant feel to public areas that comprise a lobby-cum-lounge with ornate gilt light fittings, and a cosy wood-panelled bar with tapestry panels where breakfast is also served; there is no restaurant. Bedrooms, though mostly not large, are stylishly decorated and offer all sorts of comforts from mini-bar and room safe to multi-channel TV and good bathrooms, all with showers over tubs. Most rooms are air-conditioned. Room service till 9pm. No parking of their own but the hotel can reserve spaces in a nearby garage. The street is named after the composer of the *Marseillaise*. ***Rooms** 53. Amex, Diners, Mastercard, Visa.*

MERCURE GALANT ★ 1100F

Tel 42 96 98 89 Fax 42 96 08 89 Map C1.37 **R**
15 rue des Petits Champs 75001 Mº Pyramides

The restaurant takes its name from a famous magazine, founded nearby in 1676; among other things, the journal gave the addresses of good restaurants and, were it still being printed, Pierre Ferranti's 19th-century restaurant near the Palais-Royal would surely be listed among them. Classic cooking in tranquil comfort is the order of the day with dishes such as a terrine of duck, foie gras and sweetbreads; lobster salad with fresh peaches; *feuilleté* of fresh snails with mushrooms; fillets of sole with artichoke and celery 'crisps'; steamed turbot with seaweed and young vegetables; *chausson de veau en crépinette au risotto de morilles*; calf's liver with sherry vinegar and buttered cabbage, and fillet of Charolais beef with bone marrow *en papillote* among the offerings. Desserts might include *nougat glacé* with pistachio nuts and morello cherries, *fondant au chocolat* with almonds and raisins, *soufflé glacé* Grand Marnier and *mille et une feuilles du Mercure*. The wine list is strong in Bordeaux. Set L 210F Set D 280F & 400F. ***Seats** 80. L 12.15-2.30 D 7.15-10.30. **Closed** L Sat, all Sun & Public Holidays. Amex, Mastercard, Visa.*

MEURICE 3500F

Tel 44 58 10 10 Fax 44 58 10 17 Map A1.38 **HR**
228 rue de Rivoli 75001 Mº Tuileries

Dating from the time when Préfect Haussmann was replanning Paris, the Meurice, with its location overlooking the Tuileries Gardens, quickly established itself as a favourite of the Imperial Court. More recently it has become a haunt of the literati with the jury of a new literary prize 'Le Jury Du Prix Novembre' making their home here. Following the hotel's acquisition by the Ciga group in 1988 considerable refurbishment has returned the sparkle to the stunning Salon Pompadour with its elaborate gilt decoration, and other public rooms and restored the hotel's position amongst the best in Paris. Antique furniture, fresh flowers, original paintings and the occasional marble fireplace are among the elements that bring individuality and luxury to the bedrooms and the 37 suites. Bathrooms are marble and standards of service high. ***Rooms** 180. Amex, Diners, Mastercard, Visa.*

Le Meurice ★ 1100F

Marc Marchand's menu changes with the seasons in this exquisitely appointed restaurant, but on Wednesdays you might get all four seasons at once, as Vivaldi is often included in the musical 'saveurs lyriques' evenings. Cannelloni of lobster in a Jura wine-flavoured stock, terrine of eel with blinis and Sevruga caviar, fillet of whiting with a lemon butter and asparagus sauce, calf's liver with aged vinegar, roast goose, fillet of lamb with prunes, preserved lemons and oriental spices, and *filet mignon* poached in consommé with vegetables from the *pot-au-feu* are typical choices. Palette of chocolate tastes and mandarin soufflé with a cocoa-flavoured iced cream is a speciality dessert. Set L 330F Set D (inclusive of wine) 410F. ***Seats** 60. L 12.15-2.30 D 7.30-10.30.*

Molière 592F

Tel 42 96 22 01 **Fax 42 60 48 68** Map B1.39 **H**
21 rue Molière 75001 M° Palais-Royal/Pyramides

Handily situated for many of the major Parisian sights, this is a small hotel of charm and character, with particularly pleasant staff and a reservation book that's generally filled with regulars. It's typically 19th-century in appearance, and the bedrooms, spread over seven floors and ranging in style from Louis XV to 1930s, look out on to either a little flowery courtyard or the small street. Top-floor rooms have sloping ceilings, some rooms have balconies and all are sound-proofed and have room safes: cable TV includes English channels. 11 of the rooms have shower and WC only (doubles with bathtub are 650F and twins with bath 720F). Singles are 470F. No restaurant. ***Rooms** 32. Amex, Diners, Mastercard, Visa.*

Montana-Tuileries 580F

Tel 42 60 35 10 **Fax 42 61 12 28** Map B1.40 **H**
12 rue St-Roch 75001 M° Tuileries

The building dates from 1800 and became a hotel in 1945. Bedrooms are individual in their detail, with generally simple modern furnishings and the expected modern comforts. Just three rooms with shower and WC only are 580F, the remainder, with bathtubs, are 780F. Rooms on the fifth floor have little balconies. The hotel is just across the road from the Louvre and the Tuileries. Room service in the daytime only. No restaurant. ***Rooms** 25. Amex, Diners, Mastercard, Visa.*

Brasserie Munichoise 300F

Tel 42 61 47 16 Map B1.4 **R**
5 rue Danielle Casanova 75001 M° Pyramides/Opéra

First-floor restaurant with Alpine chalet decor, a friendly welcome and a menu of German/French inspiration. Dishes include salami and Baltic herrings to start, then beef goulash, *cochon de lait* (suckling pig) and their two particular specialities of roast knuckle of pork moistened with beer, and an assortment of grilled sausages, both served with choucroute. Round off a hearty, convivial meal with apple strudel. Alsace is the most favoured region on the wine list but most people drink beer, of which there is a wide variety on tap. Try Bitburger, a German pils which takes five minutes to serve properly. If all you want is a

See over

nibble they serve grilled sausages along with the beer at a small bar on the ground floor. ***Seats*** *60. Meals noon-1am (Sat from 5.30).* ***Closed*** *L Sat, all Sun. Mastercard, Visa.*

NORMANDY 1275F

Tel 42 60 30 21 **Fax 42 60 45 81** Map B1.41 **H**
7 rue de l'Echelle 75001 Mº Musée du Louvre/Palais-Royal

Built in 1877 to a Haussmann design, the hotel is three stone-faced buildings which have kept their original style. In the hall are marble columns and three enormous chandeliers that came from the liner *Normandie*; the reception desks are all in wood, as is the English bar with its velvet curtains and leather seats. In the bedrooms, which include eight suites, the same sense of tradition prevails, and some of the bathrooms retain their splendid old fittings. Room service from 6.30am to 9.45pm. ***Rooms*** *123. Amex, Diners, Mastercard, Visa.*

PAOLO PETRINI 650F

Tel 42 60 56 22 **Fax 42 36 55 50** Map B1.42 **R**
9 rue d'Argenteuil 75001 Mº Pyramides

Promoting foreign food in the capital of French gastronomy might seem like an uphill struggle, but Paolo Petrini's classic Italian cooking has proved very popular in this tiny restaurant near the Palais Royal. His seasonal menu might include starters like *taccole alla marinara* (salad of mangetout, squid and prawns) and carpaccio with rocket, lemon, olive oil and parmesan. Pasta dishes are mainly simple although *tagliatelle nere con ragù di calamari, scampi, gamberi e vongole* (octopus ink tagliatelle with a squid, scampi, prawn and clam sauce) is more unusual. A speciality is *filetto di bue al sale grosso con intingolo di erbe aromatiche* (fillet of beef cooked in green salt with herbs). The wine list manages to stay as purely Italian as the menu. ***Seats*** *30. L 12-2.30 D 8-11.* ***Closed*** *L Sat, all Sun & Aug. Amex, Diners, Mastercard, Visa.*

LA PASSION 650F

Tel 42 97 53 41 Map B1.43 **R**
41 rue Petits-Champs 75001 Mº Pyramides/4 Septembre

One wall of this little restaurant is covered with a *trompe l'oeil* of windows opening on to the Place des Victoires, another is largely mirrored. Add fresh flowers on the tables and some foodie watercolours and the whole effect is quite charming. Chef-patron Gilles Zellenwarger puts his own signature, and slight Alsace accent, on traditionally-based dishes: *foie gras de canard,* lobster (both specialities), mussel soup, fricassee of sole *fines herbes, daube de boeuf, croustade de pigeon à la bordelaise,* millefeuille of skate wing with tarragon. Set L 120F Set L & D 170F, 200F & 360F (*dégustation*). ***Seats*** *45. L 12-2.30 D 7.30-10.* ***Closed*** *L Sat, all Sun. Amex, Mastercard, Visa.*

PHARAMOND 750F

Tel 42 33 06 72 **Fax 40 28 01 81** Map D1.44 **R**
24 rue de la Grande Truanderie 75001 Mº Les Halles

Listed as a historic monument for its extravagant Belle Epoque interior (painted glass panels, giant mirrors, an amazing spiral staircase), this restaurant near Les Halles features traditional Normandy cuisine: *andouillettes, tripes à la mode de Caen,* galette of rabbit, *pied de cochon*, cod stew with sweet garlic. In winter *coquilles St Jacques au cidre* are a particular speciality. Among the desserts look out for crème brulée, *fondant au chocolat* and *nougat glacé*. The menu changes with the seasons. Set L 180F Set D 250F. ***Seats*** *95. L 12-2.30 D 7.30-10.30.* ***Closed*** *L Mon, all Sun. Amex, Diners, Visa.*

Au Pied de Cochon 520F

Tel 42 36 11 75 **Fax 45 08 48 90** Map C1.45 **R**
6 rue Coquillière 75001 Mº Les Halles

Open day and night (*every* day and *every* night), this brasserie has a warm place in the hearts of Parisians, out-of-town French and visitors from overseas. In bright, convivial surroundings helped along by young, relaxed staff, they tuck into what they've always tucked into: onion soup, fish soup, oysters and clams, snails, foie gras, the renowned pig's trotters (grilled with béarnaise sauce or *farci périgourdine*), grilled salmon and grilled steaks, fruit tarts and profiteroles. The wine list majors on Beaujolais (with all the Crus Beaujolais coming from Duboeuf) but all the main French regions are covered. House wine is a Costières de Nimes from the owner's own vineyard. ***Seats** 220 (+ 40 outside). **Meals** 24 hours a day. Amex, Diners, Mastercard, Visa.*

Pierre au Palais-Royal 700F

Tel 42 96 09 17 **Fax 42 96 09 62** Map B1.46 **R**
10 rue Richelieu 75001 Mº Palais-Royal

Nicole and Daniel Dez have been welcoming guests to their charming restaurant *du quartier* for the last 10 years and chef Roger Leplu has been here even longer. The handwritten, twice-weekly-changing menu is very much driven by the markets and the seasons with only the freshest of ingredients used in dishes like langoustine salad, duck terrine, duck foie gras (something of a speciality) served hot with sherry vinegar and cold in a terrine, *quenelles de brochet* (a popular dish almost always included on the carte), grilled John Dory with a beurre blanc sauce, *blanc de volaille* with fresh morels, cassoulet, *boeuf ficelle à la ménagère* and, among the desserts, *Paris-Brest*, vanilla crème brulée and *nougat glacé*. Exclusively French wine list is strongest in Bordeaux. Set menu 225F. ***Seats** 50. L 12-2.30 D 7-10. **Closed** Sat, Sun, Aug & Public Holidays. Amex, Diners, Mastercard, Visa.*

Hotel de la Place du Louvre 682F

Tel 42 33 78 68 **Fax 42 33 09 95** Map C2.47 **H**
21 rue des Pretres-St-Germain-l'Auxerrois 75001 Mº Louvre/Pont-Neuf

An ancient building opposite the church which gives the street its name. Bedrooms, each named after a different artist and boasting a print of his work, come with mini-bars, safes, numerous TV channels and all the usual modern conveniences. There's no restaurant, but breakfast is served either in bedrooms or in the 14th-century Cellar of the Musketeers. Room service during the day. Laundry service. ***Rooms** 20. Amex, Diners, Mastercard, Visa.*

Le Poquelin 600F

Tel 42 96 22 19 **Fax 42 96 05 72** Map B1.4 **R**
17 rue Molière 75001 Mº Palais-Royal

Next to the Comédie Française, the decorative theme is the Comédie and Molière (Jean Baptiste Poquelin). This charming little restaurant has been run by Michel (in the kitchen) and Maggy (the charming and outgoing hostess) Guillaumin since the early 70s. Among the starters look out for the duck foie gras, a speciality, perhaps atop a dish of duck fillet resting on a bed of lychees, fried with fresh figs or alongside some red tuna. Main dishes emphasise market-fresh seafood: salmon grilled *unilatéral* with a chive sauce, saffron-flavoured bouillabaisse, steamed lobster with a creamy garlic sauce, stewed turbot with smoked bacon. On the meat front there might be veal kidneys simply roasted with garlic and fillet of beef with creamed mushrooms. Dessertwise, the freshly-baked individual apple tart (order at the beginning of the meal) is so popular that it has never been off the menu since the restaurant opened but other choices like a *croustillant* of chocolate with orange zest or *oeufs en neige sous une pluie de pralines roses* also tempt. The fixed-price menu changes monthly, the *carte* seasonally. In addition to the regular wine list there is always a good value

See over

Bordeaux of the month at 120F and, also changing monthly, a selection of four wines from some of the more obscure French regions. Set menu 189F. ***Seats** 45. L 12-2 D 7.30-10.30. **Closed** L Sat, all Sun & 1st 3 weeks Aug. Amex, Diners, Mastercard, Visa.*

REGINA PARIS — 1520F

Tel 42 60 31 10 **Fax 40 15 95 16** Map B1.49 **H**
2 place des Pyramides 75001 M° Palais-Royal/Tuileries

Elegant public areas at this traditional hotel opposite the Louvre include a chandeliered lobby with carved mahogany desk and a wood panelled bar with red leather upholstery. Antique-furnished bedrooms come with all the usual amenities (safe, mini-bar) and all now have air-conditioning. ***Rooms** 130. Amex, Diners, Mastercard, Visa.*

LE RELAIS DU LOUVRE — 800F

Tel 40 41 96 42 **Fax 40 41 96 44** Map C2.50 **H**
19 rue des Pretres-St-Germain-l'Auxerrois 75001 M° Louvre/Pont-Neuf

Just 18 bedrooms and 2 suites in a charming hotel with a long and interesting history. From 1800 to 1941 it was the seat of the *Journal des Débats* – the French Hansard – and its ground floor was the famous *Café Momus*, the setting for an act in Puccini's *La Bohème*. Individually appointed bedrooms have antique furniture and rich co-ordinating fabrics, plus modern amenities like points for fax and computers. Five singles have shower and WC only. Breakfast is served only in the bedrooms. ***Rooms** 20. Amex, Diners, Mastercard, Visa.*

RITZ — 3730F

Tel 43 16 33 33 **Fax 43 16 36 68** Map A1.51 **HR**
15 place Vendome 75001 M° Opéra

Since being opened by César Ritz in 1898, this hotel, and his name, have become a synonym for opulence and luxury. Still in private hands, and unconnected with other hotels bearing the name, the Ritz continues to live up to its own legend. Day rooms in the 18th-century former private residence retain their authentic period atmosphere but today are joined by facilities such as the Ritz Health Club with its hi-tech fitness centre and romanesque pool and the Ritz Club for dancing until the small hours; for the less energetic, high tea is served in the Vendome garden to the sound of a harp. The Vendome Bar is spacious and overlooks the gardens while the Hemingway Bar, panelled and more intimate, has books and letters of the great man and other literary giants, and cocktails shaken by an Englishman. Antique-furnished bedrooms include nearly 50 full suites, some especially luxurious named after the Duke of Windsor, Coco Chanel and Scott Fitzgerald. Air-conditioning and all the usual up-to-date amenities combine with the sort of service that runs to a 24-hour valet – all in all making you feel well and truly pampered. Own parking. ***Rooms** 187. Amex, Diners, Mastercard, Visa.*

L'Espadon ★ 1500F

A Second Empire room of delicate elegance, where the exact shade of turquoise in a *trompe l'oeil* sky is picked up in the trimmings for the elaborate drapes that adorn high windows (which open on to the Vendome gardens for summer dining) and matching mirrored 'windows' that surround the room, giving it a satisfying symmetry. Add Venetian glass 'flower vase' lights set on sconces around the walls and you have a setting into which the wing-collared, be-tailed waiters fit perfectly. A typically thoughtful Ritz touch is the little gilt hook discreetly tucked away on the side of each chair to accommodate handbags. The first chef at the Ritz was the great Auguste Escoffier, who also designed the original kitchens, and it is from his classic tradition that long-serving chef Guy Legay has developed his own style, taking into account modern trends. *Menus dégustation* (590F) are where a chef generally likes to 'show off' but here it is perhaps the safe choice with such dishes as foie gras fried with vine peaches and a Médoc sauce or *coeur de filet* with a panaché of mushrooms, herbs and *sauce périgourdine*. The main menu is somewhat more adventurous: here the foie gras (goose in this case) might be served cooked pink with red onions and honey or in ravioli (back to duck) with a *bouillon* of herbs and pearl barley. A respectable cheese trolley comes with their own excellent bread. The impressive wine list is full of classic names from Bordeaux and Burgundy. ***Seats*** *60. L 12-3 D 7-11.*

Le Ruban Bleu 530F

Tel 42 61 47 53
29 rue d'Argenteuil 75001
Map B1.52
M° Pyramides
R

The painted blue riband that runs around the walls of this little restaurant in the banking district remembers a former maitre d' who served on the liner *Normandie* (sometime holder of the 'blue riband' for the fastest transatlantic crossing) and gave this place both its name and its decor back in the 1940s. The present patronne presides with charm and keeps her many regular lunchtime customers returning day after day for a traditional cuisine, majoring on fish, that is executed with a light touch to satisfy the health-conscious executive: smoked Loire eel in aspic; noisettes of monkfish with peppercorns; bass with spices and sorrel; mignons of veal with summer vegetables; gratin of red fruits; croustade of apples and calvados. The Loire predominates on an all-French wine list. Formerly a lunchtime only place, it was due to start opening for dinner from late 1995. ***Seats*** *40. L 12-2.15 D 7.15-9.* ***Closed*** *Sat, Sun, Aug & 1 week Christmas. Diners, Mastercard, Visa.*

Saint-James et Albany 980F

Tel 44 58 43 21 **Fax 44 58 43 11**
202 rue de Rivoli 75001
Map B1.53
M° Tuileries
R

Built as a rather grand private house for the Duc de Noailles during the reign of Louis XIV, the Saint-James et Albany now offers good modern bedrooms (mini-bars, safes, multi-channel television) to complement period public areas which include a courtyard garden. Ideally located between the posh shops of the Rue St Honoré and the Tuileries Gardens. Room service till 10pm. ***Rooms*** *212. Amex, Diners, Mastercard, Visa.*

See page 9 for a list of starred restaurants

Saint-Romain 692F

Tel 42 60 31 70 **Fax 42 60 10 69**
5 rue St-Roch 75001
Map B1.54
M° Tuileries
H

One of the three hotels in the Beaux Logis de Paris group, along with *Hotel du Continent* and the *Louvre St-Honoré* (see entries). This one has a certain country air. No restaurant, but there's a stone-vaulted breakfast room in the basement. ***Rooms*** *34. Amex, Diners, Mastercard, Visa.*

Tonic Hotel les Halles 590F

Tel 42 33 00 71 **Fax 40 26 06 86**
12-13 rue du Roule 75001
Map C1.55
M° Louvre
H

Totally renovated in the summer of 1993, bedrooms here come with all the usual extras plus bathrooms that boast either whirlpool tubs or multi-jet showers – both incorporating a steam bath. Breakfast is included in the room price. No restaurant. ***Rooms*** *34. Amex, Diners, Mastercard, Visa.*

The best way to get around Paris is by bus or metro –
buy a book (carnet) of tickets at any metro station and save money

La Tour de Montlhéry 450F

Tel 42 36 21 82 Map C1.56 **R**
5 rue des Prouvaires 75001 M° Chatelet/Les Halles

Lovely old restaurant near Les Halles with timbered exterior and tiled floor, old beams, exposed stone walls and red check table-cloths inside. With some famous faces among its clientele it's worth booking for dishes such as *haricot de mouton* (served out of huge porcelain dishes), *terrine de poisson*, braised salmon with mustard sauce, *cote de boeuf*, gateau of chicken livers with Madeira sauce, blanquette of veal and *cote d'agneau grillée*. Blackboard menu. Drink the house Brouilly. ***Seats** 60. **Open** 24 hours a day (although sometimes with a break 7-11 in the morning and 6-8 in the evening). **Closed** Sat, Sun & 14 Jul-15 Aug. Mastercard, Visa.*

Hotel des Tuileries 790F

Tel 42 61 04 17 Fax 49 27 91 56 Map B1.57 **H**
10 rue Saint-Hyacinthe 75001 M° Tuileries/Pyramides

Built for Marie Antoinette's first lady-in-waiting, this 18th-century mansion, just 100 metres from the Louvre, is now a small hotel that has been owned and run by the Vidal family for three generations. Quiet, double-glazed bedrooms, combine a period feel – antique furniture, chandeliers – with modern conveniences such as direct-dial phones, TVs, safes and mini-bars. No restaurant. ***Rooms** 26. Amex, Diners, Mastercard, Visa.*

Velloni 500F

Tel 42 21 12 50 Map D1.58 **R**
22 rue des Halles 75001 M° Chatelet/Les Halles

Here since 1982, chef-patron Stefano Cuccini continues to please with his classic Italian cooking at this smart modern restaurant by Les Halles. Antipasti range from Parma ham carved from the bone to warm escalope of foie gras with apple and *insalata Caprese*. Pasta dishes might include garganelli with fresh tomato and basil, spaghetti or rigatoni with a devilled sauce and taglierini with a ragout of fresh crab while meat dishes might include a fillet of beef in the style of Stefano's native Tuscany, veal with rosemary and sauté of lamb. Fish dishes vary daily according to the market. Finish with some Italian cheeses or a pud such as bitter chocolate terrine with coffee sauce or *cantuccini de Toscani e vino santo*. An excellent all-Italian wine list may include a Chianti from the vineyard of Stefano's father. Set menu 130F. ***Seats** 65. L 12-2.30 D 7.30-11. **Closed** Sun & 2 weeks mid-Aug. Amex, Diners, Mastercard, Visa.*

Willi's Wine Bar 450F

Tel 42 61 05 09 Fax 47 03 36 93 Map B1.59 **R**
13 rue des Petits-Champs 75001 M° Bourse/Palais-Royal

Posters by local artists adorn the white walls of a wine bar whose speciality is wines from the Rhone Valley but where New World wines also get a look in. A shortish menu changes daily to reflect the markets and the season: cassolette of cockles with artichokes and leeks, terrine of guinea fowl with a red onion compote, roast cod with an aubergine and basil marmalade, calf's liver with sage, fricassee of chicken with tarragon, sauté of lamb with rosemary, *croquant* of raspberries and terrine of bitter chocolate show the style. A dozen wines, changing weekly, are available by the glass or carafe. In the same ownership as *Juveniles (qv)*. Set menu 155F. ***Seats** 40. **Open** 11-11 (L 12-2.30 D 7-11, light snacks served at the bar at other times). Mastercard, Visa.*

2nd Arrondissement

Places of Interest

Bourse, 42 33 99 83, M° Bourse
Bibliothèque Nationale, 47 03 81 26, M° Bourse
Théatres des Variétés, 42 60 09 92, M° Bourse/Rue Montmartre
Opéra Comique, 42 60 04 99, M° Richelieu-Drouot
Boulevard des Italiens
Galerie Colbert – covered arcade, M° Bourse
Galerie Vivienne – covered arcade, M° Bourse

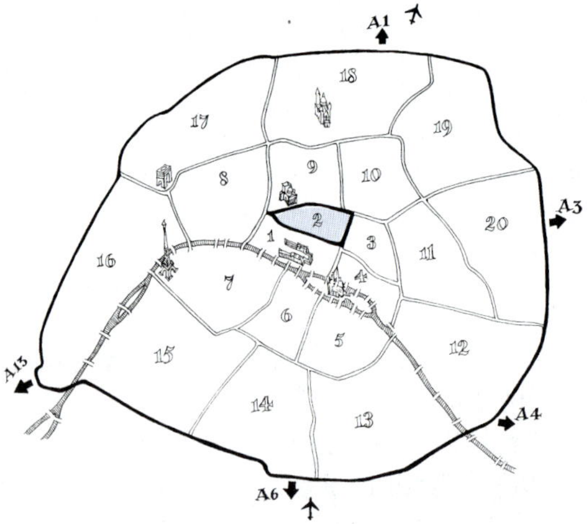

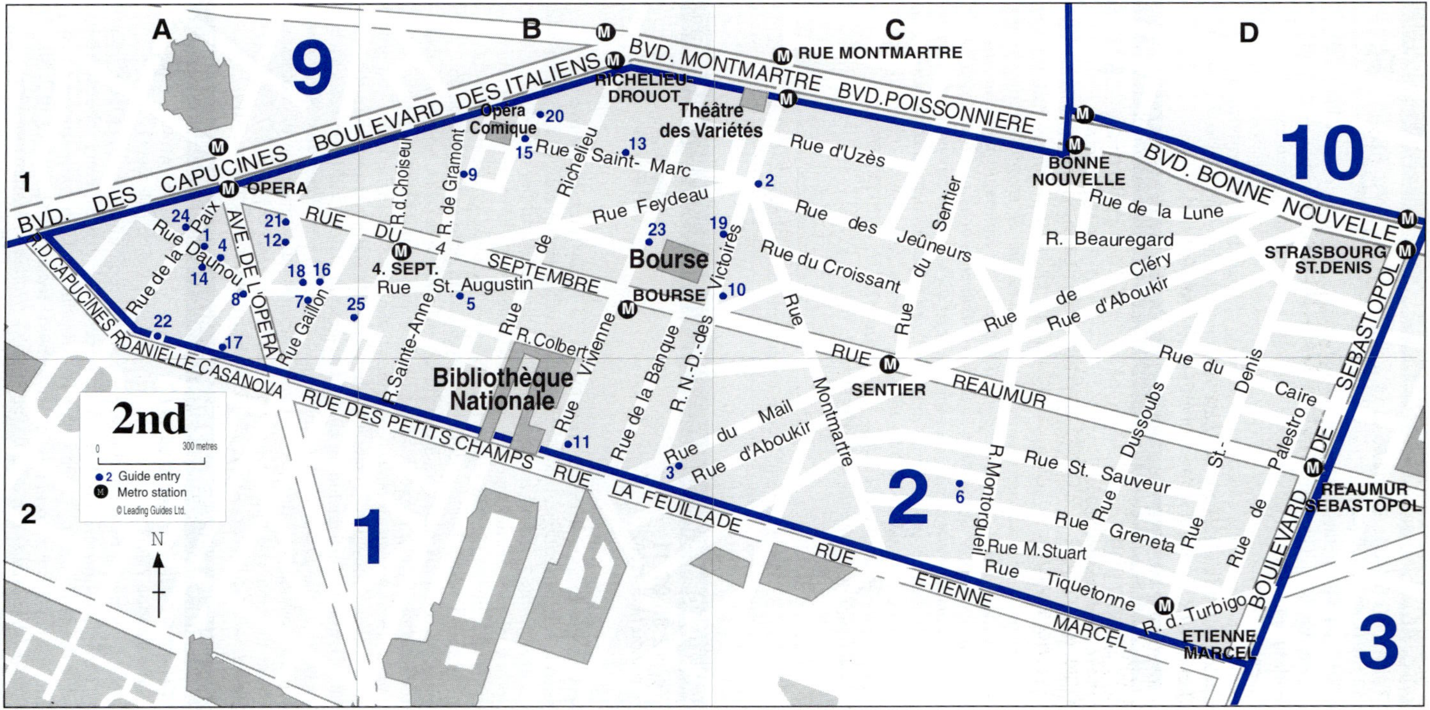
2nd
0
300 metres
2 Guide entry
Metro station
© Leading Guides Ltd.
N
A
B
C
D
1
2
9
10
1
2
3
BVD. DES CAPUCINES
BOULEVARD DES ITALIENS
BVD. MONTMARTRE
BVD.POISSONNIERE
BVD. BONNE NOUVELLE
BOULEVARD DE SEBASTOPOL
RUE ETIENNE MARCEL
RUE LA FEUILLADE
RUE DES PETITS CHAMPS
R.DANIELLE CASANOVA
R.D.CAPUCINES
RUE DU 4 SEPTEMBRE
RUE REAUMUR
AVE. DE L'OPERA
OPERA
RICHELIEU-DROUOT
RUE MONTMARTRE
BONNE NOUVELLE
STRASBOURG ST.DENIS
REAUMUR SEBASTOPOL
ETIENNE MARCEL
SENTIER
BOURSE
4. SEPT.
Opéra Comique
Théâtre des Variétés
Bourse
Bibliothèque Nationale
Rue de la Paix
Rue Daunou
Rue Gaillon
R.d.Choiseul
R. de Gramont
Rue Sainte-Anne
Rue St. Augustin
Rue de Richelieu
Rue Saint- Marc
Rue Feydeau
R.Colbert
Rue Vivienne
Rue de la Banque
R. N.-D.-des Victoires
Rue d'Uzès
Rue des Jeûneurs
Rue du Croissant
Rue du Sentier
Rue Montmartre
Rue du Mail
Rue d'Aboukir
Rue de la Lune
R. Beauregard
Rue de Cléry
Rue d'Aboukir
Rue du Caire
Rue St.-Denis
Rue Dussoubs
Rue St. Sauveur
Rue Greneta
Rue de Palestro
R.Montorgueil
Rue M.Stuart
Rue Tiquetonne
R. d. Turbigo
1
2
3
4
5
6
7
8
9
10
11
12
13
14
15
16
17
18
19
20
21
22
23
24
25

Arco Tapas y Vinos — 500F

Tel 42 60 07 20 **Fax 42 60 45 13** Map A1.1 **R**
12 rue Daunou 75002 Mº Opéra

A former English club, with high vaulted ceiling, carved wood panelling and a stone fireplace. The tapas are among the best in town, spanning fried squid, *moules piquantes*, chorizo in white wine, prawn croquettes, fried eggs with pimentos, Serrano ham and, of course, Spanish omelette. To accompany this tempting assortment is a distinguished cellar of Spanish wines majoring on Catalonia and Rioja. ***Seats*** *60.* ***Open*** *9am-midnight (hot food 12-3 & 7-11 only).* ***Closed*** *Sun & Public Holidays. Amex, Mastercard, Visa.*

Auberge Perraudin — 400F

Tel 42 36 71 09 Map C1.2 **R**
164 rue Montmartre 75002 Mº Rue Montmartre

Unpretentious restaurant-cum-wine bar with a hospitable atmosphere, where regular customers are treated more like friends. The chef-proprietor hails from St Emilion and his blackboard menus specialise in *cuisine du terroir* featuring dishes such as *cote de boeuf avec la confiture d'échalotes au vin rouge, poulet au citron, le trio de St Cochon* (comprising *saucisse de Toulouse, boudin noir* and *cote de porc)* and *andouillettes*. Save room for desserts such as *tarte aux pommes rustique, pot de crème au chocolat* and his grandmother's creation, *oeufs aux grands-mères* (a rich crème caramel). Also known as La Cave du Père Claude – Père Claude being a sister establishment in the 15th. ***Seats*** *32. L 12-2.30 D 7.30-10.* ***Closed*** *Sat, Sun & 3 weeks Aug. Mastercard, Visa.*

A glossary of French menu items starts on page 274

Chez Georges — 600F

Tel 42 60 07 11 Map B2.3 **R**
1 rue du Mail 75002 Mº Bourse

Serving simple food with fine wine has been a family tradition for five generations, currently upheld by Bernard Brouillet (along with M Devouges who has been in the kitchen here since 1968) at this archetypal brasserie – crisply-clothed tables squeezed together against banquettes down each side of a long room with mirrored walls – near the Place des Victoires. On one side of the menu (handwritten but nostalgically reproduced in pink and mauve on an ancient Roneo machine) are listed the likes of *jambon persillé, céleri rémoulade, rillettes d'oie* (which come in an earthenware pot from which you help yourself, along with a large jar of gherkins), grilled turbot with béarnaise sauce, and grilled lamb cutlets with haricots verts. On the other side is printed a wine list that is full of famous names including all the first-growth clarets, and burgundies such as Richebourg, La Tache (both from Romanée-Conti) and Echezeaux. Some dozen wines are available by the glass – if you're strong-willed that is, as the bottles are left on the table and you pay for what you drink. ***Seats*** *60. L 12-2 D 7-9.30.* ***Closed*** *Sun, 1st 2 weeks Aug & Public Holidays. Amex, Mastercard, Visa.*

Country Life — 130F

Tel 42 97 48 51 **Fax 42 60 49 67** Map A1.4 **R**
6 rue Daunou 75002 Mº Opéra

Modest vegetarian buffet to the rear of a health food shop near the Opéra, run by a religious organisation. For a fixed price of 65F (pay on entry) choose from half a dozen hot items – bean casserole, couscous, leeks in white sauce – and a simple salad bar. Air-conditioned. Unlicensed. ***Seats*** *120.* ***Open*** *L 11.30-2.30 D 6.30-10.* ***Closed*** *D Fri, all Sat, Sun & Public Holidays. Mastercard, Visa.*

Coup de Coeur 520F

Tel 47 03 45 70 **Fax 43 24 49 00** Map B1.5 **R**
19 rue St Augustin 75002 Mº 4 Septembre

A restaurant on two floors with a subtle English look to the decor. The kitchen, however, in the charge of Thierry Leblond whose background includes the *Cote St Jacques* at Joigny and the *Grand Véfour* in Paris, is strictly French with such dishes as *méli-mélo de palourdes aux champignons, salade de saucisson chaude, filets de rouget poelés à l'anis, emincé de volailles à la graine de moutarde* and *carré d'agneau roti au romarin*. Short wine list but full of familiar names, mostly from Bordeaux. Set menus 105F, 145F & 179F. ***Seats*** *60. L 12-3 D 7-10.30.* ***Closed*** *L Sat, all Sun. Amex, Mastercard, Visa.*

Aux Crus de Bourgogne 450F

Tel 42 33 48 24 **Fax 40 26 66 41** Map C2.6 **R**
3 rue Bachaumont 75002 Mº Les Halles

M Bouvier's turn-of-the-century bistro has mirrored walls, red and white check table-cloths, plenty of parlour plants and a classic bistro menu: foie gras prepared from a recipe handed down from M Bouvier's grandmother in 1932, *escargots, coq au vin* and *petit salé* typify the choice, which depends on the market. Grilled lobster is a regular fixture on Thursdays. Modest, hand-written list of some 20 exclusively French wines. ***Seats*** *80 (+ 25 outside). L 12-2.30 D 8-10.30.* ***Closed*** *Sat, Sun & 1st 3 wks Aug. Mastercard, Visa.*

Drouant ★★ 1600F

Tel 42 65 15 16 **Fax 49 24 02 15** Map A1.7 **R**
18 place Gaillon 75002 Mº 4 Septembre

A short stroll from Place de l'Opéra with a restaurant as well as a café, Drouant started out as a simple *café-tabac* back in 1880 but soon had a reputation for its good seafood and a strong literary following; the first *Prix Goncourt* was awarded here and the literary tradition continues with the *Prix Apollinaire* (for poetry) presented here each June. The restaurant is now in the same ownership as *Jules Verne (qv)*, on the second level of the Eiffel Tower, and the latter's one-time head chef now cooks here. Being close to the Paris Bourse, it's popular with the business community. Louis Grondard's cooking is of extremely well-thought-out dishes prepared in a style that's modern but retains a clear classical pedigree. Particular specialities from the carte include cassolette of girolles made with the distinctively flavoured *vin jaune* from the Jura, charlotte of langoustines with an aubergine confit, veal kidneys roasted with rosemary, and turbot roasted in a clay mould with truffles. Set L 300F Set D 650F. ***Seats*** *70. L 12-2.30 D 7-10.30.* ***Closed*** *D 25 Dec, all 1 Jan. Amex, Diners, Mastercard, Visa.*

Edouard VII 1300F

Tel 42 61 56 90 **Fax 42 61 47 73** Map A1.8 **HR**
39 ave de l'Opéra 75002 Mº Opéra

Occupying seven floors of a 19th-century building between the Opéra and the Louvre and not far from Place Vendome, the hotel enjoys a prime city-centre location. Generally spacious bedrooms (there are just four singles with shower and WC only) are traditionally furnished and come complete with double-glazing and all the usual comforts. Six have air-conditioning. ***Rooms*** *69. Amex, Diners, Mastercard, Visa.*

Restaurant Delmonico 450F

Tel 42 61 44 26

Comfortable restaurant with good service and traditional French cooking. There is a fixed-price *menu de saison* offering several choices at each stage: rabbit terrine with hazelnuts, prawn cocktail with pink grapefruit, a plate of Auvergne ham or a salad of fresh goat's cheese with artichokes to start, perhaps, followed by spiced salmon cutlets, leg of lamb infused with vanilla and accompanied by a *gratin dauphinois*, beef stroganoff with basmati rice or

See over

steamed hake with a watercress sauce. Strawberry charlotte, double chocolate mousse with a liquorice sauce and apple crumble with crème fraiche to finish. Set menus 128F & 168F. ***Seats*** *60. L 12.30-2.30 D 7.30-10.30.* ***Closed*** *Sat, Sun & Aug.*

Favart 630F

Tel 42 97 59 83 Fax 40 15 95 58 Map B1.9 **H**
5 rue Marivaux 75002 M° Richelieu-Drouot

Built in 1824 and standing opposite the Opéra Comique, the building is classed a historic monument and was the home in exile of the painter Goya. Individually decorated bedrooms, one in period style, all come with mini-bar, safe, multi-channel TV and hairdryer. Only Continental breakfast is offered and this is included in the room price. No restaurant. ***Rooms*** *37. Amex, Diners, Mastercard, Visa.*

Gallopin 460F

Tel 42 36 45 38 Fax 42 36 10 32 Map C1.10 **R**
40 rue Notre Dame des Victoires 75002 M° Bourse

With its moulded ceilings, brass and mahogany fittings, and air of comforting permanence, little seems to have changed in this famous old restaurant since it opened in 1876. The classic seasonal menu lists old favourites such as *entrecote Gallopin*, steak tartare and *foie de veau au poivre vert*. The set dinner menu (150F) might consist of *escargots de Bourgogne*, followed by sole meunière and then a *plateau de fromages*, and comes with a kir royal aperitif and half a bottle of Cotes du Rhone. ***Seats*** *120 (+ 30 outside). L 11.30-3 D 7.30-11.30.* ***Closed*** *Sat & Sun. Amex, Diners, Mastercard, Visa.*

Le Grand Colbert 500F

Tel 42 86 87 88 Fax 42 86 82 65 Map B2.11 **R**
2 rue Vivienne 75002 M° Bourse

A historic brasserie within an arcade dating from the 1830s. Decor features a fine frescoed frieze in classical style above mirrored walls stuck with current play bills. A popular haunt of the theatrical crowd (it's in the heart of the theatre district) the atmosphere really begins to buzz after the evening performances, making this a good choice for late dining. The varied menu changes daily: *morue fraiche grillée avec une purée de pommes de terre* and *cuisse de canard et pommes à l'ail.* For dessert there's a choice including *tarte fine aux pommes avec crème fraiche vanillée* or *fondant au chocolat noir avec sauce mandarine.* Champagne comes by the 50cl carafe (130F). Air-conditioned. Set menu 155F. ***Seats*** *100. Meals noon-1am.* ***Closed*** *10 days Aug. Amex, Diners, Mastercard, Visa.*

L'Horset Opéra 1320F

Tel 44 71 87 00 Fax 42 66 55 54 Map A1.12 **H**
18 rue d'Antin 75002 M° Opéra

In the heart of the city just by the Opéra, l'Horset offers modern amenities and air-conditioned comfort behind its period facade. Day rooms include the bar Le Diapason, a favourite place for cocktails. Room service throughout the day and evening. ***Rooms*** *54. Amex, Diners, Mastercard, Visa.*

Aux Lyonnais 425F

Tel 42 96 65 04 Fax 42 97 42 95 Map B1.13 **R**
32 rue Saint-Marc 75002 M° Bourse/ Richelieu-Drouot

The *plat du jour* changes daily but, apart from a few seasonal variations, the *carte* at this traditional 1900s bistro is fairly static. M Jandot's cooking has a Lyonnais slant: sausages with *salade frisée* or *pommes à l'huile, la grosse quenelle comme à Lyon, gras double à la lyonnaise* (fried tripe and onions), pike in a beurre blanc, confit of duck with sauté potatoes, chicken with tarragon and mushroom cream sauce, grilled pig's trotters. Finish with the likes of poire Belle

Hélène, coffee or chocolate Liégeois, chocolate mousse or crème caramel. Shortish wine list, mostly Beaujolais and Cotes du Rhone, with most also in half bottles. Separate list of mineral waters. Busiest at lunchtimes. Set menu 87F. ***Seats** 120. L 11.30-3 D 6.30-12. **Closed** L Sat, all Sun. Amex, Diners, Mastercard, Visa.*

LE MOÏ 400F

Tel 47 03 92 05 Map A1.14 **R**
5 rue Daunou 75002 M° Opera

Established by Mme Oggéri in 1966, this Vietnamese restaurant started life in the 16th arrondissement. The short all-day menu is simply arranged with all starters – Chinese soup with pork and egg noodles, *salade Moï, raviolis vietnamiens* – at 47F, main dishes – *crabe farcie à la vapeur* (crab stuffed with pork, mushrooms and vermicelli), *thet kho* (caramelised breast of pork, a Vietnamese speciality), *poulet au curry façon Moï* (with a coconut-flavoured rice, aubergines, courgettes and a banana-flavoured curry sauce), grilled beef with lemon grass – at 68F, a couple of fish dishes at 97F and desserts such as *crème de coco chaude à la banane* and fruit fritters, all at 35F. Just a handful of French wines and some Chinese beer. Set L 80F. ***Seats** 42. L 12-3 D 7-11 (Fri & Sat to 12). **Closed** L Sat, all Sun. Amex, Diners, Mastercard.*

LES NOCES DE JEANNETTE 320F

Tel 42 96 36 89 **Fax 47 03 97 31** Map B1.15 **R**
14 rue Favart 75002 M° Richelieu-Drouot

In the throbbing heart of the city, near the Opéra, the restaurant takes its name from a one-act comic opera by Massé. One of the street-level upstairs rooms is decorated with operetta posters, while the other is a tribute to French films of the 30s, 40s and 50s. Several upstairs rooms are used for private parties. The 159F bistrot menu is all-inclusive: aperitif, three courses, half a bottle of wine and coffee – and there's even a plate of butter with the basket of bread. Les Noces has earned its reputation with reliable, traditional bistro cooking, and a daily special always supplements the nine or ten main-course options. Monday brings navarin of lamb, Wednesday *filet de canard aux griottines et aux poires*, Friday bouillabaisse, Saturday and Sunday *curry d'agneau, riz Madras*. Salad of Roquefort, walnuts and bilberries, salmon rillettes and *emincé de fonds d'artichauts à l'huile d'olive* are typical starters; pike quenelles, sauce Nantua, grilled *andouillette AAAAA* and pork hock with green lentils are popular central dishes; and Brie de Meaux is an alternative to desserts such as *génoise au chocolat amer crème anglaise, pruneaux d'Agen au Cahors* or crème caramel. Owner Patrick Fracheboud takes excellent personal care of his customers. Set menu 159F. ***Seats** 60. L 12-2 D 7-10.30. **Closed** D 24 Dec, all 25 Dec. Amex, Diners, Mastercard, Visa.*

HOTEL DE NOAILLES 780F

Tel 47 42 92 90 **Fax 49 24 92 71** Map A1.16 **H**
9 rue de la Michodière 75002 M° Opéra/4 Septembre

A period facade conceals a hotel of striking modern design, with metal, wood and glass combining in style. Bedrooms, most of which enjoy a quiet location overlooking the courtyards, have a stylishly simple, modern theme. ***Rooms** 58. Amex, Mastercard, Visa.*

PASSY MANDARIN 500F

Tel 42 61 25 50 **Fax 42 60 33 92** Map A1.17 **R**
6 rue d'Antin 75002 M° Pyramides

A sumptuously appointed Chinese restaurant with dim sum and lacquered duck among the specialities. ***Seats** 130. **Closed** Sun, otherwise details as for entry in the 16th arrondissement.*

Pierre a la Fontaine Gaillon — 650F

Tel 42 65 87 04 **Fax 47 42 82 84** Map A1.18 **R**
place Gaillon 75002 Mº Opéra

A historic building which dates from 1672 and which had a succession of ducal owners before becoming a restaurant in the 1880s. The fountain at the front, after which it takes its name, was erected in 1707 and restored a century later by Visconti, who also built Napoleon's tomb. The interior is elegantly decorated in period style and the menu is a traditional one ranging from oysters, moules marinière, onion soup and *rosette de Lyon* to duck confit, *andouillette AAAAA*, beef stroganoff and whole sole with a lemon butter. A few modern dishes are also featured as in *petit coquelet entier à la bière, polenta croustillant* and roast fillet of lamb with sage and risotto. The daily-changing section of the menu concentrates on seafood – a speciality here. Set D 165F. ***Seats** 100. L 12-3 D 7-12.30. **Closed** L Sat, all Sun & Aug. Amex, Diners, Mastercard, Visa.*

Pile ou Face — ★ 800F

Tel 42 33 64 33 **Fax 42 36 61 09** Map C1.19 **R**
52bis rue Notre-Dame-des-Victoires 75002 Mº Bourse

A warm, cosy restaurant on two floors with burgundy red walls and a small bar/greeting area near the entrance. Everything is made on the premises, including bread (two bakings a day), petits fours and the chocolates served with coffee. Normandy farms supply much of the produce, and typifying the dishes on the *carte menu* are scrambled eggs with a purée of morels, rabbit terrine with rosemary and thyme, pigeon roasted in truffle oil with pan-fried foie gras, and oxtail pot-au-feu. For dessert, perhaps frozen yoghurt with crumbled biscuits and blackcurrant compote, or apples pan-fried in butter and served with cinnamon ice cream. Lunch is a fixed-price affair of four courses (including cheese) of dishes taken from the evening menus with about eight choices at each stage. Set menus from 235F (L) and 280F (D) to 320F. ***Seats** 40. L 12-2 D 8-10. **Closed** Sat, Sun, Aug, 24 Dec-1 Jan & Public Holidays. Mastercard, Visa.*

La Rotisserie Monsigny — 580F

Tel 42 96 16 61 Map A1.25 **R**
1 rue Monsigny 75002 Mº 4 Septembre

The latest of the Jacques Cagna Rotisseries (opened in February 1995) is located in the Bourse area right opposite the Bouffes-Parisiens Theatre. That location determines its clientele – mainly business people at lunchtime, and in the evening theatre-goers who just step across the road for a late table. It's a place of considerable space and comfort, done out in a combination of modern chic and Provençal ochres. The *menu carte* prices all entrées at 60F, main courses at 100F and desserts at 50F. The choice is an interesting combination of classic and contemporary: *terrine de foie de volaille*, beech-smoked salmon, fillets of bream *à la plancha* with a fennel fondue, *entrecote béarnaise* with *pommes Pont-Neuf*, guinea fowl half-roasted half-confit accompanied by a *jardinière* of vegetables. Desserts include splendid sorbets, *Paris-Brest* and chocolate *fondant* with vanilla ice cream. Monday to Friday lunchtimes there's a 159F no-choice three-course menu: our highly enjoyable trio of dishes comprised artichoke mousse with a delicate coulis of tomatoes and herbs, pike steak with a dense, glossy Chinon sauce, and clafoutis with mirabelles. Wines, chosen by Cagna himself, are fairly priced, with the monthly selection offering the best value. Few whites. The other Cagna Rotisseries are *La Rotisserie d'en Face* in the 6th and *La Rotisserie d'Armaillé* in the 17th (see entries). ***Seats** 150. L 12-2.30 D 7-12 (Sun & Mon till 11). **Closed** L Sat. Amex, Mastercard, Visa.*

See page 9 for a list of starred restaurants

Café Runtz — 400F

Tel 42 96 69 86 Map B1.20 **R**
16 rue Favart 75002 Mº Richelieu-Drouot

With a corner site near the Opéra Comique, Odette Leport's restaurant/*salon de thé* sports engraved glass panels and mirrors topped with pictures of some of her theatrical customers. Mealtimes bring a menu of classic Alsatian dishes: the main courses major on choucroute served with black pudding and apples, ham, sausages and bacon as well as the slightly more unusual monkfish or mixed fish, while hors d'oeuvre include the likes of *salade strasbourgeoise*, smoked Alsace ham and a warm onion tart. A house speciality is *jambonneau à la Strasbourg* served with a warm potato salad. Throughout the week there are daily specials such as Tuesday's *andouillette de Troyes* or Thursday's *bäckeoffa* – a stew of beef, mutton and pork with wine, potatoes and onions. From 9am to midnight (except while lunch is being served) you can drop in just for one of their own home-baked pastries. The wines of Alsace are well represented on a short list. ***Seats** 95. **Open** 9am-11.30pm (L 11.45-2.30 D 6.30-11.30) **Closed** Sat, Sun & Aug. Amex, Diners, Mastercard, Visa.*

Le Saint Amour — 750F

Tel 47 42 63 82 Map A1.21 **R**
8 rue Port Mahon 75002 Mº Opéra

By the Bourse and the major banks, a restaurant of refinement, busy at lunchtime but still intimate. Cooking is classic and careful, typified by *foie gras de canard, oeufs meurette* and lobster salad to start; turbot hollandaise, monkfish with lentils, veal kidneys with shallots and thyme-infused rack of lamb for mains; and *crème brulée, millefeuille* and *nougat glacé* to finish. The restaurant has a history going back 60 years. Set menu 155F. ***Seats** 70. L 12-2.30 D 7-10.15. **Closed** L Sat, all Sun & mid Jul-mid Aug. Amex, Diners, Mastercard, Visa.*

Le Stendhal — 1510F

Tel 44 58 52 52 **Fax 44 58 52 00** Map A1.22 **H**
22 rue Danielle-Casanova 75002 Mº Pyramides

In a building once occupied by the author after whom it is named, Le Stendhal is an intimate hotel of considerable luxury and comfort. Bedrooms, which include several suites, boast designer fabrics and all sorts of modern comforts from air-conditioning and double-glazing to mini-bar, room safe, and a second phone line for your fax. There's a clubby day room with dado panelling, green-shaded lights and shelves of books and the stone-vaulted basement houses the breakfast room. Room prices include Continental breakfast but there's also an à la carte selection of more substantial items, if required. Room service 24 hours. ***Rooms** 20. Amex, Diners, Mastercard, Visa.*

Vaudeville — 550F

Tel 40 20 04 62 **Fax 49 27 08 78** Map B1.23 **R**
29 rue Vivienne 75002 Mº Bourse

Classic turn-of-the-century brasserie opposite the Paris Bourse, part of the popular Café Flo group. Marble walls, mirrors, art deco light fittings, closely packed tables and friendly, efficient service from waiters who carry trays shoulder-high laden with the oysters and other shellfish that are a speciality here and which can also be bought from a pavement stall to take away. The lengthy menu caters for meat- and fish-eaters with such offerings as mussel soup with saffron, duck terrine with pistachios, warm oysters in champagne sauce among the starters. For a main course the range includes salmon escalope with sorrel, chicken fricassee with morels and noodles, *saucisse de campagne avec purée de pommes de terre* and calf's kidneys in a mustard sauce. From 6 to 11am breakfast (39F) is served in either the bar or the main restaurant. Set D (and L Sun & Public Holidays) 195F and a lunch and night-owls' menu (served from 10pm) at 112F. ***Seats** 145 (+ 100 outside). L 12-3.30 D 7-4am. **Closed** D 24 Dec. Amex, Diners, Mastercard, Visa.*

WESTMINSTER 1800F

Tel 42 61 57 46 **Fax 42 60 30 66** Map A1.24 **HR**
13 rue de la Paix 75002 Mº Opéra

Handily placed between the Opéra and Place Vendome, the Westminster boasts a lobby in traditionally grand style – marbled columns, coffered ceiling, large floral display – that sets the tone for elegant, individually decorated bedrooms and suites with antique-style furniture and coloured marble bathrooms. 24-hour room service. Private parking for 10 cars. ***Rooms*** *102. Amex, Diners, Mastercard, Visa.*

Restaurant Le Celadon 1100F

Tel 47 03 40 42

A beautiful dining-room with glittering chandeliers and polished service where Emmanuel Hodencq offers a carte featuring modern Mediterranean dishes, some with exotic Oriental spicing. Terrine of duck foie gras with *pain perdu*, red mullet with pistou and tomatoes, grilled lobster with cinnamon sticks and shallots, pan-fried John Dory with courgette flowers, lamb roasted with cumin and aubergines, and wild strawberries with a hint of liquorice show the range. Set menus 220F & 290F. ***Seats*** *55. L 12-2 D 7.30-10.* ***Closed*** *Sat, Sun, Public Holidays & Aug.*

3rd Arrondissement
Places of Interest

Archives Nationales, 40 27 62 18, M° Rambuteau
Musée Picasso, 42 71 25 21, M° St-Paul/Chemin Vert
Musée Carnavalet (History of Paris), 42 72 21 13, M° St-Paul/Chemin Vert
Place des Vosges, M° Bastille/Chemin Vert/St-Paul
Place de la République
Musée Cognacq-Jay (18th-century collection), 40 27 07 21, M° St-Paul
Hotel Guénégaud, Musée de la Chasse et la Nature, 42 72 86 43, M° Rambuteau
Musée de la Poupée (dolls), 42 72 55 90, M° Rambuteau

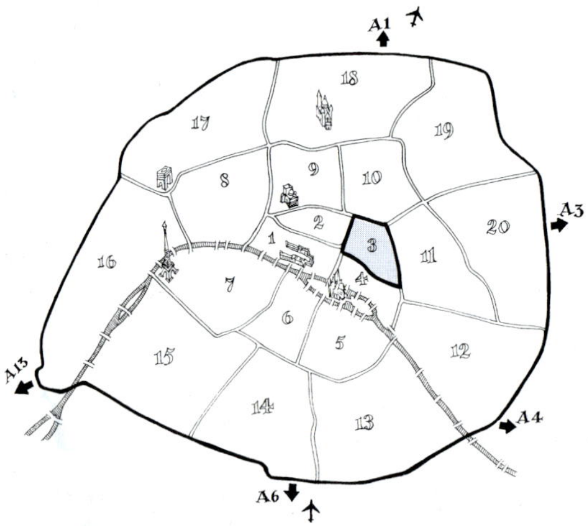

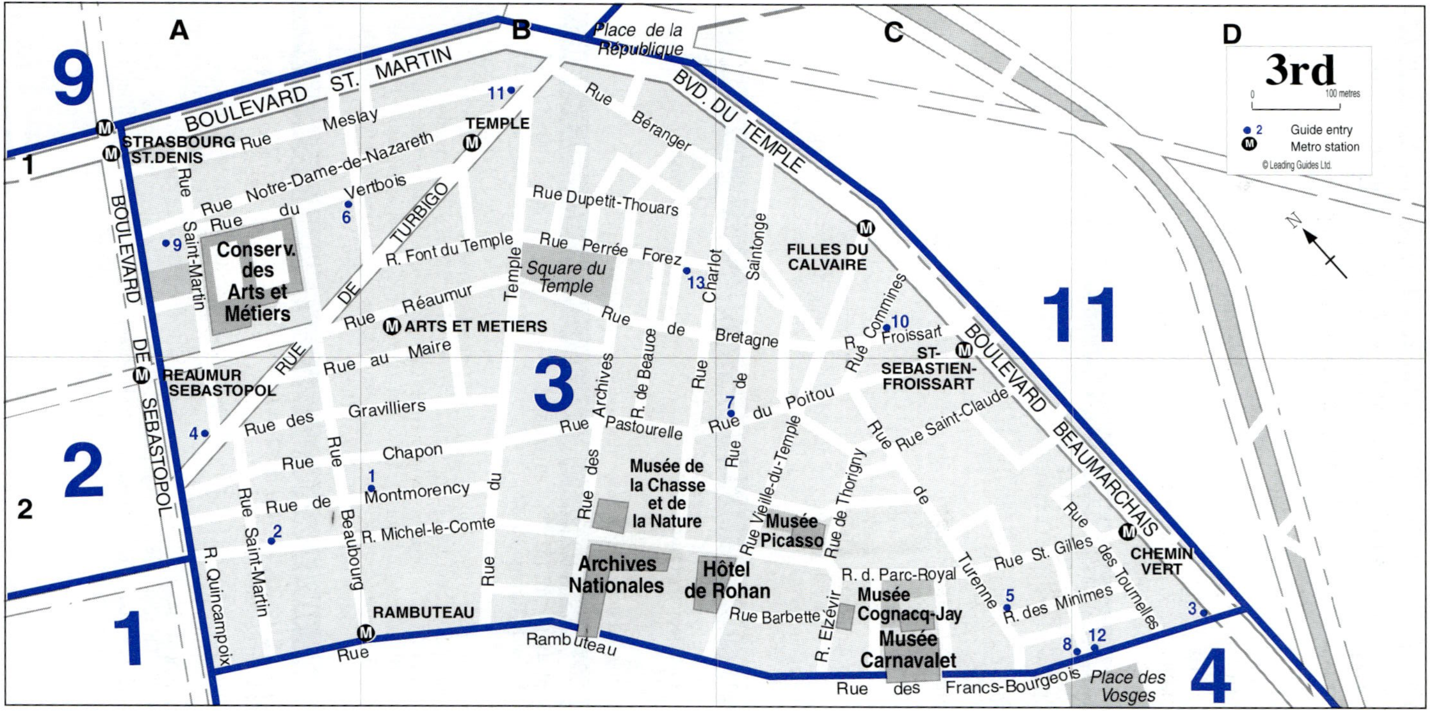
3rd
0
100 metres
2 Guide entry
M Metro station
© Leading Guides Ltd.
N
A
B
C
D
9
11
3
2
1
4
BOULEVARD ST. MARTIN
Place de la République
BVD. DU TEMPLE
BOULEVARD BEAUMARCHAIS
BOULEVARD DE SEBASTOPOL
STRASBOURG ST.DENIS
TEMPLE
FILLES DU CALVAIRE
ARTS ET METIERS
REAUMUR SEBASTOPOL
ST-SEBASTIEN-FROISSART
CHEMIN VERT
RAMBUTEAU
Conserv. des Arts et Métiers
Square du Temple
Musée de la Chasse et de la Nature
Archives Nationales
Hôtel de Rohan
Musée Picasso
Musée Cognacq-Jay
Musée Carnavalet
Place des Vosges
Rue Meslay
Rue Notre-Dame-de-Nazareth
Rue du Vertbois
Rue Saint-Martin
RUE DE TURBIGO
R. Font du Temple
Rue Réaumur
Rue au Maire
Rue des Gravilliers
Rue Chapon
Rue de Montmorency
Rue Beaubourg
R. Michel-le-Comte
Rue du Temple
R. Quincampoix
Rue Rambuteau
Rue Béranger
Rue Dupetit-Thouars
Rue Perrée
Forez
Charlot
Saintonge
Rue de Bretagne
Rue des Archives
R. de Beauce
Rue Pastourelle
Rue de Poitou
Rue Vieille-du-Temple
Rue de Thorigny
Rue Saint-Claude
R. Commines
Froissart
Rue de Turenne
R. d. Parc-Royal
Rue Barbette
R. Elzévir
Rue St. Gilles
R. des Minimes
Rue des Tournelles
Rue des Francs-Bourgeois
1
2
3
4
5
6
7
8
9
10
11
12
13

L'ALISIER 400F

Tel 42 72 31 04 **Fax 42 72 74 83** Map B2.1 **R**
26 rue Montmorency 75003 M° Rambuteau

Twin brothers run L'Alisier, Jean-Luc Dodeman in the kitchen, Jean-François in the dining-room, which is done out in traditional Paris bistro style (there is also a private room in Louis XV style). The menu (175F) mixes modern and traditional: pan-fried escalope of foie gras, tartlet of cantal cheese with tomato, terrine of salt cod with anchovy cream, fried red mullet in a raspberry vinegar sauce and veal fillet with a grain mustard sauce among a selection of starters and main dishes. For dessert there's an interesting choice including a caramelised apple tart, and a soup of exotic fruits. ***Seats*** *45. L 12-2 D 7.30-10.* ***Closed*** *Sat, Sun & Aug. Amex, Mastercard, Visa.*

AMBASSADE D'AUVERGNE 500F

Tel 42 72 31 22 **Fax 42 78 85 47** Map A2.2 **R**
22 rue du Grenier St Lazare 75003 M° Rambuteau

Appropriately named, as the rustic decor is as authentic as the food representing the Auvergne region of France. Six separate dining-rooms, each holding from 6 to 40 people, are individually decorated – one with cooking utensils, another with old paintings, a third with tapestries, and so on. Specialities include cabbage and Roquefort soup, *fromage de tete au jambon d'Auvergne; tripoux à l'estragon, pommes fondantes*, cassoulet with Puy lentils and *boudin aux chataignes* – a black pudding with chestnuts served with a chestnut sauce. Choose à la carte or from the *menu gourmet* (160F). There is also 'La Balade en Auvergne de l'Ambassade', a 300F menu gourmand of 8 dishes of the Auvergne and including wine from the region. ***Seats*** *100. L 12-2 D 7.30-10.30.* ***Closed*** *2 weeks Aug. Amex, Mastercard, Visa.*

BAR À HUITRES 500F

Tel 48 87 98 92 **Fax 48 87 04 42** Map D2.3 **R**
33 bd Beaumarchais 75003 M° Bastille

Restaurant de poissons. See entry in 14th arrondissement.

BELLEVUE ET DU CHARIOT D'OR 390F

Tel 48 87 45 60 **Fax 48 87 95 04** Map A1.4 **H**
39 rue de Turbigo 75003 M° Réaumur-Sebastopol

An old building, now renovated, near the Centre Pompidou. Lofty reception and breakfast room. Modern bar. Functional bedrooms, all with bath/WC, comprise 30 twins, 24 doubles and 5 triples. The Chariot d'Or recalls an alley behind the hotel down which a bride-to-be rode in a chariot with her dowry (usually flowers and gold). Her betrothed would meet her at the other end. The hotel has no restaurant. Only Continental breakfast is served, and is included in the room prices. ***Rooms*** *59. Amex, Diners, Mastercard, Visa.*

HOTEL DES CHEVALIERS 572F

Tel 42 72 73 47 **Fax 42 72 54 10** Map C2.5 **H**
30 rue de Turenne 75003 M° St-Paul/Bastille

The Place des Vosges and the Picasso Museum are both a few steps away from this friendly little Marais hotel, whose comfortable modern bedrooms (done out in pink, blue or yellow) are spread over five floors; rooms at the top have sloping roofs. There is no restaurant proper but breakfast is served in the vaulted 17th-century cellar or in the bedrooms. This hotel is a popular choice with fashion and cinema people. ***Rooms*** *24. Amex, Mastercard, Visa.*

Chez L'Ami Louis 1400F

Tel 48 87 77 48 Map A1.6 **R**
32 rue du Vertbois 75003 Mº Arts et Métiers

A restaurant since 1924, and for many years (though sadly, no longer) using an old wood-fired oven for preparing most of the main courses, which mainly take their inspiration from the South West. Portions are enormous, preparation simple, prices on the à la carte-only menu very high. Foie gras, snails, *coquilles St Jacques à la provençale*, roast lamb, and game in season are the specialities and the chips are impressively large and perfectly cooked. Most renowned of all the dishes is perhaps the marvellous roast Challans chickens. Long wine list (343 bins – all French). ***Seats*** *50. L 12-2.30 D 8-11.* ***Closed*** *Mon & Tue. Amex, Diners, Mastercard, Visa.*

Chez Nénesse 450F

Tel 42 78 46 49 Map C2.7 **R**
17 rue Saintonge 75003 Mº Filles-du-Calvaire

A fine old neighbourhood bistro, very typical of the *quartier*, with menus that change with market availability; chef-patron Alain Le Meur is particularly happy preparing fish and game in season. A salad of spinach and warm foie gras, *blanc de turbot, sauce vigneronne* (turbot with a red wine sauce), lamb's kidneys with fresh ceps and *figues farcies à la crème d'amandes* (figs filled with an almond cream) typify an early autumn menu. ***Seats*** *42. L 12-2 D 7.45-10.* ***Closed*** *Sat, Sun, 1 week Feb & all Aug. Mastercard, Visa.*

La Guirlande de Julie 350F

Tel 48 87 94 07 Map D2.8 **R**
25 place des Vosges 75003 Mº Bastille

Part of the Tour d'Argent group (as is *Coconnas*, also in Place des Vosges but in the 4th arrondissement), Julie is open long hours every day for teas, snacks and full meals. *Pot au feu* is the house speciality – a classic cold-weather dish. Also popular is the excellent navarin of lamb Oriental-style, prepared with cinnamon, coriander and cumin, prunes and almonds. A feature of the restaurant is the 40-seater terrace, a boon in warm weather. The à la carte choice is quite varied, and there are set menus at 66F (plat du jour L Mon-Fri), 87F (L *formule rapide* Mon-Fri) & 168F (L & D daily). ***Seats*** *50. Meals noon-midnight.* ***Closed*** *3 weeks Jan, 1 week Feb. Mastercard, Visa.*

Little Palace Hotel 590F

Tel 42 72 08 15 Fax 42 72 45 81 Map A1.9 **H**
4 rue Salomon-de-Caus 75003 Mº Strasbourg-St-Denis

Opposite the Square Chautemps in the old Arts et Métiers quarter. The building is old, but inside is modern. Nearly half the bedrooms have bath/WC, and these overlook the courtyard. The rest, with shower/WC, face the front. ***Rooms*** *57. Amex, Mastercard, Visa.*

Hotel du Marais 390F

Tel 48 87 78 27 Fax 48 87 09 01 Map C1.10 **H**
2bis rue Commines 75003 Mº St Seb-Froissart/Filles-du-Calvaire

Simple modern accommodation to the east of the old Marais quarter, between Bastille and République. All rooms have satellite TV and mini-bar, 12 have bath/WC, the rest shower/WC. ***Rooms*** *39. Amex, Mastercard, Visa.*

Meslay République 630F

Tel 42 72 79 79 Fax 42 72 76 94 Map B1.11 **H**
3 rue Meslay 75003 Mº République

A listed building in one of the oldest parts of Paris, just a few steps from Place de la République. All the bedrooms are en suite and accessories include TVs, hairdryers, automatic alarms, direct-dial phones and mini-bars. No restaurant. ***Rooms*** *39. Amex, Diners, Mastercard, Visa.*

Pavillon de la Reine 1700F

Tel 42 77 96 40 **Fax 42 77 63 06** Map D2.12 **H**
28 place des Vosges 75003 Mº Chemin Vert/Breguet Sabin

Set back from one of the finest and most beautiful squares in Paris (built in the 17th century and exquisitely renovated over the last few years), the entrance to this hotel is an attractive hall with massive exposed beams and stone-tiled floor. Comfortable furnishings and handsome antiques complete the attractive picture. Tastefully decorated and well maintained bedrooms, all air-conditioned, vary in size and colour, and overlook either the garden or the flowered courtyard. 24-hour reception and room service. Porter, concierge, laundry service. Breakfast 95F Continental 140F English. No restaurant. Private parking (free for 20 cars). ***Rooms*** *50. Amex, Diners, Mastercard, Visa.*

Hotel du Vieux Saule 460F

Tel 42 72 01 14 **Fax 40 27 88 21** Map B1.13 **H**
6 rue Picardie 75003 Mº République

The facade dates from 1830, but the vaulted cellars are three centuries older. Rooms differ in detail floor by floor; simple in their decor, they are quite well equipped: cable TV, hairdryer, safe, trouser press and iron. Eight have baths, the rest showers. Garage 60F for a day or a night. Buffet breakfast 45F. Sauna. A decent address in the Marais, and part of the vast Inter-Hotel network. ***Rooms*** *31. Amex, Diners, Mastercard, Visa.*

4th Arrondissement
Places of Interest

Centre Georges Pompidou, 42 77 11 12,
M° Hotel de Ville/Rambuteau
Notre Dame, 42 34 56 10, M° Cité
Hotel de Ville, 42 76 40 40, M° Hotel de Ville
Pavillon de l'Arsenal (town planning, architecture), 42 76 33 97,
M° Sully-Morland/Bastille
Place des Vosges
Maison Victor Hugo, 42 72 10 16, M° Bastille/St-Paul/Chemin Vert
Théatre de la Ville, 42 74 22 77, M° Chatelet

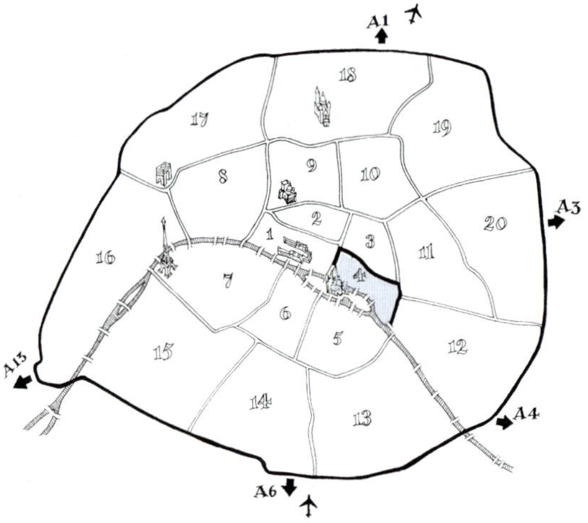

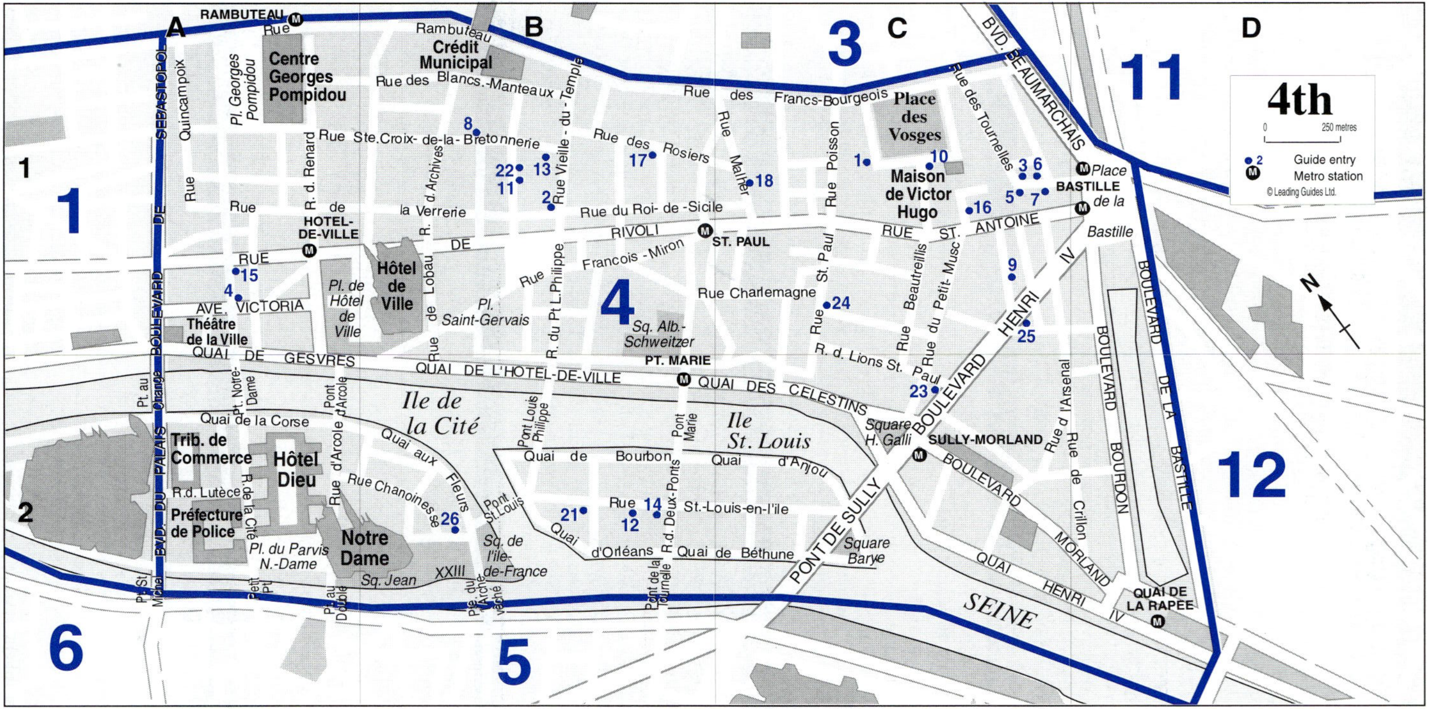

4th
250 metres
Guide entry
Metro station
© Leading Guides Ltd.
RAMBUTEAU
Centre Georges Pompidou
Pl. Georges Pompidou
Crédit Municipal
Rue des Blancs.-Manteaux
Rue Ste.Croix-de-la-Bretonnerie
Rue Vieille-du-Temple
Rue des Rosiers
Rue des Francs-Bourgeois
Place des Vosges
Maison de Victor Hugo
Rue des Tournelles
BVD. BEAUMARCHAIS
Place de la Bastille
BASTILLE
Rue du Roi-de-Sicile
RUE DE RIVOLI
RUE ST. ANTOINE
ST. PAUL
HOTEL-DE-VILLE
Hôtel de Ville
Pl. de Hôtel de Ville
Théâtre de la Ville
AVE. VICTORIA
BOULEVARD DE SEBASTOPOL
QUAI DE GESVRES
QUAI DE L'HOTEL-DE-VILLE
QUAI DES CELESTINS
PT. MARIE
Sq. Alb.-Schweitzer
Rue Charlemagne
Rue Francois-Miron
Pl. Saint-Gervais
BOULEVARD HENRI IV
SULLY-MORLAND
BOULEVARD MORLAND
BOULEVARD BOURDON
BOULEVARD DE LA BASTILLE
QUAI DE LA RAPEE
QUAI HENRI IV
PONT DE SULLY
Ile de la Cité
Ile St. Louis
Hôtel Dieu
Notre Dame
Trib. de Commerce
Préfecture de Police
BVD. DU PALAIS
SEINE

L'AMBROISIE ★★ 1600F

Tel 42 78 51 45 Map C1.1 **R**
9 place des Vosges 75004 M° Bastille/St-Paul

A beautiful 17th-century square in the narrow streets of the Marais district is a fitting setting for Bernard Pacaud's elegant and exclusive restaurant. The interior maintains the period atmosphere with a hanging tapestry, Thonet chairs, stone floors and dark wood. Bernard's charming wife Danielle works *en salle* while her husband produces consistently superb food in the kitchen. Dishes change with the seasons: in summer you might find *feuillantine* of langoustines with sesame seeds and a curry sauce, *dos de Saint-Pierre à la feuille de laurier, barigoule d'artichauts* (John Dory served on a laurel leaf with artichoke stuffed with mushrooms, shallots, butter and parsley) and *millefeuille léger à la crème citronée, compote de mangue* (light millefeuille of lemon cream with a mango compote). Sommelier Pierre Le Moullac's excellent cellar includes the wildly expensive burgundy Romanée-Conti 1972 at 6900F. ***Seats*** *35. L 12-1.30 D 8-9.30.* ***Closed*** *Sun, Mon, 2 weeks in Feb & 1st 3 weeks Aug. Amex, Mastercard, Visa.*

AXIAL BEAUBOURG 662F

Tel 42 72 72 22 Fax 42 72 03 53 Map B1.2 **H**
11 rue du Temple 75004 M° Hotel de Ville

A six-storey hotel in the Marais, close to the Hotel de Ville and the Centre Pompidou. The period building was remodelled about five years ago and bedrooms offer simple modern comforts with direct-dial phones and satellite TVs. All have en suite shower rooms with WC. No restaurant, but there's a 16th-century breakfast room in the basement. Both breakfast and city tax are included in the price quoted. ***Rooms*** *39. Amex, Diners, Mastercard, Visa.*

BASTILLE SPERIA 622F

Tel 42 72 04 01 Fax 42 72 56 38 Map C1.3 **H**
1 rue de la Bastille 75004 M° Bastille

If arriving by metro, take the Rue St Antoine exit (not the Rue Faubourg St Antoine) from the station to find this family-run hotel, where visitors can expect a warm welcome. It's a peaceful old corner building which was completely modernised internally in recent years and offers bedrooms that have all the basic modern comforts including multi-channel TV and mini-bar. A few rooms, at the lower rate of 556F, come with shower and WC only. No restaurant. ***Rooms*** *42. Amex, Diners, Mastercard, Visa.*

BENOIT ★ 1000F

Tel 42 72 25 76 Fax 42 72 45 68 Map A1.4 **R**
20 rue Saint-Martin 75004 M° Chatelet/Hotel de Ville

With its parquet floors, red velvet banquettes, white napery and plants, this elegant bistro has a refined but relaxed atmosphere. The cooking is blissfully simple, with classic dishes prepared slowly and lovingly, such as calf's head with *sauce ravigote*, roast pigeon with *petit chou farci* and monkfish steaks *au poivre*. *Gigot d'agneau* is cooked in Pauillac wine, chicken roasted with chanterelles in a salt crust, and supreme of turbot poached and served with a Noilly sauce. Set menu 200F. ***Seats*** *55. L 12-2 D 8-10. Closed Aug. No credit cards.*

LE BISTROT DU DOME ★ 500F

Tel 48 04 88 44 Fax 48 04 00 59 Map C1.5 **R**
2 rue de la Bastille 75004 M° Bastille

An offshoot of the renowned Brasserie Dome and a sister restaurant to the Montparnasse Bistrot (14th arr, see below), with the same effective decor mix of rag-painted walls, fish tiles and plastic grapes as table lights and on the vine overhead, and the same à la carte ideas on the blackboard menu. The menu is all fish, the cooking skilful and relatively unembellished: *salade de pates aux coques, sardines ou anchois grillées, raie aux choux, rascasse purée à l'huile d'olive, maquereaux à la polenta.* St Nectaire farmhouse cheese, or simple sweets like dark chocolate tart, pineapple or gratin of pears round off a good, reasonably priced meal. All the wines are 98F a bottle. ***Seats*** *80. L 12-2.30 D 7.30-11.30. Amex, Mastercard, Visa.*

Bofinger — 550F

Tel 42 72 87 82 **Fax 42 72 97 68** Map C1.6 **R**
7 rue de la Bastille 75004 Mº Bastille

Five magnificent rooms with stunning Belle Epoque decor make up one of the capital's best-known classic brasseries. Opened in 1864, it has seen a few ups and downs, but with the current owners its status as one of the 'musts' for visitors has been restored. If you're eating classic Bofinger you're eating oysters and other shellfish, foie gras, choucroute, steak tartare, grills and home-produced patisserie and ices. But there's plenty more besides on the menus, where the best value is provided by the 169F all-in *prix-fixe* of three courses and a half-bottle of wine. ***Seats*** *300. L 12-3 D 6.30-1am (Sat & Sun noon-1am). Amex, Diners, Mastercard, Visa.*

Le Bistrot de Bofinger — 400F

Tel 42 72 05 23 Map C1.7 **R**
6 rue de la Bastille 75004 Mº Bastille

The Brasserie has spawned a bistro, directly opposite and quite grand in its own right, with 40s' frescoes, light wood, brass, huge mirrors and potted plants. Oysters, foie gras, raw marinated salmon, venison terrine and fish soup are typical starters, while main courses include cassoulet, *andouillette*, and fillet of plaice. *Mousseline de poissons fins coulis de carottes, quenelles de rouget façon brandade* and *paletot de canard roti à la maniguette* were interesting companions on a recent menu. Steak tartare is a speciality cold dish, salad of citrus fruits a trademark dessert. A la carte, or set menus at 98F (lunch except Sunday) and 165F including an aperitif (kir), three courses, half a bottle of wine and coffee. All the wines are available by the glass. ***Seats*** *150. L 12-3 D 7-12. Amex, Diners, Mastercard, Visa.*

Hotel de la Bretonnerie — 620F

Tel 48 87 77 63 **Fax 42 77 26 78** Map B1.8 **H**
22 rue Ste-Croix-de-la-Bretonnerie 75004 Mº Hotel de Ville

A four-storey 17th-century building renovated with style and taste. A continuing programme keeps things spick-and-span in bedrooms that are individually decorated in either Louis XIII or Louis Philippe style, and whose bathrooms (all with tubs) are modern and roomy. Rates range from 620F to 800F depending largely on the size of the room, and extra guests can be put up for 100F. New this year is double glazing to all the bedrooms and cable TV was due to be installed before the end of 1995. Day rooms (lots of beams in evidence) are quiet and relaxing, and the vaulted cellar is used as a breakfast room. No restaurant. ***Rooms*** *30.* ***Closed*** *Aug. Mastercard, Visa.*

Hotel Castex — 340F

Tel 42 72 31 52 **Fax 42 72 57 91** Map C1.9 **H**
5 rue Castex 75004 Mº Bastille/Sully-Morland

Blaise Bouchand is the fourth generation of his family to run this modest but friendly and neatly kept budget hotel near Place de la Bastille. Newly-carpeted bedrooms (21 doubles, 5 singles, 1 triple) are fairly basic and without TVs, although they do have direct-dial phones. Eight rooms (at the lower rate of 300F for a double) have showers and washbasins in the room but share four separate loos along the corridor. Breakfast/TV room and patio. ***Rooms*** *27.* ***Closed*** *Aug (possibly). Mastercard, Visa.*

Coconnas 500F

Tel 42 78 58 16 Map C1.10 **R**
2bis place des Vosges 75004 Mº Chemin Vert/Bastille

When the weather's fair, the terrace is the place to be, set in the cloisters of one of the most stunning squares in Paris. The menu at this offshoot of *La Tour d'Argent* is old-fashioned and more or less invariable: classic preparations of foie gras, duck, whiting and specialities *poule au pot du Bon Roy Henry, petit salé* and hot soufflés. Set menu 170F. See also *La Guirlande de Julie* in the same Place but in the 3rd arrondissement. ***Seats** 60 (+ 70 outside). L 12-2 D 7.30-10.15 (must book). **Closed** Mon & Tue. Amex, Diners, Mastercard, Visa.*

Le Coude Fou 450F

Tel 42 77 15 16 Map B1.11 **R**
12 rue du Bourg-Tibourg 75004 Mº Hotel de Ville

Traditional bistro with a modern touch. Simple wooden tables and chairs, and original 'naive' frescoes depicting country scenes provide a slightly unusual setting for some excellent cooking. Some dishes are well established in the bistro repertoire – terrines, *foie gras de canard, crottin de chèvre chaud, foie de veau vinaigre de framboise*, saddle of lamb with tarragon sauce – while others may be on the way – *couscous d'anchois frais au citron vert, langoustines roties au beurre de réglisse*. Specialities include *poulet au citron* and *entrecote au Bleu d'Auvergne*. Wine is taken seriously here too, and a solid list of mostly recent vintages is supplemented by a monthly-changing selection of about 16 wines by the glass. Book for dinner. Set L 110F (three courses and two glasses of wine) Set D 130F (Sun-Thu only). ***Seats** 70. L 12-2.15 D 7.30-12. **Closed** L Sun. Amex, Mastercard, Visa.*

Hotel des Deux-Iles 830F

Tel 43 26 13 35 Fax 43 29 60 25 Map B2.12 **H**
59 rue St-Louis-en-l'Ile 75004 Mº Pont-Marie

17th-century building with the feeling of a family home. Pretty bedrooms (4 singles, 13 doubles), have Provençal-style fabrics, cane furniture and blue Portuguese bathroom tiles. Facilities include multi-channel TV, radio and hairdryers. Virtually next door (65) and offering similar facilities is the **Hotel Lutèce** (Tel 43 26 23 52). The **Galiléo**, in the 8th arrondissement (Tel 47 20 66 06) is in the same ownership. Plans for next year include installing air-conditioning both here and at the **Lutèce**; it is already in place at the **Galiléo**. At the time of going to press they were planning to start accepting Visa and Mastercard. No restaurant. ***Rooms** 17.*

Le Fond de Cour 500F

Tel 42 74 71 52 Fax 48 04 91 12 Map B1.13 **R**
3 rue St-Croix-de-la-Bretonnerie 75004 Mº Hotel de Ville

A pretty, gently lit restaurant at the end of a courtyard, where tables are set outside in the summer. A new chef is keeping up high standards with such dishes as *quenelle de rascasse et caviar d'aubergine*, fricassee of chicken with morels, rabbit fillet in a herb crust and tournedos with *sauce périgourdine*. Set L 113F & 163F Set D 149 & 189F. ***Seats** 80 (+ 45 outside). L 12-2 D 7-11. Amex, Mastercard, Visa.*

Au Gourmet de l'Isle 400F

Tel 43 26 79 27 Map B2.14 **R**
42 rue St Louis-en-l'Ile 75004 Mº Pont-Marie

The secret corners of the charming Ile St Louis are secrets no longer. The whole place is awash with tourists, most of whom at some time or other seem to be queuing at the excellent Berthillon ice cream shops. There's a big choice of restaurants, many of them blatantly touristy, some more obviously traditional Parisian. One of the best of the latter, especially in terms of value for money, is this interesting little place with two rooms of tables under old beams, and a vaulted stone basement. The 130F menu (there's also an à la carte) includes classics such as *boudin, terrine de foie de volaille, ris d'agneau* with a port sauce, *andouillette AAAAA (Association Amicale des Amateurs d'Andouillettes Authentiques)*, guinea fowl with cabbage or lentils, crème caramel, compote of apples and pears in red wine. A particular speciality is *fond d'artichaut* topped with a poached egg and *sauce gribiche*. ***Seats** 60. L 12-2 D 7-10. **Closed** Mon & Tue. Mastercard, Visa.*

LE GRIZZLI — 400F

Tel 48 87 77 56 — Map A1.15 — **R**
7 rue St-Martin 75004 — M° Chatelet/Rambuteau

Classic fin-de-siècle bistro just a few steps away from a Marks & Spencer store in the Rue St-Martin. Cooking is a mix of bistro standards and dishes from the south-west of France. Among the specialities are *haricots tarbais, calamars à l'encre, cassoulet, fricot de veau aux cèpes séchés, foie gras, jambon au couteau, confit de canard* and salmon, sole, lamb cutlets or *faux-filet* of beef grilled and served on a slate. Set L 115F Set L & D 150F. ***Seats** 50 (+ 35 outside). L 12-2.30 D 7.30-11 (also open between lunch and dinner for lighter snacks). **Closed** Sun. Amex, Mastercard, Visa.*

See page 9 for a list of starred restaurants

A L'IMPASSE (CHEZ ROBERT) — 400F

Tel 42 72 08 45 — Map C1.16 — **R**
4 impasse Guéménée 75004 — M° Bastille

Run by the fourth generation of the family Collard, this splendid little bistro is located in a cul-de-sac moments away from Place des Vosges and Place de la Bastille. The atmosphere is intimate, with carefully restored ceiling beams and exposed sandstone walls, red-tiled floors and candles on tables bedecked with white linen cloths and serviettes. Cooking by chef M Vulcain is traditional, and many visitors (including us!) cite the *blanquette de veau à l'ancienne* as among the best in Paris. Other choices could include *soupe de poisson avec sa rouille*, minted skate terrine (in summer), *gateau de foie de volaille à la bressane*, terrine of rabbit, cod on a lentil purée, calf's liver with creamed leeks, *boeuf bourguignon*, their special way with sweetbreads (cream sauce with morels and cognac) and *pain de poisson à la basquaise*. Familiar desserts include chocolate profiteroles, *ile flottante* and the ubiquitous crème caramel. A short wine list (by bottle, pichet and glass), and a couple of dozen beers. If having three courses, go for the *menu formule* (new this year) which for 130F gives a full choice from the carte otherwise priced at 35F, 85F and 35F for starters, main dishes and desserts respectively. ***Seats** 60 (+ 20 outside). L 12-1.45 D 7.30-11. **Closed** L Sat & Mon, all Sun & Aug. Mastercard, Visa (Eurocheques not accepted).*

JO GOLDENBERG — 250F

Tel 48 87 20 16 Fax 42 78 15 29 — Map B1.17 — **R**
7 rue des Rosiers 75004 — M° St-Paul

In a street of similar establishments, this is the best known Jewish caterer in town, open all day, 364 days a year, as both deli and restaurant. The deli/take-away is at the front, the restaurant behind it, and in summer a large terrace comes into its own. Zakouskis (15 different fillings), blinis, home-cooked pastrami, gefilte fish and smoked salmon are among the snack favourites, while daily dishes run from stuffed cabbage leaves to escalope Vienna-style, moussaka, goulash and chicken with paprika.
***Seats** 100 (+ 60 outside). Meals 9am to midnight. **Closed** Jewish day of atonement. Amex, Diners, Mastercard, Visa.*

HOTEL MALHER 570F

Tel 42 72 60 92 **Fax 42 72 25 37** Map C1.18 **H**
5 rue Malher 75004 Mº St-Paul

Spick-and-span accommodation in a prime location for visiting the Marais. Family-run for three generations and redecorated throughout two years ago. Eight of the bathrooms have shower and WC only, while all bedrooms have direct-dial phone, cable TV, mini-bar and hairdryer. In high season (Sep-Oct, May-Jun and a period around Christmas) the room rate increases to 670F. Breakfast room in the vaulted cellars. No restaurant. ***Rooms*** *31. Amex, Mastercard, Visa.*

AU MONDE DES CHIMÈRES 500F

Tel 43 54 45 27 Map B2.21 **R**
69 rue St Louis-en-l'Ile 75004 Mº Pont-Marie

This charming Ile St Louis bistro in a 17th-century building with exposed stone walls and beams serves the traditional, bourgeois French family cooking (chef Cécile Ibane) which is rapidly disappearing along with the way of life it represents. The menu could suggest mussel soup (served as main course), *brandade de morue, rognon de veau en cocotte*, sole meunière, chicken with 40 garlic cloves or Pauillac lamb preceded by the house speciality *L'Oeuf de Jean* – a pan-fried escalope of foie gras, deglazed with vinegar and honey and served with a poached egg. Puddings are all the classics – floating islands, *fondant au chocolat, nougat glacé* or a hot apple tart (20 minutes wait). Set L 85F Set L & D 155F. ***Seats*** *35. L 12-2.30 D 7.30-10.30.* ***Closed*** *Sun, Mon & Feb school holidays. Amex, Mastercard, Visa.*

A glossary of French menu items starts on page 274

RIVOLI NOTRE DAME 630F

Tel 42 78 47 39 **Fax 40 29 07 00** Map B1.22 **H**
19 rue du Bourg-Tibourg 75004 Mº Hotel de Ville

17th-century stone-faced building in the historic Marais quarter. Bedrooms are equipped with satellite TV, mini-bar and hairdryer and all the bathrooms have a bathtub with shower above. Breakfast can be served in either the bedrooms or the vaulted cellars. No restaurant. ***Rooms*** *31. Amex, Diners, Mastercard, Visa.*

HOTEL SAINT-LOUIS-MARAIS 610F

Tel 48 87 87 04 **Fax 48 87 33 26** Map C2.23 **H**
1 rue Charles V 75004 Mº Bastille/St-Paul/Sully-Morland

An old building (once a convent) in the ancient Marais district. Bedrooms are traditional in style with few accessories other than direct-dial phones. There are no TVs. En suite facilities are modern, most with shower and WC only but the five largest bedrooms (710F) with a bath as well. No restaurant. ***Rooms*** *15. Mastercard, Visa.*

HOTEL DU 7e ART 410F

Tel 42 77 04 03 **Fax 42 77 69 10** Map C1.24 **H**
20 rue St-Paul 75004 Mº St-Paul

17th-century building in the classic mould, in the historic Marais quarter. The hotel was renovated quite recently, and takes the American cinema (especially 40s to 60s) as its decorative theme. Reception resembles a cinema cash desk, every inch of space being covered with posters, photos and bills. Room rates range from 410F to 650F for the largest of two junior suites on the top floor. Prices are for the room whether for single or double occupancy. All the accommodation is double-glazed and provided with direct-dial phones, safes, cable TV and en suite bath or shower. Four floors, no lift, and no room service but sandwiches and snacks are available in the bar. ***Rooms*** *23. Amex, Diners, Mastercard, Visa.*

Le Vieux Bistro 650F

Tel 43 54 18 95 Fax 44 07 35 63
14 rue du Cloitre-Notre-Dame 75004

Map B2.26
Mº Cité

R

Real bistro food in a real bistro in the tourist hubbub north of Notre Dame. The bar and furniture are all authentic pieces from the beginning of the century, offset by an original tiled floor, old mirrors and claret-coloured table-cloths. Lunch and candle-lit dinners share the same menu of classics, prepared by long-serving chef M Verlataine: *poireaux vinaigrette, saucisson chaud pommes à l'huile*, sole grilled or meunière, *andouillette au Sancerre, rognons de veau sauce moutarde, coeur de filet à la moelle en papillote*. Particular specialities are *paté de tete à l'ancienne, civet de canard,* profiteroles with chocolate sauce and *tarte tatin flambée au Calvados avec crème fraiche*. Meats are served very rare. There are 60 or so wines on a list that favours Beaujolais – the house wine is a Fleurie. Quick, young, friendly service. ***Seats*** *50 (+ 15 outside). L 12-2 D 7.30-10.30 (book).* ***Closed*** *24 & 25 Dec. Mastercard, Visa.*

Woolloomooloo 650F

Tel 42 72 32 11 Fax 42 72 32 21
36 bd Henri IV 75004

Map C1.25
Mº Bastille

R

Everything about this airy, clean-cut restaurant, from head chef Bernard Plaisted and all the front-of-house staff to the background tape of natural 'outback' sounds (interspersed with music tracks), is determinedly Australian. Bold, modern Antipodean cooking combines the flavours of the Asia Pacific rim with those of the Mediterranean. Marinated quail with black noodles, mint and lime dressing; Thai-style chicken and coconut soup; baked tomato salad with ricotta, rocket and basil dressing; braised duck with sticky black rice and ginger glaze; monkfish fillets in chick pea batter with sweet potato chips; banana and coconut pudding with passion fruit syrup, and grilled figs with lime curd and shortbread demonstrate Bernard's unrestrained style. The majority of the wines are Australian, with several available by the glass. Set menus 120F & 140F. ***Seats*** *60 (+ 25 outside). L (Sat & Sun only) 12-3 D 7.30-11.* ***Closed*** *L Mon-Fri, all 24 & 25 Dec. Mastercard, Visa.*

5th Arrondissement
Places of Interest

Sorbonne, M° Cluny La Sorbonne
Panthéon (tombs of Voltaire, Rousseau, Hugo, Zola), 43 54 34 51, M° Cardinal Lemoine/Maubert-Mutualité
Jardin des Plantes, 40 79 30 00, M° Gare d'Austerlitz/Jussieu
Muséum d'Histoire Naturelle
Institut du Monde Arabe, 40 51 38 38, M° Jussieu/Cardinal Lemoine/Sully-Morland
Musée National du Moyen-Age Thermes de Cluny, 43 25 62 00, M° St-Michel/Cluny La Sorbonne
Institut Océanographique, 46 33 08 61, M° Luxembourg (RER)
Rue Mouffetard (market)
Musée de la Police, 44 41 51 00, M° Maubert-Mutualité
Sainte-Etienne du Mont, 43 54 11 79, M° Cardinal Lemoine

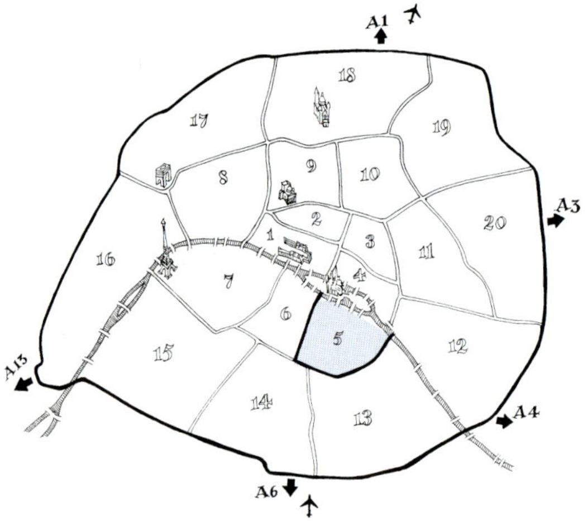

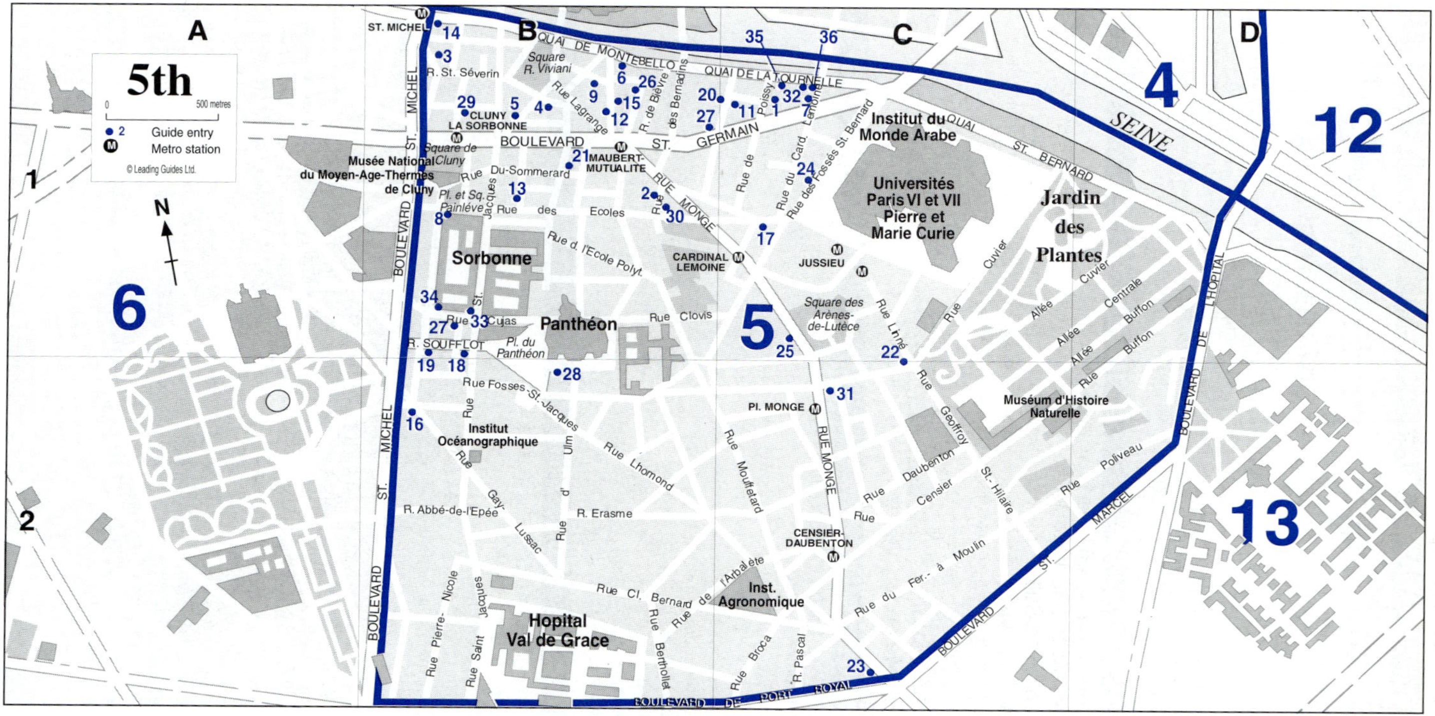
5th
0 500 metres
Guide entry
Metro station
© Leading Guides Ltd.
N
A
B
C
D
1
2
4
5
6
12
13
SEINE
ST. MICHEL
QUAI DE MONTEBELLO
QUAI DE LA TOURNELLE
QUAI ST. BERNARD
Square R. Viviani
R. St. Séverin
CLUNY LA SORBONNE
BOULEVARD ST. GERMAIN
Musée National du Moyen-Age-Thermes de Cluny
Square de Cluny
MAUBERT-MUTUALITE
Rue Du-Sommerard
Pl. et Sq. Painlévé
Rue des Ecoles
Rue Lagrange
R. de Bièvre
des Bernardins
Poissy
Lemoine
Rue du Card.
Rue des Fossés St. Bernard
Institut du Monde Arabe
Universités Paris VI et VII Pierre et Marie Curie
Jardin des Plantes
RUE MONGE
CARDINAL LEMOINE
JUSSIEU
Sorbonne
Rue d. l'Ecole Polyt.
Rue Cujas
R. SOUFFLOT
Pl. du Panthéon
Panthéon
Rue Clovis
Square des Arènes-de-Lutèce
Rue Linné
Rue Cuvier
Allée Centrale
Allée Buffon
Rue Buffon
Muséum d'Histoire Naturelle
Rue Geoffroy St.-Hilaire
Rue Daubenton
Rue Censier
Rue Poliveau
Pl. MONGE
Rue Fosses-St.-Jacques
Institut Océanographique
Rue Gay-Lussac
Rue d'Ulm
Rue Lhomond
Rue Mouffetard
R. Erasme
R. Abbé-de-l'Epée
CENSIER-DAUBENTON
Rue du Fer-à-Moulin
Rue de l'Arbalète
Inst. Agronomique
Rue Cl. Bernard
Rue Berthollet
Rue Broca
R. Pascal
Hopital Val de Grace
Rue Pierre-Nicole
Rue Saint Jacques
BOULEVARD ST. MICHEL
BOULEVARD DE PORT ROYAL
BOULEVARD ST. MARCEL
BOULEVARD DE L'HOPITAL
1
2
3
4
5
6
7
8
9
11
12
13
14
15
16
17
18
19
20
21
22
23
24
25
26
27
28
29
30
31
32
33
34
35
36

Restaurant A 500F

Tel 46 33 85 54 Map C1.1 **R**
5 rue de Poissy 75005 M° Maubert-Mutualité

An enormous sign with the letter A marks the location of this otherwise discreet restaurant down a narrow street off the eastern end of Boulevard St-Germain. The largely local crowd who frequent the restaurant can relax in an attractive interior and enjoy classical Chinese dishes, many of which are from the Imperial Court. Try Imperial prawns (prepared with sugar, salt, pepper and honey), a Hunan speciality of ham cooked with honey and a *marmite de canard maison* – a duck dish with lotus nuts and mushrooms which requires 48 hours notice. ***Seats*** *50. L 12-3 D 7-11.* ***Closed*** *L Mon. Amex, Mastercard, Visa.*

Agora St-Germain 750F

Tel 46 34 13 00 Fax 46 34 75 05 Map B1.2 **H**
42 rue des Bernardins 75005 M° Maubert-Mutualité

Just to the south of Boulevard St-Germain, the hotel has a small, warmly decorated marble-floored reception and cosily decorated bedrooms which have the advantage of being quite well soundproofed. Half look out over the street while the rest, and quietest, have views over a small courtyard garden. All have a good range of amenities and there's a characterful brick-lined, stone-floored basement breakfast room where a 45F buffet breakfast is served. ***Rooms*** *39. Amex, Diners, Mastercard, Visa.*

Hotel d'Albe 540F

Tel 46 34 09 70 Fax 40 46 85 70 Map B2.3 **H**
1 rue de la Harpe 75005 M° St-Michel

Located in a busy pedestrianised street in the very heart of the Latin Quarter, the hotel has a well-maintained modern decor throughout. The reception is compact, as are the bedrooms, but this is compensated by the use of bright colours and good lighting. There's a lift to the first five of the six floors. Rooms have all been attractively redecorated and feature en suite facilities with half having shower and WC facilities. All have satellite TVs, direct-dial phones, hairdryers and room safes. Breakfast is taken in a modern, café-like dining-room. ***Rooms*** *45. Amex, Diners, Mastercard, Visa.*

Auberge des Deux Signes 900F

Tel 43 25 46 56 Fax 46 33 20 49 Map B1.4 **R**
46 rue Galande 75005 M° Maubert-Mutualité

George Dhulster's is one of the most characterful of all Parisian restaurants thanks to a splendid location and very appealing decor. A Gothic window, all that remains of the 13th-century Chapelle Sainte-Blaise which was destroyed in 1770, now forms part of one of the thick stone walls. Heavy beams, vaulted ceilings and an early Louis XIII-style decor on the inside and exterior views over a charming square and the church of St Julien-Le-Pauvre as well as the more distant Notre Dame create a suitably impressive setting for what is largely traditional country-style cooking from his native Auvergne. *Foie gras de canard poelé aux épices et figues confites* with a glass of Sauternes, *ravioli de boeuf à la potée de choux et gingembre, salade périgourdine (frisée, foie gras, lamelles de canard confit, cerneaux de noix et l'huile de noix)* typify the choice of starter. For a main course, try *sole soufflée aux queues de langoustines, petite rognonnade de veau bourgeoise* or *confit d'oie maison*. Delicious desserts such as champagne sabayon with fresh fruit, *fondant d'ananas à la crème* or *chiboust à la sauce cannelle* round off a well-balanced meal. Set L Mon-Fri 150F Set L & D 250F. ***Seats*** *170. L 12-2.30 D 7.30-10.30.* ***Closed*** *L Sat, all Sun & Aug. Amex, Diners, Mastercard, Visa.*

Brasserie Balzar 400F

Tel 43 54 13 67 **Fax 44 07 14 91** Map B1.8 **R**
49 rue des Ecoles 75005 M° Cluny la Sorbonne

Traditional brasserie with restrained 30s decor, serving classic brasserie cuisine from noon till past midnight. Specialities include *moules marinière, rillettes de saumon, choucroute garnie, foie de veau poelé, steak au poivre* and *raie au beurre fondu*. Of the wines about a dozen are available by the generous glassful (15cl). ***Seats*** *85. Meals noon-12.30am.* ***Closed*** *Aug, 1 week Christmas. Amex, Mastercard, Visa.*

Bar à Huitres 500F

Tel 44 07 27 37 **Fax 43 26 71 62** Map B1.5 **R**
33 rue Saint-Jacques 75005 M° Maubert-Mutualité

Restaurant de poissons. See entry in 14th arrondissement.

Le Bistro du Port 400F

Tel 40 51 73 19 Map B1.6 **R**
13 quai Montebello 75005 M° Maubert-Mutualité

Overlooking Ile de la Cité, the quayside terrace of this attractive bistro offers a splendid view of Notre Dame. The fixed-price menu changes with the seasons and though it is traditionally based, creative flourishes abound and there's excellent use of spices and herbs. Begin with *pressé de jambon blanc à la graine de coriandre, vinaigrette à la vanille Bourbon; ravioli d'escargots à la crème d'ail doux et jus de persil* or *millefeuille de tartare de saumon à l'huile de crustacés*. Main courses could be *filet de canette sur lit de vin à la purée de pois épicées,* or *mitonné d'agneau confit au miel et aux raisins de Smyrne* (sultanas). Cheese is offered as an alternative to a dessert such as *pot pourri d'épices et fruits séchés au chocolat noir et blanc façon tartelette* or *gratin de mangue avec un sabayon de gingembre et poivre de Sichuan*. Set menu 138F. ***Seats*** *30 (+ 15 outside). L 12.30-2.30 D 8-10.30.* ***Closed*** *L Tue, all Mon & 10 days Aug. Mastercard, Visa.*

Le Bistrot d'à Coté 500F

Tel 43 54 59 10 **Fax 43 29 02 08** Map C1.7 **R**
16 bd St-Germain 75005 M° Maubert-Mutualité

Michel Rostang's tremendously successful restaurant has spawned three other branches, all following the same formula of serving modern versions of traditional dishes in a lively atmosphere. House specialities include *brochettes de moules poelées, salade de champignons, rognon de veau à la compotée de pieds de porc, gratin macaroni* (veal kidneys with a compote of pig's trotters and macaroni cheese) and *pot de crème au chocolat à l'ancienne*. There is a choice of seven or eight dishes for each course: two cost 139F, three are 185F. The other Bistrots d'à Coté are at 16 avenue de Villiers, 75017 Paris (tel: 47 63 25 61), 10 rue Gustave Flaubert, 75017 Paris (tel: 42 67 05 81), and 4 rue Boutard at Neuilly 92200 (tel: 47 45 34 55). ***Seats*** *65. L 12-2 D 7-11.* ***Closed*** *L Sat, all Sun (all Sat in Aug). Amex, Diners, Mastercard, Visa.*

La Bucherie 920F

Tel 43 54 78 06 **Fax 46 34 54 02** Map B1.9 **R**
41 rue de la Bucherie 75005 M° St-Michel

Bernard Bosque has been keeping his customers well fed for over 30 years, offering comforting winter dishes such as warm oysters in champagne sauce, langoustines with cabbage (the latter replaced by lentils in the summer). Game is a speciality in season, jugged hare being a fine example. Otherwise the selection includes fillets of red mullet with basil, beef fillet with a truffle jus and sautéed lamb with aubergines among a selection of delicious standards. There's classical background music and the decor features much attractive woodwork and contemporary art around the walls. In the afternoon (3-6pm) you can also take

See over

tea and pastries – rhubarb tart, chocolate cake – at armchairs around the fireplace with magazines and the day's newspapers provided. Set menu 230F. ***Seats** 100 (+ 30 outside). L 12-2.30 D 7-12.30. Amex, Diners, Mastercard, Visa.*

CHEZ TOUTOUNE 430F

Tel 43 26 56 81 Map C1.11 **R**
5 rue Pontoise 75005 Mº Maubert-Mutualité

A comfortable bistro just off the Boulevard St-Germain where Colette (Toutoune) Dejean's fixed-price menu offers good-value Provençal-inspired cooking. A soup course precedes the starters – country terrine with aspic and olives, *escabèche, céleri rémoulade,* snail gougère with garlic butter – and a cheese of the day between main dish – guinea fowl with rosemary and ratatouille, roast cod with a fennel and extra virgin olive oil purée – and dessert. The latter might include *tarte tatin* with quince, *gateau au chocolat très noir* or fresh roast figs with a passion fruit coulis. Wines from Colette's native Midi. Set menu 158F. ***Seats** 60. L 12-2 D 7.45-10.45. **Closed** L Mon, all Sun. Amex, Mastercard, Visa.*

CHIENG-MAI 400F

Tel 43 25 45 45 Map B1.12 **R**
12 rue Frédéric Sauton 75005 Mº Maubert-Mutualité

One of the best Thai restaurants in town – popular too, so worth booking – with seating on two air-conditioned floors. Order prawn soup with lemon grass; beef salad with galangal (an aromatic root); spiced fish steamed in a banana leaf; pork satay; sautéed beef with peppers; duck and chicken fried with ginger; and to finish a cooling and unusual Thai red bean and coconut milk ice cream or coconut milk jelly with fruits and ice cream. A novelty on the otherwise French wine list is an offering from China 'Nuit de Chine', both red and white. Several set menus from 120 to 173F per person plus à la carte. ***Seats** 100. L 12-2.30 D 7-11.30. **Closed** Sun, 1st 2 weeks Aug & 2 weeks Christmas. Amex, Mastercard, Visa.*

See page 9 for a list of starred restaurants

HOTEL DU COLLÈGE DE FRANCE 500F

Tel 43 26 78 36 Fax 46 34 58 29 Map B1.13 **H**
7 rue Thénard 75005 Mo Maubert-Mutualité/St-Michel

In a quiet back street near the Sorbonne in the heart of the Latin Quarter. All bedrooms have TV, radio, alarms, while rooms on the sixth floor are the largest and most characterful with beams and balconies but need to be reserved five or six months in advance. 24-hour room service, no restaurant. Continental breakfast is 33F and can be served in the bedrooms if required. ***Rooms** 29. Amex, Mastercard, Visa.*

LE DÉPART DE SAINT-MICHEL

Tel 43 54 24 55 Fax 46 33 87 21 Map B1.14 **R**
1 place Saint-Michel 75005 Mº St-Michel

Tables and chairs are arranged in outward-facing rows in order to watch the 'theatre of life' from this all-hours brasserie at a very busy crossroads by the Seine. The menu is quite extensive and varied, ranging from light snacks and pastries to a few more substantial dishes such as a speciality of *pavé au poivre*, a thick peppered steak served with French fries, French beans or spaghetti. Pride of place, however, must go to the *croque campagnard*, a *croque monsieur* that ranks among the best in Paris. It is prepared on a long slice of excellent country bread, the gruyère cheese topping nicely browned. ***Open** 24 hours. Amex, Diners, Mastercard, Visa.*

DODIN-BOUFFANT 800F

Tel 43 25 25 14 **Fax 43 29 52 61** Map B1.15 **R**
25 rue Frédéric Sauton 75005 M° Maubert-Mutualité

Somewhere in character between a bistro and a *grande brasserie de luxe*, Dodin-Bouffant's combination of outstanding modern French cooking and realistic (by top Parisian standards) pricing make it a very popular, bustling sort of place. A non-smoking room on the first floor is a little more peaceful and cosy. American Mark Singer's menu is strong on seafood, with some unusual offerings: *dos de mérou au jus et pied de veau* (grouper steak with calf's trotter), skate wing with fresh thyme, *tournedos de colinot au jus de bouchot* (hake with a mussel liquor), along with hearty bistro fare and market specials such as *carré d'agneau en croute d'herbes* or roast guinea fowl with girolles. Good wine list. Set menu 220F. ***Seats*** *60 (+ 40 outside). L 12-2.15 D 7.30-11.* ***Closed*** *L Sat, all Sun. Amex, Diners, Mastercard, Visa.*

E MARTY 450F

Tel 43 31 39 51 **Fax 43 37 63 70** Map C2.23 **R**
20 ave des Gobelins 75005 M° Les Gobelins

Near the junction of Avenue des Gobelins, Boulevard de Port Royal and Boulevard St-Marcel, the first-floor brasserie with decorative hints of its 30s origins offers a selection of very fresh and delicious shellfish including a good choice of various oysters, a mixed grill of fish (scallops, bream, mullet and salmon) and poached turbot with hollandaise sauce. In the ground-floor restaurant the *plateaux de fruits de mer* are popular and excellent choices. There's a short but varied choice of meat dishes too: *tete de veau à l'auvergnate sauce ravigote, aiguillettes de canard au poivre vert, chateaubriand grillé sauce béarnaise*. Set menu: Brasserie 120F, Restaurant 189F. ***Seats*** *95. L 12-2.30 D 7-10.30. Amex, Diners, Mastercard, Visa.*

ELYSA LUXEMBOURG 720F

Tel 43 25 31 74 **Fax 46 34 56 27** Map B2.16 **H**
6 rue Gay-Lussac 75005 M° Luxembourg (RER)

Near the Luxembourg Gardens and close to the heart of the Latin Quarter. Neat bedrooms, with satellite TV, radio-alarms, phone, mini-bars and hairdryers, are decorated in pastel shades and feature en suite marble bathrooms. Breakfast can be taken either in your room or in a cellar-like basement room with characterful exposed stone walls. ***Rooms*** *30. Amex, Mastercard, Visa.*

FAMILIA 395F

Tel 43 54 55 27 **Fax 43 29 61 77** Map C1.17 **H**
11 rue des Ecoles 75005 M° Cardinal Lemoine/Maubert-Mutualité

A family-run hotel with triple-glazing in all bedrooms which ensures peace and tranquillity from the exterior bustle of Paris. Inside, some walls have been decorated with frescoes and others hung with artwork, both by fine arts students. Well-equipped bedrooms have multi-channel TV (including BBC), phone, mini-bar and hairdryer. A number of rooms have private balconies. No room service. ***Rooms*** *30. Amex, Diners, Mastercard, Visa.*

LES FONTAINES 500F

Tel 43 26 42 80 Map B1.18 **R**
9 rue Soufflot 75005 M° Luxembourg (RER)

This corner café/brasserie between the Luxembourg Gardens and the Panthéon has kept everything very traditional – the decor as much as the cuisine. Little known by the tourists, it's extremely popular with its regular clientele of university staff, editors and other locals. Everyone sits elbow-to-elbow to enjoy such specialities as *magret de canard au poivre vert, cote de veau normande pommes sautées*, and *fricassée de lapin aux champignons*, with salmon, hake and red mullet among the fish offerings. There's always a home-made fruit tart to

See over

finish. As in many Parisian cafés, business starts at 7.45am and finishes at 12.30am. No set menu. ***Seats** 80. L 12-2.45 D 7.15-10.30. **Closed** Sun, Mon & Aug. Mastercard, Visa.*

La Gueuze 300F

Tel 43 54 63 00 Fax 43 54 12 59 Map B1.19 **R**
19 rue Soufflot 75005 Mº Cluny la Sorbonne/Luxembourg (RER)

A few paces from the Luxembourg Gardens, the speciality here is the vast selection of some 150 beers from around the world. There are 66 bottled Belgian beers with 13 more on draught. The menu is familiar, headed by moules marinière and the almost obligatory *frites*. Portions are hearty and Belgian favourites include *carbonnade flamande*. There's a short daily list of blackboard specials as well as *choucroute* and a selection of grills and salads and, to finish, enjoyable minty profiteroles. ***Seats** 170. Meals noon-2am (Fri & Sat till 4.30am). Mastercard, Visa.*

Inajiku 500F

Tel 43 54 70 07 Fax 40 51 74 44 Map C1.20 **R**
14 rue Pontoise 75005 Mº Maubert-Mutualité

Relatively inexpensive Japanese teppan-yaki bar with each table (for 7-8 people – it's normal to share) having its own hot plate at which the prawns, scallops, beef and salmon are cooked before your very eyes. Teppan-yaki menus include tofu, rice and vegetables and begin at 88F (for *beignets de blanc de poulet*, salad and dessert). Also sushi and sashimi menus at 168F and 188F (both 148F at lunchtime). Finish with jasmine tea-flavoured sorbet. Drink Japanese beer. ***Seats** 55. L 12-2.30 D 7-10.45. **Closed** Sun & Aug. Mastercard, Visa.*

Le Jardin de Cluny 775F

Tel 43 54 22 66 Fax 40 51 03 36 Map B1.21 **H**
9 rue du Sommerard 75005 Mº Maubert-Mutualité

The stone-vaulted basement breakfast room here may be of ancient origin but bedrooms above are rather more up-to-date with remote-control cable TVs (including English language channels), direct-dial phones and mini-bars. 24 have air-conditioning. No restaurant, but all-day room service includes the provision of breakfast in your room, if required. ***Rooms** 40. Amex, Diners, Mastercard, Visa.*

Le Jardin des Plantes 510F

Tel 47 07 06 20 Fax 47 07 62 74 Map C1.22 **H**
5 rue Linné 75005 Mº Jussieu

In fine weather, start the day with breakfast on the fifth-floor terrace of this appealing hotel, which stands facing the Botanical Gardens in a quiet street. Bedrooms, all with phone, TV, mini-bar and hairdryer, have floral wall coverings, a different flower for each floor, and matching bedcovers and curtains. A brasserie/tea room on the ground floor closes at 7pm; while the breakfast room is in the vaulted basement. ***Rooms** 33. Amex, Diners, Mastercard, Visa.*

Moissonnier 500F

Tel 43 29 87 65 Map C1.24 **R**
28 rue des Fossés St Bernard 75005 Mº Jussieu

Authentic old-fashioned family-run bistro with simple decor and homely atmosphere. Lyonnais and Franche-Comté specialities (in huge portions) include about a dozen assorted hors d'oeuvre from giant *saladiers lyonnaises (salades de pied de veau, de gras double, de cervelas, de boeuf); petit salé, couennes et lentilles; civet de lapereau aux pates fraiches; tablier de sapeur* ('fireman's apron' – breadcrumbed tripe with *sauce gribiche*); *meringues glacées, sauce chocolat chaud; entremets citron, coulis de framboises*. Wines, many from Beaujolais, include some recherché items like *vin jaune* from the Jura. No set menu. ***Seats*** *70. L 12-2.30 D 7-10.* ***Closed*** *D Sun, all Mon & Aug. Mastercard, Visa*

HOTEL DES NATIONS 600F

Tel 43 26 45 24 **Fax 46 34 00 13** Map C1.25 **H**
54 rue Monge 75005 Mº Cardinal Lemoine/Place Monge

On the busy Rue Monge, but double-glazing throughout keeps the traffic noise away from the bedrooms, which are simple and modern, all decorated in soft pastel shades. A few look out on to a plant-filled courtyard; some can accommodate up to four people. All have a phone, safe, TV and radio. Public rooms include a bar and lounge area. No restaurant, but breakfast can be served in your room, or there's a buffet service in the breakfast room. ***Rooms*** *38. Amex, Diners, Mastercard, Visa.*

HOTEL DE NOTRE DAME 690F

Tel 43 26 79 00 **Fax 46 33 50 11** Map B1.26 **H**
19 rue Maitre Albert 75005 Mº Maubert-Mutualité

In a quiet side street between the Boulevard St-Germain and the Seine and opposite Notre Dame. The reception/bar area is given a slightly rustic feel by timber ceiling beams that also feature in many of the bedrooms which are mostly furnished in a classical style. All have TV, mini-bar and hairdryer as well as a wall safe. No restaurant, but there's a breakfast room on the ground floor or breakfast can be taken in your room. ***Rooms*** *34. Amex, Mastercard, Visa.*

AU PACTOLE 750F

Tel 46 33 31 31 **Fax 46 33 07 60** Map B1.27 **R**
44 bd St-Germain 75005 Mº Maubert-Mutualité

Designed to resemble a rather smart private dining-room – pictures, shelves of books, crystal chandeliers – Roland Magne's restaurant has enormous charm as well as fine food. The cuisine is classically-based but interpreted with Roland's own inventiveness: *raviolis d'escargots à la crème d'ail*, fricassee of lobster with girolles, stuffed pig's trotter, escalope of salmon in a pesto sauce, *tarte au chocolat, crème brulée aux parfums des iles*. In addition to the à la carte there's a set five-course *menu gourmand* (279F) and a limited-choice business lunch. There's a public car park across the street. ***Seats*** *48. L 12.15-2.30 D 7-10.30.* ***Closed*** *L Sat, 1 May, 24 & 25 Dec. Amex, Mastercard, Visa.*

HOTEL DU PANTHÉON 770F

Tel 43 54 32 95 **Fax 43 26 64 65** Map B2.28 **H**
19 place du Panthéon 75005 Mº Maubert-Mutualité/Luxembourg (RER)

Near the Luxembourg Gardens, an 18th-century mansion facing the Panthéon. Spacious, individually decorated bedrooms, some with fabric-covered walls, feature exposed beams and country-style furniture. All have air-conditioning, mini-bars and cable television. The **Hotel des Grands Hommes** (Tel 46 34 19 60), next door, and in the same ownership, is similar in style and pricing. ***Rooms*** *34. Amex, Diners, Mastercard, Visa.*

PARC ST-SÉVERIN 600F

Tel 43 54 32 17 **Fax 43 54 70 71** Map B1.29 **H**
22 rue de la Parcheminerie 75005 Mº St-Michel/Cluny la Sorbonne

A 1930s hotel renovated in 1988. Bright bedrooms have a mix of antique and modern furniture and boast cable TV, hairdryers, mini-bars, private safes and well-lit bathrooms. In the past year just over half the rooms have had air-conditioning and double-glazing installed, with the remainder to follow in the winter period. Four rooms have balconies, the best (at 1500F) a large terrace overlooking the church of St Severin and the rooftops of the Latin Quarter. ***Rooms*** *27. Amex, Diners, Mastercard, Visa.*

HOTEL RÉSIDENCE HENRI IV 750F

Tel 44 41 31 81 **Fax 46 33 93 22** Map B1.30 **H**
50 rue des Bernardins 75005 M° Maubert-Mutualité

By Square Paul-Langevin and Rue des Ecoles, this intimate hotel boasts some nice moulded ceilings and other period features. The nine bedrooms and five apartments vary considerably in size but all have kitchenette, mini-bar, phone, hairdryer and cable TV. ***Rooms*** *14. Amex, Mastercard, Visa.*

HOTEL RÉSIDENCE SAINT-CHRISTOPHE 550F

Tel 43 31 81 54 **Fax 43 31 12 54** Map C2.31 **H**
17 rue Lacépède 75005 M° Place Monge

The bedrooms and public areas are furnished in Louis XV style at an elegant little hotel near the Botanical Gardens. The owner loves greenery, so lush foliage abounds. Those rooms whose numbers end in 2 (12, 22 etc) are special in that they enjoy excellent views over the Jardin des Plantes. Satellite TVs, mini-bars and hairdryers are standard features. Bathrooms have either bath or shower. No restaurant, but there is a pretty breakfast room or breakfast can be taken in the privacy of your room. ***Rooms*** *31. Amex, Diners, Mastercard, Visa.*

LA ROTISSERIE DU BEAUJOLAIS 440F

Tel 43 54 17 47 **Fax 44 07 12 04** Map C1.32 **R**
19 quai de la Tournelle 75005 M° Maubert-Mutualité

Quayside bistro with view of Notre Dame from a covered terrace, in the same ownership as, and across the road from, the renowned *Tour d'Argent*. Many of the ingredients come direct from Lyons (as does the antique bar counter) for a menu that might include the likes of *saucisse lyonnaise avec pommes tièdes; filet de hareng, pommes à l'huile; escargots de Bourgogne* and *salade frisée avec gésiers* as starters. Main dishes include *magret de canard, coq au vin, pigeon roti au choux* and *tete de veau sauce ravigote*. Spit-roasted meats are a speciality of the kitchen, which is open to the dining-room. For dessert try the *crème brulée, granité de pommes au Calvados, iles flottantes* or a delicious *gateau de riz*. The short wine list concentrates on Beaujolais. No set menu. ***Seats*** *50. L 12-2.30 D 7.30-11.* ***Closed*** *Mon. Mastercard, Visa.*

> The best way to get around Paris is by bus or metro – buy a book (carnet) of tickets at any metro station and save money

SELECT 650F

Tel 46 34 14 80 **Fax 46 34 51 79** Map B1.33 **H**
1 place Sorbonne 75005 M° Cluny la Sorbonne/Luxembourg (RER)

A 15th-century facade conceals a very modern interior centering on a plant-filled atrium. Among the double-glazed bedrooms, all now redecorated in a smart, contemporary style, some have exposed ceiling beams and some natural stone walls. All are air-conditioned and have TVs, phones and hairdryers. Breakfast is served in a stone-vaulted basement. ***Rooms*** *68. Amex, Diners, Mastercard, Visa.*

HOTEL DE LA SORBONNE 410F

Tel 43 54 58 08 **Fax 40 51 05 18** Map B1.34 **H**
6 rue Victor-Cousin 75005 M° Cluny la Sorbonne/Luxembourg (RER)

Small family-run hotel by the Sorbonne, just round the corner from the Luxembourg Gardens. A little rattan-furnished conservatory sitting area looks on to a plant-filled courtyard. En suite bedrooms – 11 with bathtub, the rest with shower/WC only – have country-style decor in a variety of colour schemes and such conveniences as cable TV, phones and hairdryer. ***Rooms*** *37. Amex, Mastercard, Visa.*

La Timonerie ★ 800F

Tel 43 25 44 42 Map C1.35 **R**
35 quai de la Tournelle 75005 M° Maubert-Mutualité

A charmingly decorated restaurant by the Seine. Chef-patron Philippe de Givenchy has an eclectic, refined style of cooking, and the influence of the Mediterranean is evident on the seasonal carte in dishes such as *grosse tapénade aux anchois et mozzarella en salade de basilic*, roasted sweet pepper ravioli and stuffed aubergines. Tempting main courses include *dorade rotie à l'estragon et piment et son jus de matelote réduit* (bream roasted with tarragon and chilis served with its own jus) and pig's trotters stuffed with Spanish peppers and Serrano ham and roasted in olive oil. Desserts are simple: *crepes aux fraises* and *tarte fine au chocolat*, for instance. Set L 230F. ***Seats** 20. L 12-2.30 D 7.30-10.30.* ***Closed** L Mon, all Sun, 2 weeks Feb & 3 weeks Aug. Mastercard, Visa.*

La Tour d'Argent ★★★ 2400F

Tel 43 54 23 31 **Fax 44 07 12 04** Map C1.36 **R**
15 quai de la Tournelle 75005 M° St-Paul

Almost a historic monument, this is the restaurant that once-in-a-lifetime visitors to Paris head for – if their pockets are deep enough. Even their speciality dish, a duck *à la presse* with cherries, has been on the menu for over 100 years and comes with a numbered certificate; on our most recent visit they'd reached 835,817! Duck is what the Tour d'Argent is best known for, but there are other specialities, too, including *quenelles de brochet* and *peches flambées à l'eau de vie de framboise*. There are also some lighter dishes on an essentially traditional carte that competes with luxurious surroundings, spectacular views of the Seine and Notre Dame from the coveted window tables and a fabulous cellar which also contains a museum of wine. If the prices are beyond your reach (there is a more manageable set lunch menu at 375F) head for their shop opposite, *Comptoirs de la Tour d'Argent*, where souvenirs bearing the restaurant's logo are sold – tinned foie gras, tableware, silk ties and the like. ***Seats** 110. L 12-2.30 D 8-10.30.* ***Closed** Mon. Amex, Diners, Mastercard, Visa.*

Hotel des Trois Collèges 450F

Tel 43 54 67 30 **Fax 46 34 02 99** Map B1.37 **H**
16 rue Cujas 75005 M° Cluny la Sorbonne/Luxembourg (RER)

Between the Panthéon and the Luxembourg Gardens, a period building conceals a simple modern interior. Bedrooms have claret-coloured carpets contrasted with either white or beech furniture and beige walls. All have TV, phone and hairdryer. The spacious breakfast room makes way for a delightful *salon de thé* where from noon till late (except Sat and Sun), a classic selection of light snacks, gateaux and teas is served. ***Rooms** 44. Amex, Diners, Mastercard, Visa.*

6th Arrondissement
Places of Interest

Jardin du Luxembourg
Saint-Sulpice
Saint-Germain-des-Prés
Musée Delacroix, 43 54 04 87, M° St-Germain-des-Prés
Latin Quarter, Boulevard St-Germain, Boulevard St-Michel
Hotel des Monnaies, 40 46 55 35, M° Pont Neuf
Institut de France, 44 41 43 35, M° Pont Neuf/Odéon

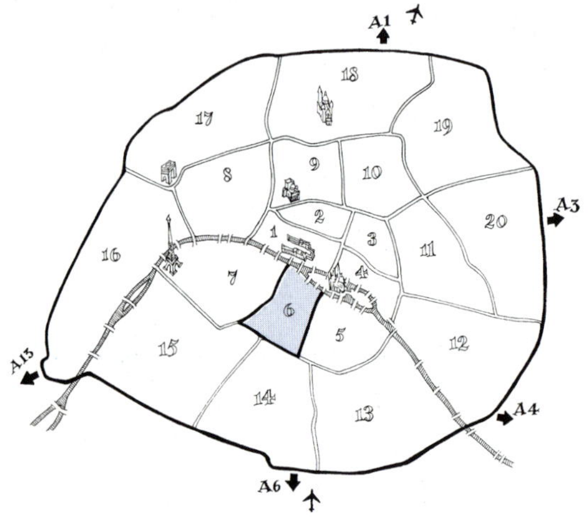

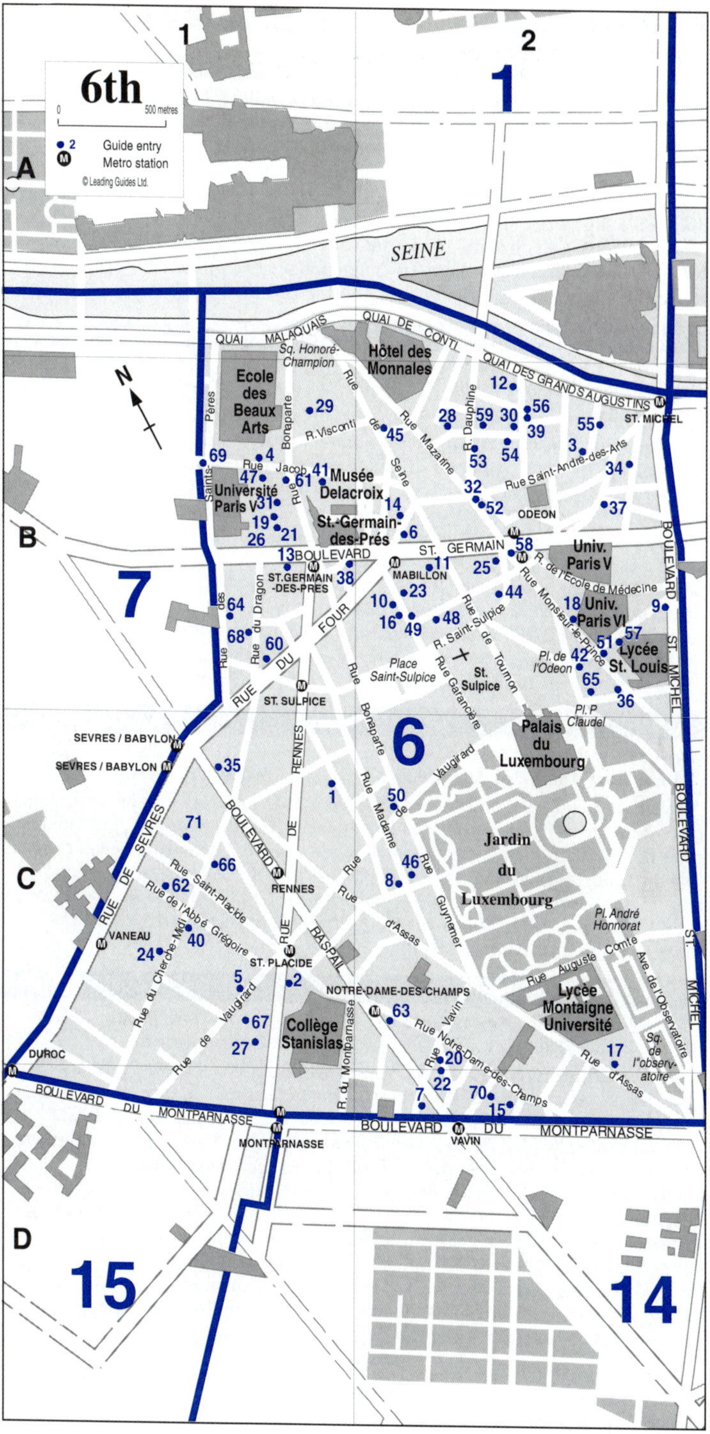
6th
0
500 metres
Guide entry
Metro station
© Leading Guides Ltd.
SEINE
Hôtel des Monnaies
Ecole des Beaux Arts
Musée Delacroix
Université Paris V
St.-Germain-des-Prés
Univ. Paris V
Univ. Paris VI
Lycée St. Louis
St. Sulpice
Palais du Luxembourg
Jardin du Luxembourg
Lycée Montaigne Université
Collège Stanislas
QUAI MALAQUAIS
QUAI DE CONTI
QUAI DES GRANDS AUGUSTINS
BOULEVARD ST. GERMAIN
RUE DU FOUR
BOULEVARD ST. MICHEL
BOULEVARD RASPAIL
RUE DE RENNES
RUE DE SEVRES
BOULEVARD DU MONTPARNASSE
Rue d'Assas
Rue de Vaugirard
Rue Notre-Dame-des-Champs
ST. MICHEL
ODEON
MABILLON
ST.GERMAIN -DES-PRES
ST. SULPICE
SEVRES / BABYLON
RENNES
VANEAU
ST. PLACIDE
NOTRE-DAME-DES-CHAMPS
DUROC
MONTPARNASSE
VAVIN
Place Saint-Sulpice
Pl. de l'Odeon
Pl. P Claudel
Pl. André Honnorat
Sq. de l'observatoire

HOTEL DE L'ABBAYE SAINT-GERMAIN 980F

Tel 45 44 38 11 **Fax 45 48 07 86** Map C1.1 **H**
10 rue Cassette 75006 Mº St-Sulpice

Its sacred role is far in the past, but this former convent, situated between a courtyard and a garden (where alfresco breakfasts can be taken), remains a place of peace and calm. Bedrooms are comfortable (air-conditioning has been installed in all rooms since last year), though not all are particularly roomy. The rate quoted above is for a standard room; larger rooms are priced much higher, and at the top of the range are four duplex suites (1900F-2000F) with their own usable balconies. Bathrooms all have tubs. Room service till midnight. Three lounges, one with a real log fire in winter, and a modern bar (also open till midnight). No restaurant. ***Rooms*** *46. Amex, Mastercard, Visa.*

ACACIAS SAINT-GERMAIN 750F

Tel 45 48 97 38 **Fax 45 44 63 57** Map C1.2 **H**
151bis rue de Rennes 75006 Mº St-Placide

In the Left Bank triangle of the Latin Quarter, Saint-Germain-des-Prés and Montparnasse, this hotel (built in 1856 and a private house till 1930, now a listed building) offers space and comfort, plus a delightful little summer garden (overlooked by five family rooms). Top-floor rooms are spacious, with sloping ceilings and views over the Paris rooftops. 20 bedrooms were recently refurbished in a classic English style and it is intended that the remainder should receive the same treatment soon. All have satellite TV, mini-bar, hairdryer and safe. Among the offerings are 24-hour room service and 24-hour availability of breakfast (Continental as well as cooked), laundry, baby-sitting and fluent English. There is a 50F supplement for the rooms with bathtubs, the others have shower and WC only. Special low rates in winter, July and August, and interesting package deals. ***Rooms*** *41. Amex, Diners, Mastercard, Visa.*

ALLARD 650F

Tel 43 26 48 23 Map B2.3 **R**
41 rue Saint-André-des-Arts 75006 Mº Odéon/St-Michel

A lively, authentic bistro, its decor splendidly unchanged since it opened at the turn of the century, its appeal as strong as ever. The handwritten menu offers time-honoured specialities that include *jambon persillé, saucisson chaud lyonnais*, sole meunière, poached turbot with beurre blanc, Bresse chicken with girolles, roast guinea fowl with lentils and – perhaps most famous of all – duck with olives. Set L 150F Set L & D 200F. ***Seats*** *65. L 12-2 D 7.30-11.* ***Closed*** *23 & 24 Dec. Amex, Diners, Mastercard, Visa.*

HOTEL D'ANGLETERRE 800F

Tel 42 60 34 72 **Fax 42 60 16 93** Map B1.4 **H**
44 rue Jacob 75006 Mº St-Germain-des-Prés

Once the British Embassy, and later home to Ernest Hemingway, this charming hotel has its own delightful patio garden, the perfect spot to enjoy a leisurely breakfast or a quiet drink in fine weather. Character abounds in the elegant reception rooms which feature period furniture, objets d'art and fine paintings, and the bedrooms (some on the small side, some with four-posters, all with satellite TV, direct-dial telephone, hairdryer and small safe) are generally attractive, with original beams, exposed stone walls, comfortably large beds and generous seating. Bathrooms, with basins set in freestanding antique vanity units, have painted tiles and give the impression of being old-fashioned, but are in fact up-to-date, with decent plumbing. There are a few small rooms at a lower price (600F) and three suites at 1250F. Room service is round the clock but there is no restaurant. ***Rooms*** *27. Amex, Diners, Mastercard, Visa.*

Aramis Saint-Germain 600F

Tel 45 48 03 75 **Fax 45 44 99 29** Map C1.5 **H**
124 rue de Rennes 75006 Mº St-Placide

An appealing hotel offering high standards of comfort and traditional hospitality to a largely non-French clientele. Bedrooms vary in detail, all having been redecorated in the last couple of years, but all are attractive and relaxing with satellite TV, mini-bar and hairdryer; 15 are air-conditioned, and nine have whirlpool baths. All but a few bathrooms have both bathtub and shower. A pianist sometimes plays in the bar. The vaulted cellar makes an atmospheric function/meeting room for up to 30. No restaurant. 24-hour public parking 100 metres away. ***Rooms*** *42. Amex, Diners, Mastercard, Visa.*

L'Arbuci 440F

Tel 44 41 14 14 **Fax 44 41 14 10** Map B2.6 **R**
25 rue de Buci 75006 Mº Mabillon

Brasserie on two floors specialising in oysters, shellfish and various meat and fish dishes cooked on the rotisserie. A 78F menu offers pork, beef and chicken brochettes *à volonté* – you can eat as much as you want! – with mashed potato, while the 133F menu offers oysters *à volonté* and the 128F menu brings brochettes with nine oysters no. 5. In addition there are just a few starters (*soupe à l'oignon, salade de chèvre chaud aux épices*, snails and stuffed mussels), a couple of fish dishes (roast salmon with herbs, sea bream with fennel and giant prawns provençale) and steaks, plus roast lamb. From Thursday to Sunday evenings a pianist plays until the early hours in the ground-floor dining-room. There's a Jazz club in the basement. ***Seats*** *220.* ***Meals*** *noon-1.30am. Amex, Mastercard, Visa.*

Atelier Montparnasse 712F

Tel 46 33 60 00 **Fax 40 51 04 21** Map D2.7 **H**
49 rue Vavin 75006 Mº Vavin

Recently redecorated, Marie-José Tible's modern hotel is near, but not quite amid, the bustle of Montparnasse. Each bedroom is named after a famous impressionist artist, and each floor has a different colour scheme. All rooms are double-glazed and feature TV and mini-bar. Bathrooms all have both tub and shower and a mosaic made up of reproductions of the artist after whom the room is named. ***Rooms*** *17. Amex, Diners, Mastercard, Visa.*

See page 9 for a list of starred restaurants

Hotel de l'Avenir 450F

Tel 45 48 84 54 **Fax 45 49 26 80** Map C2.8 **H**
65 rue Madame 75006 Mº St-Placide/Notre-Dame-des-Champs

In a quiet street a few paces from the Luxembourg Gardens between Montparnasse and the Latin Quarter, l'Avenir offers the usual facilities in bedrooms plus double-glazing and room safes. The price quote above is for a room with en suite shower and WC only; larger rooms with bath (the majority) range from 530F to 650F. The only room service is of breakfast, which is also served in the ground-floor breakfast room. No restaurant. ***Rooms*** *35. Amex, Mastercard, Visa.*

Belloy St-Germain 860F

Tel 46 34 26 50 **Fax 46 34 66 18** Map B2.9 **H**
2 rue Racine 75006 Mº Odéon/Cluny la Sorbonne

The building is turn-of-the-century, reception is after Louis XIII and renovation carried out a few years ago has brought a contemporary look to the bedrooms, which include three suites. All have cable TV, hairdryer and mini-bar. Public parking 200 metres away. ***Rooms*** *50. Amex, Mastercard, Visa.*

BISTRO DE LA GRILLE 420F

Tel 43 54 16 87 Map B2.10 **R**
14 rue Mabillon 75006 Mº Mabillon

A real old-fashioned Parisian bistro popular with both locals and tourists. Its reputation is based firmly on traditional French cuisine, typified by, depending on the season, *terrine de lapin, saucisses, boudin noir, pot-au-feu de boeuf, sauté de veau aux olives, tete de veau, magret de canard, daube provençale, fondant au chocolat* and gratin of fruits. The bistro is decorated with black and white photographs of stars of the early French cinema. Set L 90F (plus carte) Set D 150F (no carte). ***Seats*** *80 (+ 30 outside).* ***Meals*** *noon-12.30am. Mastercard, Visa.*

LE BISTROT D'ALEX 500F

Tel 43 54 09 53 Map B2.11 **R**
2 rue Clément 75006 Mº Odéon/Mabillon

The decor is red and gold, and numerous paintings by Moretti adorn the walls. The cooking is a lightened mix of Lyonnais and Provençal: *rosette de Lyon, saucisson pistaché, gras double* (tripe), salad of lamb's trotters, grilled sea bream, scallops, *daube de boeuf* with pasta, Bresse chicken cooked *en vessie* with mushrooms, *pot-au-feu* (the last two winter dishes). The carte changes with the seasons and there are also dishes of the day and of the week. Desserts include a good *flan à l'orange* and *mousse au chocolat.* There is no house wine though a traditional Lyonnais *pot de Beaujolais* is available (46cl – 30F). Set menus 140F (Provençal) & 190F (Lyonnais). ***Seats*** *40. L 12-2 D 7.30-10.* ***Closed*** *L Sat, all Sun & 1 week Christmas. Amex, Mastercard, Visa.*

LES BOOKINISTES ★ 500F

Tel 43 25 54 94 **Fax 43 25 23 07** Map B2.12 **R**
53 quai des Grands Augustins 75006 Mº St-Michel

Decor is a stylish 'designer-distressed' blend of soft creamy hues with small colourful highlights gouged out of the plaster on the walls. Napery is a summery pale yellow and with minimalist black chairs and cleverly diffused lighting the ambience complements the short, modish menu. A blackboard lists a further brief but enticing selection of the day's specials. Both this and the menu proper feature innovative and well-prepared dishes that are composed with attention to detail. A carpaccio of paper-thin slices of raw tuna comes with raw baby vegetables dribbled with anchovy essence and topped with a crisp round of fine parmesan-flavoured pastry, chicken liver terrine is accompanied by an apple chutney and pumpkin soup has a garnish of potato rissoles, ham and tapénade. Main dishes could be milk-fed veal braised with mushrooms served with a gratin of marrows, or breast of young chicken marinated in spices and roasted with cabbage and a confit of lemons. ***Seats*** *70. L 12-2.30 D 7-12.* ***Closed*** *L Sat, all Sun. Amex, Mastercard, Visa.*

HOTEL BUCI-LATIN 970F

Tel 43 29 07 20 **Fax 43 29 67 44** Map B2.14 **H**
34 rue de Buci 75006 Mº Mabillon

A few yards from Boulevard St-Germain, the hotel was created in 1992 and a great deal of thought went into the decor, which is stylish and impressively modern. The foyer, with its collection of old toys, is spacious and welcoming. There's a small bar just inside the entrance and the breakfast room/coffee shop with its water garden and Mediterranean decor is on the lower ground floor. Breakfast is included in the room price. Bedrooms are all identically furnished in a warm, appealing style, with terracotta-coloured walls and curved lightwood furniture with good-size beds. Each has 21-channel TV, a mini-bar and ample storage space in Oriental wardrobes. Rooms overlooking the street are air-conditioned and all are double-glazed. Bathrooms are splendidly up to date (but note the old-fashioned taps) and boast a host of extras. Just a few rooms have shower and WC only and are let at the lower rate of 850F. ***Rooms** 27. Amex, Diners, Mastercard, Visa.*

Le Caméléon — 450F

Tel 43 20 63 43 **Fax 43 27 97 91** Map D2.15 **R**
6 rue de Chevreuse 75006 Mº Raspail/Vavin

Montparnasse bistro strongly evocative of 20s Paris, with its original decor of black banquettes, marble-topped tables, and painted flowery wallpaper. But the food's the thing here: straightforward bistro fare with some modern touches spans marinated courgettes, lobster ravioli, salad of oxtail, salt cod *provençale*, breast of veal with fresh pasta, *confit de canard*, *soufflé glacé au thé*, pear *clafoutis* and chocolate and orange mousse. ***Seats** 45. L 12-2 D 8-10.30. **Closed** Sat, Sun & 3 weeks Aug. Amex, Mastercard, Visa.*

Aux Charpentiers — 450F

Tel 43 26 30 05 **Fax 46 33 07 98** Map B2.16 **R**
10 rue Mabillon 75006 Mº Mabillon

Once the eating place of the guild of carpenters (their museum is next door), the restaurant has the timeless quality of a typical French bistro. Starters include fresh duck foie gras – best with a chilled glass of Sauternes, *fromage de tete avec échalotes* and *soupe de poissons*. Mains like roast duck with an olive and port sauce (on the menu here for the last 130 years), roast Bresse chicken, and beef fillet cooked *en papillote* with carrots and bone marrow, are supplemented by daily specials: veal Marengo on Monday, *boeuf à la mode* on Tuesday, *petit salé* with lentils on Wednesday, pot-au-feu on Thursday (*jarret de veau* in summer), *aïoli* of cod on Friday, stuffed cabbage on Saturday and roast leg of lamb on Sunday. Simple sweets to finish such as tarte tatin, crème caramel, a *clafoutis* of mirabelles, and a particular speciality, *entremet chocolat amer.* Set L 122F Set D 153F (inc wine). ***Seats** 100 (+ 20 outside). L 12-3 D 7-11.30. Amex, Diners, Mastercard, Visa.*

Le Chat Grippé ★ — 800F

Tel 43 54 70 00 **Fax 46 33 13 05** Map C2.17 **R**
87 rue d'Assas 75006 Mº Port-Royal

A small, quiet, elegantly appointed restaurant with a restrained decor of deep burgundy and grey with smoked mirror panelling, pink napery and tall, black, rattan chairs. The menu is a studied example of carefully thought-out modern combinations, with the use of subtle spicing put to good effect. The *menu dégustation* (dishes taken from the carte) is a perfect and well-balanced option, served only to the whole table, which changes with the seasons. Terrine of duck foie gras with fig purée might be followed by oysters roasted *en crépinette* with leek 'chips' and a meat jus. Next a dish of scallops with shavings of parmesan before a main dish of roast pigeon. A delicious Cabécou de Rocamadour follows, dribbled with olive oil, a side salad and nut and raisin bread served alongside. The dessert could be *feuillantines aux poires caramélisés, lait d'amande glacé.* Coffee and petits fours round off a classy meal in welcoming surroundings. Set L 160F Set L & D 225F & 240F. ***Seats** 35. L 12-2.30 D 7.30-10.30. **Closed** L Sat, all Mon & Aug. Mastercard, Visa.*

Chez Maitre Paul — 450F

Tel 43 54 74 59 **Fax 46 34 58 33** Map B2.18 **R**
12 rue Monsieur-le-Prince 75006 Mº Odéon

The Jura/Franche-Comté region of eastern France provides the inspiration for the menu at this grand little restaurant which has been in the same family since opening some 30 years ago. The specialities are basically unchanged down the

See over

years – splendid smoked sausages (*brésil*) and other charcuterie, sole fillets cooked with Chateau Chalon, calf's sweetbreads with morels, chicken cooked in Arbois (the yellow wine of the Jura), chocolate gateau, the day's fruit tart. Game is a speciality during the hunting season with dishes such as pheasant with wild mushrooms. Set menu 180F. ***Seats*** *50. L 12.15-2.30 D 7.15-10.30.* ***Closed*** *L Sat, all Sun. Amex, Diners, Mastercard, Visa.*

CRYSTAL HOTEL 600F

Tel 45 48 85 14 Fax 45 49 16 45 Map B1.19 **H**
24 rue St-Benoit 75006 Mº St-Germain-des-Prés

Just seconds from Boulevard St-Germain, the Crystal provides charm and comfort in traditional surroundings, with affable service provided by the *directrice* and her staff. Bedrooms are fairly simple, but bright and cheerful, some also being air-conditioned, and there's one suite. The price quoted above is for one of the six rooms with shower and WC only, rooms with bath are at 700F, or 820F for the larger 'de luxe' rooms. All have satellite TV, mini-bar, safe and hairdryer. Room service of breakfast only. ***Rooms*** *26. Amex, Diners, Mastercard, Visa.*

See page 9 for a list of starred restaurants

DANEMARK 690F

Tel 43 26 93 78 Fax 46 34 66 06 Map C2.20 **H**
21 rue Vavin 75006 Mº Vavin/Notre-Dame-des-Champs

A neat little hotel, in business for 100 years and now with completely renovated bedrooms. Outside is painted a cheerful blue, while in the public area there's something of the look of the 30s, with blues and greys in evidence. Bedrooms have a smart contemporary decor, with furniture in mahogany, oak or ash (depending on the storey). Satellite TV, mini-bar and hairdryer are common to all, as are tubs in bathrooms; room 10 boasts a whirlpool bath. ***Rooms*** *15. Amex, Diners, Mastercard, Visa.*

CAFÉ DES DEUX MAGOTS

Tel 45 48 55 25 Map B1.21 **R**
6 pl Saint-Germain-des-Prés 75006 Mº St-Germain-des-Prés

Opened in 1885, this, one of the typical Parisian boulevard cafés, stands on a corner opposite the church of St-Germain-des-Prés. Rows of tables and chairs spill out on to the pavement. Hugely popular as a meeting place, it is the haunt of writers, artists, politicians and tourists. Former patrons have included Simone de Beauvoir, Hemingway and Truman Capote. If you're hungry for conversation, this is the place to be. ***Open*** *7.30am-1.30am. Amex, Mastercard, Visa.*

DOMINIQUE 500F

Tel 43 27 08 80 Map C2.22 **R**
19 rue Bréa 75006 Mº Vavin

Though it has recently changed hands, this long-established Russian restaurant/take-away/bar/shop remains much as it has always been with its 'Kremlin-style' decor and reliable cooking that is wholesome and full of flavour. Caviar, borsch, blinis, and *zakouskis* (hors d'oeuvre) like stuffed peppers, smoked sturgeon, smoked salmon, *fromage blanc aux herbes* and chicken liver paté are followed by substantial dishes such as sturgeon *à la russe* (with tomato and paprika sauce), beef stroganoff, chicken Kiev and wiener schnitzel. Round things off with *vatrouchka* (tart with fromage blanc and fruit preserve), chocolate and nut gateau, apple strudel or a cold fruit soup. To accompany this gutsy food there's a short list of wines, mainly Bordeaux and champagne, and a long list of vodkas. Set L 98F (2-course in bar only), Set L & D 170F. ***Seats*** *100. L 12-2.30 D 7.15-11.* ***Closed*** *L Mon, all Sun & 15 Jul-15 Aug. Amex, Diners, Mastercard, Visa.*

L'ECAILLE DE PCB — 600F

Tel 43 26 73 70 **Fax 46 33 07 98** Map B2.23 **R**
5 rue Mabillon 75006 M° Odéon/Mabillon/St-Germain-des-Prés

Mahogany and brass give this splendid place the look of a grand motor yacht, which is quite appropriate for a restaurant specialising totally in seafood. Simple preparation, mainly by roasting, emphasises the quality and freshness of the fish, which is often prepared with olive oil and fresh herbs. Where sauces are involved they are generally served separately. Dishes include *escabèche* of fresh sardines, Scottish salmon *à l'unilatéral*, roast John Dory with grain mustard sauce (a particular favourite), osso buco of monkfish *orientale* and Brittany lobsters grilled, poached or cooked *en papillote*. Options include a three-course *menu minceur* (600 calories) at 210F, *menu d'affaires* at 190F and a set menu at 125F. Sister restaurant to the nearby *Aux Charpentiers* (see above). ***Seats** 40 (+ 10 outside). L 12-3 D 7.30-11. **Closed** L Sat, all Sun. Amex, Mastercard, Visa.*

L'EPI DUPIN — ★ 410F

Tel 42 22 64 56 Map C1.71 **R**
11 rue Dupin 75006 M° Sèvres-Babylone

The restaurant's name comes from the way chef-patron François Pasteau bakes his bread rolls in little connected chains (like ears of corn) known as *épi*, together with a pun on the name of the street. The building dates back to the 17th century and features exposed timbers and bare stone walls. Open only since March 1995, the restaurant was an instant success (booking advisable), not just because the four-course menu (there's no à la carte) is so reasonably priced but because François' cooking is so good that the combination represents incredible value for money. His daily trips to the Rungis market help to keep costs down and ensure the best of ingredients for starters such as a *charlotte tiède de fenouil aux pommes anisées*, a *pissaladière* with tuna and herbs, salmon with pistou on a bed of fresh tagliatelle or a simple, perfectly dressed, green salad with a few thin slices of foie gras terrine topped with flakes of rock salt, and mains like *croustillant* of salmon with citrus sauce, *barigoule de céleri et Saint Jacques*, duck fillet with honey and ginger and *roulade de tete de veau* with saffron-flavoured boulangère potatoes. Desserts are no less tempting: *crepe soufflée au citron flambée à la vodka*, a pastilla of dried fruits, *poire roti en suprise au lait d'amande* and, on a recent visit, a wonderful, hot *dariole au coulant de chocolat sauce pistache* in which the mould conceals a liquid chocolate centre that blends deliciously with the surrounding pistachio sauce. There are about half a dozen choices at each stage except the cheese. Busy waiters provide swift service. Short list of wines with only the fizz breaching the 200F barrier. It seems unlikely that you will be able to enjoy François Pasteau's cooking at these prices for very long so take advantage while you may. Set menu 153F. ***Seats** 40 (+ 12 outside). L 12-2.30 D 7.30-10 30. **Closed** L Sat, all Sun & 25 Dec. Mastercard, Visa.*

FERRANDI — 580F

Tel 42 22 97 40 **Fax 45 44 89 97** Map C1.24 **H**
92 rue du Cherche-Midi 75006 M° Vaneau

Newly installed air-conditioning has brought an extra degree of comfort to this discreet and charming bed-and-breakfast hotel peacefully situated in an early 19th-century building opposite the *Musée Hébert* (paintings by Ernest Hébert), just north of the Montparnasse area. The entrance hall has an open fireplace with an elaborate gilt mirror above and chandelier, and individually decorated bedrooms (on four floors, there is a lift) have period freestanding furniture, heavy drapes and pink marble bathrooms (all with tubs as well as showers). One room has a four-poster bed and all are double-glazed and come with such mod cons as satellite TV, hairdryer and telephone. Room rates range up to 980F and there is one suite at 1280F. Six parking spaces (100F per day) can be reserved when you book. Room service till 8pm. Bar. Patio. ***Rooms** 42. Amex, Diners, Mastercard, Visa.*

HOTEL DE FLEURIE 850F

Tel 43 29 59 81 **Fax 43 29 68 44** Map B2.25 **H**
32 rue Grégoire-de-Tours 75006 M° Odéon/St-Germain-des-Prés

Exceptionally pleasant little hotel, just off the Boulevard St-Germain, where family owners are continuously making improvements. The latest project is the installation of computer modems in each of the air-conditioned bedrooms. All are bright and spacious, traditional in style (although with mod cons like satellite TV), and their bathrooms are clad in marble, with hairdryers and heated towel rails. Double rooms all have bathrooms en suite, single rooms (650F) have either bath or shower. Children under 12 stay free in parents' room. No restaurant but breakfast is served in a bright stone-lined cellar, or in bedrooms at no extra charge. Room prices include the city tax. ***Rooms** 29. Amex, Diners, Mastercard, Visa.*

CAFÉ DE FLORE

Tel 45 48 55 26 Map B1.26 **R**
172 bd Saint-Germain 75006 M° St-Germain-des-Prés

Along with *Les Deux Magots* among the most renowned *cafés littéraires* and the birthplace of existentialism, the café is a good place for people-watching, less so for its savouries. ***Open** 7am-1am. Amex.*

GRAND HOTEL LITTRÉ 815F

Tel 45 44 38 68 **Fax 45 44 88 13** Map C1.27 **H**
9 rue Littré 75006 M° Montparnasse

Bedrooms in this 19th-century building come in various sizes but all are traditional in style, with amply-sized beds, solid furnishings and large bath or shower rooms. All have satellite TV and some also have hairdryers and safes. The English bar is contrastingly more modern, with plain wood panelling. Room service till 8.45pm. There are 15 reservable parking spaces in a private garage (120F for 24 hours). ***Rooms** 97. Amex, Diners, Mastercard, Visa.*

L'HEURE GOURMANDE 260F

Tel 46 34 00 40 Map B2.28 **R**
22 passage Dauphine 75006 M° Odéon

Passage Dauphine is a charming alleyway which connects Rue Mazarine to Rue Dauphine. Step down to enter a cosy dining-room with extra table space on a mezzanine level. The feel is charming and feminine, with antique furniture, Liberty fabrics and mismatched crockery. Until 3pm there are savoury dishes like *assiette jardin* (steamed vegetables with a butter sauce), *mezza luna* (crescent-shaped ravioli filled with mushrooms and cheese) plus more elaborate *assiettes gourmandes* (*petit salé aux lentilles, brandade de morue*). Their speciality savoury *tartes* (provençale, broccoli, courgette) are always available as are their delicious home-made pastries (*tarte au chocolat amer, clafoutis*, or *crumble aux fruits rouges*), hot chocolate *à l'ancienne,* fresh fruit juices and Berthillon ice cream. On Friday and Saturday there is an additional brunch menu at 138F. ***Seats** 55. **Meals** 11-7 (Sun from 2). **Closed** Aug & Public Holidays. Mastercard, Visa.*

L'HOTEL 1000F

Tel 43 25 27 22 **Fax 43 25 64 81** Map B1.29 **HR**
13 rue des Beaux-Arts 75006 M° Mabillon

In the late 19th century, when it was known as the Hotel d'Alsace, Oscar Wilde first took refuge, then died here ("I am dying beyond my means") in 1900. Restored by owner Guy-Louis Duboucheron and re-opened in 1968, the hotel retains many original features, with Wilde's room reconstructed and the furniture of Mistinguett (another habitué) restored. Spacious and air-conditioned bedrooms are in a mixture of styles (even Baroque) and offer cable TV and mini-bars among the usual facilities. The price quoted above is for a room with shower and WC only; rooms with bath range from 1700F to 2300F. Room service is available till 2am. Breakfast is served in vaulted cellars. ***Rooms** 27. Amex, Diners, Mastercard, Visa.*

Le Belier 500F

Red walls, green carpet, paintings (changing exhibition – for sale) and sculpted steel animals; the busy decor is crowned by a noisy stone fountain with gigantic flower arrangement. Chef Christian Schuliar offers a classic cuisine of well-presented, precisely cooked dishes. From the *menu carte: oeufs pochés en meurette aux champignons*, onion soup with port and quail's eggs, osso buco of monkfish with preserved tomatoes, pike-perch with cabbage and bacon, loin of lamb with morel mushrooms, *riz condé* with apricot compote, crème brulée with cognac. Set L 140F Set D 195F. ***Seats** 100. L 12-2 D 7.30-12.*

Jacques Cagna 1200F

Tel 43 26 49 39 Fax 43 54 54 48 Map B2.30 **R**
14 rue des Grands-Augustins 75006 M° St-Michel

A discreet doorway on a narrow, ancient street in the St-Germain area near the Seine, leads up to this charming first-floor restaurant. The 16th-century decor of heavy beams and partially oak-panelled walls hung with old oil paintings contrasts with Jacques Cagna's energetic, eclectic cooking. He prides himself on the freshness of his ingredients and on rarely repeating a dish from one menu to the next, but examples of typical starters are *salade tiède de homard breton, légumes de Provence aux aromates* (warm lobster salad with Provençal vegetables and aromatic herbs) and *carpaccio de dorade rose, rémoulade de céleri et caviar Sévruga* (carpaccio of sea bream with a rémoulade of celery and Sevruga caviar). Mains include *canard de Challans aux zestes d'orange et citron* (Challans duck cooked with orange and lemon zest, served with a red burgundy sauce) and roast Houdan chicken with wild mushrooms. For chocolate addicts, the plate of five different chocolate desserts is a must. Set L 270F Set D 490F. ***Seats** 60. L 12-2 D 7.30-10.30. **Closed** L Sat, 3 weeks Aug & Christmas-New Year. Amex, Diners, Mastercard, Visa.*

A glossary of French menu items starts on page 274

Latitudes Saint-Germain 940F

Tel 42 61 53 53 Fax 49 27 09 33 Map B1.31 **H**
7-11 rue St Benoit 75006 M° St-Germain-des-Prés

Practical modern hotel (opened in 1988) which retains its turn-of-the-century facade. Air-conditioning, satellite TV, mini-bar, and hairdryer come as standard in the spacious, pastel-hued bedrooms. Some rooms on the first floor have just been refurbished in bolder Provençal colours and earn a 100F supplement. En suite facilities include bath and shower in every room. No room service except for breakfast, which can also be taken in a cellar breakfast room which five nights a week (Tue-Sat) becomes a jazz club with bar. The hotel is just a few steps away from the bustle of the Boulevard St-Germain, but those few steps are enough to provide a fair measure of peace and quiet (unless you're in the cellar listening to the jazz). Room prices vary considerably depending upon the time of year; that quoted above is the high season price for a standard double. ***Rooms** 117. Amex, Diners, Mastercard, Visa.*

Left Bank 990F

Tel 43 54 01 70 Fax 43 26 17 14 Map B2.32 **H**
9 rue de l'Ancienne Comédie 75006 M° Odéon

The building dates from 1750, but it has been a hotel only since 1989. It offers high standards of comfort and service. It's a handsome place, too, with antique furniture, tapestries, stone walls and fine wood panelling, oak beams and a little interior garden. Bedrooms are very well appointed – air-conditioning, double-glazing, safes, direct-dial phones, mini-bars, multi-channel TV, marble bathrooms with hairdryers. One room is equipped for disabled guests. Room service is limited to breakfast. ***Rooms** 31. Amex, Diners, Mastercard, Visa.*

Brasserie Lipp 560F

Tel 45 48 53 91 Fax 45 44 33 20 Map B1.13 **R**
151 bd Saint-Germain 75006 M° St-Germain-des-Prés

Perhaps the capital's most famous brasserie, founded in 1880 by Léonard Lipp. It now has a 20s decor of ceramics, mirrors and painted ceiling (it's classed as a historic monument). It was, and is, the haunt of the famous, from Malraux to Speilberg, from Hemingway to Tom Cruise. Throughout its long opening hours it serves a classic brasserie menu, and listed as specialities are *cervelas rémoulade*, Bismarck herrings, grilled stuffed pig's trotters, and choucroute with pork knuckle. The choice is extensive and each day there are additional dishes such as poached haddock beurre blanc, navarin of lamb and Provençal stuffed vegetables. Set menu 195F. ***Seats** 150. Meals 10am-1am. Amex, Mastercard, Diners, Visa.*

La Lozère 320F

Tel 43 54 26 64 Fax 44 07 00 43 Map B2.34 **R**
4 rue Hautefeuille 75006 M° St-Michel

This beamed, stone-walled (and air-conditioned) restaurant is owned by the tourist office of the Lozère region of central France, and the tables and chairs were made by craftsmen from that area. The menu has a similar provenance, and among the hearty *spécialités lozériennes* are warming winter soups, omelettes and *tripoux* as well as *filet de truite saumonée de Lozère au jambon, entrecote 'fleur d'Aubrac' poelée,* and *andouillettes*. Thursday evening (and Thursday lunchtime by prior order) brings *l'aligot d'Aubrac*, a potato purée with melted Tomme cheese, garlic and crème fraiche served with Lozère sausage. Desserts include *fromage blanc au cassis* and a chestnut and chocolate charlotte. Wines are mostly from the Languedoc-Roussillon. Adjacent to the restaurant is the tourist office where you can book your *gite rural* and a shop selling craft goods and produce from the region. Set L 92F (inc wine or beer) Set L & D 125F & 155F. ***Seats** 38. L 12-2 D 7.30-10.15. **Closed** Sun, Mon, Aug, 1 week Easter & Christmas-New Year. Mastercard, Visa.*

Hotel Lutétia 1280F

Tel 49 54 46 46 Fax 49 54 46 00 Map C1.35 **HR**
45 bd Raspail 75006 M° Sèvres-Babylone

This grand old hotel opened in 1910 and is one of the most famous on the Left Bank. In 1983, Sonia Rykiel oversaw a major refurbishment which restored it to its full art deco glory. Public rooms are well proportioned, decorated in marble, gilt and velvet and furnished with Taki's sculptures, Lalique and elegant glass screens. The Bar Lutèce, overlooking the huge reception area, is still a favourite meeting place for the chic set who gossip, sip cocktails and listen to live piano or jazz. Bedrooms are equipped with air-conditioning and all modern amenities but, with their mahogany wardrobes, octagonal bedheads and ornate furnishings, have an elegant period atmosphere. Business needs are not overlooked and 12 conference rooms are available for meetings and receptions. 24-hour room service. Public parking 120F. ***Rooms** 271. Amex, Diners, Mastercard, Visa.*

Le Paris ★ 1000F

Tel 49 54 46 90

As a disciple of Escoffier, chef Philippe Renard has a classical pedigree, but he loves to experiment. His seasonal carte includes *cannelloni de foie gras de canard à la truffe noire du Périgord, tournedos de boeuf à la moutarde de Brive, palet de pommes aux amandes* (tournedos of beef in Brive mustard, served with apple and almond rings) and *petit coeur sablé au coco et aux framboises, violettes cristallisées* (heart-shaped cocoa and raspberry shortbread with crystallised violets). Set L 250F & 350F Set D 350F, 495F & 550F. **Brasserie Lutétia**, the hotel's informal second restaurant, is also open from 7.30 for breakfast and, later, serves excellent seafood platters as well as other light dishes. ***Seats** 43. L 12-2 D 7.30-10.30. **Closed** Sat, Sun & Aug.*

Luxembourg — 755F

Tel 43 25 35 90 **Fax 43 26 60 84**
4 rue de Vaugirard 75006
Map C2.36
M° Odéon
H

Peace, comfort and a charming welcome a few steps from the Luxembourg Gardens and Palace. Bedrooms are of reasonable size and furnished with reproduction Louis XVI pieces; they all offer modern amenities such as satellite TV, mini-bar, hairdryer and safe and bathrooms all have both tub and shower. A buffet breakfast is served in the vaulted cellars. Small courtyard garden. No restaurant. ***Rooms** 33. Amex, Diners, Mastercard, Visa.*

Hotel du Lys — 460F

Tel 43 26 97 57 **Fax 44 07 34 90**
23 rue Serpente 75006
Map B2.37
M° St-Michel
H

In a narrow street right in the very heart of the Latin Quarter, the hotel occupies a well-preserved 17th-century building. The location is excellent, being close to the junction of the Boulevards St-Michel and St-Germain yet in a surprisingly quiet side street. Run by the second generation of the same family, it has an atmosphere that is both welcoming and homely. Bedrooms, reached by characterfully narrow and irregular stairs (there's no lift), are individually decorated and furnished with care and taste and have considerable charm. All have satellite TV, hairdryer and neat, simple bathrooms (half with bath and half with shower). Breakfast and the city tax are both included in the room rate. ***Rooms** 22. No credit cards.*

Madison — 1012F

Tel 40 51 60 05 **Fax 40 51 60 01**
143 bd Saint-Germain 75006
Map B1.38
M° St-Germain-des-Prés
H

Set slightly back from the Boulevard, a handsome hotel with bedrooms (some with balconies) overlooking either street or courtyard. Features include double-glazing, air-conditioning, 10-channel TV, direct-dial phone, mini-bar and, in bathrooms that all have both tub and shower, hairdryers. Continental breakfast is served in your room or a buffet breakfast is offered in the dining-room. 24-hour bar/*salon de thé*. Children under 12 stay free in parents' room. Major renovation of public areas involved the hotel being closed from 15th to 31st December 1995. ***Rooms** 55. Amex, Diners, Mastercard, Visa.*

> The best way to get around Paris is by bus or metro –
> buy a book (carnet) of tickets at any metro station and save money

Mariage Frères

Tel 40 51 82 50 **Fax 44 07 07 52**
13 rue des Grands-Augustins 75006
Map B2.39
M° Odéon
R

Both an experience in *savoir vivre* and a trip back in time, the menu of this exceptional tea shop located in a 17th-century building offers an almost never-ending list (actually 450) of teas. The colonial atmosphere of the first-floor dining-room with its high ceiling and green plants contrasts with the vaulted basement so typical of St-Germain-des-Prés. The menu is almost entirely focused on tea with *escalope de saumon au thé vert Mat Uji* (salmon scented with green tea – 85F), *charlotte d'un jardin de thé* (scented with Casablanca tea), *financier de thé* (a cake flavoured with Japanese green tea) and *madeleines au thé*, scones and muffins served with tea jelly. A place highly recommended for afternoon teas and pastries, but unfortunately not to the budget traveller. The original shop is in the centre of Le Marais at 30 rue du Bourg-Tibourg, Tel 42 72 28 11. ***Seats** 28. Open 12-7. Amex, Mastercard, Visa.*

La Marlotte 460F

Tel 45 48 86 79 **Fax 45 44 34 80** Map C1.40 **R**
55 rue Cherche-Midi 75006 M° Sèvres-Babylone

A very civilised spot, with smart customers and staff. The room is rustic-elegant with old paintings on papered walls, attractive flower displays and candle-light in the evening. Cooking is careful and traditionally based but with innovative touches. Dishes on an autumn menu ranged from terrine of turbot with an olive coulis and duck foie gras to coquilles St Jacques with basil butter, *boeuf gros sel à la moëlle*, fresh lemon tart and profiteroles with bitter chocolate. ***Seats*** *80 (+ 30 outside.) L 12-3 D 8-11.* ***Closed*** *Sat, Sun & Aug. Amex, Diners, Mastercard, Visa.*

Hotel des Marronniers 700F

Tel 43 25 30 60 **Fax 40 46 83 56** Map B1.41 **H**
21 rue Jacob 75006 M° St-Germain-des-Prés

Peace is a commodity in plentiful supply at this really delightful little hotel, whose ancient origins may still be traced (one wall of the basement dates from the time of Henri IV). Bedrooms (all with either bath or shower and WC en suite) have a romantic, rustic appeal. One of the most attractive features is a little informal garden. Ask for a room overlooking this garden (there's a 100F supplement); the topmost room also has a view of the belfry of St-Germain-des-Prés. ***Rooms*** *37. No credit cards.*

La Méditerranée 500F

Tel 43 26 02 30 **Fax 43 26 18 44** Map B2.42 **R**
place de l'Odéon 75006 M° Odéon

With a new manager has come a change of style so that the carte now gives about equal emphasis to meat and fish. The chef remains the same, however, and seafood specalities such as *brandade de morue, bouillabaisse*, fillets of John Dory with garlic and fresh tomatoes, *éventail* of salmon with parsley sauce, sea bream in red wine and *soupe de poissons* are still to be found alongside *confit de canard*, calf's liver (simply fried in butter), *tournedos bordelaise* and *andouillettes*. The elegant decor of the main room is the work of the renowned set designer Bréard. ***Seats*** *160 (+ 20 outside). L 12-3 D 7-11. Amex, Diners, Mastercard, Visa.*

Hotel de l'Odéon 760F

Tel 43 25 70 11 **Fax 43 29 97 34** Map B2.44 **H**
13 rue St-Sulpice 75006 M° Odéon

16th-century building in the Latin Quarter, with no bedroom the same as its neighbour. Tasteful period furnishings and a generally cosy feel make up for a lack of size in some rooms; all have private bathrooms, just two with shower rather than bathtub. All are now air-conditioned and have cable TV, safe and hairdryer. Most rooms overlook a little interior garden. ***Rooms*** *29. Amex, Diners, Mastercard, Visa.*

La Palette 200F

Tel 43 26 68 15 Map B2.45 **R**
43 rue de Seine 75006 M° Odéon/Mabillon/St-Germain-des-Prés

In amongst the tiny streets of the Left Bank is a corner café appropriately named given the number of galleries in the vicinity. Relatively unchanged since the early 1900s, the walls are wood-panelled and have colourful faïence tiling as well; it is best experienced in the summer when seating is placed under the trees or on the pavement. This is a family business where good home cooking is only on offer at lunchtime when various *assiettes* (ham, charcuterie, cheese, rillettes), grilled sausages, croques monsieur and madame, and country ham with country bread are supplemented by a *plat du jour* (55F) that might be tenderloin of pork with lentils, roast beef with potato purée or breadcrumbed escalope with petits pois. The patronne's fruit tarts are well worth saving space for – raspberry, tatin or lemon. Sandwiches and coffee are on offer at other times. ***Seats*** *100 (+ 100 outside). Open 8am-2am (meals 12-3).* ***Closed*** *Sun, Aug & 8 days Feb/Mar (school holidays). No credit cards.*

PERREYVE 450F

Tel 45 48 35 01 **Fax 42 84 03 30** Map C2.46 **H**
63 rue Madame 75006 Mº Notre-Dame-des-Champs/St-Placide

Comfort and style on a small scale in a modernised hotel near the Luxembourg Gardens. There's a pleasant sitting-room on the ground floor. No restaurant, but room service is available till 11pm. ***Rooms*** *30. Amex, Mastercard, Visa.*

LE PETIT ST BENOIT 250F

Tel 42 60 27 92 Map B1.47 **R**
4 rue St Benoit 75006 Mº St-Germain-des-Prés

Very homely cooking in friendly surroundings – the terrace is a favourite spot for a lively discussion on any topic under the sun. Outside or in, regulars tuck into familiar dishes like *hachis parmentier, boeuf bourguignon, gigot d'agneau* or *blanquette de veau*, with *museau vinaigrette* or herring fillets to start and a fruit tart to round things off. The place has a very traditional look, with old mirrors and clocks, railway-style luggage racks for coats, plain wooden tables and red tablecloths. ***Seats*** *50 (+ 50 outside). L 12-2.30 D 7-10.30.* ***Closed*** *Sat, Sun & 2 weeks Aug. No credit cards.*

LE PETIT VATEL 200F

Tel 43 54 28 49 Map B2.48 **R**
5 rue Lobineau 75006 Mº Odéon/Mabillon

A restaurant in the tradition of the Latin Quarter, long popular with students and artists. Chef-patronne Marie's home cooking covers such dishes as vegetable soup, *hachis parmentier*, roast pork with thyme, Toulouse sausages, *boeuf bourguignon* and daily fish and vegetarian specials. There are also regular *plats du jour* with, for example, Monday bringing *endive au jambon* in winter and *courgette gratin* in summer, and Tuesday stuffed peppers in winter and *poivron oriental* in summer. On Thursday it's always *pain de viande à la provençale*, a particular speciality. To finish, a couple of cheeses, crème caramel, Mont-Blanc, chocolate gateau. Set L 61F Set D 87F. ***Seats*** *22 (+ 10 outside). L 12-3 D 7-12 (Sat all day noon-1am).* ***Closed*** *L Sun, all Christmas-New Year. Amex, Mastercard, Visa.*

LA PETITE COUR 500F

Tel 43 26 52 26 **Fax 44 07 11 53** Map B2.49 **R**
8 rue Mabillon 75006 Mº Mabillon

The level of the original Rue Mabillon was several feet below the present one and the restaurant, located on the old street, now more of a courtyard, is approached across a narrow stone bridge and down a series of steps. In summer, tables and parasols provide a delightful spot for alfresco dining and the interior is no less charming with rich burgundy velour seating, which could have come from the boudoirs of courtesans, and soft-apricot silky fabric-covered walls hung with oil paintings in traditional gilt frames providing a very romantic setting. The food is up-to-date with offerings such as ravioli of langoustines with tarragon, *gateau de canette aux figues*, smoked salmon and cod with potato salad and fried ceps with fresh herbs among the starters of a seasonally-changing menu that continues with dishes such as *encornets sautés à la provençale*, calf's liver with balsamic vinegar, and fillet of beef *à la lie de vin de Bordeaux*. Sweets might include a vanilla crème brulée, a gratin of peaches with red wine sabayon, coffee and almond tartlet and *soufflé glacé à la noix de coco*. Set L 165F (*formule*, with a glass of wine) & 178F Set D 198F. ***Seats*** *48 (+ 36 outside). L 12-2.30 D 7-11.30. Mastercard, Visa.*

Au Plaisir des Pains

Tel 45 48 40 45 Map C2.50 **R**
62 rue de Vaugirard 75006 M° Saint-Sulpice

Appetising pastries, jars of honey and traditional jams decorate the window. The shop has a tiny, light-green dining-room on the first floor with darkwood tables and chairs. M Arella is in charge, wielding his mighty whisk to create deliciously light savouries: *tarte à la tomate, feuilleté au Roquefort, sandwich aux poivrons grillés* (grilled peppers served in warm Greek bread), and mouth-watering desserts such as *fondant au chocolat* and Berthillon ice cream making it an unusual and high-quality sandwich shop. ***Open*** *10am-8pm.* ***Closed*** *Sun & Public Holidays. No credit cards.*

> The best way to get around Paris is by bus or metro – buy a book (carnet) of tickets at any metro station and save money

Polidor 240F

Tel 43 26 95 34 Map B2.51 **R**
41 rue Monsieur-le-Prince 75006 M° Odéon

One of the real survivors, not greatly changed in the past 100+ years. The art deco lighting is quite a feature, the uneven ceiling may look as though it's about to fall down and the floor is not quite even but it's all part of the charm, and it would be a shame to change it. Long-serving waitresses distribute homely, traditional dishes like pumpkin soup, home-made duck foie gras terrine, *escargots bourguignon, blanquette de veau, boeuf bourguignon, poulet basquaise* and duck with petits pois, many of which have been on the menu from the start. Finish with tarte tatin, their excellent patisserie, the chocolate tart, a speciality, being always in great demand, or home-made ice creams and sorbets. Set L 55F Set L & D 100F. ***Seats*** *120. L 12-2.30 D 7-12.30 (Sun to 11). No credit cards.*

Le Procope 500F

Tel 43 26 99 20 Fax 43 54 16 86 Map B2.52 **R**
13 rue de l'Ancienne Comédie 75006 M° Odéon

The oldest café in Paris, now restored to its 17th-century splendour. The menu calls it "Le Rendezvous des Arts et des Lettres" and indeed in its 300-year history Le Procope has entertained many leading lights of French literature, from Balzac to Voltaire. The menu sticks mainly to reasonably prepared brasserie food, with oysters, whiting Colbert, duck à l'orange, fillet of beef béarnaise and guinea fowl with calvados among the popular choices. Sorbets and ice creams are the speciality desserts, all made on the premises. Rhone bottles head the wine list. Set L 72F & 99F Set L & D 169F. Late night menu (from 11pm) 119F. ***Seats*** *250. Meals 11am-1am. Amex, Diners, Mastercard, Visa.*

Le Régent 750F

Tel 46 34 59 80 Fax 40 51 05 07 Map B2.53 **H**
61 rue Dauphine 75006 M° Odéon

Traditional and modern features blend happily at the Régent, an 18th-century mansion in the heart of St-Germain-des-Prés. Old stonework and painted beams take the eye in reception, and the breakfast room is a vaulted cellar. Bedrooms are decorated in a variety of pleasing, well-co-ordinated styles and shades, all are air-conditioned and double-glazed, with direct-dial phone, satellite TV, mini-bar and digitally-coded safe. Bathrooms (seven with shower and WC only) feature marble or hand-painted Italian tiles. Children under 12 are accommodated free with parents in the larger rooms. There's no restaurant, but the *Café des Deux Magots (qv)* in the same ownership is not far away. ***Rooms*** *25. Amex, Diners, Mastercard, Visa.*

Relais Christine 1630F

Tel 43 26 71 80 **Fax 43 26 89 38** Map B2.54 **H**
3 rue Christine 75006 Mº St-Michel

You enter through wrought-iron gates and a bricked courtyard, resplendent with small trees and shrubs. The hotel, quite close to Notre-Dame and situated just south of the river in a quiet street near St-Germain-des-Prés, was once a 16th-century abbey (note the stone-vaulted medieval breakfast room and discreet panelled lounge with leather sofas), and still has lots of character in the bedrooms, which overlook either the small, pretty garden or courtyard, and provide every comfort from air-conditioning to satellite TV alongside period furniture and fine paintings. The *Pavillon de la Reine (qv)* in the 3rd arrondissement is under the same ownership. Garden. ***Rooms*** *51. Amex, Diners, Mastercard, Visa.*

Relais Hotel du Vieux Paris 990F

Tel 43 54 41 66 **Fax 43 26 00 15** Map B2.55 **H**
9 rue Gît-le-Coeur 75006 Mº St-Michel

A hotel with a history going back to 1480. It once belonged to the Duc de Luynes and more recently was a favourite with the Beat generation including Kerouac, Burroughs and Ginsberg as well as the artists Picasso, Matisse and Giacometti. Completely renovated in 1991, it is a comfortable, roomy and well-appointed place; the more so since the installation of air-conditioning last year. Accommodation comprises 13 rooms and 7 suites; three of the latter have mezzanines and magnificent views over the rooftops. Exposed timber beams, handsome furnishings, 20-channel TV, mini-bar, safe and marble-finished bathrooms (whirlpool baths in suites) all make for a pleasant stay. The suites range in price from 1370F to 1650F. ***Rooms*** *20. Amex, Diners, Mastercard, Visa.*

Relais Louis XIII ★ 1000F

Tel 43 26 75 96 Map B2.56 **R**
8 rue des Grands-Augustins 75006 Mº St-Michel

Built on the remains of the Grands-Augustins monastery (dating back to the early 17th century), the restaurant retains many relics of the past. Magnificent beams and timbered walls have been perfectly preserved and are the back-drop to tapestries and objets d'art of the period. The classical French cuisine offers scallops with ginger, Landes duck foie gras and langoustine ravioli with tarragon followed perhaps by a panaché of seafood with basil butter, fricassee of Breton lobster with Sauternes, wild duck (for two) or fillet of beef with Périgord truffles. Finish with *aumonière de pommes*, chocolate mousse or crème brulée. Set L 195F & 250F Set D 250F & 350F (*dégustation*). ***Seats*** *55. L 12.15-2.15 D 7.30-10.15.* ***Closed*** *L Mon, all Sun & mid Jul-mid Aug. Amex, Diners, Mastercard, Visa.*

See page 9 for a list of starred restaurants

Relais Médicis 995F

Tel 43 26 00 60 **Fax 40 46 83 39** Map B2.57 **H**
23 rue Racine 75006 Mº Odéon

Two 18th-century buildings of three storeys are separated by a pretty little patio garden with a fountain. The whole place has been designed to give a country feel, and the well-appointed bedrooms feature flowery Impressionist-style fabrics and warm, pastel-coloured walls. Painted woodwork, antiques and old photographs add to the period appeal, while air-conditioning and double-glazing keep things peaceful and comfortable. All rooms have mini-bars, safes and hairdryers. The handsome marble bathrooms have separate WCs. Room price includes breakfast and city tax. ***Rooms*** *16. Amex, Diners, Mastercard, Visa.*

Relais St Germain 1500F

Tel 43 29 12 05 **Fax 46 33 45 30** Map B2.58 **H**
9 carrefour de l'Odéon 75006 Mº Odéon

The building is 17th-century, and the inside of this delightful little place is done out in colourful country style, with flowery fabrics, antique furniture and beams. Modern comforts include air-conditioning, double-glazing, cable TV, mini-bar, safe and hairdryer. Bathrooms, finished in marble, have tubs, showers and separate WCs. The top-floor suite, which has a terrace, is reached by a little staircase from the 5th floor (other floors are served by a lift). A generous Continental breakfast (included in room price) is served in the rooms or downstairs. New this year is a wine bar (11am-1am, closed Sun) connecting to the hotel. The hotel stands at the bustling Odéon crossroads. ***Rooms** 20. Amex, Diners, Mastercard, Visa.*

La Rotisserie d'en Face 520F

Tel 43 26 40 98 **Fax 43 54 54 48** Map B2.59 **R**
2 rue Christine 75006 Mº Odéon/St-Michel

Across the road from his main restaurant, this is one of Jacques Cagna's three cheaper dining options (see also *La Rotisserie Monsigny* in the 2nd, and *La Rotisserie d'Armaillé* in the 17th). The setting is lively, modern and informal and the menu offers a good choice of dishes bearing the Cagna hallmark of care and quality. Snail ravioli in a tarragon bouillon, poached eggs with mussels in a curry sauce and duck and foie gras *paté en croute* could be your starter, followed perhaps by sautéed sea scallops with layered Provençal vegetables, *andouillette* with mustard sauce or something from the rotisserie – free-range chicken with mashed potatoes, rack of lamb with ratatouille or rib of beef with Noirmoutier potatoes deep-fried in their skins. Seasonal game could feature wild duck with figs and polenta or a *tourte* of young boar with foie gras and wild mushrooms. The day's fruit tart is always a good bet for dessert. Reds outweigh whites on a wine list selected by Jacques himself – look for the bottles of the month. Set L 145F Set D 195F. ***Seats** 85. L 12-2.30 D 7-11 (Fri & Sat to 11.30). **Closed** L Sat, all Sun. Amex, Mastercard, Visa.*

Hotel de Saint-Germain 695F

Tel 45 48 91 64 **Fax 45 48 46 22** Map B1.60 **H**
50 rue du Four 75006 Mº St-Sulpice/Sèvres-Babylone

Each floor of bedrooms at this civilised litle hotel has its own colour scheme; blue and yellow on the first, blue and red on the second and blue and green on the third. All rooms offer direct-dial phone, satellite TV, mini-bar and safe. About half the bathrooms have shower and WC only. ***Rooms** 30. Amex, Diners, Mastercard, Visa.*

Hotel Saint-Germain-des-Prés 950F

Tel 43 26 00 19 **Fax 40 46 83 63** Map B1.61 **H**
36 rue Bonaparte 75006 Mº St-Germain-des-Prés

A traditionally run hotel decorated in a quaintly old-fashioned style and located in an old street at the heart of St-Germain-des-Prés. Bedrooms, though not large, are comfortably appointed – air-conditioning, double-glazing, TV (it was planned that all should have cable by 1996), safe, direct-dial phone, mini-bar – and many have beamed ceilings. Four rooms have shower and WC only. There are three larger de luxe rooms and two suites. ***Rooms** 30. Mastercard, Visa.*

Saint-Grégoire 930F

Tel 45 48 23 23 **Fax 45 48 33 95** Map C1.62 **H**
43 rue de l'Abbé-Grégoire 75006 Mº St-Placide

An 18th-century mansion modernised into a charming hotel with a snug, brightly decorated lounge, a little garden and a cellar breakfast room. Bedrooms (two with balconies) feature pastel colour schemes, a largely traditional decor and some handsome antiques. Two rooms on the 6th floor are air-conditioned but plans were afoot to extend this to the rest of the hotel during the winter of 1995/96. Two smaller rooms are priced at 790F and there are two rooms, one a junior suite and one with balcony, at 1390F. The hotel is between Boulevards Raspail and Montparnasse. ***Rooms*** *20. Amex, Diners, Mastercard, Visa.*

SAINTE-BEUVE 700F

Tel 45 48 20 07 **Fax 45 48 67 52** Map C2.63 **H**
9 rue Ste-Beuve 75006 Mº Notre-Dame-des-Champs

Accommodation at this 19th-century building just off Boulevard Raspail comprises standard, superior and de luxe rooms plus a junior suite and four apartments. Price varies according to size, with the apartments at the top of the range at 1700F. Furnishings are a careful blend of old and new, David Hicks being responsible for the interior design. Facilities include satellite television, room safe and mini-bar. Attractive tiled bathrooms all have both tub and shower. Garden bar. ***Rooms*** *23. Amex, Mastercard, Visa.*

A glossary of French menu items starts on page 274

HOTEL DES SAINTS-PÈRES 720F

Tel 45 44 50 00 **Fax 45 44 90 83** Map B1.64 **H**
65 rue des Saints-Pères 75006 Mº St-Germain-des-Prés/Sèvres-Babylone

Built in the 17th century by Louis XVI's architect Gittard, the hotel has kept a certain traditional style and charm while being considerably modernised. Most of the bedrooms have a quiet setting overlooking the courtyard garden where, when the weather's kind, breakfast and tea can be taken. Rooms have all the usual amenities and nine are air-conditioned. There are lounges and a bar but no restaurant. ***Rooms*** *39. Amex, Mastercard, Visa.*

HOTEL SÉNATEUR 750F

Tel 43 26 08 83 **Fax 46 34 04 66** Map B2.65 **H**
10 rue Vaugirard 75006 Mº Odéon

Completely renovated in 1992, the Sénateur has a contemporary, functional designer look, with a little greenery to brighten the public areas; bedrooms use carefully co-ordinated colour schemes and have en suite facilities (some with shower and WC only), satellite TV, safe and mini-bar. Top-floor rooms enjoy splendid views. There's a public car park next to the hotel, which is in the heart of St-Germain-des-Prés. ***Rooms*** *41. Amex, Diners, Mastercard, Visa.*

TAVERNE BASQUE 450F

Tel 42 22 51 07 **Map C1.66** **R**
45 rue du Cherche-Midi 75006 Mº St-Placide/Sèvres-Babylone

Run by Pierre Alcorta and his family, this is very much a homely, local restaurant. The decor has warmth and character too, with dark wood-strip panelled walls hung with colourful pictures and Basque artefacts suspended from the beamed ceiling. The food is simple, flavoursome and well prepared. Specialities from the South-West region of France include a hot starter of pipérade – a scrambled egg mixture with tomato and onion – that comes topped with slices of raw cured ham, *ttoro* (fish soup), cold goose confit, roast duck breast with honey from the Pyrenees and Toulouse cassoulet. *Boudin de volaille au foie gras* is a recent addition to the menu. There are daily specials, too, such as venison medallions *Grand Veneur*, tuna steak *basquaise* and poached haddock. Good desserts round things off well: *clafoutis* with cherries and honey, *tarte aux pommes* with Izarra (a Basque liqueur). Service is charming. Set menus 150F (*saison*) & 190F (incl drink). ***Seats*** *560. L 12-2.30 D 7.30-10.30.* ***Closed*** *L Sat, all Sun & 1st 2 weeks Aug. Amex, Diners, Mastercard, Visa.*

Victoria Palace Hotel 940F

Tel 45 44 38 16 Fax 45 49 23 75 Map C1.67 **H**
6 rue Blaise-Desgoffe 75006 Mº St-Placide/Montparnasse

A choice of accommodation in a large, old-fashioned hotel between Montparnasse and St-Germain-des-Prés. All rooms have satellite TV, and all but a few have a bathtub as well as a shower in the en suite facilities. Prices range from 880F for a single to 1420F for a de luxe double. The bar, and room service, operate 24 hours a day. Private parking for 12 cars (130F for 24 hours). ***Rooms*** *111. Amex, Diners, Mastercard, Visa.*

La Vigneraie 500F

Tel 45 48 57 04 Map B1.68 **R**
16 rue Dragon 75006 Mº St-Germain-des-Prés/Sèvres-Babylone

An old-fashioned *bistro à vins*, where you can drop in for a glass of wine (Bordeaux a speciality) or settle down for a full meal. The menu sticks to classics old and new: salad of spinach and chicken livers, goat's cheese on toast, salmon *à l'unilatéral, pot-au-feu, gigot d'agneau à la fleur de thym, délice au chocolat.* Set L 75F Set L & D 168F. ***Seats*** *60. L 12-2.30 D 7-11.30.* ***Closed*** *L Sun. Amex, Diners, Mastercard, Visa*

La Villa 800F

Tel 43 26 60 00 Fax 46 34 63 63 Map B1.69 **H**
29 rue Jacob 75006 Mº St-Germain-des-Prés

An ultra-modern hotel whose striking design has been a talking point since its opening half a dozen years ago. Accommodation ranges from '3rd category with shower' to a senior suite with two bedrooms and a sitting-room (1950F). All rooms are double-glazed and air-conditioned and come with mini-bar, satellite TV and even a telephone extension in the bathroom. Among the hotel's many unique attractions is its cocktail bar, open from 6, with the top names in jazz performing live after 10.30pm Monday to Saturday. ***Rooms*** *32. Amex, Diners, Mastercard, Visa.*

Villa des Artistes 650F

Tel 43 26 60 86 Fax 43 54 73 70 Map D2.70 **H**
9 rue de la Grande-Chaumière 75006 Mº Vavin

Just steps away from Boulevard du Montparnasse, a welcoming hotel with public rooms done out in art deco style and built around a neat little courtyard garden with a central fountain. Standard rooms (about half the total) have shower and WC only while de luxe accommodation (850F) offers many extras including bathtubs, air-conditioning and mini-bar. All rooms have safes. Room rate includes breakfast and city tax. ***Rooms*** *59. Amex, Diners, Mastercard, Visa.*

7th Arrondissement
Places of Interest

Musée d'Orsay, 40 49 48 14, M° Solferino/RER Musée d'Orsay
Assemblée Nationale, M° Assemblée Nationale
Hotel National des Invalides, 44 42 37 72,
M° Latour-Maubourg/Varenne/RER Invalides
Musée de l'Armée (tomb of Napoleon I)
Tour Eiffel, 45 50 34 56, M° Bir Hakeim/RER Champs de Mars
Champ de Mars, M° Ecole Militaire
Ecole Militaire, M° Ecole Militaire
Les Egouts de Paris (sewers), 47 05 10 29, M° Alma-Marceau/RER Pont de l'Alma
Musée Auguste Rodin, 44 18 61 31, M° Varenne

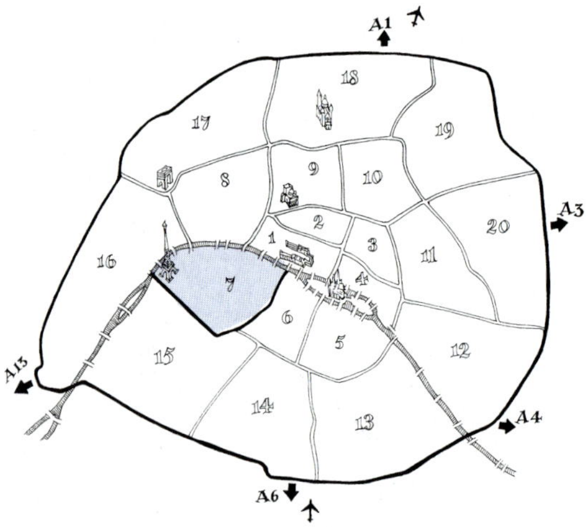

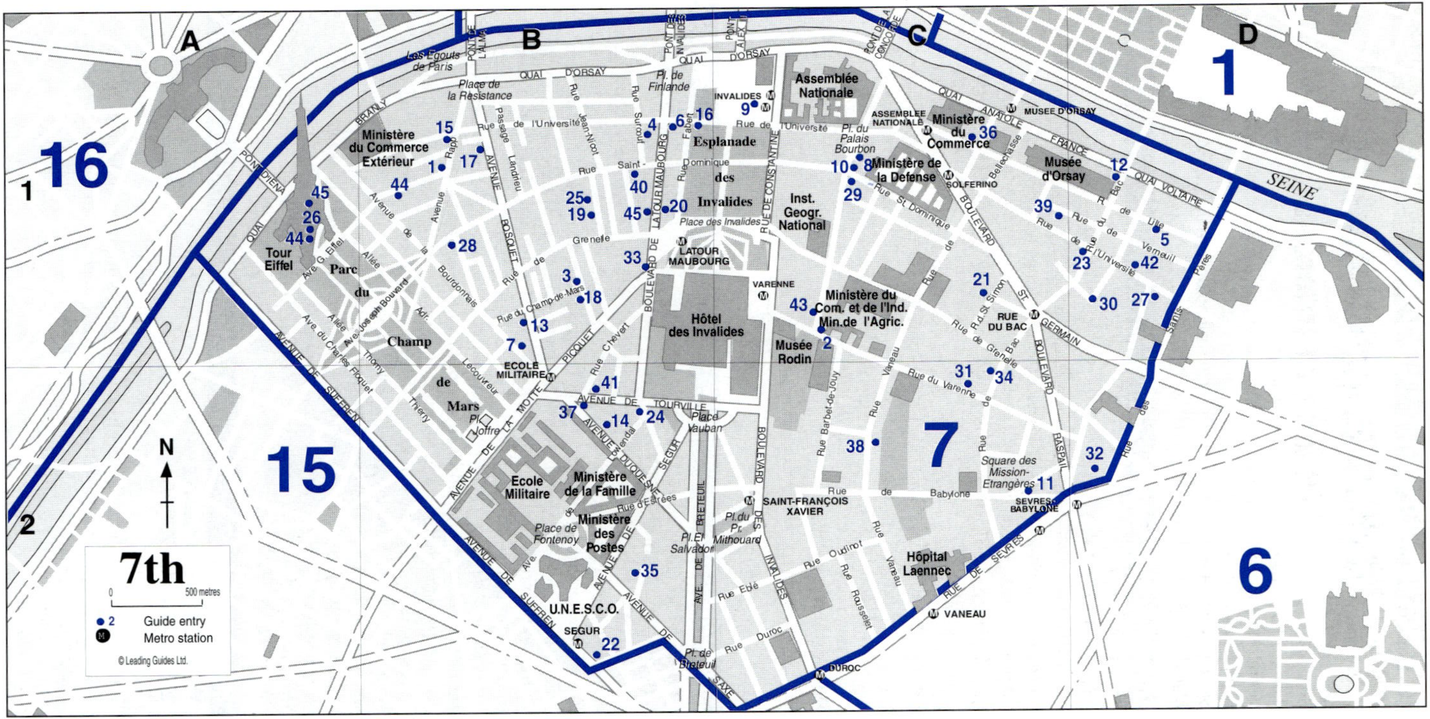
7th
0
500 metres
2 Guide entry
Metro station
© Leading Guides Ltd.
N
A
B
C
D
1
2
16
15
7
6
1
SEINE
Tour Eiffel
Parc du Champ de Mars
Ministère du Commerce Extérieur
Esplanade des Invalides
Hôtel des Invalides
Assemblée Nationale
Inst. Geogr. National
Ministère de la Defense
Ministère du Commerce
Musée d'Orsay
Ministère du Com. et de l'Ind. Min.de l'Agric.
Musée Rodin
Ecole Militaire
Ministère de la Famille
Ministère des Postes
U.N.E.S.C.O.
Hôpital Laennec
Square des Mission-Etrangères
Les Egouts de Paris
Place de la Résistance
Pl. de Finlande
Pl. du Palais Bourbon
Place des Invalides
Place Vauban
Pl. Joffre
Place de Fontenoy
Pl. El Salvador
Pl.du Pr. Mithouard
Pl. de Breteuil
INVALIDES
ASSEMBLEE NATIONALE
MUSEE D'ORSAY
SOLFERINO
LATOUR MAUBOURG
VARENNE
RUE DU BAC
ECOLE MILITAIRE
SAINT-FRANÇOIS XAVIER
SEVRES-BABYLONE
VANEAU
DUROC
SEGUR
QUAI D'ORSAY
QUAI ANATOLE FRANCE
QUAI VOLTAIRE
QUAI BRANLY
PONT DE L'ALMA
PONT DES INVALIDES
PONT ALEX III
PONT DE LA CONCORDE
PONT D'IENA
AVENUE RAPP
AVENUE BOSQUET
BOULEVARD DE LATOUR MAUBOURG
RUE DE CONSTANTINE
BOULEVARD DES INVALIDES
BOULEVARD ST. GERMAIN
BOULEVARD RASPAIL
AVENUE DE LA MOTTE PICQUET
AVENUE DE TOURVILLE
AVENUE DUQUESNE
AVENUE DE SUFFREN
AVENUE DE SEGUR
AVE. DE BRETEUIL
AVENUE DE SAXE
RUE DE SEVRES
Rue de l'Université
Rue Saint-Dominique
Rue de Grenelle
Rue de Lille
Rue de Verneuil
Rue du Bac
Rue de Bellechasse
Rue de Varenne
Rue de Babylone
Rue Vaneau
Rue Barbet-de-Jouy
Rue Oudinot
Rue Rousselet
Rue Eblé
Rue Duroc
Rue des Saints Pères
Rue Jean-Nicot
Rue Surcouf
Rue Fabert
Passage Landrieu
Avenue de la Bourdonnais
Rue du Champ-de-Mars
Rue Chevert
Rue Cler
Ave. G. Eiffel
Allée Ave. Joseph Bouvard
Allée Thomy Thierry
Ave. du Charles Floquet
Adr. Lecouvreur
Rue d'Estrées
Ave. de Lowendal
R.d.St. Simon
Rue de Grenelle
1
2
3
4
5
6
7
8
9
10
11
12
13
14
15
16
17
18
19
20
21
22
23
24
25
26
27
28
29
30
31
32
33
34
35
36
37
38
39
40
41
42
43
44
44
45
45

ALTITUDE 95 — 400F

Tel 45 55 20 04 **Fax 47 05 94 40** Map A1.45 **R**
1ère étage Tour Eiffel 75007 Mº Bir Hakeim/RER Champs de Mars

95 metres up, on the first level of the Eiffel Tower, chef Fabrice Brossard presents menus based on French regional cuisine – each dish identified by region. The cooking may not scale the heights of the*Jules Verne* on the level above, but neither do the prices. Foie gras, oysters, snails, onion soup, *andouillettes, moules poulette* and *jambonette de lapin aux pruneaux confits* illustrate the broad choice. Set L 97F & 148F Set D 235F Children's menu 46F. ***Seats** 260. L 11.30-3 D 6.30-11. Amex, Diners, Mastercard, Visa.*

ANTOINE ET ANTOINETTE — 450F

Tel 45 51 75 61 Map B1.1 **R**
16 ave Rapp 75007 Mº Alma Marceau

A delightful little restaurant where chef-patron Jean-Claude Pernot has been preparing a selection of classic French country dishes since 1984. There is nothing complex about the food, which ranges from starters such as *fondant de canard aux raisins, brouillard aux morilles, marinade de sardines à l'aneth* and *salade tiède de foie de volaille*. For a main course the choice could be *aile de raie à l'embeurrée de choux, aiguillettes de canard, carré d'agneau roti au thym* or *supreme de dorade aux poireaux.* Desserts include *aumonières de crepes aux pommes confites* and *nougat glacé au miel.* Millefeuille with red berries is a speciality dessert to order at the beginning of the meal. Set L & D 130F. ***Seats** 45 (+ 22 outside). L 12.15-2 D 7.30-10. **Closed** Sat, Sun & 2 weeks Aug. Amex, Diners, Mastercard, Visa.*

See page 9 for a list of starred restaurants

L'ARPÈGE ★ — 2400F

Tel 45 51 47 33 **Fax 44 18 98 39** Map C1.2 **R**
84 rue de Varenne 75007 Mº Varenne

There are few better restaurants in Paris than L'Arpège, but food this good does not come cheaply. The minimalist decor (bare pink stuccoed plaster, white napery, charcoal grey furniture) seems designed to distract the diner's attention as little as possible from Alain Passard's cooking. He has spent time with Boyer in Reims and Senderens at *Lucas Carton* but shows a distinctive originality in his interpretations of traditional dishes. Typical starters from the carte are *crème de cèpes du pays de Brive aux oeufs et parmesan* (cream of ceps mushroom soup with eggs and parmesan) and *homard de Bretagne et navets en vinaigrette aigre-douce au romarin* (lobster and turnip in a sweet and sour dressing with rosemary). Tempting mains include *sole de l'ile d'Yeu farcie au gingembre, jus d'oignon blanc* (sole stuffed with ginger and served with white onion jus) and *dragée de pigeonneau vendéen à l'hydromel* (young pigeon cooked in mead). Desserts include the decidedly strange *tomate confite farcie aux douze saveurs* (baked tomato stuffed with 12, mainly citrus, 'flavours'). Set L 390F Set D 790F. ***Seats** 40. L 12.30-1.30 D 7.30-10.30. **Closed** L Sun, all Sat & 5-21 Aug. Amex, Diners, Mastercard, Visa.*

BEAUGENCY — 660F

Tel 47 05 01 63 **Fax 45 51 04 96** Map B1.3 **H**
21 rue Duvivier 75007 Mº Ecole Militaire

A modern building close to Hotel des Invalides and not far from the Eiffel Tower. Brightly decorated, double-glazed bedrooms, some quite compact, have satellite TV, mini-bar and hairdryer. Breakfast is included in the room rate and is available from room service or it can be taken in the cheerful breakfast room with its white rattan furniture and wall-length mural. ***Rooms** 30. Amex, Diners, Mastercard, Visa.*

Le Bellecour H 1000F

Tel 45 55 68 38 **Fax 45 50 30 11** Map B1.4 **R**
22 rue Surcouf 75007 M° Invalides

Located near the Esplanade des Invalides, south of the Quai d'Orsay, this restaurant is renowned for its earthy Lyonnais specialities such as *andouillette au vin de Macon* and *salade de clapotons* (lamb's trotters). A second carte lists more refined dishes like lobster salad with white peaches, French beans and lobster egg vinaigrette, and fillet of beef with a confit of shallots and potato gratin. Set L 160F & 250F Set D 250F & 420F. ***Seats*** *35. L 12-2 D 7.30-10.30.* ***Closed*** *L Sat (all Sat in Jun/Jul), all Sun & Aug. Amex, Diners, Mastercard, Visa.*

Bersoly's Saint-Germain 580F

Tel 42 60 73 79 **Fax 49 27 05 55** Map D1.5 **H**
28 rue de Lille 75007 M° Rue du Bac/St-Germain-des-Prés

Highlights at this one-time monastery include a warm, friendly welcome, antiques from the nearby specialist shops, a pretty little interior courtyard and an atmospheric vaulted cellar where breakfast is served from 6.30 to 10.30. It is also served in the cosy bedrooms, which are named after French Impressionist painters. All have cable TV, hairdryer and safe. ***Rooms*** *16.* ***Closed*** *Aug. Mastercard, Visa.*

La Boule d'Or 500F

Tel 47 05 50 18 **Fax 47 05 91 21** Map B1.6 **R**
13 bd de Latour-Maubourg 75007 M° Invalides

Contemporary decor, a civilised band of regulars, a charming owner and a chef with skill and imagination. Dishes are in the traditional French mainstream, from *compote de canard à la biere et pain d'épice* and *escargots à la crème de langoustines et basilic* through fillet of bream Parisian-style with shallots, chicken poached in the yellow wine of Arbois and pork cheek with lemon and ginger to a speciality hot lemon soufflé or sweet apple tart with cinnamon, both to be ordered at the beginning of the meal. Set menu 175F. ***Seats*** *55. L 12.15-2.30 D 7.30-10.30.* ***Closed*** *L Sat, some Public Holidays. Amex, Diners, Mastercard, Visa.*

La Bourdonnais 650F

Tel 47 05 45 42 **Fax 45 55 75 54** Map B1.7 **HR**
111 ave de la Bourdonnais 75007 M° Ecole Militaire

This turn-of-the-century building offers comfortable accommodation in traditional Parisian style. Limited room service. Public parking 56F. Garden. ***Rooms*** *60. Amex, Diners, Mastercard, Visa.*

La Cantine des Gourmets ★ 1000F

Tel 47 05 47 96 **Fax 45 51 09 29**

Next door to La Bourdonnais at no 113, this restaurant is not only one of the most popular in the city, but also one of the friendliest. Philippe Bardau's cooking is firmly rooted in Provence, as can be witnessed by starters such as *confit d'aubergines au basilic, tartines de maïs à l'ail doux* (confit of aubergines with basil, served with small garlic-flavoured corn tartlets) and *millefeuille de Saint-Pierre au concassé d'olives et de fenouil* (millefeuille of John Dory with olives and fennel). Main courses are also blessedly simple and evocative of the sun-drenched South-East. For example, Lozère lamb with ratatouille, and pan-fried red mullet with spaghetti *pimentés et aromates*. Desserts include *macaron glacé choco-caramel* with toasted hazelnuts. Set L 180F & 220F Set D 280F & 380F. ***Seats*** *60. L 12-2.30 D 8-12.* ***Closed*** *1 May, 25 Dec.*

A glossary of French menu items starts on page 274

Bourgogne et Montana 870F

Tel 45 51 20 22 Fax 45 56 11 98 Map C1.8 **H**
3 rue de Bourgogne 75007 M° Invalides/Assemblée Nationale

Opposite the Palais Bourbon and very near the Assemblée Nationale, this traditionally run hotel is in a late 18th-century building. Major refurbishment in the past year has modernised the interior while still retaining the fine pieces of antique and period furniture that graced both its public areas and bedrooms. All the bedrooms are warm and comfortable and are well equipped, with cable TV, mini-bar and hairdryer. The room rate includes Continental breakfast served in the bedrooms or there's a buffet offered in the restaurant (closed for main meals Sat, Sun and 1st 3 weeks Aug). ***Rooms*** *34. Amex, Diners, Mastercard, Visa.*

Chez Françoise 500F

Tel 47 05 49 03 Fax 45 51 96 20 Map C1.9 **R**
Aérogare des Invalides 75007 M° Invalides

Not advertised on the esplanade outside – look for it in the basement of the Invalides Air France bus terminal. A sort of up-market brasserie, it has made its reputation as the MPs' canteen, with a relaxed, enjoyable atmosphere. Langoustine salad with guacamole, *foie gras de canard frais maison*, scallops *provençale, confit de canard, civet de marcassin*, roast rack of lamb with dauphinoise potatoes, *lièvre à la royale*, veal kidneys with sherry sauce – nothing is missing from the classical repertoire and certainly not quality. Finish with the likes of *parfait glacé au café* and tarte tatin. Monday to Thursday evenings there's a pianist and on Friday and Saturday, a small combo usually plays jazz. Private parking with access in front of 2 rue Fabert. Set menu 168F. ***Seats*** *150 (+ 50 outside). L 12-3 D 7-12. Amex, Diners, Mastercard, Visa.*

Chez Marius 700F

Tel 45 51 79 42 Fax 47 53 79 56 Map C1.10 **R**
5 rue de Bourgogne 75007 M° Invalides/Assemblée Nationale

Affable chef-patron Michel Perrodo runs a delightful restaurant specialising in the cuisine of the Mediterranean and particularly seafood. Oysters, from *belons* down to *papillons* could precede John Dory with saffron, grilled line-caught bass with a *sauce vierge*, bouillabaisse, rack of lamb with thyme flowers, Bresse chicken with morels, calf's sweetbreads and langoustines with a shellfish sauce or breast of duck with raspberry vinegar. Good choice of desserts too, including a bitter chocolate fondant with a mint sauce, hot apple tart, *nougat glacé* with red fruits and crème brulée with brown sugar. Set menu 180F. ***Seats*** *55. L 12-3 D 7.30-10.30.* ***Closed*** *L Sat, all Sun & Aug. Amex, Diners, Mastercard, Visa.*

Chomel 550F

Tel 45 48 55 52 Fax 45 48 89 76 Map C2.11 **H**
15 rue Chomel 75007 M° Sèvres-Babylone

Regular maintenance keeps everything ship-shape in this comfortable and traditional Left Bank hotel. There are six floors, served by a lift, and bedrooms have either shower or bath and WC as well as the usual extras of phone, hairdryer and mini-bar. The TVs show an English channel. Breakfast may be taken in the bedrooms or in the little lounge. Parking available below the nearby *Bon Marché* store. ***Rooms*** *23. Amex, Diners, Mastercard, Visa.*

> The best way to get around Paris is by bus or metro –
> buy a book (carnet) of tickets at any metro station and save money

CHRISTIAN CONSTANT

Tel 47 03 30 00 **Fax 42 86 97 97** Map D1.12 **R**
26 rue du Bac 75007 Mº Rue du Bac

An excellent pastry shop open all day for fine baking and a few light savouries. A must are the chocolate delicacies for which Christian Constant has won a well-deserved reputation. *Fleurs de Chine* is a light, bitter chocolate mousse with a cocoa sorbet and jasmine ice cream and *Sonia Rykiel* is a chocolate and banana tart named after the famous dress designer because she liked it so much (both 25F). Ice creams and sorbets, and *entremets glacés* like *soufflé glacé Rothschild* with fruit confit and Cointreau and *truffes glacées à cacao amer, crème à la vanille de Tahiti* are other specialities. On the savoury front there are quiches (salmon 31F, mussel), croque monsieur and other sandwiches (smoked salmon 36F), and salads. Also at 37 rue d'Assas in the 6th (same hours and menu) and as we were going to press they were about to open a *salon de thé* in the Old England shop in the Boulevard des Capucines. ***Open*** *8-8. Mastercard, Visa.*

CLÉMENTINE 420F

Tel 45 51 41 16 Map B1.13 **R**
62 ave Bosquet 75007 Mº Ecole Militaire

Chef-patron Bernard Przybyl specialises in the cuisine of the South-West (Cahors) in his snug little restaurant with up-market bistro decor offering cassoulet, foie gras and dishes such as *fricassée de rognons de veau* with mustard, *confit de dinde à la landaise, filet de poulet grillé au gros sel et citron* and *médaillons de roussette à l'ail*. Reliable cooking, kind prices, regional wines. Set menu 149F. ***Seats*** *60 (+ 12 outside). L 12-2.30 D 7.30-10.30.* ***Closed*** *L Sat, all Sun & 2 weeks Aug. Amex, Mastercard, Visa.*

DERBY EIFFEL 690F

Tel 47 05 12 05 **Fax 47 05 43 43** Map B2.14 **H**
5 ave Duquesne 75007 Mº Ecole Militaire

Not far from the Eiffel Tower and close to Hotel des Invalides, the Derby's public areas include a relaxing modern lounge and a courtyard garden. There are also two meeting rooms, for 10 to 40 people. Bedrooms are neat and practical, with satellite TV, mini-bars, hairdryers and private safes. Underground car park close by. ***Rooms*** *43. Amex, Diners, Mastercard, Visa.*

LES DEUX ABEILLES

Tel 45 55 64 04 Map B1.15 **R**
189 rue de l'Université 75007 Mº Alma Marceau

A family-style tea room with smart 30s decor and careful management by the lady owner and her daughter. There are three rooms: the first quaintly English and old-fashioned; the second airy and bright with a glass skylight; the third sombre, and this is where smokers are assigned. Light savoury dishes such as *flan à la ciboulette, courgettes farcies, blanquette de veau au citron* or *poulet à l'estragon* are offered throughout the day but the real treats are the home-made pastries on display: *fondant au chocolat, crumble aux poires et fruits rouges*, or *gateau au fromage blanc* (cheesecake). ***Open*** *9-7.* ***Closed*** *Sun & Aug. Mastercard, Visa.*

LE DIVELLEC ★★ 1300F

Tel 45 51 91 96 **Fax 45 51 31 75** Map B1.16 **R**
107 rue de l'Université 75007 Mº Invalides

Jacques Le Divellec is one of the prime exponents of modern fish cookery. His restaurant, overlooking the Esplanade des Invalides, has a suitably nautical theme with numerous paintings of boats, fish and the sea and a lobster tank in the dining-room. The cooking style is excitingly innovative yet relatively uncomplex, the quality and flavour of the fish taking precedence over elaborate saucing and obsequious garnishes. A favourite is the juxtaposing of foie gras and

See over

seafood as in langoustines with foie gras terrine (scallops replace the langoustines in winter), or tournedos of tuna with truffled duck foie gras. Exquisite starters such as a salad of lobster with coral vinaigrette, a tartare of bass, salmon and mullet with virgin olive oil and clams stuffed with garlic and thyme could precede John Dory with tapénade and a tomato and olive coulis or roast turbot with a lobster béarnaise and fried potatoes. The lobster press is an invention of M Le Divellec and is based on the famous duck press at *La Tour d'Argent*; it is used in the preparation of *homard à la presse*. There are a couple of meat dishes for the determined carnivore. Among the desserts look out for Jacques' latest creation, herb sorbet. Set L 290F & 390F. ***Seats** 60. L 12-2 D 7.30-10.* ***Closed** Sun, Mon & 22 Dec-3 Jan. Amex, Diners, Mastercard, Visa.*

DUQUESNOY ★★ 1200F

Tel 47 05 96 78 Fax 44 18 90 57 Map B1.17 **R**
6 ave Bosquet 75007 M° Ecole Militaire

Jean-Paul Duquesnoy prepares haute cuisine dishes for a smart, civilised clientele in his handsomely decorated, wood-panelled restaurant just south of Pont d'Alma. His skill, finesse and light touch are evident throughout an exceptionally enticing carte: *soupe crémeuse de girolles au cerfeuil et grosses langoustines*, crab-stuffed courgette flowers, line-caught turbot with a fine 'minestrone' of vegetables and sauce pistou, *rouelles d'abats de la "Saint Cochon"*, beef with truffles in a Graves wine sauce with quenelles of bone marrow and ethereal pommes soufflées, a spectacular dessert of four different chocolate creations. Choosing is a delightful, but difficult task, and Jean-Paul will do it for you if you (and all at your table) order the *menu dégustation* of four specialities served in small portions. The 250F lunchtime menu provides great value for money. Classic wines accompany the classic food. Françoise Duquesnoy is a charming and knowledgable hostess. Set L 250F Set L & D 450F & 520F (*dégustation*). ***Seats** 45. L 12-2 D 8-10.* ***Closed** L Sat, all Sun, 1st 2 weeks Aug, 25 Dec & 1 Jan. Amex, Mastercard, Visa.*

A glossary of French menu items starts on page 274

ECAILLE ET PLUME 500F

Tel 45 55 06 72 Fax 45 51 38 35 Map B1.18 **R**
25 rue Duvivier 75007 M° Ecole Militaire

In a romantic setting of soft lights, candles and hunting scenes, chef-patronne Marie Naël presents a seductive menu of classical dishes based on the freshest seasonal produce. That means plenty of fish in summer (*tournedos de lotte au fumet de Bordeaux, polenta frite*; roast scallops and watercress; and some unusual shellfish – razor shells, limpets) and game in winter, including wild duck, wild boar, hare and grouse flambéed in whisky. The *menu club* at 150F is now available to first-timers if mentioned when booking. Throughout the year look out for special tasting menus with various themes – a mushroom feast in October – and national cuisines. ***Seats** 40. L 12-3 D 7.30-11.* ***Closed** L Sat, all Sun, 1 week Feb & all Aug. Amex, Mastercard, Visa.*

EIFFEL PARK HOTEL 835F

Tel 45 55 10 01 Fax 47 05 28 68 Map B1.19 **H**
17bis rue Amélie 75007 M° Latour-Maubourg

Modern, comfortable hotel opened in 1989, possessing well-appointed, up-to-date bedrooms with satellite TV, safe, mini-bar and hairdryer. There's a splendid view over the Paris roof-tops from the sun-terrace on the 5th floor. Meeting rooms for up to 30; bar; reading room. ***Rooms** 36. Amex, Diners, Mastercard, Visa.*

Elysées Maubourg 710F

Tel 45 56 10 78 **Fax 47 05 65 08** Map B1.20 **H**
35 bd de Latour-Maubourg 75007 M° Latour-Maubourg

A hotel with stylish, up-to-date bedrooms featuring quality furnishings and cable TV, hairdryer and mini-bar. Intimate bar, indoor garden, a meeting room for 15 people and the unusual (for Paris) feature of a sauna in the basement. Parking des Invalides is 300 metres away. ***Rooms*** *30. Amex, Diners, Mastercard, Visa.*

La Ferme Saint-Simon ★ 600F

Tel 45 48 35 74 **Fax 40 49 07 31** Map C1.21 **R**
6 rue de Saint-Simon 75007 M° Rue du Bac

A smart, well-respected restaurant in a quiet residential area, La Ferme combines cosy dining-rooms with a charming, intimate atmosphere. The menu is thoroughly up-to-date and demonstrates the chef's creativity and imagination. Dishes include marinated mackerel with a tomato and basil coulis and stuffed courgette flowers, *feuilleté de girolles et ris de veau poelés, terrine de tete de veau tiède, vinaigrette aux olives, dorade grillé jus au safran et artichauts, lotte et moules en petite bourride parfumée à la marjolaine* and a speciality *'Grillardine Denise Fabre'*– a lobster feuilleté with a basil-flavoured lobster sauce. Among the meat dishes are braised shin of veal, *fricassée de poularde de Bresse, jus au foie gras et girolles parmentière* and lamb noisettes with stuffed baby vegetables. For dessert there are some delicious confections such as *feuillantine à la pistache,* crème brulée with apricots and *clafoutis*. Set L 170F Set D 190F. ***Seats*** *90. L 12-2 D 7.30-10.15.* ***Closed*** *L Sat, all Sun & 5-15 Aug. Amex, Diners, Mastercard, Visa.*

Foc-Ly 600F

Tel 47 83 27 12 Map B2.22 **R**
71 ave de Suffren 75007 M° La Motte Picquet Grenelle

Specialising in Chinese and Thai cooking, the restaurant has smart lightwood panelling, a comfortable ambience and staff who provide friendly and efficient service. The menu is short and lends a French influence to the cooking with generally mild spicing and the assumption that diners conform to having a starter, main course and dessert. There's a selection of deep-fried and steamed dim sum. Other dishes from a largely simple and uncomplicated selection include *marmite de coquilles St Jacques et crevettes au pates de soja, marmite de canard à la mangue*, and *poulet sauté à l'ail*. Relatively inexpensive wine list. Also at 79 Avenue Charles de Gaulle, Neuilly sur Seine. Set L 110F & 130F Set D 140F & 160F. ***Seats*** *70. L 12-2.30 D 7-11.* ***Closed*** *Mon in August. Amex, Diners, Mastercard, Visa.*

Gaya Rive Gauche 600F

Tel 45 44 73 73 Map D1.23 **R**
44 rue du Bac 75007 M° Rue du Bac

Sister restaurant to *Gaya Rive Droite* (*qv*) across the river, with which it shares the successful formula of serving only the best and freshest of fish each day, in simple, uncomplicated fashion. Decor has a nautical flavour with old photos of boats, fishermen and the like around wood-panelled walls. ***Seats*** *50 (+ 10 outside). L 12-2.30 D 7-11.* ***Closed*** *Sun & 2 weeks Aug. Amex, Mastercard, Visa.*

Grand Hotel de France 490F

Tel 47 05 40 49 **Fax 45 56 96 78** Map B2.24 **H**
102 bd de Latour-Maubourg 75007 M° Ecole Militaire

Practical, reasonably priced accommodation with cable TV featuring a few English-speaking channels and mini-bars in a modern (1980s) hotel opposite Invalides and five minutes from the Eiffel Tower. Hotel bar. There is room service of breakfast, or it can be taken in the pleasant breakfast room. ***Rooms*** *60. Amex, Mastercard, Visa.*

Les Jardins d'Eiffel 860F

Tel 47 05 46 21 **Fax 45 55 28 08** Map B1.25 **H**
8 rue Amélie 75007 M° Invalides

A bourgeois building from the beginning of the century has been turned into a hotel of real comfort and character. Individually decorated, all rooms have attractive period-style furnishings, neat private bathroom and separate WCs, sound-proofing, satellite TV, mini-bar, safe, direct-dial phone, electric blinds, trouser press and hairdryer. 36 rooms are air-conditioned and are designated 'executive' but more rooms are gradually being converted; rooms with views of the Eiffel Tower attract a supplement. Parking for 32 cars. ***Rooms** 80. Amex, Diners, Mastercard, Visa.*

Jules Verne ★ 1500F

Tel 45 55 61 44 **Fax 47 05 29 41** Map A1.26 **R**
2ème Etage Tour Eiffel 75007 M° Bir Hakeim/Champs de Mars

This is a stunning setting for those prepared to book 6 to 7 weeks in advance and who don't mind being a third of the way up on the second level of the Eiffel Tower, 120m above ground. The effort is well worth while as the views and Alain Reix's cooking are superb. The interior decor purposefully doesn't detract from what's outside, with everything in black and grey, even the artwork. On offer is a menu that is both highly imaginative and very sophisticated. The choice of starters ranges from a langoustine 'bouillabaisse' with spinach ravioli and a salad of obster with a confit of goose gizzard and artichokes to a fricassee of baby squid with chives and pan-fried foie gras. Main dishes include excellent fish dishes as in *morceau de bar au consommé de tomatoes, fondue d'aubergine* and *panier vapeur de Saint Pierre, ragout de legumes à la crème de bacon*. Among the meaty offerings are *cocotte de ris de veau et rognons, gratin de spaetzli*, oxtail wrapped in lettuce with cumin-flavoured carrots, and roasted Bresse chicken with a nutmeg-flavoured jus. Super desserts, too, as in a *léger flan de semoule à la banane sèche de Tahiti, glace vanille*, hot cherry and almond soufflé (to be ordered at the start of the meal) or a *soupe de vin de Loupiac, melon et fruits rouges* with a white peach sorbet. Set L (Mon-Fri) 290F Set D 660F. Valet parking. ***Seats** 100. L 12-2.30 D 7-10.30. Amex, Diners, Mastercard, Visa.*

Hotel Lenox 590F

Tel 42 96 10 95 **Fax 42 61 52 83** Map D1.27 **H**
9 rue de l'Université 75007 M° Rue du Bac

The location is a relatively quiet street a short distance from the heart of St-Germain. Sister to the *Lenox* in the 14th (*qv*), it is virtually identical in its decor and style. There's a spacious and welcoming entrance hall-cum-lounge and bedrooms have attractive traditional furnishings complemented by modern amenities. ***Rooms** 34. Amex, Diners, Mastercard, Visa.*

Londres 555F

Tel 45 51 63 02 **Fax 47 05 28 96** Map B1.28 **H**
1 rue Augereau 75007 M° Ecole Militaire

A few paces from Champs de Mars and the Eiffel Tower, a straightforward business and tourist hotel with friendly, helpful staff. Ten of the cheerful bedrooms have bath/WC, and are at the back of the hotel, where it's quieter; the rest have shower/WC. All have cable TV, mini-bar and hairdryer. ***Rooms** 30. Amex, Diners, Mastercard, Visa.*

The best way to get around Paris is by bus or metro –
buy a book (carnet) of tickets at any metro station and save money

MICHEL COURTALHAC 500F

Tel 45 55 15 35 Map C1.29 **R**
47 rue de Bourgogne 75007 Mº Varenne

Several choices on the short, monthly-changing menus are replaced daily depending on the market availability of produce which is purchased fresh each morning and cooked to order at this simple, pleasant, beamed restaurant located in an area of Government offices. *Gazpacho andalou, caviar d'aubergines* and *entrecote poelé, pommes de terre à la fourme* could appear alongside the day's specials: eggs poached with herbs, monkfish *à la mediterranéenne* and sauté of rabbit with savory. Cheeses from Barthélemy in Rue Grenelle are offered as an alternative to, say, chocolate ganache with coffee sauce or the dessert of the day, perhaps raspberry millefeuille. ***Seats** 50. L 12.30-2.45 D 7.45-10.30. **Closed** L Sat, all Sun, Aug & 1 week Christmas. Amex, Mastercard, Visa.*

MONTALEMBERT 1625F

Tel 45 49 68 68 **Fax 45 49 69 49** Map D1.30 **HR**
3 rue Montalembert 75007 Mº Rue du Bac

The restored splendour of its 1926 origins incorporates the well-conceived use of many luxurious materials, including marble, leather, wrought iron, cast bronze and a variety of woods. Beyond the entrance the first striking feature is a rug woven to reproduce the handwriting of the Count of Montalembert. Some of the bedrooms have contemporary furniture, others are in Louis-Philippe style. All are equipped with up-to-the-minute accessories including video recorder (the hotel has a tape library). Bathrooms are particularly luxurious in both look and appointments, with Portuguese marble, chrome and generous towelling and toiletries. There's 24-hour room service. The bar is a popular place for the literary world to meet, and there's an adjoining lounge for quiet relaxation, and a delightful garden patio. ***Rooms** 56. Amex, Diners, Mastercard, Visa.*

Restaurant 700F

As stylish as the rest of the hotel, with lightwood panelling and black and white photographs. Snacks and more substantial dishes, both traditional and contemporary, are available, but Sunday brunch (a 180F buffet) is what it's best known for. Specialities are vine leaf rolls filled with duck and foie gras, *soupe au pistou*, sea bass grilled with thyme, salmon roasted with poppy seed and served with leeks, lamb kebab with beetroot crisps and celery, grilled veal fillet with green beans and a lemon butter sauce and tarte tatin with a green apple sorbet. Set menu 170F. ***Seats** 30 (+ 20 outside). **Meals** noon-10.30pm.*

PAUL MINCHELLI 1000F

Tel 47 05 89 86 **Fax 45 56 03 84** Map B1.45 **R**
54 bd de Latour Maubourg 75007 Mº Latour-Maubourg

Rather masculine restaurant, near the Hotel des Invalides, with mock-wood panelling in a shade of yellow emphasised by the curtains that shield the interior from outside view. Eat at crisply-clothed tables or sitting on high stools at a black bar occupying the centre of the room and featuring a lobster tank. Despite the tank (and specialities like lobster with honey and spices, and clams sautéed with thyme, plus oysters, whelks and other shellfish), Paul insists that this is a *fish* rather than a seafood restaurant. The two particular specialities are the raw *(crues)* fish and shellfish starters – tuna, scallops, brill and scallop tartare, *poisson des iles* with lime (there are up to a dozen choices in summer) – and fish steamed in a glass bowl with edible seaweed: fillet of brill, cod, skate wing with tarragon vinegar. Other options on the daily-changing carte (the mysterious letters that appear after some of the dishes are obscure, often political, jokes) might include *brandade de morue* or a bold dish of baby monkfish tails in a fricassee with garlic and smoky bacon. Desserts from the trolley – a slice of *baba au rhum* was given an extra slurp of spirit at the table – or various ices. Shortish list of wines includes a fair number of famous names. ***Seats** 70. L 12-2 D 8-11.30. **Closed** Sun, Mon, Aug & week between Christmas and New Year. Mastercard, Visa.*

LE PETIT LAURENT 700F

Tel 45 48 79 64 Fax 45 44 15 95 Map C2.31 **R**
38 rue de Varenne 75007 M° Sèvres-Babylone/Rue du Bac

In civilised Louis XVI surroundings chef Sylvain Pommier prepares a range of dishes in which classic skills are blended with contemporary touches. Sea bream roasted with mango and lime, calf's liver with juniper, pan-fried spatchcocked quail and fillet of beef with shiitake mushrooms typify his style. Set menus 185F & 250F. ***Seats*** *35. L 12-2 D 7.30-10.* ***Closed*** *L Sat, all Sun & Aug. Amex, Diners, Mastercard, Visa.*

LE RÉCAMIER ★ 1000F

Tel 45 48 86 58 Fax 42 22 84 76 Map D2.32 **R**
4 rue Récamier 75007 M° Sèvres-Babylone

A really splendid place for late spring and summer when its open-air terrace comes into its own. Extending into a delightful, pedestrianised street awash with flowers long-established, the restaurant majors on solid classics from the Burgundy region like *boeuf bourguignon* with fresh noodles and *jambon persillé*. Modern influences also appear as in an escalope of tuna with pesto or fillets of red mullet with basil and mashed potato. Gratin dauphinois is a favourite accompaniment, appearing with the likes of rack of lamb, Auvergne-style calf's liver and various steaks. The wine list is phenomenal – particularly strong in Bordeaux and champagne. Set L 300F (also 230F on Saturday, when there's no à la carte). ***Seats*** *80. L 12-2.30 D 7.45-10.30.* ***Closed*** *Sun. Amex, Diners, Mastercard, Visa.*

RÉSIDENCE LATOUR-MAUBOURG 670F

Tel 47 05 16 16 Fax 47 05 16 14 Map B1.33 **H**
150 rue de Grenelle 75007 M° Latour-Maubourg

Directly across from Hotel des Invalides between Rue Fabert and Boulevard de Latour-Maubourg, the accommodation here is comfortable and homely. All rooms are now double-glazed and each has a TV, two phone lines for the use of lap-tops and fax machines, and a hairdryer in the bathroom. At the rear of the ground floor is a lounge which in the morning becomes an informal breakfast room – breakfast is included in the room price and offers fresh orange juice and excellent Italian coffee. ***Rooms*** *10. Mastercard, Visa.*

A glossary of French menu items starts on page 274

SAINT-GERMAIN 570F

Tel 45 48 62 92 Fax 45 48 26 89 Map C2.34 **H**
88 rue du Bac 75007 M° Rue du Bac

An old mansion whose conversion to a hotel has not spoilt its original character. Beams, moulded ceilings, stone walls and period furniture all make their contribution, in the individually and very attractively appointed bedrooms as well as in elegant day rooms. Bathrooms have been smartened up in the past year and now feature marble cladding. ***Rooms*** *29. Amex, Mastercard, Visa.*

SAXE-RÉSIDENCE 638F

Tel 47 83 98 28 Fax 47 83 85 47 Map B2.35 **H**
9 villa de Saxe 75007 M° Ségur

A particularly peaceful hotel with a neat, functional, 50s look, set in a residential area south of Invalides by the Ecole Militaire and the UNESCO building. Private facilities, mini-bar, safe, cable TV, direct-dial phone and hairdryer in all rooms. Resident's bar, meeting room and lounge. Private parking (free) for five cars. ***Rooms*** *52. Amex, Diners, Mastercard, Visa.*

SOLFÉRINO — 532F

Tel 47 05 85 54 Fax 45 55 51 16 Map C1.36 **H**
91 rue de Lille 75007 M° Solférino/Musée d'Orsay (RER)

Purpose-built for the Gare d'Orsay (now the Musée d'Orsay) 150 years ago, the Solférino has a quiet, old-fashioned charm, highlighted by bright bedrooms decorated in creamy pastel shades and flowery wallpaper, a delightful and very homely little lounge and a cheerful sky-lit breakfast room (Continental breakfast is included in the room rate). TVs are currently available on request. ***Rooms*** *32.* ***Closed*** *23 Dec-4 Jan. Mastercard, Visa.*

SPLENDID — 780F

Tel 45 51 24 77 Fax 44 18 94 60 Map B2.37 **H**
29 ave de Tourville/1 ave Duquesne 75007 M° Ecole Militaire

A fine Haussmann building whose triangular construction affords views of the Eiffel Tower from all its bedrooms, though from many you have to crane your neck out of the window! A few have balconies and the three small suites have private telephone lines. There is a welcoming mirror-lined reception, very stylish bar and bright, well-decorated bedrooms which are art deco in style. All rooms have satellite TV, mini-bar, safe and hairdryer. There is 24-hour room service and, if not taken in your bedroom, the Continental breakfast is served in the basement breakfast room. ***Rooms*** *48. Amex, Diners, Mastercard, Visa.*

HOTEL DE SUÈDE — 652F

Tel 47 05 00 08 Fax 47 05 69 27 Map C2.38 **H**
31 rue Vaneau 75007 M° Vaneau/François Xavier/Sèvres-Babylon

Located south of the Musée d'Orsay with rear rooms overlooking its own gardens and the *Jardin de Matignon*, the hotel has a very conservative and traditional air. Panelled public areas are decorated in an elegantly restrained manner and bedrooms, while not large, have a stylish decor with pale grey velour-upholstered armchairs and Directoire-style furniture. Satellite TV and direct-dial phone in all rooms. There's a pleasant little interior courtyard/garden where breakfast or tea may be taken. All-day room service. ***Rooms*** *39. Amex, Mastercard, Visa.*

TAN DINH — 700F

Tel 45 44 04 84 Fax 45 44 36 93 Map C1.39 **R**
60 rue de Verneuil 75007 M° Rue du Bac/Musée d'Orsay (RER)

Robert Vifian introduced Paris to the delights of Vietnamese cooking, and his pastel-toned restaurant continues to produce traditional Vietnamese dishes with an innovative slant; there's an exceptional wine list to boot. Steamed Vietnamese ravioli with smoked goose, Saigon chicken rolls, mango salad with crab, sea trout with a lime sauce, sautéed chicken in a star anise sauce and sautéed lamb with spices and coconut are typical of the MSG-free delights on the menu. ***Seats*** *60. L 12-2 D 7.30-11.* ***Closed*** *Sun, Aug & some Public Holidays. No credit cards.*

THOUMIEUX — 300F

Tel 47 05 49 75 Fax 47 05 36 96 Map B1.40 **R**
79 rue St-Dominique 75007 M° Latour-Maubourg

The robust dishes of Corrèze in the southern Limousin are among the most popular orders at this roomy, relaxed restaurant, which has been run by three generations of the same family since 1922. *Cassoulet, confit de canard* and foie gras are some of the familiar treats on offer, and other choices include *milhassou d'aubazine* (paté with potatoes, herbs and bacon), *salade corrézienne* (frisée, smoked goose fillet, duck gizzard and chestnuts) and *boudin limousin aux chataignes garni avec pommes frites.* Familiar bistro fare includes *assiette de crudités, artichaut vinaigrette, soupe de poissons, omelette aux cèpes* and steaks. A speciality is *La flognarde de Treignac* – a version of clafoutis with apples.

See over

Thoumieux is also a hotel with 10 modern bedrooms (600F double). Set menus 72F & 150F (*menu corrézien*). ***Seats*** *120 L 12-3.30 D 6.45-12. Sun meals 12-12.* ***Closed*** *1 May. Mastercard, Visa.*

LE TOURVILLE 690F

Tel 47 05 62 62 Fax 47 05 43 90 Map B2.41 **H**
16 ave de Tourville 75007 M° Ecole Militaire

A short distance from Les Invalides, the hotel is ideally located for visiting some of the more important Parisian sights. Behind its classical facade the lounge and bar have a refined, stylish decor and bedrooms are warmly and tastefully decorated in soft pastels. Furnishings are a mix of period and modern. All are air-conditioned and equipped with satellite TV, phone and hairdryer. Breakfast can be taken in your room or in the charming, vaulted basement breakfast room. Best of the accommodation are four rooms with private terraces (1390F) and two junior suites with whirlpool baths (1690F). 24-hour room service. ***Rooms*** *30. Amex, Diners, Mastercard, Visa.*

HOTEL DE L'UNIVERSITÉ 800F

Tel 42 61 09 39 Fax 42 60 40 84 Map D1.42 **H**
22 rue de l'Université 75007 M° Rue du Bac/St Germain-des-Prés

17th-century appeal lives on in the shape of beams, antiques and traditional fabrics retaining much of the charm of the private residence which it once was. Accommodation, though not spacious, is comfortable and ranges from singles with shower only (600F) to top-floor apartments with terraces (from 1200F for a double to 1500F for a triple). All rooms are now air-conditioned and have cable TV and hairdryer. Some have a mini-bar. There is all-day room service with breakfast served either in your room or in the pleasant foyer. ***Rooms*** *27. Amex, Mastercard, Visa.*

HOTEL DE VARENNE 550F

Tel 45 51 45 55 Fax 45 51 86 63 Map C1.43 **H**
44 rue de Bourgogne 75007 M° Varenne

Done out in "le style anglais", the Varenne is situated in an area of government offices just a few paces from Les Invalides. Some bedrooms face the street (these are double-glazed) while the rest look over a flowery courtyard where breakfast is served in the summer. Each room is equipped with phone and TV, and a hairdryer in the bath/shower room. ***Rooms*** *24. Amex, Mastercard, Visa.*

VIN SUR VIN 700F

Tel 47 05 14 20 Fax 45 56 02 74 Map B1.44 **R**
20 rue de Montessuy 75007 M° Alma Marceau

A small and very select restaurant whose menu is based round a splendid wine list of some 400 different wines selected by owner Patrice Vidal. Joachim Grafford, the chef, has been here for 3 years. Having previously worked at *L'Arpège (qv)*, his menus are imaginative: for instance, a terrine of whole rabbit with foie gras, baby mackerel in white wine, fricassée of squid with garlic and basil potatoes, fillet of John Dory with avocado and knuckle of veal with a compote of vegetables. ***Seats*** *25. L 12-2.30 D 8-10.* ***Closed*** *L Sat & Mon, all Sun, 23 Dec-2 Jan & 2 weeks Aug. Mastercard, Visa.*

8th Arrondissement

Places of Interest

Champs Elysées
Place de la Concorde – Obélisque, M° Concorde
Place de la Madeleine, La Madeleine Church, 44 51 69 00, M° Madeleine
Arc de Triomphe, 43 80 31 31, M° Charles de Gaulle-Etoile
Grand Palais, 44 13 17 17, M° Champs Elysées-Clemenceau
Palais de la Découverte (science, planetarium)
Petit Palais, 42 65 12 73, M° Champs Elysées-Clemenceau
Saint-Augustin, M° St-Augustin
Parc Monceau, M° Monceau
Musée Cernuschi (Chinese art), 45 63 50 75, M° Villiers/Monceau
Musée Nissim de Camondo (18th-century residence), 45 63 26 32, M° Villiers/Monceau
Galérie National du Jeu de Paume (former Impressionist, now contemporary), 42 60 69 69, M° Concorde/Tuileries
Pont Alexandre III, M° Invalides/Champs Elysées-Clemenceau/Concorde

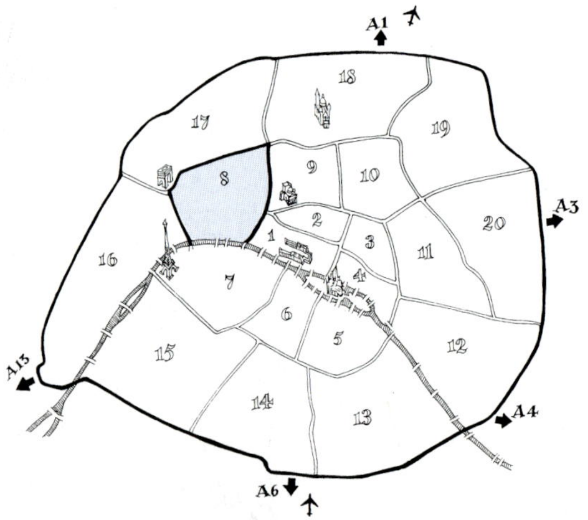

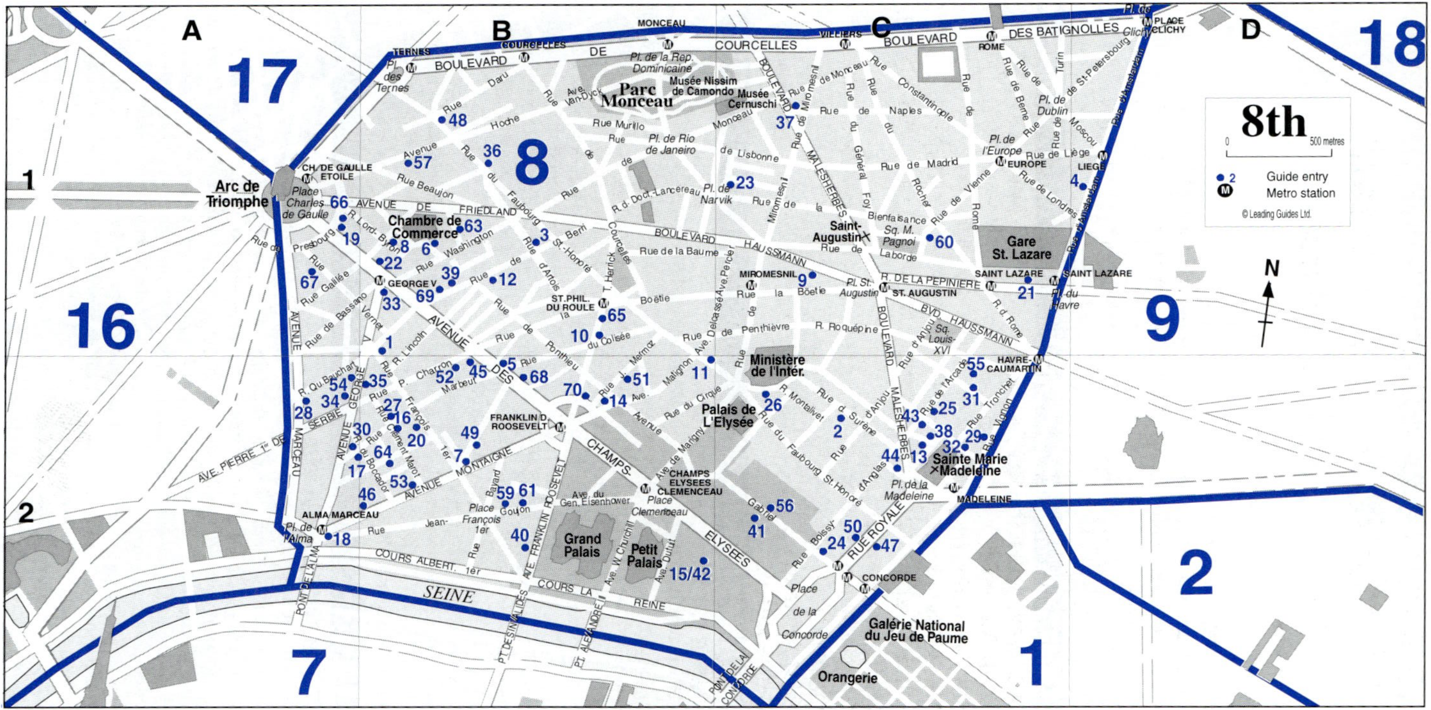
8th
0
500 metres
Guide entry
Metro station
© Leading Guides Ltd.
N
A
B
C
D
1
2
8
9
16
17
18
7
1
2
Arc de Triomphe
Place Charles de Gaulle
CH. DE GAULLE ETOILE
TERNES
COURCELLES
MONCEAU
VILLIERS
ROME
PLACE CLICHY
EUROPE
LIEGE
SAINT LAZARE
ST. AUGUSTIN
MIROMESNIL
HAVRE-CAUMARTIN
MADELEINE
CONCORDE
CHAMPS ELYSEES CLEMENCEAU
FRANKLIN D. ROOSEVELT
GEORGE V
ST.PHIL. DU ROULE
ALMA MARCEAU
Parc Monceau
Musée Nissim de Camondo
Musée Cernuschi
Chambre de Commerce
Saint-Augustin
Gare St. Lazare
Ministère de l'Inter.
Palais de L'Elysée
Sainte Marie Madeleine
Grand Palais
Petit Palais
Galérie National du Jeu de Paume
Orangerie
SEINE
BOULEVARD DE COURCELLES
BOULEVARD DES BATIGNOLLES
AVENUE DE FRIEDLAND
BOULEVARD HAUSSMANN
BOULEVARD MALESHERBES
AVENUE DES CHAMPS ELYSEES
AVENUE MONTAIGNE
AVENUE MARCEAU
AVENUE GEORGE V
RUE ROYALE
COURS ALBERT 1er
COURS LA REINE
Place de la Concorde
Pl. de la Madeleine
Rue du Faubourg St. Honoré
Rue de Rome
Rue de Madrid
Rue de Naples
Rue de Londres
Rue de Vienne
Rue de Miromesnil
Rue de la Boëtie
Rue de Penthièvre
Rue d'Anjou
Rue de la Baume
Rue Beaujon
Rue Washington
Rue Lord Byron
Rue Galilée
Rue de Bassano
Rue Marbeuf
Rue François 1er
Rue Clément Marot
Rue du Boccador
Rue Boissy d'Anglas
Rue Tronchet
Rue Vignon
Rue de l'Arcade
Rue de Surène
PONT DE L'ALMA
PONT DE LA CONCORDE
PT. DES INVALIDES
PT. ALEXANDRE
AVE. PIERRE 1er DE SERBIE

Al Ajami 550F

Tel 43 59 55 37 **Fax 42 56 60 08** Map B1.1 **R**
58 rue François 1er 75008 Mº George V

Well-established Lebanese restaurant with sister establishments in Beirut and Riyadh. Reflecting its fashionable location this is a refined, art deco-style dining-room with elegant Oriental touches. The menu offers plenty of choices, especially the cold and hot starters, including some slightly more unusual dishes among the selection of familiar items. Houmus is served in its common form as well as with either fried pine kernels or slices of hot lamb. There are also little turnovers of lemony spinach, braised and marinated slices of beef, shish kebabs and grilled lamb cutlets flavoured with thyme. There's little in the way of fish with only a brochette on offer. Good choice of desserts. Set L 105F (weekdays) Set L & D 125F & 155F. ***Seats*** *80 (+ 20 outside).* ***Meals*** *noon-midnight. Amex, Diners, Mastercard, Visa.*

Alison 690F

Tel 42 65 54 00 **Fax 42 65 08 17** Map C2.2 **H**
21 rue Surène 75008 Mº Madeleine/Concorde

Between the Madeleine and the Elysée Palace, near all the smart shops of the Faubourg Saint Honoré, the Alison provides modest comfort in the heart of the city. Rooms all have TV, hairdryer and safe. No restaurant, but there's a stone-vaulted breakfast room-cum-lounge in the basement. ***Rooms*** *35. Amex, Diners, Mastercard, Visa.*

See page 9 for a list of starred restaurants

Aux Amis du Beaujolais 400F

Tel 45 63 92 21 **Fax 45 62 70 01** Map B1.3 **R**
28 rue d'Artois 75008 Mº George V/St-Philippe-du-Roule

In the same family since 1924, this modest bistro, done out in a cheerful shade of yellow, on the corner of the Rue d'Artois and the Rue du Berri, can be relied on for some sound, unpretentious cooking. Bernard Picolet credits his grandmother for the *cuisine familiale* that features rillettes, fish, foie gras, wild boar terrines, *salade de gésiers* and *rosette du Beaujolais* amongst the starters and braised tuna with carrots, bass with fennel, *pot-au-feu*, daube of beef with olives and *andouillette du Beaujolais* as main dishes on the daily-changing menu. Beaujolais, not surprisingly, dominates the list of wines with the Chénas and Moulin à Vent arriving by cask to be bottled at the restaurant. Gents have an old-fashioned hole-in-the-floor loo, ladies are more comfortably accommodated. ***Seats*** *95. L 12-3 D 6.30-9.* ***Closed*** *Sun, 1 week from 15 Aug & 1 week Christmas. Amex, Mastercard, Visa.*

Androuët 600F

Tel 48 74 26 93 **Fax 49 95 02 54** Map D1.4 **R**
41 rue d'Amsterdam 75008 Mº Gare St-Lazare

Recently returned into private ownership, this is one of the famous Parisian fromageries, founded in 1909. In the restaurant above the shop, cheese-lovers can indulge to the full in the likes of *croquette de Camembert, ravioles de chèvre frais, homard au Roquefort, saumon au Bleu de Causses, magret de canard au lou picadou* and *filet de boeuf au Roquefort*. Asterisks on the menu indicates those few dishes (apart from desserts) that do not involve cheese in one way or another. When it comes to choosing from the splendid cheese tray a good plan is to leave the selection to the knowledgeable waiters who will even advise on the order in which they should be eaten. Set L 175F Set L & D 230F/250F Set D 195F. ***Seats*** *100. L 12-2.30 D 7-10.15.* ***Closed*** *L Sat, all Sun. Amex, Diners, Mastercard, Visa.*

L'APPART 500F

Tel 53 75 16 34 **Fax 53 75 16 39** Map B2.5 **R**
9 rue du Colisée 75008 Mº Franklin D Roosevelt

Busy, trendy and elegantly appointed restaurant on two floors just off the Champs Elysées. Waitresses in smart black suits offer swift service at closely packed tables, or you can eat at the bar downstairs (where there are also tables) from a reasonably priced carte: rémoulade of pig's trotters with leeks and balsamic vinegar, ravioli of fromage frais with a parsley cream, roast salmon with a dill vinaigrette, fillets of red mullet on a bed of vegetable ribbons, and rack of lamb roasted with thyme. The hot apple flan is large and square and needs to be ordered at the beginning of the meal; other desserts include warm chocolate tart with gingerbread ice cream, a feuillantine of pears with a caramel sauce or a minestrone of fresh fruits with basil served with a lemon sorbet. Shortish wine list plus lots of cocktails. Set L 100F, 145F & (Sunday brunch) 160F. ***Seats*** *125. L 12-2.30 D 7.30-12.* ***Closed*** *24 Dec. Amex, Mastercard, Visa.*

ATALA 950F

Tel 45 62 01 62 **Fax 42 25 66 38** Map B1.6 **H**
10 rue Chateaubriand 75008 Mº George V

Located a short distance east of the Arc de Triomphe, the hotel boasts a spacious, wood-panelled, marble-floored lobby which opens on to a pretty courtyard garden that is the ideal spot for summer breakfasts. Pleasant bedrooms in art deco style all have a mini-bar, direct-dial phone and satellite TV and some have a balcony or terrace. Private parking for just three cars. ***Rooms*** *50. Amex, Diners, Mastercard, Visa.*

L'AVENUE 700F

Tel 40 70 14 91 **Fax 49 52 08 27** Map B2.7 **R**
41 ave Montaigne 75008 Mº Alma-Marceau/Franklin D Roosevelt

Haute couture meets haute cuisine at this art deco restaurant much favoured by the fashion world – Dior, Céline and Christian Lacroix are nearby. Actually it's more a *brasserie de luxe* with a menu offering modish *meridional*-style dishes such as piccata of monkfish with lime and tomatillos, fricassee of red mullet with ratatouille and tapénade, calf's liver with mushroom ravioli and a poulette sauce, fillet of roast pork with a chutney of pineapple and guava, and grilled lamb chops with rosemary and baked tomatoes. A section of the menu headed *Sur le Pouce* offers quick snacks such as a club sandwich, gazpacho of tomatoes, fennel, cucumber and basil, steak tartare, or a plate of select cheeses. Good wines from *Taillevent's* wine shop. ***Seats*** *150. L 12-2.30 D 8-12.* ***Closed*** *25 Dec. Amex, Mastercard, Visa.*

> The best way to get around Paris is by bus or metro –
> buy a book (carnet) of tickets at any metro station and save money

BALZAC 1830F

Tel 45 35 18 00 **Fax 42 25 24 82** Map B1.8 **H**
6 rue Balzac 75008 Mº George V

Although only just off the bustling Champs Elysées the Balzac (named, as is the street, after the 19th-century writer) is a haven of peace and luxury. Built for an aristocrat in 1910, this Belle Epoque townhouse was completely renovated in 1985. Oil paintings and antique tapestries grace elegant public areas while air-conditioning, double-glazing, marble bathrooms and twin telephone lines add comfort and convenience to the bedrooms, of which 14 are suites. Discreet, attentive service extends to a 24-hour room menu and valet parking. ***Rooms*** *70. Amex, Diners, Mastercard, Visa.*

Le Bistrot du Sommelier — 800F

Tel 42 65 24 85 **Fax 53 75 23 23** Map C1.9 **R**
97 bd Haussmann 75008 Mº St-Augustin/Miromesnil

The owner, Philippe Faure-Brac, won awards for best sommelier in France in 1988 and 'World's Best Sommelier' in 1992. The wine list is phenomenal, with 900 bottles and no less than 40 wines available by the glass. The decor is themed strongly on wine and the menu is unfussy, short and modern. Starters include *supreme de volaille farci de son foie, salade aux acidulés de noisette*, parsleyed haddock, and lamb's sweetbreads with a lightly vinegared sauce and warm duck foie gras in a spiced gingerbread crust on a bed of onions. Among the main dishes are fillet of brill with aniseed-flavoured snails, fricassee of scallops and langoustines with shredded cabbage and a shellfish cream, Bresse chicken with Jura wine and morels as well as saddle of rabbit with prune jus flavoured with plum eau de vie and entrecote bordelaise with marrow sprinkled with sea salt. There's good game in season, too. To finish there are delicious desserts such as fresh mango with thin leaves of chocolate, crème brulée flavoured with ginger and orange zest cooked in Grand Marnier, or a bitter chocolate marquise with pistachioed crème anglaise. There's a good selection of cheeses from Alléose in the 17th. A *menu surprise* (390F D only) offers a selection of 6 dishes with 6 glasses of complementary wines. ***Seats*** *50. L 12-2.30 D 7.30-11.* ***Closed*** *Sat, Sun, Aug & 25 Dec-1 Jan. Amex, Mastercard, Visa.*

Le Boeuf sur le Toit — 500F

Tel 43 59 83 80 **Fax 45 63 45 40** Map B1.10 **R**
34 rue du Colisée 75008 Mº St-Philippe-du-Roule

Part of the excellent *Flo* group of traditional Parisian brasseries, this one in art deco style is full of mirrors, plants and bustling waiters. Oysters and other shellfish are a speciality but there is much else besides: *feuilleté de foie gras chaud aux pommes, sole de ligne à la planche, confit de canard, selle d'agneau aux herbes, andouillettes*, steak tartare with matchstick potatoes, rump steak with maitre d'hotel butter, brill with butter sauce, and excellent crepes flambées to finish. Set L 112F (inc wine) Set D 189F & 112F (from 10pm). ***Seats*** *230.* ***Meals*** *noon-2am.* ***Closed*** *D 24 Dec. Amex, Diners, Mastercard, Visa.*

Le Bristol — 3600F

Tel 42 66 91 45 **Fax 42 66 34 16** Map B2.11 **HR**
112 rue du Faubourg St Honoré 75008 Mº Miromesnil

First opened in 1925 but much extended since, Le Bristol is a luxurious oasis of peace and tranquillity set among the exclusive shops of Rue du Faubourg St-Honoré. Down a few steps from the spacious lobby, there is a timeless feel to the main public area where marble floors are strewn with Oriental rugs, baronial-style stone walls are hung with tapestries and wood panelling sports fine paintings, all lit by sparkling crystal and gilt chandeliers. One of the lifts still has some fine art deco wrought-iron gates. An unexpected delight at the heart of the hotel is a charming garden, while up on the top floor, with views over the rooftops of Paris, is a swimming pool made to resemble the prow of a luxury yacht and created by the naval architect who designed yachts for Onassis and Niarchos. The air of peace and tranquillity extends to air-conditioned bedrooms, most of which overlook the garden or one of the inner courts (there is in any event very little traffic noise after 9pm) and all of which have their own lobby between room and corridor. The style is firmly traditional, with period, often gilt-trimmed, furniture, chandeliers and fine, individually-chosen soft furnishings. Nearly a quarter of the rooms are suites of various sizes but even the most modest rooms (a relative term) boast splendid white marble bathrooms, all with twin washbasins and shower cubicles in addition to generously-sized bathtubs, separate loos and Hermès toiletries. High levels of service include a helpful concierge desk, room service that can provide hot meals 24 hours a day and the proper servicing of rooms in the evening. Free parking. Our Paris Hotel of the Year for 1996.

Restaurant 1600F

The location of the restaurant changes between winter and summer. The Restaurant d'Hiver is an elegant, oval room with fine wood panelling, a large Flemish tapestry and glittering chandeliers while the Restaurant d'Eté has a tent-like ceiling, cushioned rattan chairs, and tables that spill out into the garden when the weather is fine. Chef Emile Tabourdiau, who has been in charge of the kitchen for more than ten years, offers plenty of options with two fixed-price menus, one of which indicates those dishes that can be served swiftly, and a couple of dishes based on the day's market in addition to an à la carte. Lobster bisque served with an oyster flan, medallions of monkfish with thyme butter and aubergine 'crisps', roast Bresse pigeon with a tatin of carrots and onions, and fillet of beef *en feuillantine* with mushrooms and Sichuan pepper show the style. Things such as crepes Suzette flambées and hot soufflés offer an alternative to the dessert trolley. Set L 345F Set D 460F/630F. ***Seats** 60. L 12-2.30 D 7-10.30.*

HOTEL CALIFORNIA 1800F

Tel 43 59 93 00 Fax 45 61 03 62 Map B1.12 **H**
16 rue de Berri 75008 M° George V

Between the Champs Elysées and Boulevard Haussmann, the California is a hotel with its own distinct personality, part of a small family-run group. Some 3000 original paintings are scattered throughout the bedrooms and public areas and there's a small art gallery dedicated to encouraging young artists. Dating from the 1920s, but totally refurbished in 1992, the light, airy lobby boasts chandeliers and rug-strewn marble floors and the leather-upholstered piano bar, a collection of model boats, another of owner Monsieur Leroy's interests. Air-conditioned throughout, the individually decorated bedrooms include a number of full suites, some arranged for business travellers with a meeting room, others for leisure and tourists with extra large TVs and one even with a piano. All rooms come with little extras like sweets from Cambrai (the family's home town). Bathrooms are marble, a few with shower/WC only. 24-hour room service, staffed business centre, fitness room and valet parking. ***Rooms** 173. Amex, Diners, Mastercard, Visa.*

A glossary of French menu items starts on page 274

CAVIAR KASPIA 800F

Tel 42 65 33 32 Fax 42 66 60 11 Map C2.13 **R**
17 place de la Madeleine 75008 M° Madeleine

A very smart, first-floor restaurant above a shop specialising in caviar and smoked fish. The menu is composed of luxury snack items ranging from smoked trout, smoked sturgeon, *oeufs Guriev* – poached eggs on a bed of Sevruga – and hot borsch, to wild Norwegian or Swedish smoked salmon, a plate of mixed smoked fish and a selection of caviars served in portions beginning at 30gms (174F for Sevruga and 509F for Beluga), Cheeses, a selection of pastries, and desserts are also available. Set L 260F & 300F. ***Seats** 60. **Meals** noon-midnight. **Closed** Sun. Amex, Diners, Mastercard, Visa.*

CENTRE-VILLE MATIGNAN 890F

Tel 42 25 73 01 Fax 42 56 01 39 Map B2.14 **H**
3 rue de Ponthieu 75008 M° Franklin D Roosevelt

Not far from the *haute couture* shops of the Faubourg St Honoré, this stylish hotel features up-to-date equipment including individually controllable air-conditioning, mini-bar, TV, room safe and a Minitel terminal in each room. A sister hotel near the Arc de Triomphe (*Centre-Ville Etoile* Tel 43 80 56 18) is very similar in style with identical prices. ***Rooms** 23. Amex, Diners, Mastercard, Visa.*

Le Cercle Ledoyen 600F

Tel 47 42 76 02 **Fax 47 42 55 01** Map B2.15 **R**
carré des Champs Elysées 75008 Mº Champs Elysées-Clemenceau

The second restaurant of the two-starred *Ledoyen (qv)* and housed in the same delightful pavilion near the Petit Palais. Here the decor features a pale, bird's-eye-view map of Paris painted on walls and ceilings within wood-panelling of the same shade. The cooking and the menu could not be more straightforward with starters – cold cauliflower cream soup, chicory salad with scallops, vinaigrette of ox cheek – all at 60F, mains – grilled salmon with anchovies, pan-fried grouper with fennel and spices, stew of wild boar, mixed grill – all 100F and desserts such as feuilleté of apples with a caramel sauce, fresh pineapple with a coconut sauce and macaroon with pistachios and rhubarb compote. There's a separate chocolate section including chocolate tart, chocolate tiramisu and cocoa sorbet with a praline feuilleté each priced at 50F, all adding up to excellent value for money. Booking is advisable. ***Seats*** *80 (+ 80 outside). L 12-2 D 7-11.30.* ***Closed*** *Sun. Amex, Diners, Mastercard, Visa.*

Chez André 500F

Tel 47 20 59 57 **Fax 47 20 18 82** Map B2.16 **R**
12 rue Marbeuf 75008 Mº Alma-Marceau/Franklin D Roosevelt

A short distance to the south of the Champs Elysées, this classic bistro has paper cloths but linen napkins and swift friendly service. Specialities include sole meunière, *saumon grillé sauce hollandaise, tete de veau sauce ravigote, gigot d'agneau roti avec purée maison* and *magret de canard avec cèpes*. There are also various *plateaux de fruits de mer* (from 121F) as well as dishes of the day of which some are regulars such as *hachis parmentier* on Mondays and *brandade de morue* on Thursdays. Several wines are available by the glass or carafe and about half the shortish list also comes in half bottles. ***Seats*** *100.* ***Meals*** *noon-1am. Amex, Diners, Mastercard, Visa.*

Chez Edgard 520F

Tel 47 20 51 15 **Fax 47 23 94 29** Map A2.17 **R**
4 rue Marbeuf 75008 Mº Alma-Marceau

A lively atmosphere pervades this attractive art deco-styled restaurant. The menu is of familiar, classic starters and grills with a quite lengthy specials section which changes daily. The latter includes fish and shellfish dishes typical of South-West France – grilled red mullet with olive oil – as well as the likes of grilled sea bass with fennel, skate wing with pickled nasturtium seeds, *civet de lapin*, and grilled entrecote with matchstick potatoes. The day's desserts might include a gratin of raspberries and a caramelised pear tart to supplement such straightforward items as crème brulée, pear Belle Hélène and chocolate liégois to be found on the main menu. Set menu 195F. ***Seats*** *180 (+ 40 outside). L 12-3 D 7.30-12.30.* ***Closed*** *Sun, 25 Dec & 1 Jan. Amex, Diners, Mastercard, Visa.*

Chez Francis 600F

Tel 47 20 86 83 **Fax 47 20 43 26** Map A2.18 **R**
7 place de l'Alma 75008 Mº Alma-Marceau

Immortalised as the setting for a scene in the play *The Mad Woman of Chaillot* by Jean Giraudoux, this smart, classic brasserie by the Pont d'Alma has been a fashionable meeting place for over a century. From the terrace you can admire the Eiffel Tower, from within, yourself – reflected in the ornately framed amber mirrors, alongside glittering chandeliers. The cooking is traditional and uncomplicated and majors on excellent seafood, such as haddock marinated with dill, moules marinière and a superb *plateau de fruits de mer.* The kitchens also produce dishes such as *escalope de thon à la provençale, cote de boeuf aux échalotes confites*, pan-fried calf's liver with raspberry vinegar and roast rack of lamb with thyme. Amongst the wines one white (Muscadet) and one red (Bordeaux) are served by the glass. Set menu 190F. ***Seats*** *160 (+ 180 outside).* ***Meals*** *noon-1am. Amex, Diners, Mastercard, Visa.*

CHIBERTA ★ 650F

Tel 45 63 77 90 **Fax 45 62 85 08** Map A1.19 **R**
3 rue Arsène-Houssaye 75008 Mº Etoile

Just off the top end of the Champs Elysées, very close to the Arc de Triomphe, this stylishly modern restaurant features magnificent displays of flowers and is a fine setting for Philippe de Silva's culinary skills. His dishes are well thought-out, superbly constructed and beautifully presented. There is an underlying complexity to what, on paper, appears relatively simple and straightforward. His art is in successful marriages of ingredients in perfect balance. To begin you might choose from chilled lobster soup with baby vegetables, lobster cannelloni, red mullet salad with saffron vinaigrette or pan-fried langoustines with aubergine purée or ravioli with truffles and parsley. Main dishes will include fish such as steamed bass with caviar and champagne and turbot roasted with horseradish. Meat dishes could be roast pigeon with pistachios, pan-fried calf's liver with sesame seeds and duck roasted with honey. Finish with desserts such as a light pastry with apple, sesame seeds and cinnamon sorbet; *millefeuille à la vanille*, and a chocolate tart with acacia honey ice cream. Good selection of red Bordeaux. Three wines are available by the glass – whites from Burgundy and Graves and a red from the Médoc. Set menu 290F. ***Seats*** *75. L 12-2.30 D 7.30-11.* ***Closed*** *Sat, Sun, Public Holidays, Aug & 25 Dec-1 Jan. Amex, Diners, Mastercard, Visa.*

CLARIDGE-BELLMAN 1000F

Tel 47 23 54 42 **Fax 47 23 08 84** Map B2.20 **H**
37 rue François 1er 75008 Mº Franklin D Roosevelt

Located between the Seine and the Champs Elysées in an area of Paris much favoured by leading couturiers and perfume houses, this is a small hotel of considerable charm. Public areas include a panelled reception, cosy bar and sitting-room with tapestry covering one wall. Characterful bedrooms – an antique here, chandelier there or old marble fireplace – all come with air-conditioning, cable TV and mini-bars along with other modern comforts. Room service from 7am to 9pm. There's also a delightful breakfast room on the ground floor. ***Rooms*** *42. Amex, Diners, Mastercard, Visa.*

CONCORDE SAINT-LAZARE 1160F

Tel 40 08 44 44 **Fax 42 93 01 20** Map C1.21 **H**
108 rue Saint-Lazare 75008 Mº Gare St-Lazare

Splendid old railway hotel built by Gustave Eiffel in 1889. The impressive lobby (with plenty of button-backed leather seating) is three storeys high and is listed as a national monument, as is the billiard room. Bedrooms are smartly decorated in shades of pink or blue and have the usual modern comforts including cable TV. About half the rooms are air-conditioned. 24-hour room service. Valet parking. ***Rooms*** *300. Amex, Diners, Mastercard, Visa.*

COPENHAGUE 850F

Tel 44 13 86 26 **Fax 42 25 83 10** Map B1.22 **R**
142 ave des Champs Elysées 75008 Mº Etoile/George V

Towards the top end of the Champs Elysées, the restaurant is on the first floor of the *Maison du Danemark* and, as the name suggests, the food is Scandinavian in style. The menu includes an *Hommage au Saumon Nordique*, the salmon served smoked, marinated, hot with spinach and mushrooms and *unilatéral*. Set menus include the 'Danish Table' (for 2 people) at 538F and the menu of the day at 240F which includes a glass of aquavit and another of draught Carlsberg (or half a bottle of wine). Not all is exclusively Nordic, with other dishes including the likes of jellied chicken consommé with fish roe, lobster with truffle oil, plaice meunière and spiced reindeer cutlet and fillet. Good selection of Chablis and Bordeaux. On the ground floor, next to a shop selling Danish specialities and filled baguettes to take away, is the simpler **Flora Danica** with unclothed tables

See over

and a less expensive menu in similar style to that above. ***Seats*** *80. L 12-2.30 D 7.15-10.30.* ***Closed*** *L Sat May-Sep, all Sun, Public Holidays, 1 week Jan & all Aug. Amex, Diners, Mastercard, Visa.*

LE CRÉTOIS 300F

Tel 45 63 34 17 Fax 45 61 48 97 Map C1.23 **R**
19 rue Treilhard 75008 Mº Miromesnil

Small, modest bar-bistro with 1960s-style decor run by a mother and son team who have local business folk queuing up for their simple blackboard lunch menu. The likes of warm leeks with raspberry vinaigrette, *saucisse sèche d'Auvergne, andouillette*, beef skirt with shallots, and herring fillets with *pommes à l'huile* are washed down with a choice of some 17 wines, which include most of the *crus Beaujolais*, all available by the glass as well as the bottle. Throughout the day there is a short list of *tartines* (various things on toast – ham, cheese, rillettes etc) and lunchtime hot dishes like a escalope of veal normande and *canette rotie avec cèpes*. Cheerful, friendly atmosphere. ***Seats*** *45 (+ 20 outside). Open 7am-6.30pm. (L 12-3.30).* ***Closed*** *Sat & Sun. Amex, Mastercard, Visa.*

See page 9 for a list of starred restaurants

HOTEL DE CRILLON 3500F

Tel 44 71 15 00 Fax 44 71 15 02 Map C2.24 **HR**
10 place de la Concorde 75008 Mº Concorde

This fabulous *palace*, owned by the Taittinger family, continues to uphold the high standards which made its reputation. The central hall of Siena and Portor marble manages to maintain intimate proportions and the *salons* have been carefully restored to their former glory. Many of the spacious, quiet, air-conditioned bedrooms have been tastefully decorated in traditional style by Sonia Rykiel and all have lavish marble bathrooms. The hotel's first floor, dedicated to conferences and receptions, has a series of linked historic rooms: *salon Marie-Antoinette* with its pretty terrace, *salon des Aigles* and *salon des Batailles*, all looking out on to the famous obelisk. 24-hour room service. ***Rooms*** *163. Amex, Diners, Mastercard, Visa.*

Les Ambassadeurs ★★ 1600F

Tel 44 71 16 16 Fax 44 71 15 00

Everything about this magnificent restaurant radiates quality and refinement, from its chequered floors to its trompe l'oeil skies. The gilded mirrors, painted friezes of cherubs, night-blue curtains and tables sparkling with crystal and silver might seem overwhelming in their opulence if the classical proportions of the room were not perfect. Instead, the atmosphere is of intimacy and comfort; a feeling which the impeccable but friendly service enhances. The setting is perfect for chef Christian Constant's outstanding cooking. Although classically trained, he is continually experimenting and prides himself on rarely repeating a dish from one seasonal menu to the next. Examples of his best dishes are starters like *confit de foie gras d'oie, poivre et sel, purée de figues et pruneax* (confit of foie gras with salt and pepper and puréed figs and prunes), and *moelleux de pommes rattes, médaillons de homard à la civette* (lobster medallions with rattes potatoes and chives) and mains such as *darne de bar clouté aux anchois, meunière de poivrons et aubergines à l'huile d'olive* (roast fillet of bass studded with anchovies, served with aubergines and peppers 'meunière' in olive oil) and *carré d'agneau de Pauillac roti sous la cendre, tomate farcie de pied et épaule d'agneau* (rack of Pauillac lamb roasted in embers with tomatoes stuffed with lamb shoulder and trotters). Constant's desserts are of an equally high quality, as in *macaron au fenouil frais glacé, fruits rouges et noirs dans leur jus* (iced fresh fennel macaroon with red and black fruits in their juice). The wine list is heftily-priced but includes some of the best bottles in France. Set L 340F Set D 610F. ***Seats*** *60. L 12-2.30 D 7-10.30.*

L'Obélisque 600F

Different in style and atmosphere from *Les Ambassadeurs*, the hotel's second restaurant feels more like a club, with its low ceilings, panelled walls and Lalique chandeliers. It has a separate entrance on the Rue Boissy d'Anglas and is invariably packed at lunchtimes. Christian Constant supervises the kitchen and offers a good value set menu at 270F. A typical meal might consist of *mousseline d'avocat aux crabes, coeur de laitue vinaigrette* (mousseline of avocado and crab served with a dressed lettuce heart), *daurade rotie* (roast fillets of sea bream) *à l'huile d'olive avec ratatouille niçoise*, and *crème brulée à la vanille Bourbon*. Look out for the occasional fortnights of foreign cooking. Set menu 270F. ***Seats** 90. L 12-2.30 D 7-10.30.*

Daniel Météry 700F

Tel 42 65 53 13 **Fax 42 66 53 82** Map C2.25 **R**
4 rue de l'Arcade 75008 M° Madeleine

As we go to press the ground floor is being enlarged with the addition of 10 tables. This is an attractive, modern restaurant offering sound modern cooking by chef-patron Daniel Météry. The choice of fish has been extended to include some seven different dishes. Begin with a feuilleté of chicken livers and leeks or tabbouleh of cockles with paprika, and follow with perch stuffed with anchovy and basil, cod with grain mustard or pork fillet with ginger. A speciality here is the 260F 'all vinegar' menu which changes daily. *Cassolette de pieds de mouton au vinaigre de Xérès à l'orange* to start, *rascasse au vinaigre de champagne, jus de truffes* as the main course, followed by *figues fraiches au vinaigre de figues* for dessert. A meat alternative to the fish main course could be *souris d'agneau au vinaigre de noix de coco*. Choose from two fixed-price menus (180F/200F). ***Seats** 45. L 12-2.15 D 7.30-10.15. **Closed** L Sat, all Sun, 24, 25 Dec & 1 Jan. Amex, Mastercard, Visa.*

Hotel de l'Elysées 600F

Tel 42 65 29 25 **Fax 42 65 64 28** Map C2.26 **H**
12 rue des Saussaies 75008 M° Miromesnil

Theatres, the Elysées Palace, the Madeleine and shopping in the fashionable Rue du Faubourg St-Honoré are all within a short walk of this moderately priced, traditionally-run hotel decorated in Restoration style. Bedrooms vary in size and decor, but all are air-conditioned and have satellite TV. A few have a four-poster or canopied bed. Two suites under the mansard roof have mini-bars. Continental breakfast can be taken in your room or in the lounge, and includes freshly squeezed orange juice. ***Rooms** 32. Amex, Diners, Mastercard, Visa.*

L'Etage Baumann 500F

Tel 47 20 11 11 **Fax 47 23 69 65** Map B2.27 **R**
15 rue Marbeuf 75008 M° Franklin D Roosevelt

A smart brasserie-style restaurant just off the Champs Elysées, majoring on traditional Alsatian cuisine: *foie gras de canard maison, choucroute strasbourgeoise*, and a house speciality of *choucroute aux poissons* – monkfish, cod and smoked fish accompanied by a beurre blanc sauce. A sister restaurant, *Baumann Ternes (qv)*, is in the 17th (other branches are to be found in Strasbourg). Set menu 173F. ***Seats** 130. L 12-2.30 D 7.30-12.30am. **Closed** L Sat, all 12-21 Aug. Amex, Diners, Mastercard, Visa.*

Fakhr el Dine 400F

Tel 47 23 44 42 **Fax 47 27 11 39** Map A2.28 **R**
1/3 rue Quentin Bauchart 75008 M° George V

With a splendid and authentic-looking decor, this spacious restaurant is the setting for a range of familiar and traditional Lebanese specialities. The menu changes very little though there is plenty of variety on offer. Tabbouleh and houmus are among the starters, together with *rkakat* (feuilleté filled with cheese) or *sambousek* (meat rissoles with pine nuts), followed by *chawarma* (marinated

See over

lamb, chopped and roasted on a brochette). Oriental patisserie makes for a sweet ending. If you're feeling adventurous, pick one of the mezze (*mezze extra* for 2 people – 10 dishes 330F). Lebanese wines, alcohols and liqueurs are available. Also at 30 rue de Longchamp 75016 (Tel 47 27 90 00) and the Institut du Monde Arabe (Tel 46 33 47 70). Set menus 150F & 160F. ***Seats*** *50. L 12-4 D 8-12. Amex, Diners, Mastercard, Visa.*

Fauchon-Le 30 — 800F

Tel 47 42 56 58 **Fax 47 42 96 02** Map C2.32 **R**
30 place de la Madeleine 75008 M° Madeleine

Occupying the north-eastern corner of a splendid square, Fauchon ranks among the world's best and most renowned food shops. Mouthwatering window displays give a good measure of what is available within. Additional to the shop side of the operation there are several eating places, including a caviar bistrot, café/tea room, Italian trattoria and seafood brasserie. The shop occupies a corner of Place de la Madeleine, and the restaurant (at no 30) is on the first floor looking across to the church. Smartly decorated in pastel peach colours, the Roman villa-style restaurant also has a pretty patio terrace garden as well as tasteful table settings. Chef Bruno Deligne's *carte* might include a tartare of tuna marinated in lime juice, *gazpacho andalou*, fillet of cod with a tapénade jus, duck breast with glazed turnips, pistachios and stewed apricots, and rack of lamb with boulangère potatoes. There are also some marvellous desserts/pastries/cakes created by *patissier* Pierre Hermé. Excellent coffee, scrumptious petits fours, ordinary wine list. Set D 245F. ***Seats*** *80 (+ 36 outside). L 12.15-2.30 D 7.30-10.30.* ***Closed*** *Sun & some Public Holidays. Amex, Diners, Mastercard, Visa.*

La Ferme St Hubert — 400F

Tel 47 42 79 20 **Fax 47 42 46 97** Map C2.29 **R**
21 rue Vignon 75008 M° Madeleine/Havre-Caumartin

The cheese shop came first, with a stuffed goat in the window and wonderful smells emanating from within. A few years later Henry Voy opened this little restaurant next door. There's nothing fancy – just paper napkins and squares on closely packed tables and a huge black and white photograph of a couple of cows in a field on one wall. Virtually everything on the menu involves cheese in one way or another from starters like a plate of seven cheeses, goat's cheese baked in a tomato on a bed of salad, camembert croquettes with a sherry vinegar-dressed salad, and a *gratin dauphinois* with smoked bacon, to main dishes such as *andouillette* with roquefort, spinach and *gratin dauphinois*, sirloin with a roquefort sauce or a gratin of chicory with Livarot,
a fine Normandy cheese. Raclettes are for two people, and come with a selection of preserved meats and potatoes ad lib. A few simple desserts include crème brulée and crème caramel. This is very much a place for informal eating, from just a snack (breakfast served from 8am) to a three-course affair. ***Seats*** *42. L 12-3.30 D 7-11.* ***Closed*** *Sun, 25 Dec. Amex, Mastercard, Visa.*
Also at:
17 Rue d'Antin 75002 Tel 42 65 42 74

La Fermette Marbeuf — 600F

Tel 53 23 08 00 **Fax 53 23 08 09** Map A2.30 **R**
5 rue Marbeuf 75008 M° Franklin D Roosevelt

In the smart 'Golden Triangle' area, just off the Champs Elysées, the splendid fin-de-siècle decor is almost, but not quite, as big a draw as the cooking. The classic menu features a few dishes which are modern and imaginative. Begin with a terrine of cucumber and horseradish, mussel soup with saffron or Brittany langoustines with a jus of green apples and hazelnut oil. The restaurant is known for its feuilletés, too, such as one with a mousseline of scorpion fish in red butter or snails in a light garlic butter. Main courses could be grilled breast of lamb with *sauce Choron*, fillet of beef with a pepper sauce, breast of duck with fresh figs and rosemary, fillet of brill with sesame seeds and semolina or cod in a sweet

and sour sauce. To finish there are desserts such as crème brulée with orange zest or a bitter chocolate mousse tart. Park in the George V or Rue François 1er car park and present your ticket at the restaurant for 2 hours free parking.
Set L & D 169F. ***Seats** 150. L 12-3 D 7-11.30. Amex, Diners, Mastercard, Visa.*

HOTEL FOLKESTONE 812F

Tel 42 65 73 09 Fax 42 65 64 09 Map C2.31 **H**
9 rue Castellane 75008 Mº Madeleine/Havre-Caumartin

Smart little hotel just north of the Madeleine. Bedrooms feature stylish matching fabrics, cable TV, mini-bar, hairdryer and room safe. Rooms on the fifth floor are air-conditioned, with plans for the remainder to follow in late spring. One of the two comfortable lounges boasts a stained-glass panel depicting irises and they are particularly proud of their buffet breakfast. Room service of Continental breakfast only, from 7 to 11. ***Rooms** 50. Amex, Diners, Mastercard, Visa.*

FOUQUET'S 800F

Tel 47 23 70 60 Fax 47 20 08 69 Map B1.33 **R**
99 ave des Champs Elysées 75008 Mº George V

Brass plaques commemorating each year's winners of the French cinema's 'César' awards pave the entrance to this institution (listed as a historic building in 1988) and remind one that it is still very much a haunt of the famous. The *Menu Tradition* (265F) offers a varied selection of classic dishes beginning with duck foie gras terrine, snails in garlic butter, moules marinière, and fish soup with rouille and croutons. Fishy main courses could be quenelles of scorpion fish with a lobster sauce, fresh sardine fritters with a tartare sauce and cod with garlic mayonnaise. For meat choose between the likes of daube of beef, *hachis parmentier* (French shepherd's pie) and grilled entrecote with parsley butter. Eat on the veranda to see and be seen, inside or upstairs in the 'Raimu' room (except weekends) to soak up the atmosphere. The all-French wine list has an emphasis on the Loire and Bordeaux. A snack menu – croque-monsieur, omelettes, quiche lorraine, *rillettes de canard*, sandwiches, salads – is served in the bar or on the terrace from 11am to 11pm with breakfast from 8am. Open every day of the year. Pronounce it 'Fooketts'. Set menu 265F. ***Seats** 300 (+ 50 outside). L 12-3 D 7-1am. Amex, Diners, Mastercard, Visa.*

GEORGE V 3200F

Tel 47 23 54 00 Fax 47 20 40 00 Map A2.34 **HR**
31 ave George V 75008 Mº George V

Named after an English king, designed by an American (in the late 1920s) and run by the international Forte group, the George V is nevertheless very much a Parisian hotel. Grand, high-ceilinged public rooms boast antique furniture, 17th-century tapestries, objets d'art and even a Renoir plus lots of fresh flowers, all helping to create an atmosphere of elegance and luxury. Whether staying in one of the many sumptuous suites or in an individually designed bedroom one can expect the same high standards of service. Numerous private function rooms include the wood-panelled Louis XIII salon with its massive stone fireplace and the Chantilly room with cool stylised classical murals. Parking 140F a day. Ten conference rooms. Valet parking. ***Rooms** 260. Access, Amex, Diners, Visa.*

Les Princes Restaurant ★ 1000F

Chandeliers above widely spaced tables with elegant place settings and a huge floral centrepiece – this is a truly grand hotel dining-room with a suitably expansive menu. Long-standing chef Joyeux's main carte is supplemented by a limited choice fixed-price menu and, in season, a special game menu. Specialities include pan-fried langoustines, St Pierre and crab in a light green onion sauce, and miniature pompoms of fowl, truffles and foie gras with an asparagus salad. If you want to go the whole hog try the no-choice tasting menu that consists of eight suitably small-sized courses. A large terrace can seat up to 70 and when in use the dining-room itself is not. Set menus 240F & 450F. ***Seats** 60. L 12-2.30 D 7-10.30.*

Les Georgiques 1000F

Tel 40 70 10 49
36 ave George V 75008

Map B2.35 **R**
Mº George V

A tranquil panelled restaurant is the setting for Katsumaro Ishimaru's excellent modern renditions of classic French haute cuisine. The menu changes according to market availability but typically could offer starters such as a *gratiné d'escargots avec noisettes, salade de homard* or *foie gras poelée aux truffes* and main dishes such as *filet d'agneau au thym, turbot farci au foie gras* or a *panaché de poissons, sauce aux fines herbes*. Excellent desserts like *charlotte aux poires au coulis de fruits rouges* or *tarte au chocolat chaud* round off a meal characterised by accomplished cooking and polished service. To appreciate his talent to the full the *Menu d'Agrément* (served only to an entire table) is worth considering. Set L 180F Set L & D 360F. ***Seats** 50. L 12-2 D 7-10.* ***Closed** L Sat, all Sun, 25 Dec & 1 Jan. Amex, Diners, Mastercard, Visa.*

Golden Tulip St-Honoré 1700F

Tel 49 53 03 03 **Fax 42 89 95 08**
218 rue du Faubourg St-Honoré 75008

Map B1.36 **HR**
Mº Etoile/Ternes

A luxurious and particularly well-appointed hotel, built in 1989, and boasting function rooms and its own car park. The rooms and suites are air-conditioned and sound-proofed, with mini-bars, marble bathrooms, safes, a keycard security system, satellite TV, fax point and hairdryer. Room service is available 24 hours a day. ***Rooms** 72. Amex, Diners, Mastercard, Visa.*

Le Relais Vermeer 700F

An elegant and stylish setting for Sylvain Lefevre's imaginative French cooking. Begin with a soup of clams and sea urchins, a mushroom tart with thin pastry, crisply sautéed potatoes with smoked salmon and caviar cream or stuffed, rolled sardine fillets with chanterelles. Choosing a starter may be difficult but selecting a main dish may prove even more of a problem, so tempting are the menu descriptions. Sautéed scallops and poached oysters with leeks, crisply sautéed sea bass with toasted sesame seeds and lobster jus, and fillets of red mullet sautéed on one side only served on coarsely chopped tomatoes and courgettes with a saffron sauce are featured among the fish dishes. Meats include roast free-range guinea fowl with chanterelles and stuffed cabbage, thinly sliced fillet of lamb with herbs served with sliced potatoes sautéed in goose fat and roast wild duck with *verjus*. In addition to the *menu du jour*, and at the same price, there's a *menu diététique* for the health-conscious. Short but well-balanced list of French wines. Set menu 180F. ***Seats** 70. L 12-3 D 7-11.* ***Closed** L Sat, all Sun & last 3 weeks Aug.*

Le Grenadin 650F

Tel 45 63 28 92 **Fax 45 61 24 76**
44 rue de Naples 75008

Map C1.37 **R**
Mº Villiers

Decorated in shades of beige with wood panelling, the restaurant has a comfortable ambience romanticised in the evening by candles on each table. Chef-patron Patrick Cirotte's cooking is appealingly individualistic with sometimes unusual combinations in light, well-balanced dishes. *Terrine de foie gras aux lentilles vertes, marinade de saumon aux caramboles,* and oysters and alfalfa sprouts with lemon cream are typical starters. For a main course there's *roti de lotte aux champignons, sauce carottes; magret de canard à la vinaigrette tiède de passe-pierres et noix*, or saddle of rabbit with courgette spaghetti and shallots. A speciality dessert is the *millefeuille minute*: a very light confection with honey-flavoured *crème patissière*. Some 450 wines on the list include all the wines of the Loire. Set menus 198F, 248F, 298F & 330F. ***Seats** 40. L 12-2.30 D 7.30-10.30.* ***Closed** Sat (except L Nov-Apr), Sun, 14 Jul, 15 Aug, 4 days Christmas & 4 days New Year. Amex, Mastercard, Visa.*

A glossary of French menu items starts on page 274

HÉDIARD 550F

Tel 43 12 88 99 **Fax 43 12 88 98** Map C2.38 **R**
21 place de la Madeleine 75008 M° Madeleine

Established 140 years ago, Hédiard stands in distinguished company among the luxury food shops of Madeleine. At its heart on the first floor is a restaurant which is open all day from breakfast until late. You can either sit at the bar and perhaps enjoy tapas, a pastry or a speciality tea (the latter is accompanied by a *madeleine* – what else!), or at one of the tables in the spacious restaurant done out in natural wood. Whether you have just one dish or the full gamut – a starter of mixed leaf salad with green beans and foie gras followed by *tortelli à la compote de lapereau aux tomates confites* and ending with a trio of cheeses or a dessert such as *tarte au citron* or *tarte tatin* – you are assured of quality and charming service. ***Seats*** *80. Meals 9am-10.30pm.* ***Closed*** *Sun. Amex, Diners, Mastercard, Visa.*

> The best way to get around Paris is by bus or metro –
> buy a book (carnet) of tickets at any metro station and save money

LANCASTER 2350F

Tel 40 76 40 76 **Fax 40 76 40 00** Map B1.39 **H**
7 rue de Berri 75008 M° George V

Located only yards from the Champs Elysées, in one of the city's most fashionable areas, the hotel retains all the elements of an elegant and stylish Parisian town house. The foyer sets the tone with its mirror-finished cream marble floor. Magnificent flower arrangements and fine antiques grace the public rooms together with tapestries, oil paintings and a collection of eighteenth-century clocks. The bar is softly lit and has pastel-coloured murals. One of the finest features of the hotel is the splendid courtyard, which provides a touch of the countryside so close to the hustle of the Champs Elysées. The whole place has a comforting, traditional and old-fashioned appeal reflected in the bedrooms with their Persian rugs, antique porcelain ornaments and exquisite 18th-century artwork. Up-to-date bathrooms feature toiletries from the best *parfumiers* as well as cosseting bathrobes. Modern influences include air-conditioning and mini-bars, though standards of service are very high, making the latter somewhat less than essential. Recently sold out of the Savoy Group. ***Rooms*** *58. Amex, Diners, Mastercard, Visa.*

LASSERRE ★★ 1600F

Tel 43 59 53 43 **Fax 45 63 72 23** Map B2.40 **R**
17 ave Franklin D Roosevelt 75008 M° Franklin D Roosevelt

René Lasserre, at the age of 12, came to Paris from Bayonne between the wars to seek his fortune and went on to found this much loved restaurant. Customers and staff are equally loyal. Regulars have their own 'Club de la Casserole' and ex-staff have their own organisation, 'Les Anciens de Lasserre', which includes such illustrious members as Gérard Boyer, Guy Savoy and Marc Haeberlin. Attention to detail, in decor, service and cooking, is the cornerstone of the restaurant's success. The surroundings are splendid, from the specially commissioned chandeliers to the famous sliding roof which retracts on summer evenings. Current chef Bernard Joinville still cooks timeless Lasserre classics like 'Le Ragout 74' and *sole soufflée au salpicon de crustacés* s well as other traditional dishes such as *grenadins de veau de lait poelées au cidre* (small slices of veal pan-fried in cider), turbot poached with hollandaise sauce or grilled with Choron sauce and *chateaubriand*. Desserts are also splendidly simple: *trois sorbets de saison* and *soufflé chaud à la liqueur d'Amaretto*, for instance. And to drink? It has to be Champagne Lasserre. ***Seats*** *100. L 12.30-2.30 D 7.30-10.30.* ***Closed*** *L Mon, all Sun & Aug. Valet parking. Amex, Mastercard, Visa.*

LAURENT ★★ 1800F

Tel 42 25 00 39 **Fax 45 62 45 21** Map C2.41 **R**
41 ave Gabriel 75008 Mº Champs Elysées-Clemenceau

Built in the 1840s, Laurent is one of the 'pavilion' restaurants in the gardens at the Place de la Concorde end of the Champs Elysées. Chef Philippe Braun is a protégé of Joël Robuchon and an exquisite chef in his own right. His seasonal menu lists deceptively simple-sounding dishes yet his subtle combinations of taste and texture are masterly. Sardines marinaded in thyme and *araignée de mer* (spider crab) *en gelée* are typically straightforward starters. Mains include grilled turbot with *artichauts à la barigoule* (artichokes stuffed with finely chopped mushrooms, shallots, parsley and butter) and superbly roasted rack of lamb with a spiced aubergine purée. Finish with a plate of French and Swiss cheeses or a dessert such as the speciality *deux soufflés Laurent*. Virtually every French wine can be found on the superb list. The terrace is a wonderful setting for summer dining. Set menu 380F. Valet parking. ***Seats*** *100 (terrace 100). L 12.30-3 D 7.30-10.* ***Closed*** *L Sat, all Sun & Public Holidays. Amex, Diners, Mastercard, Visa.*

LEDOYEN ★★ 1200F

Tel 47 42 35 98 **Fax 47 42 55 01** Map B2.42 **R**
carré des Champs Elysées 75008 Mº Champs Elysées-Clemenceau

One of the most historic restaurants in Paris, Ledoyen has, in its time, been patronised by Robespierre, painted by Tissot and written about by Maupassant. Opened in 1792 (as Chez Doyen) the setting, in a pavilion near the Petit Palais in the Jardin des Champs Elysées, is incomparable, with the most elegant first-floor dining-room looking out over the gardens. The kitchens are in the very capable hands of Ghislaine Arabian while her husband Jean-Paul looks after the front of house, a winning team who successfully maintain the long-held high standards associated with this address. Modern dishes, simply described on the menu, are prepared with precise attention to the essential details such as flavour and texture with skilful presentation an integral part of each composition. Begin with roast langoustines with a potato salad and truffle vinaigrette or an open raviolo with Brittany lobster, button mushrooms and an 'essence' of chicken and foie gras. Follow with sea bass baked in a salt crust, baked turbot flavoured with Garde beer served with fried onions, rib of roast milk-fed veal with sage and fresh tagliatelle or Chateaubriand with black grapes and bone marrow. Game in season might include a terrine of hare with rhubarb chutney, and noisettes of venison flavoured with juniper berries and served with figs cooked in red wine. Set menu 520F & (for 2 or more) 590F. On the ground floor, and also under the supervision of Ghislaine Arabian (although she is very much 'at the stove' of the gastronomic restaurant above), is *Le Cercle Ledoyen (qv).* ***Seats*** *50. L 12-2 D 7-10.* ***Closed*** *Sat, Sun & Aug. Amex, Diners, Mastercard, Visa.*

LIDO 930F

Tel 42 66 27 37 **Fax 42 66 61 23** Map C2.43 **H**
4 passage Madeleine 75008 Mº Madeleine

A small and charming traditional hotel located just off Place de la Madeleine. The panelled reception also features Oriental carpets and a beamed ceiling. There are more beams in some of the traditionally furnished bedrooms, which offer all sorts of amenities including mini-bar, cable TV, safe and, in the en suite marble bathrooms – all of which have tubs – a hairdryer. All rooms are air-conditioned. Buffet breakfast is included in the room price. ***Rooms*** *32. Amex, Diners, Mastercard, Visa.*

See page 9 for a list of starred restaurants

LUCAS CARTON ★ 2600F

Tel 42 65 22 90 **Fax 42 65 06 23** Map C2.44 **R**
9 place de la Madeleine 75008 Mº Madeleine

Bertrand Guénon has been chef de cuisine since 1980, but it is still Alain Senderens who inspires the kitchen of this stunning Belle Epoque restaurant with its blond wood panelling and etched glass. Among his renowned dishes are ravioli of baby scallops with courgettes, *foie gras au chou, canard Apicius roti au miel et aux épices*, and *tarte aux zestes d'oranges*. The carte is unique in giving the option of a glass of wine individually chosen to complement each and every dish, including the puds – a truly wonderful idea. A glass of '86 Jurançon with the cabbage-wrapped foie gras, for example, a Grand Chablis with a dish of langoustines, ginger and fried oysters; Pomerol with the wild duck and the Ch Latour '87 with the noisettes of lamb. Desserts are all prepared individually to order so it is necessary to order them along with the starter and main dish, unless leaving all decisions to the kitchen by going for the no-choice 'Menu Lucas Carton' – served only to the whole table. Valet parking. ***Seats** 100. L 12-2 D 6-10.30. **Closed** L Sat, all Sun, 21 Dec-7 Jan & most of Aug. Mastercard, Visa.*

LA MAISON D'ALSACE 550F

Tel 43 59 44 24 **Fax 42 89 06 62** Map B2.45 **R**
39 ave des Champs Elysées 75008 Mº Franklin D Roosevelt

Open throughout the day and night all year round, this spacious and popular brasserie has mirrored walls, banquette seating formed into convivial booths and a terrace on the Champs Elysées itself. As the name suggests the menu gives pride of place to the produce and cuisine of Alsace: choucroute, *escargots à Wantzeneau*, escalope of veal with horseradish sauce, foie gras in Gewurztraminer-flavoured aspic, quiche lorraine. Shellfish, including a good *plateau de fruits de mer*, is also a speciality. Finish with a delicious *clafoutis aux griottes*. A short wine list includes all the grape varieties grown in Alsace plus a few wines from other areas, or drink the *grande bière d'Alsace à la pression*. From 11pm till dawn there is a special 119F 'night menu'. ***Seats** 180 (+ 100 outside). Meals 24 hours a day. Amex, Diners, Mastercard, Visa.*

MAISON BLANCHE ★ 1100F

Tel 47 23 55 99 **Fax 47 20 09 56** Map B2.46 **R**
15 ave Montaigne 75008 Mº Alma-Marceau

On the roof of the Théatre des Champs-Elysées the decor is modern and the panoramic view of the Paris skyline stunning – especially at night with the illuminated Eiffel Tower in the middle distance. Jose Martinez' menu is as up-to-date as the surroundings. Terrine of duck foie gras with vanilla, salad of shin of beef with shallots, calf's brains with preserved lemon or oyster fritters with nine flavours are featured among the starters. For a main dish the choice could be sea bass poached in cider with vichy carrots, tuna roasted with pepper and bone marrow, skewers of scallops with lime grass, roast pigeon with quince preserve and calf's sweetbreads with chard. Finish with an apple, quince, cinnamon and rosemary crumble, coffee crème caramel, *pastilla au lait de lavande* or orange cream and conserve with chocolate. ***Seats** 200. L 12-2 D 8-11. **Closed** L Sat, all Sun, last week July & 1st 3 weeks Aug. Amex, Mastercard, Visa.*

LA MAISON DU VALAIS 550F

Tel 42 60 22 72 Map C2.47 **R**
20 rue Royale 75008 Mº Madeleine

Rustic chalet-style setting with dark timber walls and brown and white genuine cow-hide seats where Parisians come to eat Swiss fondues and raclettes (slices of gently melted raclette cheese served with hot potatoes in their skins). Start with a plate of cured ham, wafer-thin sliced air-dried beef and dried sausage or a salad of potato, salmon and shallots. Among the fish dishes, fillets of perch meunière and wild char, either grilled or meunière, are specialities as is the salmon from the tank grilled with fennel. A skewer of grilled veal kidneys flambéed with

See over

whisky and beef *pot-au-feu* are examples of the meat dishes available. The long list of desserts is mostly ice cream or sorbet-based though there's tarte tatin, chocolate profiteroles and crepes flambéed with mandarin liqueur. The wine list covers all the French regions plus the Valais area of Switzerland. The house red (Dole), white (Fendant) and rosé (Valaison) are sold by the *pichet* or the glass. Set menu 215F (inc wine). ***Seats** 80 (+ 18 outside). L 12.15-2.30 D 7.15-11.30. **Closed** Sun & Public Holidays. Amex, Diners, Mastercard, Visa.*

LA MARÉE ★ 1200F

Tel 43 80 20 00 Fax 48 88 04 04 Map B1.48 **R**
1 rue Daru 75008 Mº Ternes

On the corner of Rue du Faubourg St-Honoré. There are a couple of meat dishes on the menu here but this is overwhelmingly a seafood restaurant; the name means tide. The menu changes frequently and specialities which appear regularly include Colchester oysters as well as warm oysters in champagne, *demoiselles de Cherbourg à la nage*, ravioli of langoustines, baby turbot with mustard and a *panaché* of steamed red mullet and line-caught bass. Flemish paintings decorate the walls. The clever wine list is printed on the inside of the menu and presented by vintage – youngest first. Three Spanish, three US and a handful of rural wines apart, it is magnificently all-French and includes choice wines by the glass. ***Seats** 80. L 12-2.15 D 8-10.30. **Closed** L Easter Mon & Whit Mon, all Sat, Sun, 25 Dec, 1 Jan & Aug. Amex, Diners, Mastercard, Visa.*

LE MARIGNAN 1690F

Tel 40 76 34 56 Fax 40 76 34 34 Map B2.49 **H**
12 rue de Marignan 75008 Mº Franklin D Roosevelt

South of the Champs Elysées in an elegant neo-Gothic building with an art deco facade, Le Marignan combines traditional comforts with modern amenities. Public rooms are a stylish blend of marble-pillared classicism and the ultra-modern. Scattered throughout is a collection of sculptures while walls are hung with an exciting assortment of modern art. Bedrooms, sixteen of which are suites, include many which are duplexes or have terraces. Otherwise they are more intimate than spacious but all are air-conditioned and furnished to a good standard. Bathrooms are a blend of modern tiling and coloured marble.
A notable feature is the Salon de Thé (open 7.30am-midnight) where numerous teas are offered with home-made pastries, together with light snacks all day. ***Rooms** 73. Amex, Diners, Mastercard, Visa.*

MAXIM'S 2000F

Tel 42 65 27 94 Fax 40 17 02 91 Map C2.50 **R**
3 rue Royale 75008 Mº Concorde

For over 100 years Maxim's has been both an institution and a legend and it is now owned by Pierre Cardin. Magnificently and grandly decorated in art nouveau style (it was registered as a national historical monument in 1979), it has an original facade hidden by the glass terrace; note also the murals, mirrors, copper decorations, art deco lighting and the glass roof over the main dining-room, once the interior courtyard. Eating the traditional *cuisine* here does not come cheap, but as long-serving maitre d' Jean-Pierre Guevel says "for about eleven hundred francs each, you can enjoy a complete night out, starting at around 8.30pm for aperitifs, sitting down at, say, 9.15pm and dancing to the five-piece orchestra from 11pm to 2am with a bottle of champagne on the table". Add too the violinist who serenades the tables, taking care not to obstruct the tail-coated waiters who glide effortlessly through the dining rooms. Chef Michel Ménant, himself in situ for 30 years, oversees the classical cooking – dishes are first presented to customers before being served over flame warmers, not often seen these days – typical starters being duck terrine, langoustines in aspic with tarragon, hot or chilled Billy By soup (a creamy mussel soup) and quail's eggs with caviar. Main courses such as fillet of beef with foie gras, lamb noisettes with basil and veal kidneys with mustard are included, together with particular specialities like gratin of lobsters with chanterelles, medallions of salmon with chervil, and Challans duck with an orange sauce and figs. For dessert there's peach *cardinale, figues à la royale* and iced raspberry mousse as well as the usual ice creams and sorbets. Exalted wines at exalted prices. ***Seats*** *200. L 12.30-2 D 7.30-10.30* ***Closed*** *Sun, 25 Dec, 1 Jan, 1 May & 14 Jul. Amex, Diners, Mastercard, Visa.*

AU PETIT MONTMORENCY 900F

Tel 42 25 11 19 Map B2.51 **R**
26 rue Jean-Mermoz 75008 Mº Franklin D Roosevelt

Daniel Bouché's cooking in his peaceful restaurant is a blend of modern and classic influences with starters such as a soup of oysters in Pomerol with wild mushrooms, a salad of potatoes and truffles and a speciality of *foie gras au caramel poivrée* (a cold dish). Main courses could include *cote de veau de lait en cocotte, gros turbot à l'huile d'olive, citron et tomate* as well as game in season such as *lièvre à la royale*. Desserts, many of which need to be ordered at the beginning of the meal, are unmissable, examples being *soufflé chaud au chocolat avec glace à la vanille*, and *gratin de mures avec glace à la menthe fraiche*. ***Seats*** *45. L 12-2.30 D 7.30-10.30.* ***Closed*** *Sat (except L Easter-Sep), Sun & Aug. Mastercard, Visa.*

LE PICHET 900F

Tel 43 59 50 34 **Fax 45 63 07 82** Map B2.52 **R**
68 rue Pierre Charron 75008 Mº Franklin D Roosevelt

A smart bistro with mirrored walls and plentiful photographs of celebrity clients. The menu specialises in fish, with an excellent choice of shellfish. Particular dishes include *soupe de moules, raie pochée vinaigrette tiède, tournedos de saumon aux lentilles vertes* and *St Jacques au Saint Croix du Mont* (pan-fried scallops in a sweet white wine). Meat-eaters are not forgotten with starters such as *fricassée de petits gris* and *jambon de Salamanque* and main courses like fillet of beef Rossini, *cote de boeuf à la moëlle, sauce bordelaise* and *carré d'agneau roti au thym*. Sweets include a delicious *gourmandise de poire, sauce cannelle* as well as *feuilleté aux pommes chaudes*. Shortish wine list also includes some famous names. ***Seats*** *96. L 12-2.30 D 7-12.* ***Closed*** *Sat, Sun, 2 weeks Christmas & 3 weeks Aug. Amex, Diners, Mastercard, Visa.*

PLAZA ATHÉNÉE 3010F

Tel 47 23 78 33 **Fax 47 20 20 70** Map B2.53 **HR**
25 ave Montaigne 75008 Mº Alma-Marceau

Surrounded by the great haute-couture houses, the Plaza has its own inimitable sense of style and has long been a haunt of the famous – and sometimes infamous; Mata Hari was arrested in the hotel's darkwood and leather English bar. Other public areas include a large circular lobby, vaulted Galerie de Gobelins with pairs of columns down each side, and a verdant courtyard garden with fountains and red umbrellas that match the awnings of the balustraded bedroom windows that overlook it. There are four splendid conference rooms. Bedrooms in Louis XV, Louis XVI or Regency style are elegant and comfortable, with air-conditioning and ultra-modern bathrooms. Facilities include 24-hour room service, hairdressing salon, perfume boutique and theatre desk. Guests have free access to a fitness club, and transport to it (but not back). Parking for about a dozen cars (150F a day). Forte. ***Rooms*** *253. Access, Amex, Diners, Visa.*

Le Régence 1050F

An elegant dining-room with fluted pilasters supporting an elaborate gilded frieze, and widely spaced tables displaying silver place settings. The menu is very much Grand Hotel in both style – separate sections for grills, fish etc – and content; the starters include oysters, caviar, smoked salmon and foie gras. Amongst the other, perhaps less standard, dishes are a lobster soufflé, curried

See over

monkfish with shellfish, green noodles and sweet peppers, and breast of chicken simmered with lemon and peppermint. From a good varied choice of desserts this would be just the place to enjoy the spectacle that is crepe Suzette flambée. *Menu gourmand* 490F. Over 2000 references on the wine list, including a champagne *de la maison*. ***Seats*** *75 (+ 80 outside). L 12.30-2.30 D 7.30-10.30.*

Relais Plaza 650F

Informal, all-day eaterie with 1930s' decor and entrance direct from the street as well as from within the hotel. It's breakfast till 11am after which the full menu runs through until the early hours. With something to suit all appetites the choice ranges from club sandwiches and croque monsieur, via pasta, salads and egg dishes to lamb curry, sole meunière and grills. Set L 225F Set D 260F. ***Seats*** *103.* ***Meals*** *8am-1.30am.*

PRINCE DE GALLES 2250F

Tel 47 23 55 11 Fax 47 20 96 92 Map A2.54 **H**
33 ave George V 75008 M° George V

The Prince of Wales Hotel, which was acquired by Sheraton Hotels, re-opened in April 1994 after a top-to-toe refurbishment resulting in tip-top standards of comfort and accommodation. The tone is set by an elegant lobby with baronial-style stone walls and central carpeted island sporting a huge floral display that almost reaches up to touch the glittering chandelier above; the bar boasts red leather upholstery and carved wood-panelled walls. A unique feature of the hotel is its central patio/courtyard, overlooked by many of the bedrooms, with the enclosing walls completely covered with original 1927 mosaic tiling – right up to roof level. Air-conditioned bedrooms are all identically furnished with traditional freestanding pieces, including leather-topped desk, and with all the expected modern comforts. Complimentary newspapers are provided as well as Hermès toiletries in the bathrooms. De luxe rooms have a fax point. Peace and quiet are ensured by almost all the rooms having their own lobby and service extends to a 24-hour room menu and the turning down of beds in the evening. There is a well-equipped fitness room and a small business centre. Valet parking. ***Rooms*** *171. Amex, Diners, Mastercard, Visa.*

HOTEL QUEEN MARY 810F

Tel 42 66 40 50 Fax 42 66 94 92 Map C2.55 **H**
9 rue de Greffulhe 75008 M° Havre-Caumartin

British-owned (and mainly British-staffed), this small hotel in a quiet back street near the Madeleine was totally renovated in 1993 and offers good air-conditioned bedrooms that have attractive matching bedcovers and curtains, often with period plaster-panelled walls. All rooms have safe, mini-bar, trouser press, hairdryer, cable TV and good workspace with all but five small singles having two telephones. Fully tiled bathrooms have showers over tubs except for the singles which have shower and WC only. Nice touches include a welcoming decanter of sherry, and scrambled eggs, bacon, sausages, tomatoes and mushrooms in the buffet breakfast (69F), which is served in a bright yellow basement breakfast room. There is a small bar but no restaurant. Room service 7am to 10pm. ***Rooms*** *36. Amex, Mastercard, Visa.*

RÉSIDENCE MAXIM'S DE PARIS 2250F

Tel 45 61 96 33 Fax 42 89 06 07 Map C2.56 **H**
42 ave Gabriel 75008 M° Concorde/Champs Elysées-Clemenceau

Pierre Cardin's name is synonymous with haute couture. In 1986 he turned his attention to this grand building, which he purchased and then set about indulging all his design skills and fantasies. The result has been to create some of the most refined and elegant bedrooms and suites to be found anywhere. Individually furnished, they differ greatly one from another, ranging in style from those on the 5th floor with an ultra-modern, cool, late-20th-century decor to those with exquisite original art deco furniture and others with genuine 18th-century pieces. All except four standard bedrooms are suites but even the former are spacious and all have almost the full A to Z of amenities, from full air-conditioning to video players. Bathrooms feature highly polished marble together with stunning murals. Hallways too are extraordinary, with their beautiful antiques and fine paintings. Standards of service are exemplary and there is valet parking. A hotel of outstanding quality and merit. ***Rooms*** *33. Amex, Diners, Mastercard, Visa.*

ROYAL MONCEAU 2600F

Tel 42 99 88 00 Fax 42 99 89 90 Map B1.57 **HR**
37 ave Hoche 75008 M° Etoile

A huge, arched, marble-floored lobby with trompe l'oeil sky ceiling is at the centre of things at this luxury hotel in the business district. Amenities include a sybaritic health centre (pool, steam bath, sauna, squash, all sorts of beauty treatments), pretty gardens, news stand and choice of bars. Bedrooms and suites, some quite grand, are furnished and decorated in traditional style while being provided with every modern comfort. 24-hour room service. ***Rooms*** *219. Amex, Diners, Mastercard, Visa.*

Le Jardin 1000F

Tel 42 99 98 70

Appropriately named restaurant in a circular, glass-walled conservatory jutting out into the hotel's garden. Bruno Cirino took over the kitchen here in 1994 and offers the flavours of his native Provence – steamed spider crab in a bouillon with pistou, wild duck roasted with olives and ceps, or a menu that might also include baby cod roasted with mustard and grilled with herbs and escalopes of veal sweetbreads pan-fried with Auvergne ceps. No surprises on an expensive all-French wine list. Set L 280F & 340F Set D 430F. ***Seats*** *60 (+ 40 outside). L 12.30-2.30 D 7.30-10.30.* ***Closed*** *Sat, Sun & Public Holidays.*

Il Carpaccio 900F

Tel 42 99 98 90

For a complete change of cuisine, though not of decor as this also has something of a garden theme with trelliswork, mirrors and large troughs of flowers, the hotel's second restaurant is thoroughly Italian. Angelo Paraccuchi prepares a menu with both traditional and modern elements. The à la carte offers dishes such as ricotta ravioli, turbot with pizzaiola, grilled lamb cutlets and veal cutlets milanaise. The menu of the day is more imaginative with offerings such as warm carpaccio of grouper with a marinade of olives and tomatoes, pumpkin risotto with black truffles and parsley and roast sea bass with black pepper and marsh samphire. A modest and mostly Italian wine list is presented by region. Set L 280F. ***Seats*** *60. L 12.30-2.30 D 8-10.30.* ***Closed*** *Aug.*

SAN REGIS 2100F

Tel 44 95 16 16 Fax 45 61 05 48 Map B2.59 **HR**
12 rue Jean Goujon 75008 M° Champs Elysées-Clemenceau

Quietly elegant hotel with an intimate home-from-home atmosphere in the prestigious 'Golden Triangle' area favoured by renowned fashion houses like Christian Dior, Valentino and Ricci. Individually decorated bedrooms combine 17th- and 18th-century style furniture with well-chosen fabrics, often with matching wall-coverings, and such modern comforts as air-conditioning. Good, coloured-marble bathrooms. Day rooms include a charming lounge with antique, blond-wood panelling and a clubby bar. Unobtrusive yet attentive service. ***Rooms*** *44. Amex, Diners, Mastercard, Visa.*

Restaurant 900F

Separated from the bar by a pillared archway, the small, pretty restaurant is almost like a private dining-room. The menu – there's a version with French on one side and an English translation on the facing page – is fairly straightforward and sensibly short (about eight choices at each stage) but well-balanced: terrine with spices, shredded artichokes and stuffed tomato, shellfish bisque, John Dory with lentils vinaigrette,

See over

spring lamb with cranberries, pear and ginger in puff pastry. French list with a couple of wines served by the glass. Set menu 250F. ***Seats*** *21. L 12-2.30 D 7.30-10.30.*

LE SARLADAIS 650F

Tel & Fax 45 22 23 62 Map C1.60 **R**
2 rue de Vienne 75008 Paris Mº Eglise St-Augustin

No one goes away hungry from Jean and Josette Tartrou's unpretentiously comfortable restaurant near the Gare St Lazare. The cooking is that of the South-West of France with more than half the menu devoted to *Spécialités Périgourdines*: neck of goose stuffed with foie gras, *anchaut Périgord* (fillet of pork confit in aspic), *tourin à l'ail* (garlic soup), truffle omelette, *salade sarladaise* (confit of duck and duck's gizzard). Particular specialities are foie gras (served with seasonal produce – ceps, chestnuts or raspberries with raspberry vinegar, confit of duck with *pommes sarladaise* (sliced potatoes with onion and garlic), and *cassoulet périgourdin* which arrives in a huge terrine with a proper breadcrumb crust. A shortish wine list concentrates on the wines of the South and South-West. The lower part of the split-level dining-room is reserved for non-smokers. Set L 200F Set L & D 145F & 200F. ***Seats*** *70. L 12-2.30 D 7-10.* ***Closed*** *L Sat, all Sun, Aug & Public Holidays. Amex, Mastercard, Visa.*

LES SAVEURS 650F

Tel 45 63 17 44 **Fax 42 25 06 59** Map B2.61 **R**
Hotel Sofitel-Paris-Elysées, Mº Champs Elysées-Clemenceau
8 rue Jean Goujon 75008

On the mezzanine level of the Sofitel-Paris-Elysées, Les Saveurs is a civilised, air-conditioned restaurant with an ambience that is both classic and modern reflecting the innovative style of Didier Lanfray in the kitchen. His imaginative style is evident throughout the menus. Starters include roast Nourmoitier potatoes with crab, sardine fillets with an *escabèche* of vegetables and tapénade or prawns with grated coconut. Fish dishes range from sea bass flavoured with Szechuan spices or sole with foie gras and oysters to cold baked turbot with wild mushroom butter. In the meat section there is fillet of beef with bone marrow and *fleur de sel*, fricassee of veal kidneys with tarragon and Roquefort and duck pie with salsify and wild mushrooms. Finally, for dessert choose between a chocolate delice with coffee sauce, a crisp pear galette with hazelnut ice cream or *pain perdu* with a cinnamon custard. There's a separate list of the 'foreign' wines and another of wines offered by the glass. Set menu 155F. ***Seats*** *60. L 12.15-2.30 D 7.30-10.30.* ***Closed*** *Sat, Sun 25 Dec & Aug. Amex, Diners, Mastercard, Visa.*

TAILLEVENT ★★★ 1350F

Tel 45 61 12 90 **Fax 42 25 95 18** Map B1.63 **R**
15 rue Lammenais 75008 Mº George V

Excellence sustained over many years is the achievement of this most civilised and refined of restaurants presided over by the urbane second-generation owner Jean-Claude Vrinat. Wood-panelled walls and discreet, polished service help to create an almost club-like atmosphere relished by the good and the great of the capital's establishment. Philippe Legendre continues in the tradition of his predecessor (who was head chef here for 30 years) of acknowledging modern trends but only gradually and from a solidly classical base. Specialities include *boudin de homard Breton à la nage, poulette de Bresse en cocotte* and a *moelleux au chocolat et à thym* that shares the dessert section of the menu with such wonderfully old-fashioned sounding puds as *riz à l'impératrice* and *blanc-manger à l'ancienne* (a world away from the blancmange of children's tea parties). The legendary wine list is supported by their own wine shop, one of the best in Paris, in the nearby Rue du Faubourg Saint-Honoré. ***Seats*** *120. L 12-1.30 D 7.30-10.* ***Closed*** *Sat, Sun & 3 weeks Aug. Amex, Diners, Mastercard, Visa.*

Hotel de la Trémoille 2240F

Tel 47 23 34 20 **Fax 40 70 01 08** Map B2.64 **H**
14 rue de la Trémoille 75008 Mº Alma-Marceau

A Forte Exclusive hotel in a quiet location off Avenue George V and named after a 15th-century military hero, General Louis de la Trémoille. The hotel boasts an elegant lobby with a rug-strewn marble floor. Fresh flower arrangements and exotic palms add a further element of stylishness. Bedrooms are very comfortable, each furnished in a smart, very traditional manner with fine furniture. Facilities, though, are totally up-to-date with air-conditioning, cable TV, mini-bar and room safe. All-day room service. Valet parking. ***Rooms*** *107. Amex, Diners, Mastercard, Visa.*

Le Val d'Or 500F

Tel 43 59 95 81 Map B1.65 **R**
28 ave Franklin D Roosevelt 75008 Mº St-Philippe-du-Roule

A modest establishment with 1950s decor offering a short lunchtime menu in a basement restaurant where you will be treated to Lyonnais specialities such as *sabodet* (pig's head sausage) *poché au Brouilly* as a starter and main dishes such as *cote de veau rotie,* calf's liver with cider vinegar and Bresse chicken either roasted or served in a cream sauce with girolles. A favourite cheese is *fromage de Salers* from the Auvergne. Charcuterie and sandwiches are served throughout the day in the ground floor wine bar/café where some dozen or so mostly Burgundian wines, including most of the Beaujolais crus, are available by the glass. Both very popular with local office workers. It is advisable to book for the restaurant. Watch out for the hole-in-the-ground loos. ***Seats*** *50. L only 12-3 (wine bar/café 9-5).* ***Closed*** *Sat (except wine bar/café), Sun (except wine bar/café), Aug. Mastercard, Visa.*

Vancouver ★ 900F

Tel 42 56 77 77 **Fax 42 56 50 52** Map A1.66 **R**
4 rue Arsène Houssaye 75008 Mº Etoile

After having spent an idyllic holiday in Vancouver, Chantal Decout and her chef-husband Jean-Louis decided to name their restaurant accordingly. Set on two levels, the art deco interior resembles a 30s ocean liner with plenty of wood, etched glass, metal and light colours. Jean-Louis specialises in cooking seafood – favourite dishes are velouté of mussels with saffron and sautéed shrimps sweet sour, followed by sea bream with cider, *brandade de rouget-barbet, bouillabaisse parisienne* (as Jean-Louis likes it!), and a light *crème brulée* or *Paris-Brest craquelin* to finish. New dishes include starters such as *dim sum de langoustines avec épices au vapeur, ragout de homard breton aux champignons sauvages* and main courses like *sole farcie aux champignons sauce au vin de Bordeaux* or *gambas avec une crème au cognac*. Desserts might be *aumonière de pommes avec amandes, sabayon de peche à la vanille* and *tarte au chocolat glace à la menthe fraiche*. So Vancouver is worth a visit, and you don't have to cross the ocean to get there. Set menus 190F & 380F. ***Seats*** *45. L 12-1.30 D 7.30-10.* ***Closed*** *Sat, Sun, Public Holidays & Aug. Amex, Mastercard, Visa.*

Vernet 1850F

Tel 44 31 98 00 **Fax 44 31 85 69** Map A1.67 **HR**
25 rue Vernet 75008 Mº Etoile

Built at the turn of the century and completely refurbished in 1989, the Vernet combines period style with modern comforts. Antique-furnished bedrooms and suites are all air-conditioned and the splendid marble bathrooms all have jacuzzi tubs. Day rooms include an elegant lounge with panelled walls where afternoon tea and cocktail hour are accompanied by the piano. Guests have use of the health and beauty centre of the nearby Royal Monceau Hotel. 24-hour room service (cold food only after 11pm). Own parking (110F a day) ***Rooms*** *57. Amex, Diners, Mastercard, Visa.*

See over

Les Elysées du Vernet ★ 1000F

The magnificent, glass-roofed Belle Epoque dining-room provides a really splendid setting for some fine cooking with a sunny Mediterranean slant: *filets de rougets de roche poelés aux olives et tomates confites; langoustine royale rotie au sel de Guérande, mesclun niçoise; cote de boeuf de Chalosse, grosses frites à la graisse d'oie, sauce bordelaise à la moelle et poivre noir* (for two), *petites brioches toastées aux fruits noirs; sorbet noix de coco*. Farmhouse cheeses, good choice of coffees and teas and a comprehensive French wine list. 24 of the seats are in a non-smoking covered terrace. Set L 400F Set D 370F & 490F. ***Seats** 40 (+ 15 outside). L 12-2.30 D 7.30-10.* ***Closed** Sat, Sun, Aug & 1 week Christmas.*

Virgin Café

Tel 42 89 46 81 Fax 49 53 50 41 Map B2.68 **R**
52 ave des Champs Elysées 75008 Mº Franklin D Roosevelt

Large bright café on the second floor of the Virgin Megastore. The trendy darkwood and black decor matches the menu: duck ravioli with duck jus, potato and smoked salmon burgers, roast chicken with thyme and saffron rice, fillet of fresh salt cod with a meat jus, fried onions and spinach and crème brulée with two sugars. They also offer breakfast, brunch, afternoon teas, cocktails, children's menu and smiling service. On the drinks front there are as many cocktails (ten of them alcohol free) as wines. ***Open** 10am-11.30pm (Fri & Sat to 12.30am).* ***Closed** 25 Dec, 1 Jan & 1 May. Amex, Mastercard, Visa.*

The best way to get around Paris is by bus or metro –
buy a book (carnet) of tickets at any metro station and save money

Warwick 2670F

Tel 45 63 14 11 Fax 43 59 00 98 Map B1.69 **HR**
5 rue de Berri 75008 Mº George V

The hotel enjoys a good location just off the Champs Elysées, a few paces from the fashion shops of the Faubourg St-Honoré. To complement the setting the decor is both elegant and up-to-date. Space and comfort are watchwords in the bedrooms, with soundproofing and air-conditioning in all rooms as well as a mini-bar, cable TV and hairdryer. Additionally, junior suites have a trouser press and phone extension in the bathroom. Some rooms have terraces. Piano bar; 24-hour room service. ***Rooms** 147. Amex, Diners, Mastercard, Visa.*

La Couronne 750F

Smart restaurant where first-class service complements the reliably good cooking of long-standing chef Paul Van Gassel. His menus offer Provençal cooking with more than just a hint of innovation. Flavour combinations are superb, resulting in well-balanced dishes like warm smoked salmon with a mousseline of herbs, a salad of lobster, winkles and cockles with spring potatoes, or soft-boiled eggs with morels and asparagus to begin. Fish main dishes could include poached skate with a chive sauce, grilled red mullet with fennel, crystallised carrots and orange twists or a pilaf of crab and cockles with a saffron sauce. For those with a penchant for meat there is roast saddle of Pauillac lamb with rosemary-scented vegetables and free-range Houdan chicked roasted with hazelnut oil. Desserts follow in a similar imaginative vein with chocolate millefeuille and orange conserve, *croustillant* of almonds with poached pear and almonds, and pineapple and sultanas marinated in *marc* from Gewurztraminer. There are three set menus in addition to a short *carte*. Fine wine list covering all French regions.
Set menus 230F, 270F & 390F. ***Seats** 50. L 12-2.30 D 7.30-10.30.* ***Closed** L Sat, all Sun & Aug.*

YVAN 700F

Tel 42 89 16 69 Fax 45 63 78 69 Map B2.70 **R**
1bis rue Jean-Mermoz 75008 Mº Franklin D Roosevelt

Yvan Zaplatilek's eponymous restaurant stands just off the central section of the Champs Elysées and now offers a menu with plenty of choices of mostly modern French dishes. Begin with a cappuccino of cream of lentils with croutons, oysters with tiny fried sausages, or *escalope de foie gras poelé au céleri et muscat* and continue with a seafood main course like monkfish tail with leeks and a watercress sauce or lobster with vanilla and courgette pasta. Meat dishes include boned quail with figs, grapes and polenta, fillet of beef with oysters, artichokes and a red wine sauce and veal kidneys with basil and an olive oil mash. Excellent desserts to round off the meal could be *pain perdu* with pears and a caramel sauce, *croustillant* of pineapple with saffron or *feuilleté de chocolat à la banane*. For dinner there are four different set menus, each with three choices at each stage, from which you can mix and match; at lunchtime just one prix-fixe plus an à la carte. Set L 178F Set D 168F, 188F, 238F & 278F.
Seats *75. L 12-2.30 D 8-12.* ***Closed*** *L Sat, all Sun & Public Holidays. Amex, Diners, Mastercard, Visa.*

9th Arrondissement
Places of Interest

Place de Clichy
Trinité
Boulevard des Italiens
Opéra National de Paris Garnier, 40 17 33 33, M° Opéra
Olympia, 47 42 25 49, M° Opéra
Folies Bergères, 44 79 98 98, M° Cadet/Rue Montmartre
Musée Grévin (waxworks), 47 70 85 05, M° Rue Montmartre
Apollo Casino de Paris, 36 68 01 40, M° Trinité
Moulin Rouge, 46 06 00 19, M° Blanche

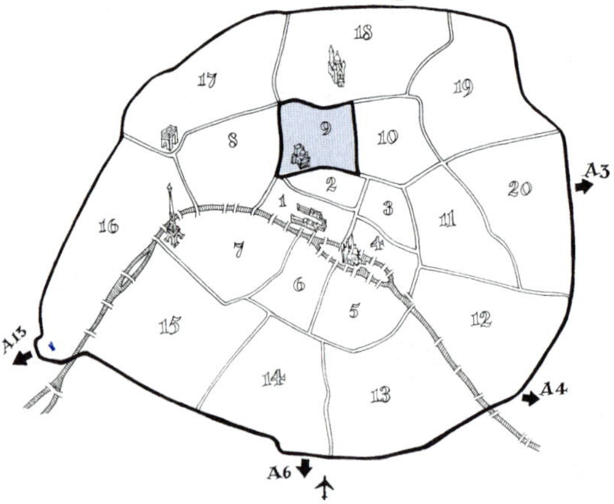

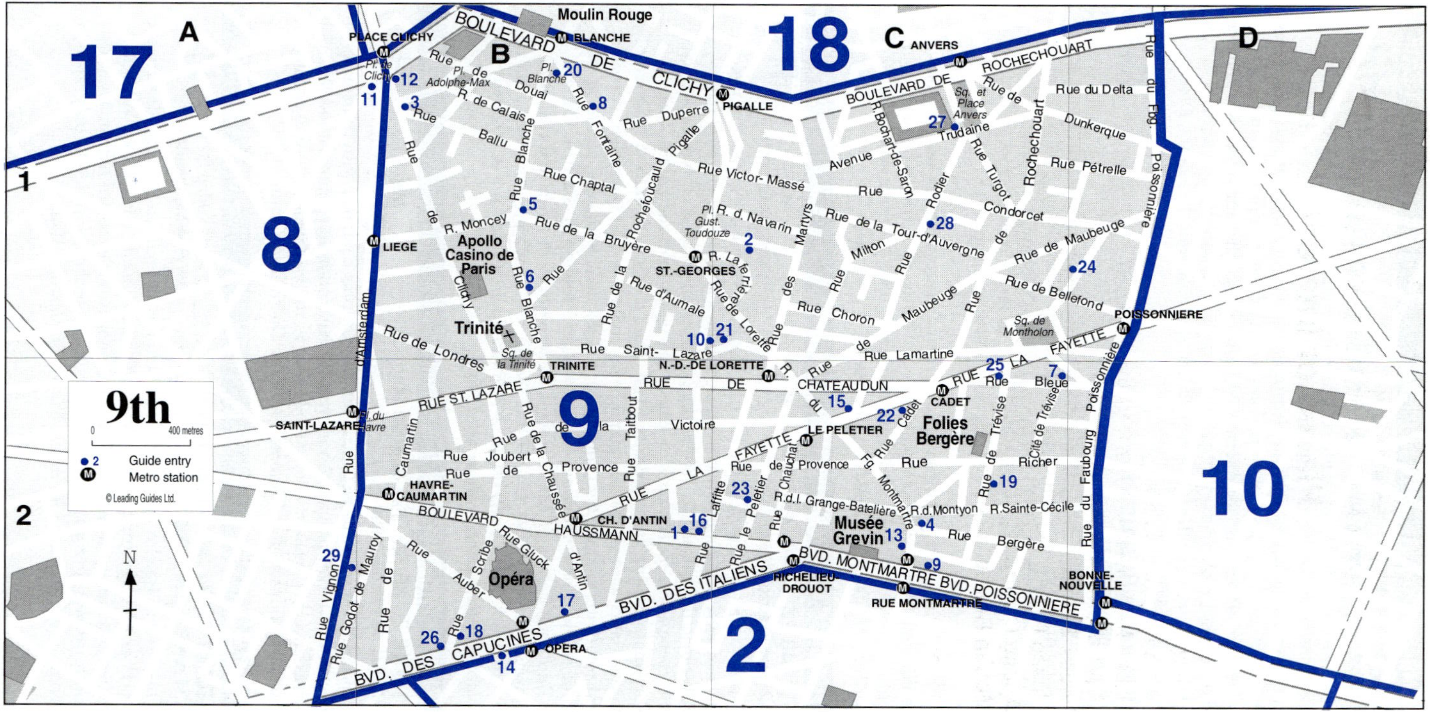
9th
0 400 metres
2 Guide entry
M Metro station
© Leading Guides Ltd.
N
17
18
8
9
10
2
A
B
C
D
1
2
Moulin Rouge
BLANCHE
PLACE CLICHY
PIGALLE
ANVERS
LIEGE
ST.-GEORGES
TRINITE
N.-D.-DE LORETTE
SAINT-LAZARE
CADET
LE PELETIER
HAVRE-CAUMARTIN
CH. D'ANTIN
HAUSSMANN
RICHELIEU-DROUOT
RUE MONTMARTRE
BONNE-NOUVELLE
POISSONNIERE
OPERA
BOULEVARD DE CLICHY
BOULEVARD DE ROCHECHOUART
BOULEVARD HAUSSMANN
BVD. DES CAPUCINES
BVD. DES ITALIENS
BVD. MONTMARTRE
BVD. POISSONNIERE
RUE ST. LAZARE
RUE DE CHATEAUDUN
RUE LA FAYETTE
Apollo Casino de Paris
Trinité
Sq. de la Trinité
Opéra
Folies Bergère
Musée Grevin
Sq. et Place Anvers
Sq. de Montholon
Pl. de Clichy
Pl. Blanche
Pl. de Adolphe-Max
Pl. du Havre
Pl. R. d. Navarin
Gust. Toudouze
Rue de Douai
R. de Calais
Rue Ballu
Rue Blanche
Rue Fontaine
Rue Duperre
Rue Pigalle
Rue Chaptal
Rue de la Rochefoucauld
Rue de la Bruyère
R. Moncey
Rue de Clichy
Rue de Londres
Rue d'Amsterdam
Rue d'Aumale
R. La ferrière
Rue de Lorette
Rue Saint-Lazare
Rue Victor-Massé
Avenue Trudaine
R. Bochart-de-Saron
Rue des Martyrs
Rue Rodier
Rue de la Tour-d'Auvergne
Rue Milton
Rue Turgot
Rue Condorcet
Rue de Rochechouart
Rue du Delta
Rue de Dunkerque
Rue Pétrelle
Rue de Maubeuge
Rue de Bellefond
Rue du Fbg. Poissonnière
Rue du Faubourg Poissonnière
Rue Choron
Rue Lamartine
Rue Bleue
Rue de Trévise
Cité de Trévise
Rue Richer
R.Sainte-Cécile
Rue Bergère
R.d.Montyon
R.d.l. Grange-Batelière
Rue du Fg. Montmartre
Rue Cadet
Rue de Provence
Rue de Châteaudun
Rue Chauchat
Rue le Peletier
Rue Laffitte
Rue de la Victoire
Rue Taitbout
Rue de la Chaussée d'Antin
Rue Joubert
Rue Caumartin
Rue Gluck
Rue Scribe
Rue Auber
Rue de Mauroy
Rue Godot de Mauroy
Rue Vignon
1
2
3
4
5
6
7
8
9
10
11
12
13
14
15
16
17
18
19
20
21
22
23
24
25
26
27
28
29

AMBASSADOR 1520F

Tel 44 83 40 40 **Fax 40 22 08 74** Map B2.1 **HR**
16 bd Haussmann 75009 M° Richelieu-Drouot/Chaussée d'Antin

Constructed in 1927, this traditional and luxurious hotel in the Groupe Concorde was completely renovated in the early 1990s combining modern comforts and amenities with an elegant decor. The bedrooms (three quarters of them air-conditioned) contain period pieces and come with well-equipped bathrooms. Room service operates 24 hours a day. There are eleven conference and function rooms (max 100 people). The hotel is conveniently located for the Opéra and many of the major department stores. ***Rooms*** *298. Amex, Diners, Mastercard, Visa.*

Venantius Restaurant 900F

Tel 48 00 06 38

Decorated in an opulent 'neo-Pompeian' style, this, the hotel's gastronomic restaurant, has its own entrance from the street. Chef Gérard Fouché's carte offers starters such as baby lobsters on a salad of fresh herbs perfumed with truffles and *foie gras de canard confit tuiles de melon poivré* before mains like fillet of sea bream with caviar, aubergine crisps and a *jus niçois*; saddle of young rabbit studded with truffles and served with broccoli fritters and risotto, and fillet of lamb with basil vinaigrette and a tian of courgettes. Desserts might include chocolate soufflé with bitter orange compote, and strawberries roasted with lavender honey and served with caramel. Set L & D 210F Set D 380F (*dégustation*). ***Seats*** *50. L 12-2.30 D 7-10.30.* ***Closed*** *Sat, Sun, Aug & 1 week Feb.*

AUBERGE LANDAISE 480F

Tel 48 78 74 40 **Fax 48 78 20 96** Map C1.2 **R**
23 rue Clauzel 75009 M° Pigalle/St-Georges

Block-stone walls give a rustic look to Dominique Morin's restaurant, which is divided into two dining areas by upright beams and a small entrance hall. Armagnac dating back to 1800 is displayed on one wall. As the name suggests, the chef-patron concentrates on dishes and wines from the South-West (Bayonne, Biarritz and Bordeaux areas). *Hors d'oeuvre landais* (a selection of meats); salad with artichokes, green beans and goose liver; *pipérade; cassoulet maison* (with mutton, duck and pork); braised duck with ceps; and *tarte tatin* with *crème fraiche* are some of the specialities leaving his kitchen. Choose a Bordelais, Cahors or Madiran wine to accompany the meal and one of 80 armagnacs to finish. Set L & D 180F Set D 130F. Two private rooms can cater for 30 people each. ***Seats*** *60. L 12-2.30 D 7-10.30.* ***Closed*** *Sun & 10 days mid-Aug. Amex, Diners, Mastercard, Visa.*

AURORE MONTMARTRE 420F

Tel 48 74 85 56 **Fax 42 81 09 54** Map B1.3 **H**
76 rue de Clichy 75009 M° Place Clichy

A neat little hotel with well-maintained bedrooms equipped with mini-bars, televisions and telephones. About half the bathrooms have shower and WC only. Breakfast (35F) is taken in a vaulted room in the basement. Children sharing parents' room stay free. ***Rooms*** *24. Amex, Diners, Mastercard, Visa.*

BERGÈRE 550F

Tel 47 70 34 34 **Fax 47 70 36 36** Map C2.4 **H**
34 rue Bergère 75009 M° Rue Montmartre

This modern hotel is conveniently located for shopping in the large department stores or visiting Montmartre. Newly air-conditioned bedrooms are all double-glazed and equipped with satellite TVs, mini-bars, direct-dial telephones, safes and hairdryers. Just a few of the bathrooms have shower and WC only. 24-hour room service. ***Rooms*** *136. Amex, Diners, Mastercard, Visa.*

Le Bistrot Blanc — 400F

Tel 42 85 05 30 Map B1.5 **R**
52 rue Blanche 75009 M° Blanche/Trinité

A welcome oasis in a fairly unremarkable street. Inside, the decor, in soft shades of cream, is both inviting and homely. The latter also aptly describes the food, which is simple and mainly Provence-inspired. Begin with a garlicky *soupe au pistou*, fricassee of scallops and clams on a fondue of tomato and basil, ravioli of Brousse (cheese), stuffed artichokes *à la barigoule* or *brandade de morue* with garlic croutons. Main dishes include carefully cooked *filets de rouget en tapénade, pieds* (of lamb) *et paquets, canette aux épices* and *filet de boeuf aux gousses d'ail roties*. Straightforward, enjoyable desserts like *nougat glacé* and *merveilleux agrumes*. Service could not be more accommodating. At the time of going to press there were plans to replace the carte with two fixed-priced, two-course menus (89F & 129F) plus an à la carte dessert list. ***Seats** 40. L 12-2 D 7-10. **Closed** Sat, Sun & Aug. Amex, Mastercard, Visa.*

> The best way to get around Paris is by bus or metro –
> buy a book (carnet) of tickets at any metro station and save money

Le Bistro des Deux Théatres — 340F

Tel 45 26 41 43 **Fax 48 74 08 92** Map B1.6 **R**
18 rue Blanche 75009 M° Blanche/Trinité

The inexpensive fixed-price menu at this friendly corner bistro gets you an aperitif, three courses, wine and coffee. There's a choice of ten dishes at each stage, and in spite of the low price there's no stinting on luxury with fixtures, on an otherwise seasonally changing menu, including duck foie gras, smoked salmon, turbot with a beurre blanc sauce, grilled rump steak béarnaise, apple tart flamed with calvados and *crème brulée à la cassonade*. Set menu 169F. ***Seats** 85. L 12-2 D 7.30-12.30am. Amex, Mastercard, Visa.*

Le Bistrot Papillon — 550F

Tel 47 70 90 03 Map C2.7 **R**
6 rue Papillon 75009 M° Poissonière/Cadet

Jean-Yves Guion's classic cooking is served in the two small dining-rooms of this auberge, whose walls are covered with suede-effect claret-coloured wallpaper and tables laid with silver cutlery and crystal glass. *Andouillettes* are a major speciality, served Vallé d'Auge-style with caramelised apples, and other great favourites include foie gras with port jelly, *sole à l'orange*, salmon steak *en papillote, confit de canard*, pan-fried lamb cutlets with tarragon and *chateaubriand béarnaise*. Round things off with a 'symphony of sorbets'. Loire and Bordeaux wines take pride of place on the 100-bottle strong list. Set menu 140F. ***Seats** 60. L 12-2.30 D 7-10. **Closed** Sat, Sun, 1 week Easter & last 3 weeks Aug. Amex, Diners, Mastercard, Visa.*

Blanche Fontaine — 559F

Tel 45 26 72 32 **Fax 42 81 05 52** Map B1.8 **H**
34 rue Fontaine 75009 M° Blanche

Since it's a little way off the busy Boulevard de Clichy, the hotel is reasonably quiet, though the action at the Moulin Rouge is just two minutes walk away. All bedrooms have double-glazing, direct-dial phone, cable TV and hairdryer, and all but one have both bath and shower. Room service ends at 9.30pm but the bar remains open longer. Room price includes breakfast – served till 11.30am. Private parking for ten cars at 40F for 24 hours. ***Rooms** 49. Amex, Diners, Mastercard, Visa.*

Brébant 890F

Tel 47 70 25 55 Fax 42 46 65 70 Map C2.9 **H**
32 bd Poissonnière 75009 Mº Rue Montmartre

An early 19th-century building houses this traditional Parisian hotel, which offers comfortable accommodation in double-glazed bedrooms decorated in pastel colours with matching curtains and bedcovers. All have satellite TV, radio, direct-dial phone, mini-bar and safe, and those on the top floor boast slanting ceilings and beams. Ten rooms have shower and WC only. Breakfast is served in the Le Vieux Pressoir restaurant, which takes its name from the old Norman cider press which the owner has installed. Three lifts serve the building and seven conference rooms (max 200 people) are available. Laundry and dry cleaning service. ***Rooms** 122. Amex, Diners, Mastercard, Visa.*

Casa Olympe 500F

Tel 42 85 26 01 Fax 45 26 49 33 Map B1.10 **R**
48 rue Saint-Georges 75009 Mº St-Georges

An informal, Mediterranean atmosphere pervades this restaurant in a quiet street in northern Paris. On the well-priced menu carte, which changes according to seasons, straightforward, basic cooking is lifted by the best-quality ingredients. Typical dishes include *sardines à la vénitienne*, pumpkin soup with mussels and coriander, salmon baked with fennel and preserved lemon, chicken with artichokes and tarragon, and roast shoulder of lamb (serves 2 or 3). For dessert, a bitter chocolate *fondant* or crème brulée with coffee. Set menu 190F. ***Seats** 32. L 12-2 D 8-11. **Closed** Sat, Sun, Aug, 25 Dec & 1 Jan. Mastercard, Visa.*

La Champagne 600F

Tel 48 74 44 78 Fax 42 80 63 10 Map B1.11 **R**
10bis place de Clichy 75009 Mº Place Clichy

Essentially for fish and shellfish lovers, this large 'brasserie de luxe' on two floors with a distinctive nautical theme offers oysters, skate with brown butter and monkfish with green pepper sauce until the early hours. Wines from Chablis, Loire and Alsace feature. ***Seats** 145. L 12-3 D 7-2am. Amex, Diners, Mastercard, Visa.*

Charlot Roi des Coquillages 600F

Tel 48 74 49 64 Fax 40 16 11 00 Map B1.12 **R**
12 place de Clichy 75009 Mº Place Clichy

Mirrors in the ceiling, 20s furnishings, engraved glass, tiles and shells make a most attractive setting for Charlot, King of Shellfish. Mediterranean seafood specialities such as *moules à la provençale, bouillabaisse marseillaise*, lobsters and langoustines from Brittany or a *grand aïoli à la provençale* dominate chef Didier Lizard's menu, which varies 'according to the season, the weather and the fishermen'. Fish such as bass or red mullet might be steamed, grilled, fried, cooked in foil or poached. Shellfish is in season when the month of the year includes an 'R', so during winter try the *plateau de fruits de mer*. To accompany the Provençal dishes choose one of several wines from the region. Desserts vary from a pear crème brulée or a Grand Marnier soufflé to *crepe pralinée*. Set menu 185F. ***Seats** 140. L 12-3 D 7-1am. Amex, Diners, Mastercard, Visa.*

Chartier 170F

Tel 47 70 86 29 Map C2.13 **R**
7 rue du Faubourg Montmartre 75009 Mº Rue Montmartre

The road is largely given over to fast food outlets, but at the end of a dim courtyard a revolving door leads into another world and almost another age. Camille Chartier's creation, which celebrates its centenary this year, is a much-loved Paris institution with the look of a grand railway station and a permanent rush-hour buzz. Clusters of globe lamps shine brightly from the glass roof, huge panelled mirrors line the walls and tall copper coat racks run between and above the tables. Waiters, clad classically in black jackets and white aprons, perform with speed and efficiency, noting your order on the paper tablecloths and rushing around with heavily laden trays. The food is, in all honesty, nothing special, but prices are amazingly low and there's no better place to watch Paris eating (and no more convivial spot, as you're quite likely to have to share a table with some of 1200 who eat here each day). Starters are priced from 9F for egg mayonnaise, beetroot salad or andouille with butter to 31F for half-a-dozen snails. Main courses start at 32F for hachis parmentier (shepherd's pie) with the most expensive dish breaching the 50F barrier (it's 51F) for the first time this year; entrecote with *frites* is 90F for 2, perch with shallot sauce 49F). Chocolate mousse, compote of peaches or an ice cream could be your dessert, and with a glass or two of wine and a cup of coffee the bill for two will struggle to reach 200F. Another Chartier outlet, with a similar menu but without the atmosphere, is *Le Drouot* at 103 Rue Richelieu in the 2nd. Tel 42 96 68 23. ***Seats** 300. L 11-3 D 6-9.30. Mastercard, Visa.*

Chez Clément Opéra — 320F

Tel 47 42 00 25 **Fax 47 42 94 02**
17 bd des Capucines 75009
Map B2.14
M° Opéra
R

Popular all-day brasserie often bursting at the seams with hungry shoppers, tourists and office workers. Oysters, shellfish, spit-roasted meats and profiteroles are the house specialities, along with hare terrine, bone marrow with salt, moules marinière and knuckle of pork with lentils. The oysters, meats and profiteroles are served *à volonté* for, respectively, 135F, 75F and 38F, and if you order the excellent camembert, you can help yourself from a board left on the table. Other Chez Cléments are in the 8th (123 ave des Champs Elysées Tel 40 73 87 00) and 17th (99 bd Gouvion-St-Cyr Tel 45 72 93 00). ***Seats** 200. Meals noon-1am. Mastercard, Visa.*

Copthorne Commodore — 1250F

Tel 42 46 72 82 **Fax 47 70 23 81**
12 bd Haussmann 75009
Map C2.16
M° Richelieu-Drouot
H

Enjoying a prime location midway between the Opéra and the Bourse (Stock Exchange) near the major department stores, this Copthorne hotel, built in 1927 in Italian rococo style, offers a high standard of comfort and service. Bedrooms are decorated in pastel shades with blue walls, grey carpet, floral curtains and furniture in the style of the roaring twenties; all have well-appointed en suite bathrooms and the usual facilities including mini-bar and satellite TV. More luxurious Connoisseur rooms come with various other extras at a 200F supplement. The glass-domed Carvery is open for breakfast and a buffet lunch. The Cancans bar/brasserie is an alternative option for lunch or dinner à la carte. Three meeting rooms, maximum capacity 28. Room service till 11pm. ***Rooms** 162. Amex, Diners, Mastercard, Visa.*

Le Grand Café Capucines

Tel 47 42 19 00 **Fax 47 42 74 22**
4 bd des Capucines 75009
Map B2.17
M° Opéra
R

An elegant brasserie with a breathtaking art deco interior of enormous mirrors and walls covered with tiles painted with Mucha drawings, sculpted stair railings and lights in the form of giant shells. It's open day and night, and fish and shellfish are a major draw – the options, both à la carte and fixed-price, are many and varied; the shellfish platter is a meal in itself, and other specialities include carpaccio of monkfish and salmon with dill, seafood tagliatelle, veal kidney with Meaux mustard, rump steak with shallots, champagne sorbet and chocolate mousse. After 11pm and until dawn there's a special late-night, fixed-price menu of 119F offering two courses and a drink. Set menus 118F & 180F. ***Open** 24 hours. Amex, Diners, Mastercard, Visa.*

GRAND HOTEL INTER-CONTINENTAL — 3040F

Tel 40 07 32 32 **Fax 42 66 12 51** Map B2.18 **HR**
2 rue Scribe 75009 Mº Auber/Opéra

Built during the Napoleon III era, this luxurious and elegant hotel is located on a corner of Place de l'Opéra, opposite the Opera House. The cental reception room, the Cour d'Honneur, is a marble-floored lounge under a huge steel and glass dome. Bedrooms include 25 spacious suites. Business facilities are particularly impressive with 18 conference rooms available for meetings of between eight and 500 people. 24-hour room service. Private parking 150F. Gymnasium. Sauna. Solarium. ***Rooms** 514. Amex, Diners, Mastercard, Visa.*

Restaurant Opéra — 800F

Tel 40 07 30 10 **Fax 40 07 33 75**
5 place de l'Opéra

This fabulously opulent restaurant, decorated in blue and gold, with its famous ceiling painted with stylised cherubs and clouds, is an appropriate setting for grand gourmet food. Truffles, lobster, foie gras and other luxury ingredients dominate a list of starters which includes Périgord chestnut cream and foie gras flan, and warm fillet of squab and truffle pie. Fish dishes are particularly fine: sea bass roasted with almonds and served with fennel purée flavoured with coriander, and crispy fillet of pike-perch with green olive cream. Surprisingly, the restaurant has recently halved the prices of all the wines on their extensive list in order to make good wine more accessible. An excellent bottle can now be had for around 100F. ***Seats** 75. L 12-3 D 7-11. **Closed** Sat, Sun, Aug & 1 week in Jan.*

Brasserie du Café de la Paix — 400F

Tel 40 07 30 20
12 bd des Capucines

Guests take breakfast in the brasserie, which runs along two sides of the hotel. It has been a popular meeting place since it opened 130 years ago and is decorated with fine 19th-century wall and ceiling frescoes. In season, oysters are a speciality on the traditional menu, which also includes dishes such as steak tartare and grilled salmon with béarnaise sauce. The glass-roofed pavement terrace is a great place for eating, drinking and people-watching. Set menu 138F. ***Seats** 220. **Meals** noon-1.15am.*

HOTEL DU LÉMAN — 450F

Tel 42 46 50 66 **Fax 48 24 27 59** Map C2.19 **H**
20 rue de Trévise 75009 Mº Cadet

A small modernised hotel with double-glazing and a cosy cellar-like breakfast room with a buffet breakfast till 10.30. Bedrooms, some with beams, are neatly decorated and extras provided include video, stereo and mini-bar. Bathrooms all have showers over tubs. Dry cleaning and laundry service. Parking at a small discount (80F for 24 hours) in a garage just 30 metres away. ***Rooms** 24. Amex, Diners, Mastercard, Visa.*

LIBERTEL LAFAYETTE — 885F

Tel 42 85 05 44 **Fax 49 95 06 60** Map C2.15 **H**
49 rue Lafayette 75009 Mº Cadet/Le Peletier

Formerly called Cidotel Lafayette, this hotel located between Opéra and the Sacré Coeur has just grown in to the next-door building adding 28 new air-conditioned bedrooms, a bar and large atrium lobby. The original part of the building has also benefited from a total refurbishment. Some rooms have little balconies and all have cable TV, mini-bar, safe, trouser press, hairdryer and tea and coffee-making kit. Most have both bath and shower in the en suite facilities. Accommodation includes six larger Superior rooms and six suites. One floor is designated no-smoking. The hotel offers laundry, dry cleaning and photographic developing services plus room service of both lunch and dinner although there is no restaurant. ***Rooms** 103. Amex, Diners, Mastercard, Visa.*

Libertel le Moulin 785F

Tel 42 81 93 25 **Fax 40 16 09 90** Map B1.20 **H**
39 rue Fontaine 75009 Mº Blanche

A new name (formerly Hotel du Moulin Rouge), but nothing else has changed at this attractive modern hotel that's part of a small group. Located a short distance from the Moulin Rouge in a pleasant street, it features smartly decorated bedrooms, some with balconies but all with mini-bars, cable TV and up-to-date marble-lined bathrooms of which just over half have shower and WC only. Laundry and dry cleaning can be arranged and there is room service at lunchtime and from 6.30 to 10.45 in the evening. ***Rooms** 50. Amex, Diners, Mastercard, Visa.*

L'Oenothèque 650F

Tel 48 78 08 76 Map C1.21 **R**
20 rue St Lazare 75009 Mº Notre Dame de Lorette

Wine and cognac merchant Daniel Hallé runs this splendid 'restaurant à vins', which is divided into two air-conditioned rooms. The first is full of bottle-laden shelves, while the second is decorated with paintings (for sale) by contemporary artists. There are 350 references on the all-French wine list, while the short menu changes on a daily basis according to what's best in the market. *Foie gras de canard, pétoncles tièdes* (small scallops) or *bavarois de poivrons* could precede rack of lamb, grilled veal kidney, *andouillette* in red wine or fillet of rascasse with lemon butter. Roast pigeon is something of a speciality. To finish, perhaps a fruit tart, chocolate marquise or crème brulée. ***Seats** 40. L 12-2.30 D 7.30-10.30. **Closed** Sat, Sun, last 3 weeks Aug & 1 week Feb. Mastercard, Visa.*

Opéra Cadet 780F

Tel 48 24 05 26 **Fax 42 46 68 09** Map C2.22 **H**
24 rue Cadet 75009 Mº Cadet

A modern hotel in a building located in a semi-pedestrianised street. The buffet breakfast is taken in a conservatory overlooking a plant-filled garden. The air-conditioned rooms offer en suite bathrooms (all with tub and shower), satellite TV, direct-dial telephone and mini-bar. A lounge bar is open all day and there are two conference rooms (max 40). Private parking (8 reservable spaces – 60F a day). Laundry service. ***Rooms** 85. Amex, Diners, Mastercard, Visa.*

Au Petit Riche 490F

Tel 47 70 68 68 **Fax 48 24 10 79** Map C2.23 **R**
25 rue Le Peletier 75009 Mº Richelieu-Drouot

Engraved glass, mirrors and wood give the correct period look to this 19th-century bistro, where good food is matched by fine wines (the Loire features very strongly). A plate of oysters, *terrine de canard, salade gourmande*, and a salad of goat's cheese are typical starters, while the main-course choice might include poached haddock *à l'aigre-doux,* tuna with ratatouille niçoise, *magret* or *confit de canard, andouillette* with Vouvray or grilled entrecote with three mustards. End with farmhouse cheeses, crème brulée, *nougat glacé* or the speciality *tarte fine aux pommes tièdes*. There are four private rooms upstairs for 8-45 people. Set menu 160F. ***Seats** 110. L 12-2.15 D 7-12.15am. **Closed** Sun. Amex, Diners, Mastercard, Visa.*

Hotel du Pré 545F

Tel 42 81 37 11 **Fax 40 23 98 28** Map D1.24 **H**
10 rue Pierre Sémard 75009 Mº Poissonnière/Cadet

Turn-of-the-century building, renovated about a dozen years ago, in the same street as a pretty little public park. It's peaceful, comfortable and family-run, with big beds and good bathrooms (all but two have both tub and shower). Buffet breakfast 50F. 24-hour reception. No room service. No restaurant. Madame du Pré also owns, in the same street, the **Relais du Pré**

See over

(Tel 42 85 19 59 Fax 42 85 70 59) and the **Résidence du Pré** (Tel 48 78 26 72 Fax 42 80 64 83). The hotels are between Gare du Nord and Opéra. Adjacent to a public car park where hotel guests enjoy a special rate of 60F for 24 hours. ***Rooms*** *41. Amex, Diners, Mastercard, Visa.*

RIBOUTTÉ-LAFAYETTE 450F

Tel 47 70 62 36 **Fax 48 00 91 50** Map C2.25 **H**
5 rue Riboutté (corner 82 rue Lafayette) 75009 Mº Cadet

A small, inexpensive and tastefully decorated hotel in a tiny street well placed for the area's department stores. The rooms are individually decorated, with en suite facilities (eight with shower and WC only) and a few have a view of Square Montholon nearby. 24-hour reception. Special tariff (80F per day) at a nearby garage. ***Rooms*** *24. Amex, Mastercard, Visa.*

LE ROYAL VIGNON "LE ROI DU POT-AU-FEU" 300F

Tel 47 42 37 10 Map A2.29 **R**
34 rue Vignon 75009 Mº Madeleine/Havre-Caumartin

Pot-au-feu is the speciality at this most convivial little bistro with a well-worn, slightly kitsch look of the 30s. First comes a bowl of steaming broth, then a generous plateful of meat and marrow bone and vegetables, accompanied by cornichons, mustard and coarse salt. ***Seats*** *40. Meals 12-10.30.* ***Closed*** *Sun & Public Holidays. Mastercard, Visa.*

SCRIBE 2200F

Tel 44 71 24 24 **Fax 42 65 39 97** Map B2.26 **HR**
1 rue Scribe 75009 Mº Opéra

A major corner site, formerly the Jockey Club, whose Napoleon III facade today conceals a busy, cosmopolitan hotel. Refurbishment over recent years has extended from the spacious lobby with its Baccarat crystal chandeliers and the luxurious, softly-lit cocktail bar to the bedrooms. Things like air-conditioning, double-glazing (for streetside rooms) and endless TV channels provide the modern comforts for rooms that are mostly furnished in Louis Philippe or Louis XVI style, although some rooms are in 'English' style and there are some suites, featuring mezzanine bedroom floors, that are more contemporary in concept. One floor of rooms is designated non-smoking. Two conference rooms. ***Rooms*** *217. Amex, Diners, Mastercard, Visa.*

Les Muses 700F

Tel 44 71 24 26

Guests at this sophisticated restaurant sit at round tables in sombre surroundings of wood panelling, black lacquer, mirrors and bouquets of flowers. The cooking is a mix of classic and modern: warm salad of sea bass in a watercress-infused oil; prawns in puff pastry with herbs and satay; lamb en *crépinette* with savory, young carrots and mushrooms; mignons of veal with asparagus and candied tomato; cinnamon-flavoured crème brulée; peanut crisp with peaches and rhubarb served with wild strawberries. Set menus 210F & 270F. ***Seats*** *40. L 12-2.30 D 7.30-10.30.* ***Closed*** *Sat, Sun, Aug & Bank Holidays.*

LA TABLE D'ANVERS ★ 900F

Tel 48 78 35 21 **Fax 45 26 66 67** Map C1.27 **R**
2 place d'Anvers 75009 Mº Anvers

Christian Conticini is the *cuisinier* and his brother Philippe the *patissier* at this restaurant overlooking the square. Christian is known for the original way in which he mixes spices, condiments, oils and vinegars in dishes that regularly feature vegetables, mushrooms and pastas. Fresh foie gras comes with *fleur de sel et pain grillé à l'huile d'olive*; red mullet with capers, parsley, lavender and risotto milanese; turbot is roasted with olive oil, haricot beans, broad beans, girolles and saffron, and veal sweetbreads come in a dish with grilled aubergine and tomato flavoured with liquorice. The special mushroom section of the carte menu might include a warm salad of potato with girolles, cheese and ham, turbot roasted with ceps and bacon, sweetbreads grilled with figs, *trompettes* and wine, pigeon with ceps and chestnuts, and a fricassee of various wild mushroonms with a nut coulis. Philippe's crafted desserts may include some irresistible chocolate creations and a *passion créole* (soaked biscuit, vanilla ice cream, rum, pineapple, pepper and coconut). On arriving at your table, choose as an aperitif a glass of one of fifteen regional wines; to clean the palate between courses the Conticini brothers offer unusual 'parfums à boire' (hot or cold drinks flavoured with hibiscus, star anise, sage or cinnamon). The extensive wine list includes a number of Italian wines and several *vins de pays*. Among the several fixed-price menus is a special Dessert Menu that brings one savoury dish followed by three desserts (*en surprise*) with four glasses of *vin doux naturel* and four *infusions*. Set L 180F Set D 190F (vegetarian), 250F, 450F (dessert) & 550F (*dégustation*). ***Seats*** *50. L 12-2.45 D 7-11.30.* ***Closed*** *L Sat, all Sun. Amex, Mastercard, Visa.*

WALLY LE SAHARIEN 600F

Tel 42 85 51 90 **Fax 45 86 08 35** Map C1.28 **R**
36 rue Rodier 75009 M° Anvers

In the 9th, just as in the 4th until a couple of years ago, Wally Shouaki entices old friends and new with his unique *menu dégustation*. There's no written menu, and the food just starts arriving once you are seated. First comes *harira* (a hearty vegetable soup) then pigeon pastilla before sardines stuffed with herbs and onion. The main event is couscous accompanied by *méchoui* and excellent merguez but with no bouillon and no vegetables; dessert is a delicate gateau with a fresh orange coulis and as much mint tea as you want. Wines from North Africa naturally accompany the food at this splendid oasis in a gastronomic semi-desert. Set menu 240F. ***Seats*** *45. L 12-2.30 D 7.30-11.30.* ***Closed*** *Sun, 1st week Jan & 1 week early Sep. No credit cards.*

10th Arrondissement
Places of Interest

Musée de Cristalleries de Baccarat, 47 70 64 30,
M^O Chateau d'Eau
Place de la République

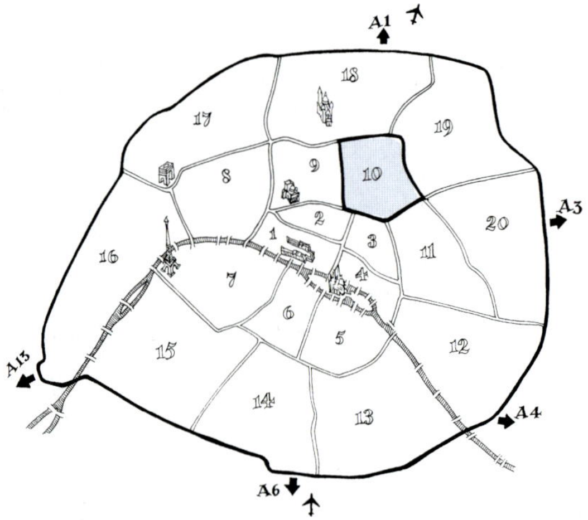

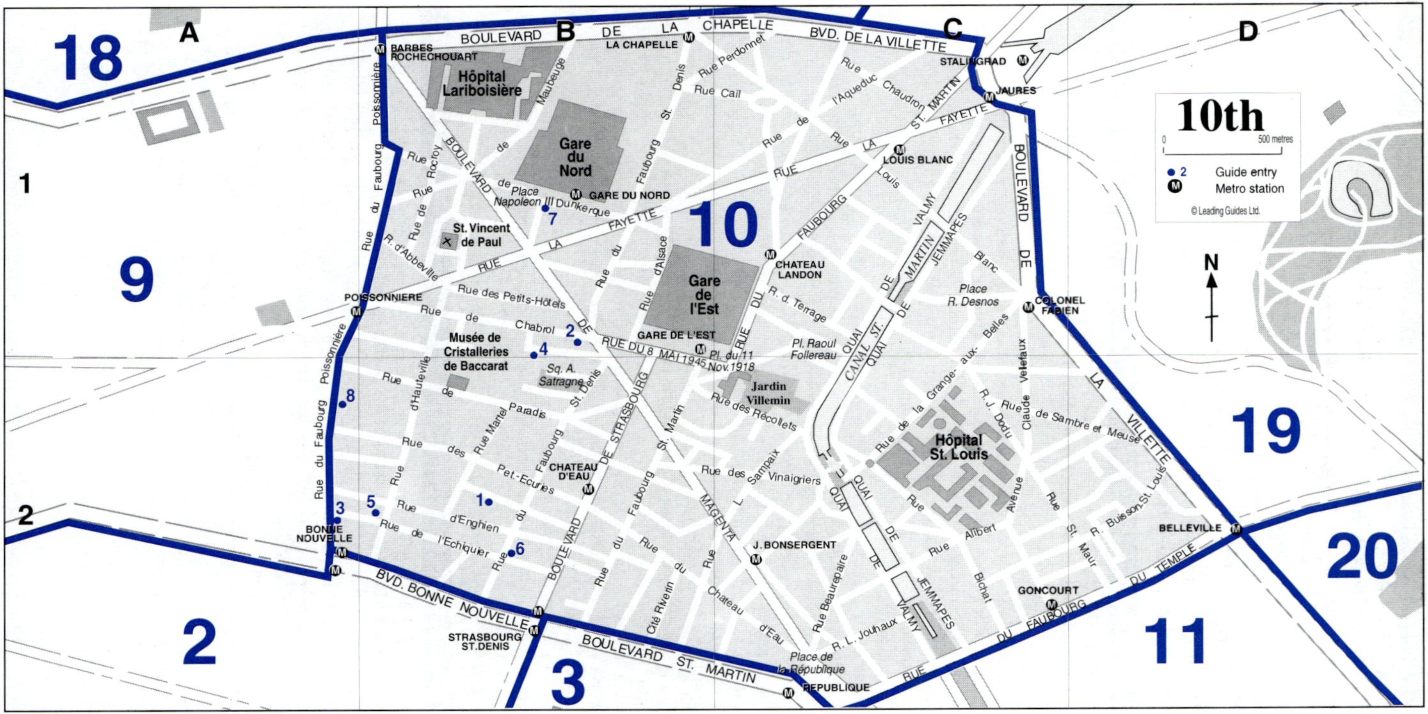
10th
0
500 metres
2 Guide entry
Metro station
© Leading Guides Ltd.
N
A
B
C
D
1
2
18
9
10
19
20
11
2
3
BOULEVARD DE LA CHAPELLE
BVD. DE LA VILLETTE
BOULEVARD DE LA VILLETTE
BVD. BONNE NOUVELLE
BOULEVARD ST. MARTIN
BOULEVARD DE STRASBOURG
BOULEVARD DE MAGENTA
RUE LA FAYETTE
RUE DU FAUBOURG ST. MARTIN
RUE DU FAUBOURG DU TEMPLE
QUAI DE VALMY
QUAI DE JEMMAPES
CANAL ST. MARTIN
RUE DU 8 MAI 1945
Hôpital Lariboisière
Gare du Nord
Gare de l'Est
St. Vincent de Paul
Musée de Cristalleries de Baccarat
Jardin Villemin
Hôpital St. Louis
BARBES ROCHECHOUART
LA CHAPELLE
STALINGRAD
JAURES
LOUIS BLANC
GARE DU NORD
CHATEAU LANDON
COLONEL FABIEN
POISSONNIERE
GARE DE L'EST
CHATEAU D'EAU
J. BONSERGENT
BONNE NOUVELLE
STRASBOURG ST.DENIS
REPUBLIQUE
GONCOURT
BELLEVILLE
Rue du Faubourg Poissonnière
Rue de Maubeuge
Rue du Faubourg St. Denis
Rue Perdonnet
Rue Cail
Rue de l'Aqueduc
Rue Chaudron
Rue Louis Blanc
Rue de Rocroy
Rue de Dunkerque
Place Napoleon III
R. d'Abbeville
Rue des Petits-Hôtels
Rue de Chabrol
Rue d'Alsace
R. d. Terrage
Pl. Raoul Follereau
Pl. du 11 Nov. 1918
Sq. A. Satragne
Rue d'Hauteville
Rue de Paradis
Rue Martel
Rue des Pet.-Ecuries
Rue d'Enghien
Rue de l'Echiquier
Rue des Récollets
Rue des Vinaigriers
Rue L. Sampaix
Rue du Château d'Eau
Cité Riverin
Rue Beaurepaire
R. L. Jouhaux
Place de la République
Place R. Desnos
Rue Claude Vellefaux
Rue de la Grange-aux-Belles
R. J. Dodu
Rue de Sambre et Meuse
Avenue Richerand
Rue Alibert
Rue Bichat
Rue St. Maur
R. Buisson St. Louis
1
2
3
4
5
6
7
8

Au Chateaubriant 550F

Tel 48 24 58 94 Map B1.2 **R**
23 rue de Chabrol 75010 Mº Poissonnière/Gare de l'Est

A fine collection of modern prints fills the walls of this warm, stylish little restaurant, where owner-chef Guy Bürkli belies its name by offering Italian cuisine both traditional and adventurous. In the first category come garlic mushrooms, *scampi fritti, penne all'arrabbiata, osso buco* and *tournedos Rossini*, in the latter lasagne with aubergines and sardines, cod steak with confit tomatoes, millefeuille of veal and *croustillant de tete de veau* with capers. Charming service by Madame Bürkli. Set menu 159F (including aperitif). ***Seats*** *40. L 12.15-2.30 D 7.30-10.15.* ***Closed*** *Sun, Mon & Aug. Amex, Mastercard, Visa.*

Aux Deux Canards 410F

Tel 47 70 03 23 **Map A2.3** **R**
8 rue du Faubourg Poissonnière 75010 Mº Bonne Nouvelle

A stable door (opened from the inside) leads from the busy street into a little haven of brass and mirrors and traditional French cooking by Bernard Ferec, a chef who rarely leaves his kitchen. The menu, which changes daily, is written on a blackboard and the voluble patron Gérard Faesch uses an extending blackboard pointer to explain at length what is on offer. (The prelude is a demonstration – sniffing included – of how they make and mature the orange honey which is an integral part of their *Barbary duck à l'orange* and chocolate mousse.) Foie gras with blueberry sauce is a permanent feature on a carte that generally follows the seasons, other choices run from *pétoncles* (little scallops) and dill-marinated salmon to *salade lyonnaise* (pork, onions, potatoes, leaves), duck terrine, veal kidneys, pig's trotters with mustard and bone marrow, *moules de bouchot* served out of their shells with hollandaise sauce, Fisherman's Dream (boned sardines grilled with basil sauce), *andouillette* and *faux filet béarnaise*. Salmon is served with two sauces – beurre blanc and beurre rouge. Munster and other cheeses, *gateau de crepe soufflé, crème brulée* (burnt at the table with a hot iron from the kitchen), *gratin de fruits sabayon,* or *oeuf à la neige* could round off the meal – or, of course, that chocolate mousse. A place full of atmosphere, run by a real enthusiast who personally oversees the ordering of wines – look for some blackboard bargains. Conviviality is guaranteed not only by the patron but also by the piano, which guests can play when the mood takes them. Having succumbed to commercial pressure, this is no longer a completely non-smoking restaurant. Set menu 110F. ***Seats*** *50. L 12-2 D 7-10. (Fri & Sat to 10.30).* ***Closed*** *L Sat, all Sun & Aug. Amex, Diners, Mastercard, Visa.*

Brasserie Flo 450F

Tel 47 70 13 59 **Fax 42 47 00 80** Map B2.1 **R**
7 cour des Petites-Ecuries 75010 Mº Chateau d'Eau/Strasbourg St Denis

The site has been a tavern/brasserie since 1886 and to the present day parquet flooring, leather banquettes, the original darkwood panelling and coffered ceiling remain. The decor sets off the colourful pictures and frescoes that evoke scenes related to the brewing of beer and landscapes of the Alsace region. Once called Hans, it changed its name after passing into the hands of the Floderer family, who owned it until 1964. Seafood is a major speciality – oysters, clams, crab, mussels, prawns, langoustines – which you can order piecemeal or in various platters. The menu changes on a very regular basis, but *foie gras gelée au Riesling*, steak tartare, grills and choucroute are among the favourites. The starter of the day might be smoked salmon with dill or *caviar d'aubergine à la provençale* and dishes such as *tripes à la mode de Caen, coq au Riesling* and fillets of red mullet with a rosemary-flavoured cream sauce typify the *plats du jour*. The entrance to the courtyard is at 63 Rue du Faubourg St-Denis. Valet parking in the evening. Set L 112F Set D 189F (and 112F after 10pm). ***Seats*** *140. L 12-3 D 7-1.30am.* ***Closed*** *D 24 Dec. Amex, Diners, Mastercard, Visa.*

FLORA — 595F

Tel 48 24 84 84 **Fax 48 00 91 03** Map B1.4 **H**
1-3 cour de la Ferme-Saint-Lazare Mº Gare de l'Est
(corner 79 bd Magenta) 75010

Being close to both Gare du Nord and Gare de l'Est, there's easy access to areas to the north and east of Paris (especially airports and ferries and the Tunnel). The hotel is pleasantly decorated in pastel colours and offers functional en suite (half with baths, half with showers) accommodation. There's no restaurant, but breakfast is served in a vaulted stone cellar. ***Rooms*** *45. Amex, Diners, Mastercard, Visa.*

L'HORSET PAVILLON — 930F

Tel 42 46 92 75 **Fax 42 47 03 97** Map B2.5 **H**
38 rue de l'Echiquier 75010 Mº Strasbourg St Denis/Bonne Nouvelle

In 1593, when the building was in forested land outside the city walls, it was used as a hunting lodge by Henri IV. He then gave it to a religious order, who were forced to hand it over to the State during the French Revolution. From the basement, subterranean passages led to the town. In 1850 it became a hotel. Located in a quiet street in the area known as 'Les Grands Boulevards', this is one of five L'Horset hotels in Paris. Genuine Belle Epoque stained glass, frescoes and wooden panelling fill the reception rooms and the fully-equipped bedrooms (air-conditioning, mini-bar, safe, cable TV, bath and shower) are done out in keeping with this era. ***Rooms*** *92. Amex, Diners, Mastercard, Visa.*

JULIEN — 450F

Tel 47 70 12 06 **Fax 42 47 00 65** Map B2.6 **R**
16 rue du Faubourg St Denis 75010 Mº Gare de l'Est

Built in 1889 but not opened until 1903; the public had a long wait to appreciate Fournier's art nouveau interior for which the establishment has now been classified a historic monument. The artist Louis Trezel, who was passionate about the theatre and modern art, painted an astonishing decor of women and flowers in the style of Mucha on glass panels on the walls of the entire brasserie; another eye-catching feature is a magnificent mahogany counter. In the same family as *Brasserie Flo* (see above), with a daily-changing menu virtually the same but without the choucroute and shellfish specialities. Popular orders include smoked salmon, foie gras, terrine of skate with tomato coulis, grills, confit and cassoulet. Set L 112F Set D 112F (after 10). ***Seats*** *180. L 12-3 D 7-1.30am.* ***Closed*** *D 24 Dec. Amex, Diners, Mastercard, Visa.*

LA P'TITE TONKINOISE — 400F

Tel 42 46 85 98 Map A2.8 **R**
56 rue du Faubourg Poissonnière 75010 Mº Poissonnière/Bonne Nouvelle

Long-established Vietnamese restaurant with red plush seating and bamboo-clad walls on which a photo of Henri Costa's former restaurant in Hai-Phong takes pride of place. Henri, along with his wife Odette, presides over La P'tite Tonkinoise (Tonkin is an area of northern Vietnam) with delightfully old-fashioned politeness and civility while son Michel cooks to the sensibly short carte, set out by courses in Western style. To start try some of his excellent steamed 'ravioli' topped with crisply-fried onion and fresh basil or traditional nems (spring rolls). The dozen or so mains, served with a bowl of rice from which you serve yourself with a scallop shell, might include stuffed chicken wings in a curry sauce, brochettes of grilled prawns, crab claws with red peppers and beef with two varieties of mushroom. A handful of wines, Tsing-Tau beer or good jasmine tea to drink. Set L 133F. ***Seats*** *40. L 12-2 D 7.30-10.* ***Closed*** *Sun, Mon & Aug-mid Sep. Mastercard, Visa.*

Terminus Nord 500F

Tel 42 85 05 15 **Fax 40 16 13 98** Map B1.7 **R**
23 rue Dunkerque 75010 Mº Gare du Nord

Directly across from the imposing facade of Gare du Nord this classic 20s brasserie is the perfect first or last stop on a Eurostar train journey or a channel port trip. There's something for everyone on the splendidly traditional, daily-changing menus. There's even a menu for children (main dish, dessert and a drink 62F). The fixed-price menus represent good value, too, with a choice of starter and main or main and dessert with an inclusive half-bottle of wine. House specialities are numerous, including tarama with toasted country bread and goose foie gras with Riesling jelly among the starters, and as a main dish, choucroute several ways and lamb's sweetbreads in puff pastry with a champagne sauce. Classic dishes include entrecote steak or chateaubriand, both with béarnaise sauce, and lamb noisettes with tarragon. The selection of seafood (shellfish make an eye-catching and mouthwatering display outside) is superb – do ask for the separate menu. Prepared fish dishes could include warm oysters in a champagne sauce, Scottish salmon with crisply cooked skin accompanied by wild mushrooms, and monkfish medallions with baby vegetables. Service from well-drilled, smartly attired staff is serious. Set menus 112F & 189F. Also open for breakfast, teas and coffees. Pavement terrace. ***Seats*** *200.* ***Open*** *11am-12.30am. Amex, Diners, Mastercard, Visa.*

11th Arrondissement
Places of Interest

Place de la Bastille/Opéra Bastille
Place de la République
Musée Edith Piaf, 43 55 52 72, M° Ménilmontant

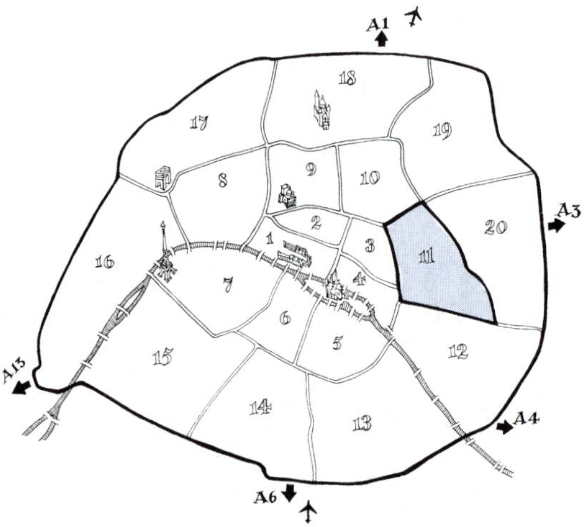

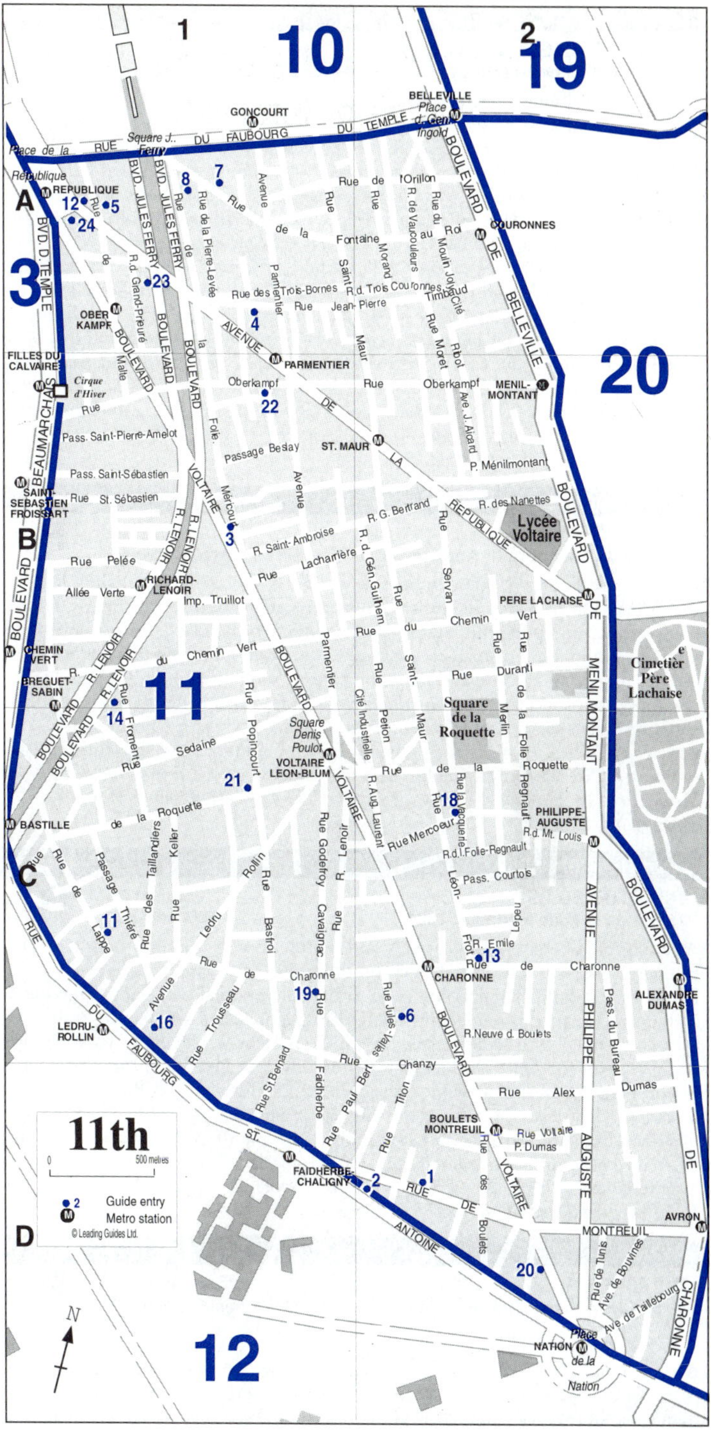
11th
0
500 metres
2 Guide entry
M Metro station
© Leading Guides Ltd.
N
A
B
C
D
1
2
3
10
11
12
19
20
GONCOURT
BELLEVILLE
Place d. Genl. Ingold
Place de la République
Square J. Ferry
RUE DU FAUBOURG DU TEMPLE
REPUBLIQUE
BVD. D. TEMPLE
BVD. JULES FERRY
Rue de la Pierre-Levée
Avenue Parmentier
Rue de la Fontaine au Roi
Rue de l'Orillon
R. de Vaucouleurs
Rue du Moulin Joly
Rue Saint Maur
Rue Morand
BOULEVARD DE BELLEVILLE
COURONNES
R.d. Grand-Prieuré
Rue des Trois-Bornes
R.d. Trois Couronnes
Rue Jean-Pierre Timbaud
Cité Ribot
Rue Moret
OBERKAMPF
AVENUE DE LA REPUBLIQUE
PARMENTIER
BOULEVARD RICHARD LENOIR
FILLES DU CALVAIRE
Cirque d'Hiver
Rue de Malte
Rue Oberkampf
MENIL-MONTANT
Ave. J. Aicard
BOULEVARD BEAUMARCHAIS
Pass. Saint-Pierre-Amelot
Pass. Saint-Sébastien
Passage Beslay
ST. MAUR
P. Ménilmontant
SAINT-SEBASTIEN FROISSART
Rue St. Sébastien
Rue Folie Méricourt
R. des Nanettes
Lycée Voltaire
R. G. Bertrand
R. Saint-Ambroise
Rue Lacharrière
R. d. Gén. Guilhem
Rue Servan
Rue Pelée
Allée Verte
RICHARD-LENOIR
Imp. Truillot
PERE LACHAISE
Rue du Chemin Vert
CHEMIN VERT
R. LENOIR
BREGUET-SABIN
Rue Popincourt
BOULEVARD VOLTAIRE
Rue Duranti
Rue de la Folie Regnault
Rue Merlin
Cimetière Père Lachaise
Square de la Roquette
Rue Froment
Rue Sedaine
Square Denis Poulot
VOLTAIRE LEON-BLUM
Cité Industrielle
Rue Petion
Rue de la Roquette
BOULEVARD DE MENILMONTANT
BASTILLE
R. Aug. Laurent
Rue la Vacquerie
Rue Mercoeur
PHILIPPE-AUGUSTE
R.d. Mt. Louis
R.d.l.Folie-Regnault
Pass. Courtois
Rue Léon-Frot
R. Emile Lepeu
Rue de Lappe
Passage Thiéré
Rue des Taillandiers
Rue Keller
Avenue Ledru Rollin
Rue Rollin
Rue Bastroi
Rue Godefroy Cavaignac
R. Lenoir
Rue de Charonne
CHARONNE
AVENUE PHILIPPE AUGUSTE
ALEXANDRE DUMAS
Pass. du Bureau
LEDRU-ROLLIN
RUE DU FAUBOURG ST. ANTOINE
Rue Trousseau
Rue Jules-Vallès
R.Neuve d. Boulets
Rue Chanzy
Rue St.Bernard
Rue Faidherbe
Rue Paul Bert
Rue Titon
Rue Alex Dumas
BOULEVARD DE CHARONNE
BOULETS MONTREUIL
Rue Voltaire
P. Dumas
FAIDHERBE-CHALIGNY
RUE DE Boulets
Rue des Boulets
MONTREUIL
AVRON
Rue de Tunis
Ave. de Bouvines
Ave. de Taillebourg
NATION
Place de la Nation
1
2
3
4
5
6
7
8
11
12
13
14
16
18
19
20
21
22
23
24

L'AIGUIÈRE 700F

Tel 43 72 42 32 **Fax 43 72 86 36** Map D2.1 **R**
37bis rue de Montreuil 75011 M° Nation/Faidherbe-Chaligny

New decor, following a fire last year, is in fresh shades of yellow, blue and white but still boasts lots of fresh flowers, and the restaurant remains a comfortable and elegant setting. *Aiguières* were originally pewter receptacles for water until Louis XIII had them made in glass and used them for wine when he dined here with his musketeers. To this day, *grands crus* wines are served in them at L'Aiguière. Chef Pascal Viallet adapts traditional recipes to modern-day tastes in dishes which show many innovative touches. The foie gras is home-prepared and one of the main-course specialities is *tournedos Yella* (fillet of Charolais beef with foie gras, sweetbreads and a Périgord sauce with truffles) which could be followed by another speciality, *feuillantine de poire en chaud froid*. Other dishes might include *terrine de gibier sauce Cumberland, cassolette de pétoncles et escargots à la nage au pistou du safran*, duck foie gras roasted with *vin de pissenlit* (dandelion wine) and *délice de glace à la fleur d'orchidée*. A la carte plus set menus at 135F (with half bottle of wine), 175F & 248F. The last (248F) menu offers a different glass of wine with each course. ***Seats** 80. L 12-2.30 D 7.30-10.30.* ***Closed** L Sat, all Sun. Amex, Diners, Mastercard, Visa.*

LES AMOGNES 480F

Tel 43 72 73 05 Map D2.2 **R**
243 rue du Faubourg St Antoine 75011 M° Faidherbe-Chaligny

Chef-owner Thierry Coué describes his cuisine as *du terroir* but slightly lighter than usual. His generous menu is a four-course affair with six choices of starters, main courses and puddings. Start with *beignets de brandade de morue* with fried sage leaves and confit tomatoes, *pétoncles aux carottes à la crème à l'aneth* or boudin noir in filo pastry, and move on to tuna with artichokes, peppers and coriander; roast monkfish *en persillade* with stuffed courgettes or oxtail-stuffed cèpes or a very special *cote de boeuf* with *truffade auvergnate*. For dessert, perhaps a feuilleté of pears with a spiced wine granita, or roast figs stuffed with red berries. French-only wine list with fair prices that match the cost of the food. *Menu carte* 180F. ***Seats** 40. L 12.30-2.30 D 7.30-11.* ***Closed** Sun & Mon. Mastercard, Visa.*

ANJOU-NORMANDIE 400F

Tel 47 00 30 59 Map B1.3 **R**
13 rue de la Folie Méricourt 75011 M° St-Ambroise

A setting of auberge quaint-cosiness: old beams, flowery curtains, assorted landscapes, seascapes and foodscapes on the walls, crisp white table linen, candles in old pewter holders. Speciality meat dishes (all seasoned with *sel de Guérande* and ground pepper) are *andouillettes* (grilled plain, grilled and flamed with calvados, grilled with shallots, baked with Comté cheese), *confit de canard*, tripe and *filet de boeuf*. Start with feuilleté of mussels or Roquefort, or *terrines maison* – you help yourself from three king-size terrines. Tarte tatin is the recommended dessert. Coffee is served with a Valrhona chocolate and a cracked fresh hazelnut – a charming touch to end a satisfying meal. Good sound cooking by Alain Langevin, service led by his wife Monique. They've been here 20 years. Set menus 137F, 165F & 60F (*menu enfant*). ***Seats** 23 (+ 30 for lunch). L 12-1.45 D 7.30-9.30.* ***Closed** D Mon, all Sat, Sun & Aug. Mastercard, Visa.*

ASTIER 380F

Tel 43 57 16 35 Map A1.4 **R**
44 rue Jean-Pierre Timbaud 75011 M° Oberkampf/Parmentier

A very popular and convivial neighbourhood bistro on two floors with a particularly appealing 135F menu for lunch or supper. The cooking is in traditional bistro style, and some of the most popular dishes are *terrine de poisson beurre blanc* , whelks with aïoli, salmon with tarragon, roast turbot with béarnaise sauce, *tete de veau vinaigrette* , sauté of hare with fresh pasta, confit of duck leg, sautéed lamb with flageolets, and *saucisse de Morteau* with lentils. The ravenous will help themselves from an excellent 20-strong cheese tray before rounding off with pears in red wine, *clafoutis* or a very refreshing terrine of orange and grapefruit. A very comprehensive (about 200 bins) and reasonably-priced wine list features many of the best growers – quite exceptional for such an unassuming place. This is a really good traditional restaurant, where the staff want you to have a jolly time whether you're a regular or a first-timer. Set menu 135F. ***Seats*** *80. L 12-2 D 8-11.* ***Closed*** *Sat, Sun, 2 weeks Easter, all Aug & 2 weeks Christmas. Mastercard, Visa.*

CARTET 550F

Tel 48 05 17 65 Map A1.5 **R**
62 rue de Malte 75011 Mº République

Raymond Nouaille, chef-owner of this tiny bistro with its 1930s decor of wood-panelled walls, mirrors, pictures and floor tiles, specialises in regional dishes from the Lyons area. *Pieds de mouton sauce poulette* or *sauce rémoulade*, crab soufflé, *quenelles de brochet, gras double flambé*, monkfish *sauce Nantua, cote de veau aux morilles* and *boeuf à la ficelle* are typical choices. Choose from the six classic desserts (lemon tart, crème caramel, chocolate mousse and floating islands are some examples) displayed on the small bar. ***Seats*** *18. L 12-2 D 7.30-9.30.* ***Closed*** *Sat, Sun, 8 days Mar, all Aug & 8 days Christmas. No credit cards.*

CHARDENOUX 500F

Tel 43 71 49 52 Map C2.6 **R**
1 rue Jules-Vallès 75011 Mº Faidherbe-Chaligny/Charonne

Owner-chef Bernard Passavant produces traditional bistro cuisine in his beautiful and genuine, listed 1900s' bistro with its etched glass doors separating the two dining-rooms, mirrors, intricately moulded ceilings and a gleaming zinc bar. The menu may feature a gratin of girolles, terrine of rabbit, *oeuf en meurette*, salad of St Jacques with hazelnut oil, cod florentine, *daurade au poivron rouge et riz sauvage*, veal kidneys cooked whole with Meaux mustard, game and mushrooms in season, fresh fig tart and a dark chocolate mousse with orange purée. Wines from the Loire and the Rhone are prominent on the list. Now open on Saturday night but with a four-course *menu carte* only (165F). ***Seats*** *40. L 12-2.15 D 8-10.* ***Closed*** *L Sat, all Sun, 1 week Feb & all Aug. Amex, Mastercard, Visa.*

CHEZ FERNAND (LES FERNANDISES) 420F

Tel 43 57 46 25 Map A1.7 **R**
17 rue de la Fontaine-au-Roi 75011 Mº République

All the regional products for which Normandy is famous – cider, butter, milk, camembert, apples, calvados – feature on the menu in chef-owner Fernand Asseline's inexpensive restaurant. Typical dishes may include *rillettes de maquereau*, calf's foot salad, *terrine de foie gras de canard*, skate with camembert, *cote de boeuf à la moëlle, poulet de ferme Vallée d'Auge, gratin de morue*, fillet of duck in a cider sauce with apples, and to finish both *crepes aux pommes* and *tarte aux pommes* come flambéed with calvados. Drink Normandy cider as an alternative to wine. Set L 100F Set D 130F. ***Seats*** *70. L 12-2 D 7.30-11.30.* ***Closed*** *Sun, Mon & Aug. Mastercard, Visa.*

> The best way to get around Paris is by bus or metro –
> buy a book (carnet) of tickets at any metro station and save money

CHEZ LÉON DE BRUXELLES 300F

Tel 43 38 28 69 Map A1.24 **R**
8 place de la République 75011 Mº République

One of the many outlets of a popular chain of restaurants specialising in various ways with mussels. These are ordered from colourful illustrated menus, and most arrive with a bowl of *frites*. Look out for the day's special offers which can include fish soup ad lib and a glass of beer together with some good mussels. ***Seats*** *120. Open 11.30am-1am. Amex, Diners, Mastercard, Visa.*

Also at:

120 rue Rambuteau 75001 Tel 42 36 18 50
3 bd Beaumarchais 75004 Tel 42 71 76 55
63 ave des Champs Elysées 75008 Tel 42 25 96 16
30 bd des Italiens 75009 Tel 42 46 36 15
1 place Pigalle 75009 Tel 42 80 28 33
82 bd du Montparnasse 75014 Tel 43 21 66 62

CHEZ PHILIPPE 650F

Tel 43 57 33 78 Map A1.8 **R**
106 rue de la Folie Méricourt 75011 Mº République

Rustic best describes the good food and cosy decor of this bistro specialising in the food of the South-West produced by long-standing chef Philippe Serbource. Alongside several Bayonne hams are cartwheels hanging from the ceiling with lights attached which illuminate a setting of exposed stone walls, beamed ceilings, red-tiled floor, wooden tables covered in white linen and cane-seated chairs. Home-prepared foie gras is available every day as a starter, and other typical offerings include *confit de canard, confit d'oie* and *cassoulet*. There's always a hearty *plat du jour*, with a tart or *clafoutis* to finish. ***Seats*** *40. L 12-2 D 7.30-10.* ***Closed*** *Sat, Sun, Aug & Public Holidays. Amex, Mastercard, Visa.*

LA GALOCHE D'AURILLAC 400F

Tel 47 00 77 15 Map C1.11 **R**
41 rue de Lappe 75011 Mº Bastille

If you haven't visited the Auvergne region of France, here's your chance to do it in Paris, in one of the most ancient of streets (now taken over mainly by clubs and tapas bars). You can come to these authentic surroundings (hams and musical instruments hang from the walls) simply to sample the wines of the region or to eat some of the regional specialities such as kidney beans cooked in goose fat, a selection of charcuterie or salad of cured country ham and Cantal cheese, followed by sausage with lentils, stuffed breast of veal, mutton tripe or a steak, and plum tart to finish. All wines are available by the glass. Wine, ham and cheese can be purchased to take home. Set menu 150F. ***Seats*** *52. L 12-2 D 7-11.30.* ***Closed*** *Sun, Mon & 6 weeks Jul-Sep. Mastercard, Visa.*

HOTEL DU GRAND PRIEURÉ 350F

Tel 47 00 74 14 Fax 49 23 06 64 Map A1.23 **H**
20 rue de Grand Prieuré 75011 Mº Oberkampf

Unpretentious, clean and quite comfortable accommodation in a quiet location a few paces from Place de la République. Bedrooms, all with mini-bar and satellite TV, are simply furnished. Bathrooms have both bath and shower facilities as well as hairdryers. Breakfast is available in a brightly decorated basement room and the staff are friendly. ***Rooms*** *32. Amex, Mastercard, Visa.*

HOLIDAY INN RÉPUBLIQUE 1540F

Tel 43 55 44 34 Fax 47 00 32 34 Map A1.12 **HR**
10 place de la République 75011 Mº République

Both the Standard and Executive categories of air-conditioned bedroom at this large chain hotel are well equipped. The building, which dates back to 1850, is now listed as a historic monument. The original attractive courtyard is popular for relaxing outside and may be hired for private functions. The largest of nine conference rooms can hold 300 theatre-style. ***Rooms** 318. Amex, Diners, Mastercard, Visa.*

La Belle Epoque 600F

Renovated in 1994, the Belle Epoque offers a *menu carte* (198F – several dishes carry supplements) of fairly standard items plus a *buffet à volonté* (160F – eat as much as you like) for lunch and dinner every day except Thursday nights and Sunday lunchtimes when a New Orleans Brunch (220F, 55F for under-12s) with live jazz takes over. On Sunday lunchtime they also lay on children's entertainment (for 4-10 year olds) in a separate room. ***Seats** 50. L 12-2.30 D 7-10.30.*

Jacques Mélac

Tel 43 70 59 27 **Fax 43 70 73 10** Map C2.13 **R**
42 rue Léon-Frot 75011 Mº Charonne

The wooden beams, stone floor tiles and the thousands of empty wine bottles covering the wall space give Jacques Mélac's *bistrot à vins* a distinct but understated charm. Wine from his own vineyard in the Languedoc (new this year having given up his former domaine in the Rhone) is included in the list of thirty, chosen every fortnight. A good selection of simple dishes is available to accompany the chosen wine, such as *andouillette au vin blanc de chez Duval, crépinettes de porc, petit salé, boeuf aux carottes* or Auvergne cheeses served with Aveyron charcuterie. For the sweet-toothed there are homely puds like *clafoutis* and crème caramel. The cooking is unpretentious and the host amiable and enthusiastic. Open for drinks from 9am. ***Open** L 12-3 D 5.30-10.30. **Closed** D Mon, all Sat & Sun, Aug, Public Holidays & 1 week Christmas. Mastercard, Visa.*

The best way to get around Paris is by bus or metro –
buy a book (carnet) of tickets at any metro station and save money

Méridional 600F

Tel 48 05 75 00 **Fax 43 57 42 85** Map B1.14 **H**
36 bd Richard Lenoir 75011 Mº Bréguet-Sabin

Modern hotel conveniently located for visiting the recently-revived Bastille and Marais areas. Double-glazed rooms are equipped with en suite bathroom, direct-dial telephone, radio alarm, TV and hairdryer. No restaurant. ***Rooms** 36. Amex, Diners, Mastercard, Visa.*

Le Passage

Tel 47 00 73 30 **Fax 47 00 14 00** Map C1.16 **R**
18 passage de la Bonne-Graine 75011 Mº Ledru-Rollin

Do not be deceived by the rather drab little alleyway which leads off Rue du Faubourg-Saint-Antoine to this bright and modern wine bar/restaurant. An international selection of wines stretches to around 270 references (twenty available by the glass). Perhaps the most outstanding feature of the menu is the selection of *andouillettes* (an entire page!), all served with a *gratin dauphinois* and either *pois cassés* or lentils (with a 10F optional extra of mustard sauce). Other choices may include ricotta with confit aubergines, whole baby artichokes with olive oil and marinated peppers, duck rillettes or smoked and matjes herrings served together with a warm potato salad. A second outlet, ***Café du Passage*** (5.30pm-2am, closed Sun), is at 12 Rue de Charonne, also in the 11th. This one is open for drinks outside meal times. ***Open** L 12-2.30 D 7.30-11.30. **Closed** L Sat, all Sun. Amex, Diners, Mastercard, Visa.*

LE ROUDOULIÉ 450F

Tel 43 79 27 46 Map C2.18 **R**
16 rue de La Vacquerie 75011 M° Voltaire

A Chilean artist has painted the eye-catching ceiling in Madame Vilar's restaurant. Also vying for attention is the food, which comes from the South-West: *salade de Roudoulié* (confit of quails, smoked magret of duck and fresh foie gras), duck *pot-au-feu, lapin au chocolat*, wing of skate with Meaux mustard, fillet of beef with morel mushrooms or fillet of red mullet *à la provençale* followed by a raspberry *clafoutis, terrine de crepe en gelée des fruits rouges* or chocolate tart. Accompanying wines like Madiran are also from the area. A daily-changing lunch menu of 62F (starter and main course) provides outstanding value for money. A bonus for those clutching a copy of this guide is a complimentary aperitif. Set L 62F, Set L & D 98F & 145F. ***Seats** 40. L 12-2.30 D 7.30-10.30. **Closed** L Sat, all Sun. Mastercard, Visa.*

A SOUSCEYRAC ★ 650F

Tel 43 71 65 30 **Fax 40 09 79 75** Map C1.19 **R**
35 rue Faidherbe 75011 M° Charonne/Faidherbe-Chaligny

One of the culinary delights of the little town of Sousceyrac in the Lot region of France is its cassoulet. This dish therefore features as one of the South-Western specialities served in this typical 1920s-30s bistro with its tiled floors, wood panelling and diplomas on the walls. Others might be their foie gras (goose or duck), *terrine de queue de boeuf au foie gras*, duck cannelloni, hare *à la royale* (in season), *sandre à la bourguignonne* or coquilles St Jacques with sorrel, followed by an apple feuilleté with armagnac or crème brulée. Brothers Patrick (in the kitchen) and Luc (front of house) Asfaux are the third generation of the founding family. Comprehensive French wine list. Set menu 175F. ***Seats** 60. L 12-2 D 7.30-10. **Closed** L Sat, all Sun & Aug. Amex, Mastercard, Visa.*

LA TABLE RICHELIEU 600F

Tel 43 72 31 23 Map D2.20 **R**
276 bd Voltaire 75011 M° Nation

La Table Richelieu is a gastronomic restaurant where the pictures on the wall are for sale and menus change four times a year. Classic cooking from chef-patron Daniel Rousseau features dishes such as lobster with Sauternes sauce and fresh pasta, *millefeuille d'artichaut au foie gras et l'huile noisette*, fricassee of lamb's sweetbreads and tongue with *pommes cocotte* and *tarte fine chaude aux pommes acidulées*. Set menus 149F inc wine (not D Sat) & 260F (*dégustation*). ***Seats** 80. L 12-2.30 D 7-11. **Closed** L Sat. Amex, Diners, Mastercard, Visa.*

THAI ELEPHANT 600F

Tel 47 00 42 00 **Fax 47 00 45 44** Map C1.21 **R**
43-45 rue Roquette 75011 M° Bastille

Resembling a Thai village, this elegant restaurant is on different levels with teak furnishings, exotic plants and flowers, roofs over the tables and centrepiece of a water fountain, bridge and pond. The menu boasts 'authentic Royal Thai cuisine' with starters including the *Kiss du Golfe du Siam* (giant stuffed prawns), chicken or pork satay and mussels with celery and basil, whilst among the main courses are *Coco Cabane* which originates from Phuket (curried beef served in a fresh coconut shell accompanied by noodles) and a chicken soufflé (presented within a banana leaf, steam-cooked and seasoned with curry, coconut and citronella). Wines are taken very seriously here, and the white house wine from Alsace admirably complements the cooking; the house red is from Bordeaux. Fair prices, even a champagne at 255F – cheap for France! Set L 150F Set L & D 275F & 300F. ***Seats** 240. L 12-2.30 (Sun till 2) D 7-12 (Sun till 11). **Closed** L Sat, 1 May & 3 days Christmas. Amex, Diners, Mastercard, Visa.*

LE VILLARET 400F

Tel 43 57 89 76 Map B1.22 **R**
13 rue Ternaux 75011 Mº Oberkampf/Parmentier

No name on the door outside, and a very modest handwritten menu, but enough people know about this place to keep it full each evening, so don't turn up without booking. Decor is 'new old' – beams, bricks, stones, tiled floor, long-backed kitchen-style chairs. Chef Olivier Gaslain changes his menu with the seasons: autumn brings mushrooms and coquilles St Jacques. Everything on the list is worth trying, including *soupe de rougets, friture de céteaux* (a small sole-like fish), *oeufs cocotte* in a foie gras cream, langoustines in a saffron-infused lobster sauce, veal sweetbreads and kidneys, fresh *morue* with a creamy garlic sauce and purées of broccoli and potatoes, quenelles of chocolate with *griottes* and a vanilla sauce. Small, personal wine list. ***Seats*** *40. D only 8-1am.*
Closed *Sun & Aug. Mastercard, Visa.*

12th Arrondissement

Places of Interest

Opéra National de Paris Bastille, Reservations 44 73 13 00, Enquiries 40 01 17 89, M° Bastille
Musée National des Arts d'Afriques et d'Océanie, 44 74 84 80, M° Porte Dorée
Palais Omnisports de Paris Bercy, 40 02 60 60, M° Bercy
Bois de Vincennes (pleasure garden, zoo, boating), M° Porte Dorée

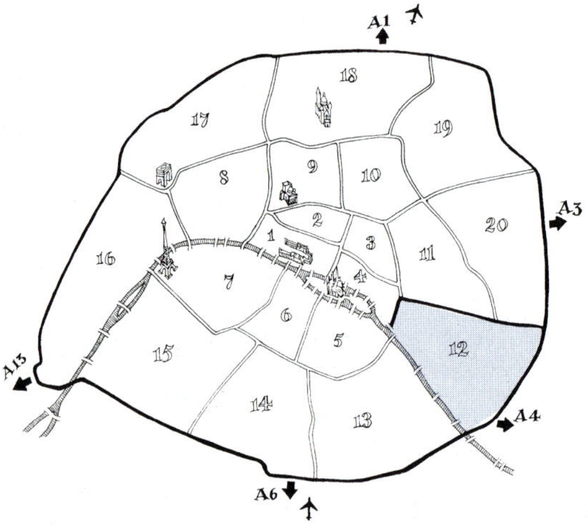

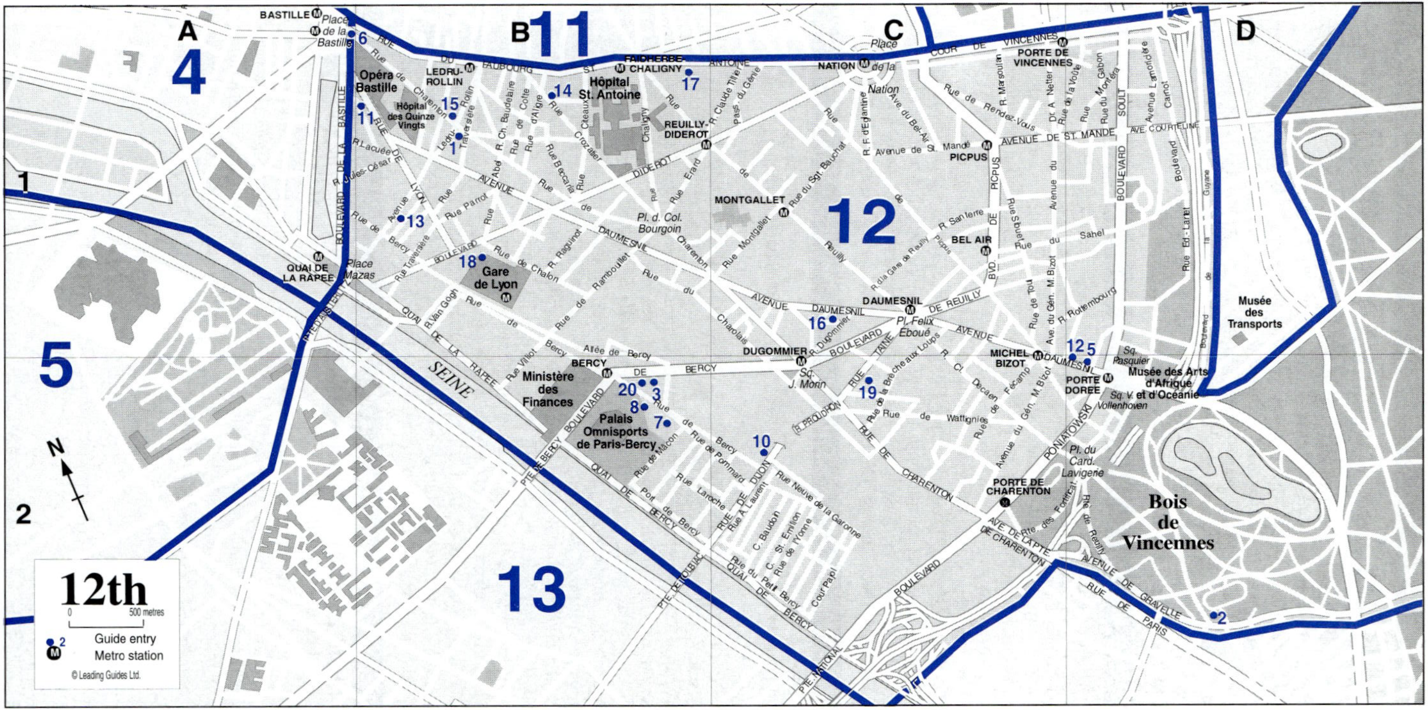

12th
0 500 metres
Guide entry
Metro station
© Leading Guides Ltd.
A
B
C
D
1
2
4
5
11
12
13
N
BASTILLE
Place de la Bastille
Opéra Bastille
Hôpital des Quinze Vingts
LEDRU-ROLLIN
FAIDHERBE-CHALIGNY
Hôpital St. Antoine
REUILLY-DIDEROT
NATION
Place de la Nation
PORTE DE VINCENNES
PICPUS
BEL AIR
MONTGALLET
DAUMESNIL
Pl. Felix Eboué
DUGOMMIER
MICHEL BIZOT
PORTE DOREE
Musée des Arts d'Afrique et d'Océanie
Sq. Pasquier
Sq. V. et d'Océanie Vollenhoven
Musée des Transports
Bois de Vincennes
PORTE DE CHARENTON
Pl. du Card. Lavigerie
QUAI DE LA RAPEE
Place Mazas
Gare de Lyon
BERCY
Ministère des Finances
Palais Omnisports de Paris-Bercy
Sq. J. Morin
Pl. d. Col. Bourgoin
SEINE
QUAI DE LA RAPEE
QUAI DE BERCY
BOULEVARD DE LA BASTILLE
AVENUE DAUMESNIL
BOULEVARD DIDEROT
AVENUE DE ST. MANDE
COUR DE VINCENNES
BOULEVARD SOULT
BOULEVARD PONIATOWSKI
RUE DE CHARENTON
AVENUE DE GRAVELLE
RUE DE PARIS
Rue de Bercy
Rue de Charenton
Rue de Lyon
Rue de Reuilly
Rue de Picpus
Rue du Faubourg St. Antoine
Rue de Rendez-Vous
Rue de Wattignies
Rue de la Brèche aux Loups
Rue Montgallet
Rue Crozatier
Rue Beccaria
Rue d'Aligre
Rue de Cotte
R. Ch. Baudelaire
Rue Abel
Rue Parrot
Rue de Chalon
R. Raguinot
Rue de Rambouillet
Rue Villiot
R. Van Gogh
Rue Traversière
R. Jules-César
R. Lacuée
Rue Erard
Rue Chaligny
Rue Cîteaux
R. Claude Tillier
Pass. du Génie
Rue du Sgt. Bauchat
R. F. d'Eglantine
Ave. du Bel-Air
Avenue de St. Mandé
R. Marsoulan
Dr. A. Netter
Rue de la Voûte
Rue du Gabon
Rue Montéra
Avenue Lamoricière
Carnot
Ave. Courteline
Rue Ed.-Lartet
Boulevard de la Guyane
Rue Sibuet
Rue du Sahel
Rue de Toul
Ave. du Gén. M. Bizot
R. Rottembourg
R. Santerre
R. d. la Gare de Reuilly
R. Dugommier
R. Cl. Decaen
Rue de Fécamp
R. Proudhon
Allée de Bercy
Rue de Pommard
Rue de Mâcon
Rue Laroche
Rue de Dijon
Rue A. Laurent
C. Baudoin
C. St. Emilion
Rue de l'Yonne
Rue Neuve de la Garonne
Rue du Petit Bercy
Cour Papi
Rue Port de Bercy
Rte. des Fortifications
Rte. de Reuilly
AVE. DE LA PTE. DE CHARENTON
PTE. DE BERCY
PTE. DE TOLBIAC
PTE. NATIONAL
PTE. D'AUSTERLITZ
1
2
3
5
6
7
8
10
11
12
13
14
15
16
17
18
19
20

Batifol 350F

Tel 40 19 02 05 Map B2.20 **R**
42 bd de Bercy 75012 Mº Bercy

This is one of a chain of almost 20 traditionally styled bistros in and around Paris. Open long hours every day (some never close), they serve a fairly straightforward selection of mainstream dishes typified by herring fillets with warm potato salad, marrowbone with rock salt and *pain de campagne*, *gratin parmentier*, confit de canard, *pot-au-feu*, and baked salmon with tagliatelle. Apple compote, *tarte à l'ancienne*, chiboust and chocolate mousse are among the favourite desserts. Set menu (with a drink) 79F *menu enfant* 37F. ***Seats** 110. **Open** (Bercy) 11am-midnight. Amex, Diners, Mastercard, Visa.*

Belle Epoque 590F

Tel 43 44 06 66 **Fax 43 44 10 25** Map B1.1 **H**
66 rue de Charenton 75012 Mº Gare de Lyon/Bastille/Ledru-Rollin

Built around a garden courtyard, the comfortably appointed rooms in this art deco hotel are numbered from 1900 upwards! The reproduction furniture was made by craftsmen using the same woods and the original designs of two famous French designers of that period, Printz and Ruhlmann. Three suites however have genuine pieces from the early 1900s. The bar is open from noon to 10pm and tea is served at around 5pm with a selection of cakes. No restaurant but the breakfast room is on the ground floor. Three meeting rooms (max 50). ***Rooms** 29. Amex, Diners, Mastercard, Visa.*

La Cipale 500F

Tel 43 75 54 53 Map D2.2 **R**
49 ave de Gravelle 75012 Mº Charenton Ecoles

Both the local velodrome (the '*piste municipale*' or '*Cipale*') and this restaurant within it (with separate entrance) are celebrating their centenary in 1996. A simple café way back in 1896, it is now a welcoming little restaurant. The patron, Bruno Frédéric, has returned to the kitchen and is again personally responsible for a carte that changes with the seasons and the market. Langoustines in a nage flavoured with lemon grass, *gateau de saumon au moutarde de violet* and a 'cake' of duck foie gras typify the starters, while mains might include *homard au beurre de vanille*, baby turbot poached with lemon thyme, *rognon de veau flambé* (at the table) and *noix de veau poelé à l'emulsion d'huile de noix. Soufflé chaud* 'after eight' (with chocolate) and a liquorice-flavoured bavarois on a passion fruit coulis give a picture of the desserts. Bruno's contact with Vendome *cavistes* produces a wine list on which he has personally tasted each reference. There is a terrace for summer dining. Set menus 160F (business) & 190F (*dégustation*). ***Seats** 32 (+ 30 outside). L 12-2 D 7.30-9.30. **Closed** L Sat, D Sun, all Mon & Aug. Mastercard, Visa.*

Hotel Claret 450F

Tel 46 28 41 31 **Fax 49 28 09 29** Map B2.3 **H**
44 bd de Bercy 75012 Mº Bercy

Formerly a post office, this building now houses a modest family-run hotel. All rooms have TV and either en suite bath or shower with WC. Some rooms are quite small and only the restaurant (Italian) has the benefit of air-conditioning. The hotel is close to the POPB (the futuristic Bercy sports complex) and Gare de Lyon. ***Rooms** 52. Amex, Diners, Mastercard, Visa.*

> The best way to get around Paris is by bus or metro –
> buy a book (carnet) of tickets at any metro station and save money

La Gourmandise 680F

Tel 43 43 94 41
271 ave Daumesnil 75012
Map D2.5
M° Porte Dorée
R

Alain Denoual has been serving his 'personalised classic cuisine' for more than a dozen years to his clients in this warm and intimate restaurant decorated in a floral style. A choice of around 140 wines is listed to accompany fixed-price menus (including one for children) as well as the à la carte. Fish is predominant: salad of langoustines and artichokes; mullet with olive oil and balsamic vinegar dressing; monkfish with mushrooms and red wine; panaché of salmon, brill and red mullet with garlic *aux épices de la mer* (seaweed), the last a speciality. On the meat side, veal kidneys and sweetbreads with mushrooms, lamb with honey and cider vinegar, and *faux filet* with two peppers are typical. Desserts include *mousse au fromage blanc* and a popular mango charlotte. Set menus 95F (*enfant*), 145F, 175F & 199F (inc wine). ***Seats*** *45. L 12-2 D 7.15-10.30.* ***Closed*** *D Mon, all Sun & 3 weeks Aug. Amex, Mastercard, Visa.*

Les Grandes Marches 550F

Tel 43 42 90 32 **Fax 43 44 80 02**
6 place de la Bastille 75012
Map A1.6
M° Bastille
R

The first floor of this large *brasserie de luxe* dominating one section of Place de la Bastille is a little more intimate (leather armchairs and wall-to-wall carpeting) than the ground floor, where the atmosphere is that of a genuine brasserie. The decor nevertheless is as contemporary as the adjacent ultra-modern Opéra Bastille building. The long menu offers something for everyone – oysters, fish soup, foie gras, *bavarois* of vegetables with a tomato coulis, millefeuille of smoked salmon, grilled sole, turbot and giant prawns, baked John Dory, calf's kidney, *andouillette, magret de canard,* chateaubriand, raspberry tart, *ile flottante*, orange mousse. Each section of the *carte* has a couple of recommended wines. Set menu 178F (ground floor only). ***Seats*** *300. Meals noon-1am.* ***Closed*** *10 days Aug. Amex, Diners, Mastercard, Visa.*

Ibis Paris-Bercy 460F

Tel 43 42 91 91 **Fax 43 42 34 79**
77 rue de Bercy 75012
Map B2.7
M° Bercy
H

A large, modern, functional and inexpensive hotel of the Ibis chain with the Bercy gardens opposite. Children under 12 stay free if sharing parents' room. Public parking in the basement at 95F for 24 hours. No room service. This is one of several Ibis hotels within the Paris area. See Around Paris section for Ibis airport hotels. ***Rooms*** *364. Amex, Diners, Mastercard, Visa.*

Novotel Paris-Bercy 760F

Tel 43 42 30 00 **Fax 43 45 30 60**
85 rue de Bercy 75012
Map B2.8
M° Bercy
H

One of the chain's hotels, built in 1987 and located opposite the lawns and gardens of the Palais Omnisports de Paris-Bercy. Well-equipped, double-glazed and air-conditioned, pastel-coloured rooms all have both tub and shower in en suite bathrooms. Two children under 16 stay free if sharing parents' room. Six conference rooms (the largest holds 120 theatre-style). This is one of several Novotels in the Paris region – call 60 77 51 51 for central reservations. ***Rooms*** *129. Amex, Diners, Mastercard, Visa.*

L'Oulette ★ 600F

Tel 40 02 02 12
15 place Lachambeaudie 75012
Map C2.10
M° Bercy/Dugommier
R

A smart modern restaurant with picture windows opening on to the terrace. The chairs and banquette seating are furnished in bold fabrics and copper cooking pans, jars of home-made preserves, plants and flowers decorate the interior. The *menu du marché* (150F) changes daily and offers simple but

See over

delicious dishes such as *salade de queue de boeuf aux oignons nouveaux* (oxtail salad with onions) and veal braised with olives. Southern French dishes are also prominent on the carte: *tarte fine croustillante aux sardines fraiches, tomates et parmesan* and fillet of gilthead pan-fried with *pipérade*, for instance. Desserts include flambéed peaches with honey and rosemary, and *parfait glacé aux noisettes caramélisées*. The four-course *menu de saison* (230F) includes wine. Public parking. ***Seats** 45 (+ 30 outside). L 12-2.15 D 8-10.15. **Closed** L Sat, all Sun. Amex, Diners, Mastercard, Visa.*

LE PAVILLON BASTILLE 955F

Tel 43 43 65 65 Fax 43 43 96 52 Map B1.11 **H**
65 rue de Lyon 75012 M° Bastille

This 19th-century building surrounds a 17th-century courtyard and fountain. The yellow and blue air-conditioned bedrooms are comfortably furnished and offer cable TV, mini-bar (soft drinks are free) and luxurious en suite bathrooms with bathrobes, magnifying mirror and hairdryer. Breakfast is served in the vaulted basement and the entrance hall becomes a relaxed bar area later in the day. No restaurant. Laundry service. ***Rooms** 24. Amex, Diners, Mastercard, Visa.*

AU PRESSOIR ★ 1100F

Tel 43 44 38 21 Fax 43 43 81 77 Map D2.12 **R**
257 ave Daumesnil 75012 M° Michel Bizot

In an ancient former wine warehouse (hence the name), the Séguins (Henri in the kitchen and Danielle welcoming customers front of house) entirely renovated their restaurant a few years ago with oak panelling, leather banquette seating and the addition of air-conditioning. A gastronomic restaurant in traditional terms, relying very much on fresh seasonal produce. *Truffe en croute de gros sel*, terrine of oxtail with an onion confit or *cassolette de raviolis d'homard* could be followed by salmon with lemon and pink grapefruit, *coeur de filet de boeuf au coulis de truffes* with fresh pasta or veal kidneys *à la orange*. Two particular specialities are hare *à la royale* (in season) and *assiette de fruits de mer tiède*. On the dessert front there's roast figs with a red fruit coulis, *mousse à la banane* and peanut ice cream. A mainly French wine list runs to some 400 bins. Two private rooms upstairs (max 12 & 20). Valet parking. Set menu 390F *(dégustation). **Seats** 50. L 12-2.30 D 7.30-10.30. **Closed** Sat, Sun, Aug & 1 week Feb (school hols). Amex. Mastercard, Visa.*

LE QUINCY 550F

Tel 46 28 46 76 Map B1.13 **R**
28 ave Ledru-Rollin 75012 M° Gare de Lyon

Chef-patron 'Boboss' has been pleasing customers with his sound country cooking, in particular from the Ardèche area of France, at this little rustic, country-style bistro for the last 25 years. Typifying the choice are *terrine fermière avec chou à l'ail, foie gras, écrevisses pattes rouges, cassoulet, lapereau au vin blanc, cote de veau aux morilles, queue de boeuf braisée, dorade à l'ancienne* and a large assortment of desserts. Wines of the region accompany (you pay by the measure and the owner drinks what you don't!) and the traditional way to round off a meal here is with a flaming plum brandy. ***Seats** 35. L 12-2 D 7-10. **Closed** Sat, Sun, Mon & mid-Aug to mid-Sep. No credit cards.*

LE RELAIS DE LYON 530F

Tel 43 44 22 50 Fax 43 41 55 12 Map B1.14 **H**
64 rue Crozatier 75012 M° Ledru-Rollin

A very quiet modern hotel with comfortable, light bedrooms; all have en suite facilities, some with bath and some with shower. There is a lobby bar open till 11pm. ***Rooms** 34. Amex, Diners, Mastercard, Visa.*

SIPARIO 400F

Tel 43 45 70 26 Map B1.15 **R**
69 rue Charenton 75012 Mº Ledru-Rollin/Bastille

Giant vegetables painted in pastel colours are the decorative highlights of this very good Italian restaurant. Southern Italian cuisine is the summer speciality, while hearty dishes from the North keep the customers full and happy in winter (the menu changes four times a year). Post-opera-goers come here for *vitello tonnato* followed by rascasse ravioli with fresh tomato, with a vanilla ice cream in a 'bath' of hot coffee sauce to finish. Set menu 100F. ***Seats** 48. L 12-2 D 7.30-11.* ***Closed** L Sat, all Sun & 15 days mid-Aug. Amex, Diners, Mastercard, Visa.*

A glossary of French menu items starts on page 274

LA SOLOGNE ★ 480F

Tel 43 07 68 97 **Fax 43 44 66 23** Map C2.16 **R**
164 ave Daumesnil 75012 Mº Daumesnil

Didier Maillet presents a seasonal menu in his comfortably appointed *terrasse* restaurant near Place Félix Eboué. Sologne is a major hunting area south of Paris, and game features prominently in winter as do wild mushrooms. Typical dishes include *salade gourmande* with coriander, terrine of calf's head and calf's foot with *sauce aigrelette, cassolette de champignons sauvages, daube de joue de boeuf au Cahors*, roast cod with cabbage confit and tartare of salmon. Among the desserts note white chocolate mousse with a peach coulis, *nougat glacé* with ginger and honey, and crème caramel with orange zest. There's plenty of interest, too, on the wine list, including a Morgon 'Marcel Lapierre', Chateau Meylet St Emilion 1989, a Macon Clessé and a 'Branger' Muscadet which is hand-produced by old-fashioned methods and comes in a 'satin-finish' bottle. The connoisseur with longer pockets will consult the list of *crus millésimés.* Virginie Maillet is a charming, concerned hostess in this really excellent little restaurant. Set L 150F. ***Seats** 45. L 12-2.30 D 7.30-10.30 (Sat to 11.30).* ***Closed** L Sat, all Sun & 2 weeks mid-Jul. Amex, Diners, Mastercard, Visa.*

LE TEMPS DES CERISES 600F

Tel 43 67 52 08 **Fax 43 67 60 91** Map B1.17 **R**
216 rue du Faubourg St-Antoine 75012 Mº Faidherbe-Chaligny/Nation

The paintings change on the walls in each of the three dining-rooms (one for non-smokers) as and when a new artist is invited to put on a show in this restaurant. Chef Bernard Bergounioux, a former sous-chef to Alain Dutournier (of *Carré des Feuillants* fame), continues to attract customers with his *cassoulet d'escargots aux noix*, duck foie gras, *daurade au jambon*, salmon with a *moutarde de violet* sauce, fillet of beef with a truffle sauce, and calf's kidneys with a coriander sauce. To finish, perhaps *croustillante framboise* or *nougat glacé*. The reliable quality, good-value menus and modestly priced wine list make this an excellent address in the area. Set menus 97F, 148F, 189F & 224F. ***Seats** 58 (+ 15 outside). L 12-2.30 D 7.30-10.30 (Fri & Sat to 11).* ***Closed** Mon. Amex, Mastercard, Visa.*

LE TRAIN BLEU 600F

Tel 43 43 09 06 **Fax 43 43 97 96** Map B1.18 **R**
Gare de Lyon 75012 Mº Gare de Lyon

Named after the legendary luxurious Paris-Cote d'Azur express of the 1920s, the buffet of the Gare de Lyon (classified as a historic monument) is truly unique. In 1900, thirty artists were commissioned to paint the most beautiful parts of

See over

France crossed by the Paris-Lyon-Marseille rail network. These paintings (41 of them) now cover the restaurant's ornate ceilings and walls and provide a wonderful backdrop to food of a high quality. Starters include duck terrine with pistachios and *saucisson lyonnais* with parsley potatoes, while typical main dishes are grilled rack of lamb with Provençal herbs and brill *(barbue)* soufflé with wild mushrooms. Set menu 250F. ***Seats*** *200. L 12-2.30 D 7-10. Amex, Diners, Mastercard, Visa.*

AU TROU GASCON ★ 800F

Tel 43 44 34 26 **Fax 43 07 80 55** Map C2.19 **R**
40 rue Taine 75012 Mº Daumesnil

Maitre-chef Alain Dutournier made his name in this 1900 bistro-style setting at the top of Rue Taine before going on to greater glory at his *Carré des Feuillants* (see entry in 2nd arrondissement). His wife Nicole runs Au Trou Gascon, a traditional haven of South-Western cuisine, but it's chef Jacques Fassat who actually delivers the goods. His cassoulet is among the finest in all Paris, with home-made sausages and beans from Tarbes. Top-quality produce is very much the keynote, all the game being guaranteed wild and all the poultry coming from farms in Chalosse. Other signature dishes are pheasant consommé with fresh chestnuts, warm paté of ceps in parsley jus, galette of potatoes, foie gras and truffles, *confit de canard* and hare *à la royale*. Desserts, some of which must be ordered at the start of the meal, include *tourtière chaude landaise*, *crème brulée cannelle et moka* and *croustade* of figs with *nougat glacé*. The long wine list covers France comprehensively and also has a fair Spanish showing. ***Seats*** *45. L 12-2 D 7.30-10.* ***Closed*** *Sat, Sun, Aug & 1 week Christmas. Amex, Diners, Mastercard, Visa.*

13th Arrondissement
Places of Interest

Gobelins (tapestry factory), 44 08 52 00, Mº Gobelins

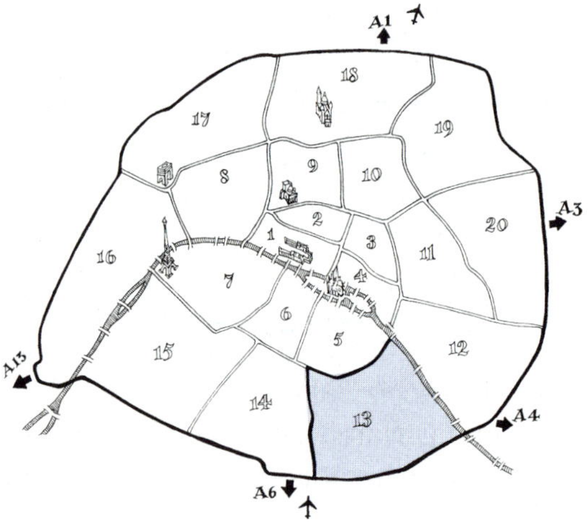

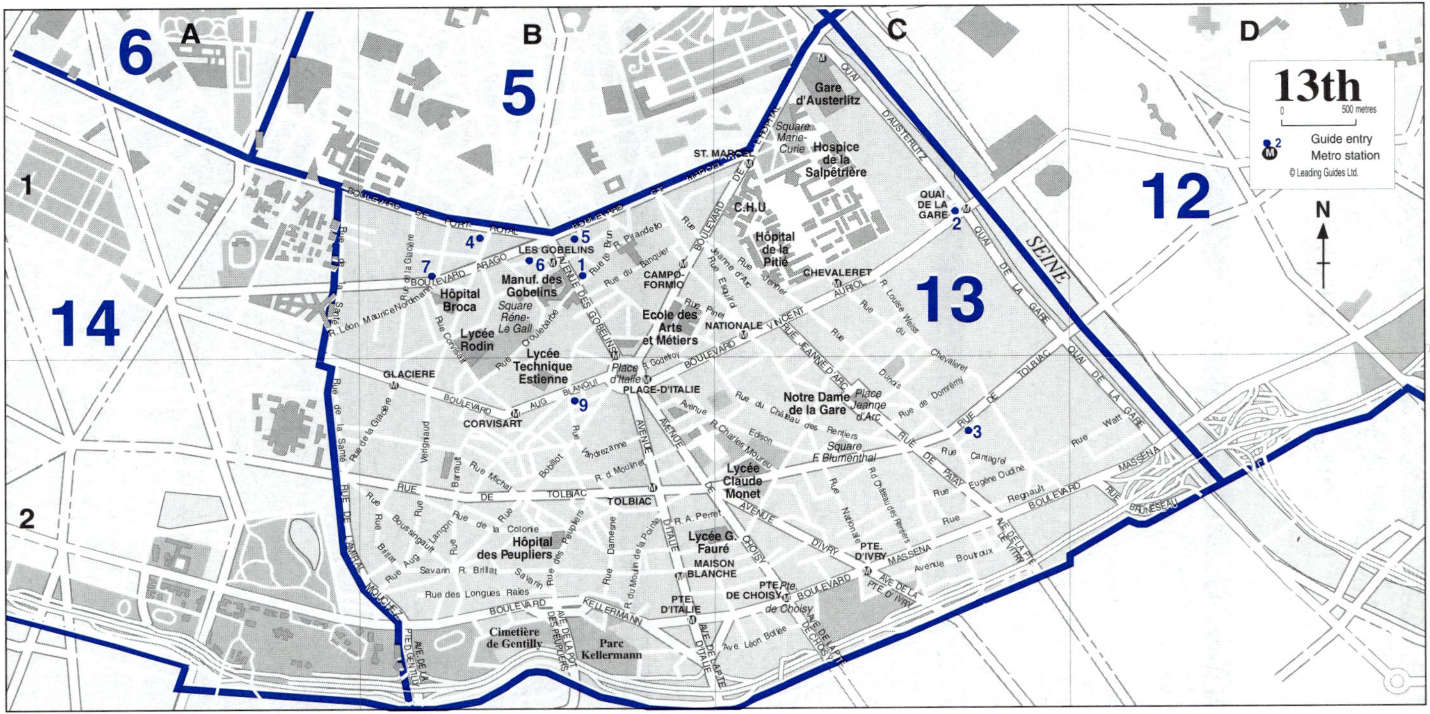
13th
0
500 metres
Guide entry
Metro station
© Leading Guides Ltd.
N
A
B
C
D
1
2
6
5
14
12
13
SEINE
Gare d'Austerlitz
Square Marie-Curie
Hospice de la Salpêtrière
ST. MARCEL
C.H.U
Hôpital de la Pitié
QUAI DE LA GARE
CHEVALERET
LES GOBELINS
CAMPO-FORMIO
Manuf. des Gobelins
Square Réne-Le Gall
Hôpital Broca
Lycée Rodin
Lycée Technique Estienne
Ecole des Arts et Métiers
NATIONALE
Place d'Italie
PLACE-D'ITALIE
GLACIERE
CORVISART
Notre Dame de la Gare
Place Jeanne d'Arc
Square F. Blumenthal
Lycée Claude Monet
TOLBIAC
Lycée G. Fauré
MAISON BLANCHE
Hôpital des Peupliers
PTE. D'ITALIE
PTE. DE CHOISY
PTE. D'IVRY
Cimetière de Gentilly
Parc Kellermann
BOULEVARD DE PORT-ROYAL
BOULEVARD ARAGO
AVENUE DES GOBELINS
BOULEVARD VINCENT AURIOL
RUE JEANNE D'ARC
QUAI D'AUSTERLITZ
QUAI DE LA GARE
RUE DE TOLBIAC
BOULEVARD MASSENA
RUE BRUNESEAU
BOULEVARD KELLERMANN
RUE DE L'AMIRAL MOUCHEZ
Rue de la Santé
BOULEVARD AUG. BLANQUI
AVENUE DE CHOISY
AVENUE D'ITALIE
AVENUE D'IVRY
Rue Nationale
Rue du Château des Rentiers
Rue de Domrémy
Rue du Chevaleret
Rue Dunois
R. Louise Weiss
Rue Watt
Rue Cantagrel
Rue Eugène Oudiné
Rue Regnault
Avenue Boutroux
Rue Edison
R. Charles Moureu
Rue Damesne
R. du Moulin de la Pointe
R. d. Moulinet
Rue Vandrezanne
Rue Bobillot
Rue Barrault
Rue Vergniaud
Rue de la Glacière
Rue Corvisart
Rue Croulebarbe
R. Léon Maurice Nordmann
Rue Michal
Rue de la Colonie
Rue des Peupliers
Rue Boussingault
Rue Brillat Savarin
Rue des Longues Raies
Rue Pinel
Rue Esquirol
Rue Jenner
Rue du Banquier
Rue le Brun
R. Pirandello
R. Godefroy
Ave. Léon Bollée
AVE. DE LA PTE. DE VITRY
AVE. DE LA PTE. D'IVRY
AVE. DE LA PTE. DE CHOISY
AVE. DE LA PTE. D'ITALIE
AVE. DE LA POT. DES PEUPLIERS
AVE. DE LA PTE. D. GENTILLY
R. A. Perret

EQUINOXE 395F

Tel 43 37 56 56 Fax 45 35 52 42 Map B1.1
40 rue le Brun 75013 Mº Gobelins
H

Well-appointed, practical hotel in a modern (1981) building. Tubs in all bathrooms, ever-open bar and private parking (50F per day – lift access) are among the pluses. Room service of drinks and snacks 24 hours a day. ***Rooms*** *49. Amex, Diners, Mastercard, Visa.*

MERCURE PARIS-BERCY 690F

Tel 45 82 48 00 Fax 45 82 19 16 Map C1.2
6 bd Vincent Auriol 75013 Mº Quai de la Gare
H

Not far from the Bibliothèque Nationale, which is currently under construction, and opposite a metro station, this ultra-modern, functional hotel offers comfortably furnished, air-conditioned and double-glazed bedrooms with mini-bars, satellite TV and, in the en suite bathrooms, both tubs and showers. Private parking for 10 cars (reservable at 80F for 24 hours). There is a bar, and room service operates until 11.30pm. Conference room for 40 delegates theatre-style. ***Rooms*** *90. Amex, Diners, Mastercard, Visa.*

MERCURE PARIS-TOLBIAC 690F

Tel 45 84 61 61 Fax 45 84 43 38 Map C2.3
21 rue de Tolbiac 75013 Mº Nationale
H

Another of the dozen Mercure hotels located inside the Périphérique offering modern, comfortably furnished bedrooms with air-conditioning, en suite bathroom, direct-dial phone, mini-bar, satellite TV, radio (with speakers in bathroom) and a room service providing light meals from Monday to Thursday, 7-11 pm. Peace and quiet are assured by each of the rooms having double windows, each of which is double-glazed (ie four panes of glass). Parking for 13 cars (reserve your place) at 70F for 24 hours. Room price quoted above is the mid-season rate; high season is 770F and low season 580F. ***Rooms*** *71. Amex, Diners, Mastercard, Visa.*

LE PETIT MARGUERY 650F

Tel 43 31 58 59 Map B1.4
9 bd du Port-Royal 75013 Mº Gobelins
R

The three Cousin brothers, Michel, Jacques and Alain, create a very friendly atmosphere at their authentic Parisian bistro. Michel and Jacques spend most of their time in the kitchen, occasionally coming out to greet customers or join in conversation. Alain makes sure all runs smoothly in the three dining-rooms with their ancient tiled floors and aged pink walls covered with mirrors. The brothers specialise in game, offal, fresh fish and regional dishes: *hure de sanglier* (a 'brawn' of wild boar), terrines of hare, partridge and pheasant, escalope of lightly smoked salmon in a cabbage leaf, *délice de rouget sauce lazienne*, roast sea bass with green lentils, veal kidney with mustard, tripe, fricassee of lamb with baby vegetables, hare *à la royale, noisettes de biche à la romaine*. To finish, perhaps a bitter chocolate cake with moka sabayon, Grand Marnier soufflé (for two – a speciality) or cherry soup with prunes in armagnac. Set L 165F Set L & D 205 (*menu carte*), 325F (*dégustation*) & 450F (*menu gibier* – in season). No à la carte. ***Seats*** *80 (+ 20 outside). L 12-2.15 D 7.30-10.30.* ***Closed*** *Sun, Mon, Aug & 8 days Christmas. Amex, Diners, Mastercard, Visa.*

The best way to get around Paris is by bus or metro – buy a book (carnet) of tickets at any metro station and save money

Pizza César

Tel 43 31 68 60 Map B1.5 **R**
81 bd St Marcel 75013 Mº Gobelins

Near the old Gobelins factory, Pizza César offers a Franco-Italian menu with the emphasis on pizzas cooked in a wood-fired oven. Best bet for the hungry is the cheap three-course menu with pizza or pasta as the centrepiece.
Open *L & D daily. Mastercard, Visa.*

Résidence des Gobelins 400F

Tel 47 07 26 90 **Fax 43 31 44 05** Map B1.6 **H**
9 rue des Gobelins 75013 Mº Gobelins

You can be certain of a warm, friendly welcome at Jennifer and Philippe Poirier's well-located hotel that also offers good clean, straightforward accommodation. All rooms are en suite, some with shower and WC only. The breakfast room looks out on to a charming courtyard with creeping ivy.
Rooms *32. Amex, Mastercard, Visa.*

Le Rhone 300F

Tel 47 07 33 57 Map B1.7 **R**
40 bd Arago 75013 Mº Gobelins

Bright, simply appointed restaurant whose scope extends in summer on to a wide pavement terrace. Jean Reuschlein and his wife specialise in the cooking of Lyons. *Andouillettes*, tripe, *boudin noir, tete de veau,* stuffed neck of goose, *quenelles de brochet, magret de canard au poivre vert* and *pavé* of beef with a Meaux mustard sauce are the principal central dishes, with marinated herrings a favourite starter and *tarte tatin* a popular finale. Plenty of simpler choices too, like egg mayonnaise, *céleri rémoulade* and *crème caramel*. There's always a daily special or two, perhaps *pot-au-feu* or *rascasse provençale.* Cotes du Tarn (Gamay) is a recommended tipple. Set menus 75F, 109F & 160F. ***Seats*** *50 (+ 30 outside). L 12-2 D 7-10.* ***Closed*** *Sat, Sun, Aug & Public Holidays. Mastercard, Visa.*

Les Vieux Métiers de France 700F

Tel 45 88 90 03 **Fax 45 80 73 80** Map B2.9 **R**
13 bd Auguste Blanqui 75013 Mº Place d'Italie

Neo-medieval is the style of this restaurant just off Place d'Italie. Its name means 'the old tradesmen of France' and various crafts are depicted on the facade. Slate floor, mock stone walls and heavy tapestries are other features. Owner-chef Michel Moisan updates classical dishes, as shown by casserole of snail and pig's trotters in Suresnes wine, *vinaigrette de homard sur taboulé aux herbes*, papillote of foie gras with cabbage, rabbit terrine with hazelnuts, turbot braised with fresh girolles, braised breast of veal Provençal-style with basil, veal kidneys cooked whole in their suet with *sauce bordelaise* and *darphin* potatoes and roast shoulder of Pauillac lamb with spices and a celery jus. Long, interesting wine list. Two private rooms for parties of up to 16. Set menus 165F & 300F (8-dish *dégustation*). ***Seats*** *60. L 12-2 D 7.30-10.30.* ***Closed*** *Sun & Mon. Amex, Diners, Mastercard, Visa.*

14th Arrondissement

Places of Interest

Montparnasse (Boulevard)
Cimetière du Montparnasse (Baudelaire, Sartre, A. Citroën, Maupassant, Serge Gainsbourg, César Frank, Saint-Saens, Samuel Beckett), 44 10 86 50, M° Edgar Quinet/Raspail
Catacombs, 43 22 47 63, M° Denfert-Rochereau
Observatoire, 40 51 22 21, M° Denfert-Rochereau/RER Port Royal

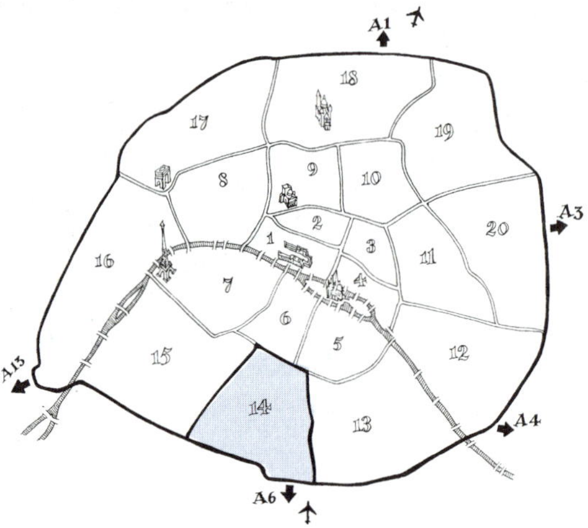

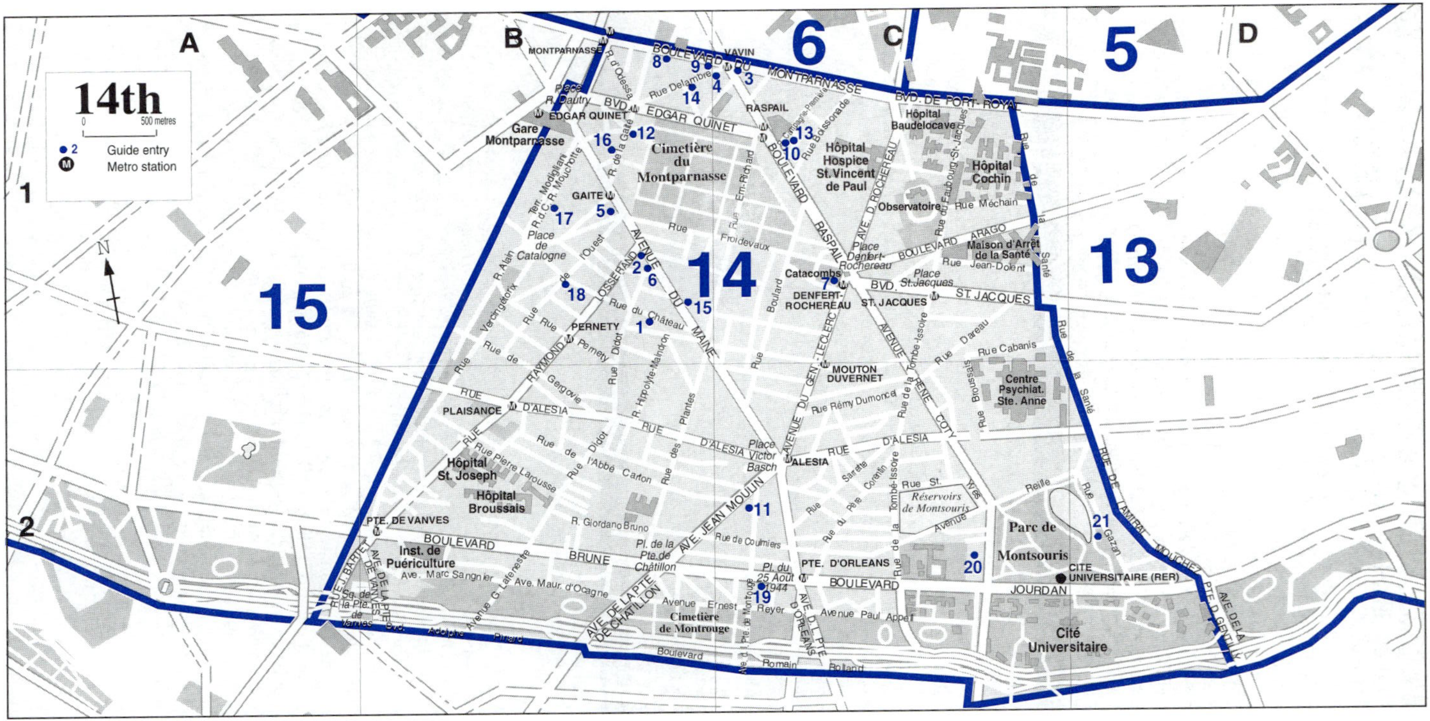

14th
0
500 metres
2 Guide entry
M Metro station
A
B
C
D
1
2
15
14
13
6
5
BOULEVARD DU MONTPARNASSE
BVD. DE PORT-ROYAL
BVD. EDGAR QUINET
BOULEVARD RASPAIL
AVENUE DU MAINE
AVENUE DU GEN. LECLERC
AVENUE RENÉ COTY
BOULEVARD ARAGO
BVD. ST. JACQUES
RUE D'ALESIA
AVE. JEAN MOULIN
BOULEVARD BRUNE
BOULEVARD JOURDAN
Gare Montparnasse
Cimetière du Montparnasse
Hôpital Baudelocave
Hôpital Cochin
Hôpital Hospice St. Vincent de Paul
Observatoire
Maison d'Arrêt de la Santé
Catacombs
Centre Psychiat. Ste. Anne
Réservoirs de Montsouris
Parc de Montsouris
Cité Universitaire
Hôpital St. Joseph
Hôpital Broussais
Inst. de Puériculture
Cimetière de Montrouge
MONTPARNASSE
VAVIN
RASPAIL
EDGAR QUINET
GAITE
PERNETY
PLAISANCE
DENFERT-ROCHEREAU
MOUTON DUVERNET
ALESIA
PTE. DE VANVES
PTE. D'ORLEANS
CITE UNIVERSITAIRE (RER)
Place de Catalogne
Place Denfert-Rochereau
Place St. Jacques
Place Victor Basch

L'Amuse Bouche 550F

Tel 43 35 31 61 Map B1.1 **R**
186 rue du Chateau 75014 M° Gaité/Mouton-Duvernet

Gilles Lambert, former sous-chef of Jacques Cagna, set up this tiny restaurant in May 1990 and continues in fine form. The elegant dining-room has apricot walls and attracts the customers with his '*classique mais renouvelée*' cuisine. Dishes on the *menu carte* are kept light with distinct flavours as in langoustine ravioli with basil (always on the menu), *foie de veau au pain d'épice*, fresh steamed cod with a warm herb vinaigrette and *épaule d'agneau à la curry de Madras*. Interesting desserts too: *croustillant* with a lime mousse; soup of medlar and cinnamon with vanilla ice cream; *mousse glacé à la banane, coulis d'abricot;* crème brulée with bergamot tea. Short well-chosen wine list. *Menu-carte* 120F/160F. ***Seats*** *24. L 12.15-2.15 D 7.15-10.30.* ***Closed*** *L Sat, all Sun & 1st 2 weeks Aug. Amex, Mastercard, Visa.*

Les Armes de Bretagne 800F

Tel 43 20 29 50 **Fax 43 27 84 11** Map B1.2 **R**
108 ave du Maine 75014 M° Gaité

From the moment of arrival at this luxurious, air-conditioned restaurant, the impeccable service takes care of your every need, including valet parking. There are two dining-rooms – one to the front with an enclosed terrace and the other at the back with a fresco by Zuber on the wall. Upstairs, a large salon can be divided into several small individual rooms for private parties. Tables are widely-spaced and the decor is Napoleon III in style. Seafood is the speciality, including oysters, clams, sea urchins, grilled sardines, *terrine de bar à la mousse de rouget, saumon à l'unilatéral*, fish soup and *petite marmite. Confit de canard, caneton à l'orange*, Lyons sausage with pistachios, *tournedos béarnaise* and saddle of lamb with truffled risotto are among the classic meat main courses with the likes of *parfait au café, fondant aux trois chocolats* and crème brulée to conclude. Set menu 200F. In the same ownership as *Pierre A la Fontaine Gaillon* in the 2nd arrondissement. ***Seats*** *120. L 12-3 D 7-11.* ***Closed*** *L Sat, all Sun & Aug. Amex, Diners, Mastercard, Visa.*

Bar à Huitres 500F

Tel 43 20 71 01 **Fax 43 21 35 47** Map C1.3 **R**
112 bd du Montparnasse 75014 M° Vavin

A great way to get things under way here is the *apéri-huitre* – one belon oyster, one claire, one spéciale and a glass of Pineau des Charentes, but the Bar à Huitres offers a lot more than just oysters! Sit in the glassed-over terrace or at the busy bar in this bright and pleasant brasserie for a plate of velvet swimming crabs, sea urchins, barnacles or sea squirts followed perhaps by skate with caper sauce, turbot with sorrel, *encornets à huile d'olive*, sautéed scallops with wild rice, *petit rouget à tapénade avec crème d'anchois* or grilled sea bass. For non-fish-eaters there are a couple of steaks and a veal fricassee. Various recent meals have shown the simplest dishes to be the best – in particular the squeaky fresh shellfish. The lengthy dessert list offers almost as much choice: *tarte fine chaude aux pommes, croustillant de tuiles aux marrons confits* (a speciality), various coupes, pear and chocolat sabayon. Set menus 98F (2 courses), 128F & 198F. Also at (with the same menu and opening hours) 33 bd Beaumarchais 75003 Tel 48 87 98 92 and 33 rue St Jacques 75005 Tel 44 07 27 37. ***Seats*** *150. Meals noon-2am. Amex, Mastercard, Visa.*

The best way to get around Paris is by bus or metro –
buy a book (carnet) of tickets at any metro station and save money

LE BISTROT DU DOME 500F

Tel 43 35 32 00 Map C1.4 **R**
1 rue Delambre 75014 Mº Vavin

Very near the famous Brasserie Le Dome, the Bistro is solely fish-orientated. The menu is renewed daily according to availability and written on slate boards which are passed around the tables. All is simply cooked – open with a tuna and salmon tartare or pan-fried shrimps, move on to roasted John Dory with herbs or skate with a vinaigrette sauce (hot) and finish with *pommes miettes* (apple crumble). ***Seats*** *60 (+ 16 outside). L 12.15-2.30 D 7.30-11.* ***Closed*** *Sun & Mon in Aug only. Amex, Mastercard, Visa.*

LA CAGOUILLE ★ 600F

Tel 43 22 09 01 **Fax 45 38 57 29** Map B1.5 **R**
Face 23 rue de l'Ouest, 12 place Constantin-Brancusi 75014 Mº Gaité

Best described as a classy bistro with attentive service, La Cagouille offers an exclusively seafood menu which changes twice a day to reflect the markets and the chef's inspiration. Oysters from Marennes, cockles from Granville, mussels, baby scallops, scrambled eggs with fresh and smoked salmon, sautéed shrimps, *calamars aux lentilles sautés à ail*, whitebait, *haddock à l'anglaise* with fresh pasta, red mullet sautéed in olive oil, fried monkfish with anchovy sauce, grilled mackerel with mustard sauce, *pavé* of tuna with ratatouille, *saumon à l'unilatéral, matelote* of eels... these are among the tempting choices you might find written up on the blackboard. Familiar desserts include *fondant au chocolat, tarte fine aux pommes* and profiteroles. Diners eat at round marble tables in surroundings decorated with items of marine interest; there's also an agreeable terrace. Note the large collection of cognacs. Set menus 150F (2 courses) 250F (3 courses and wine). ***Seats*** *70 (+ 40 outside). L 12-2 D 7.30-10.30.* ***Closed*** *1 week Christmas. Amex, Mastercard, Visa.*

LE CAROUBIER 400F

Tel 43 20 41 49 Map B1.6 **R**
122 ave du Maine 75014 Mº Gaité

Among the best couscous restaurants of the hundreds in Paris, Le Caroubier has been run by Pierre Michel for more than 20 years. The couscous comes with merguez, chicken, lamb (brochette, boulette, méchoui) and the other main-course choice is tagines – chicken, olives and preserved lemons; lamb, prunes, almonds and cinnamon; or lamb with broad beans and artichokes. Brik or pastilla to start, Oriental patisserie to finish, robust North African wines to accompany. Set menu 140F. ***Seats*** *60. L 12-2 D 7.30-10.30.* ***Closed*** *D Sun, L Mon, all Aug. Mastercard, Visa.*

LA CHAUMIÈRE DES GOURMETS 700F

Tel 43 21 22 59 Map C1.7 **R**
22 place Denfert-Rochereau 75014 Mº Denfert-Rochereau

Adjacent to the Denfert cinemas, the wooden frontage secluded by curtains hides a cosy spring-like dining-room with a strong Provençal atmosphere. It's a restaurant of rare warmth and attention to detail, shown for example in the *amuse-bouche* of *mousse de saumon* served in a precious coloured glass. Famous for his *civet de lièvre* and *chartreuse de perdreau au coulis de truffes*, Jean-Paul Huc also offers speciality fish dishes – sole grilled or meunière, *marmite dieppoise*, braised *turbotin* with mustard. Other dishes include *salade de ris de veau aux navets, filet de boeuf au jus de truffes* and *rognons de veau à la moutarde. Nougat glacé* with acacia honey, *tarte fine aux pommes tièdes* or splendid crème brulée to finish. Interesting wine list. Set menus 165F, 245F & 390F (*dégustation*). ***Seats*** *40. L 12-2.30 D 7-10.15.* ***Closed*** *L Sat, all Sun & 3 weeks Aug. Amex, Mastercard, Visa.*

La Coupole 450F

Tel 43 20 14 20 **Fax 43 35 46 14** Map B1.8 **R**
102 bd du Montparnasse 75014 M° Vavin

Good, honest food is served by very professional staff in this vast air-conditioned brasserie, beloved of Parisians and visitors alike, and busy since the day it opened in 1927. Reservations are taken only up to 8.30pm so should there be a wait for a table, order a drink at the bar to the left of the entrance and watch the comings and goings to pass the time. If you've arranged to meet friends, allow plenty of time just to find their table, so big is the place! Oysters, choucroute, snails and onion soup, grills and steak tartare are favourite choices along with cold leg of lamb with ratatouille niçoise, grilled lobster flamed with whisky, and cassoulet with goose. Starters range from melon (plain, with port, or *italienne*), rabbit terrine with cider jelly, and Welsh rarebit to Sevruga caviar with blinis and crème fraiche. A simpler menu is available on the terrace. Fish and shellfish are delivered daily. Set menus 87F (till 3pm, not Sat or Sun) & 109F (before 6pm & after 10pm). ***Seats** 450. Open 7.30am-2am (lunch served from noon). **Closed** D 24 Dec. Amex, Diners, Mastercard, Visa.*

Le Dome 700F

Tel 43 35 25 81 **Fax 42 79 01 19** Map B1.9 **R**
108 bd du Montparnasse 75014 M° Vavin

Bouillabaisse for two, oysters, clams and lobster remain among the traditional specialities at this most durable of Montparnasse institutions, and the *coquillages* can be enjoyed as a feast in the *plateau de fruits de mer* (220F for one person, 400F for two). Fruit is put to excellent use in many desserts, and Roquefort is the speciality cheese. ***Seats** 140. L 12-3 D 7-12.30. Open for coffee and snacks from 8am. **Closed** Mon, also Sun in Aug. Amex, Diners, Mastercard, Visa.*

Le Duc 900F

Tel 43 22 59 59 **Fax 43 20 46 73** Map C1.10 **R**
243 bd Raspail 75014 M° Raspail

A fashionable rendezvous for seafoodies, with the look of a classic luxury yacht. The à la carte menu is extremely varied within the fishy realm, with raw fish (sardines, bass, *poissons des iles* and coquilles St Jacques) as speciality starters. Alternatives could be *friture* of squid with (or without) garlic, *moules Madras or marinière*, warm crab mayonnaise or a selection of home-smoked fish with a vodka and *fines herbes* sauce. Main courses feature lobster *sauté à l'orange* or *seychelloise* (a house special), langoustines, plain grills and more elaborate white fish preparations – *rougets au pistou en vessie, lotte à la bohémienne (provençale* in winter), cod steamed in seaweed and grilled turbot. The cheese is Roquefort, the desserts Berthillon ices or *patisserie maison*. In the autumn of 1995 there were plans to introduce a lunchtime *menu d'affaires*. ***Seats** 50. L 12-2.30 D 8-10.30. **Closed** Sun, Mon & Public Holidays. Amex, Mastercard, Visa.*

Friant 340F

Tel 45 42 71 91 **Fax 45 42 04 67** Map C2.11 **H**
8 rue Friant 75014 M° Alésia

Situated in a quiet street, this inexpensive hotel offers small, adequately-equipped bedrooms with compact en suite bathrooms. Breakfast is taken in a glass-roofed courtyard. ***Rooms** 27. Mastercard, Visa.*

Aux Iles Marquises 640F

Tel 43 20 93 58 Map B1.12 **R**
15 rue de la Gaité 75014 M° Edgar Quinet/Montparnasse

Mathias Théry, a 'disciple' of the Troisgros brothers, presents a modern adaptation of classic cuisine in his marine-decorated restaurant lying between an Italian theatre and a naughty book/video shop. Fish soup, *salade de pétoncles en escabèche, marmite de poissons aux girolles fraiches, toutes les poissons grillées*, fillet of beef with red wine sauce – this is the Théry style, which extends to desserts such as hot passion fruit soufflé and *gateau au chocolat*. Set menus 130F & 150F. ***Seats*** *40. L 12-2 D 7-11.30.* ***Closed*** *L Sat, all Sun & 1-16 Aug. Amex, Mastercard, Visa.*

ISTRIA 530F

Tel 43 20 91 82 Fax 43 22 48 45 Map C1.13 **H**
29 rue Campagne-Première 75014 M° Raspail

Located not far from the attractions of Montparnasse and the Luxembourg Gardens, Danielle and Philippe Leroux's small hotel offers comfortable, inexpensive accommodation (showers only in the majority of rooms, four with bathtubs). All rooms have safes and hairdryers. Refurbishment in the last year has included new carpeting, bedcovers and 'Japanese' wallpaper. Breakfast is served in a charming vaulted room with exposed stone walls. No restaurant. 24-hour reception. ***Rooms*** *26. Amex, Diners, Mastercard, Visa.*

HOTEL LENOX 590F

Tel 43 35 34 50 Fax 43 20 46 64 Map B1.14 **H**
15 rue Delambre 75014 M° Vavin

The discreetly decorated Hotel Lenox with its antique furniture, paintings and old mirrors is an appealing place to stay. All rooms are double-glazed and equipped with en suite bathrooms (just eight have shower and WC only and come at the reduced rate of 540F), satellite TV, radio, direct-dial telephone and hairdryer. There's no restaurant, but light snacks and drinks are served in rooms, or the small bar from 5pm to 2am. Another Lenox, newly refurbished and with the same caring owner, is in the 7th arrondissement at 9 Rue de l'Université. ***Rooms*** *52. Amex, Mastercard, Diners, Visa.*

A glossary of French menu items starts on page 274

LOUS LANDÈS 650F

Tel 45 43 08 04 Map B1.15 **R**
157 ave du Maine 75014 M° Mouton-Duvernet

The convivial owner-chef of this auberge, Hervé Rumen, concentrates on the 'grande cuisine du Sud-Ouest' with such specialities as *foie gras de canard* ('pour apprécier 160F, pour gouter 80F'), millefeuille of foie gras with grapes and nuts in Banyuls wine, *St Pierre au bouillon de cèpes, magret* with Guérande salt and, of course, *cassoulet* (the best in Paris according to Hervé), followed by a caramelised pastry case of armagnac-soaked prunes, a mousse with red berries or a hot chocolate soufflé with vanilla ice cream. The interior of the restaurant is what the French would describe as *style anglais* and the widely spaced, white-clothed tables are laid with silver cutlery. Madiran, Cahors and Buzet (all from the South-West) are some of the 200 wines in stock. The more expensive set menu ('notre menu confiance') is a *dégustation* of six dishes to be ordered for whole parties. Set menus 195F & 310F. ***Seats*** *45 (+ 15 outside). L 12-2.30 D 8-10.30.* ***Closed*** *L Sat, all Sun, Aug. Amex, Diners, Mastercard, Visa.*

MERCURE PARIS-MONTPARNASSE 880F

Tel 43 35 28 28 Fax 43 27 98 64 Map B1.16 **H**
20 rue Gaité 75014 M° Gaité

Part of the large Mercure chain. Well-equipped bedrooms (safes, mini-bars, satellite TV) include 6 suites and 5 rooms adapted for disabled guests. There's a restaurant, bar and three conference rooms with a combined capacity of 120. Private parking for 45 cars (70F for 24 hours). In high season the room rate rises to 980F. ***Rooms*** *185. Amex, Diners, Mastercard, Visa.*

Méridien Montparnasse 1518F

Tel 44 36 44 36 **Fax 44 36 49 00** Map B1.17 **HR**
19 rue Cdt-Mouchotte 75014 Mº Montparnasse

This being one of the few skyscraper buildings (25 floors and eight lifts) in the centre of Paris, the view from the upper floors is exceptional. The comfortable bedrooms include 33 suites and six 'pied à terre' rooms with offices. All rooms are air-conditioned and soundproofed, and room equipment includes 20-channel television, radio and mini-bar. There's a business centre offering multi-lingual secretarial services and the hotel is well geared-up for conferences and banquets. 24-hour room service. Parking in public park beneath the hotel, 95F for 24 hours. Conference facilities for up to 2000. ***Rooms** 953. Amex, Diners, Mastercard, Visa.*

Montparnasse 25 1000F

Tel 44 36 44 25 Fax 44 36 49 03

This is the hotel's gastronomic dining option, where the classically-orientated carte includes some fairly elaborate dishes such as frogs' legs meunière with wild mushroom purée and foie gras, marinated mackerel with herbs and deep-fried langoustines on a salad of purslane, roast monkfish tail with a confit of young vegetables and a saffron jus, saddle of milk-fed Pauillac lamb flavoured with thyme, and roast *chapon* (a Mediterranean fish) garnished with ratatouille-stuffed squid. Desserts are just as interesting: *pastilla* of rhubarb with honey, a sabayon of mead and verbena ice cream; *cassolette* of apricot *en croute* with almond ice cream; warm feuilleté of nectarines poached in *vin de Maury*. Decor is 1920s with photos of stars of stage and screen from the period hanging on the walls next to reproduction Modigliani paintings. Tables are well spaced and service is discreetly efficient. California, Italy and Spain are featured on the wine list, as well as France. Set L 240F Set D 300F & 390F. ***Seats** 70. L 12-2.30 D 7.30-10.30. **Closed** Sat, Sun, Aug, 25 Dec-1 Jan & Public Holidays.*

Justine 700F

Tel 44 36 44 00

On the first floor of the hotel, overlooking a 100-square-metre terrace garden with trees, plants, shrubs and flowers, this brasserie resembles an enclosed veranda. The day starts with breakfast (till 10.30), the main à la carte coming on stream at midday and being available till closing. This might include such modish offerings as tomato millefeuille with fromage frais and pistou; beef carpaccio with parmesan shavings, and curried fricassee of tuna with lime-flavoured risotto, along with sole (grilled or meunière), steak with tomato provençale, béarnaise sauce and matchstick fries, and calf's liver with mashed potatoes. Lemon crème brulée, chocolate tart and caramelised pear to finish.
A special *Sur le Pouce* section of the menu lists quick bites like *croque monsieur*, club sandwich, cheeseburger and omelettes. At lunch (12-2.30) and dinner (7-10.30) there is also a fixed-price buffet. On Sundays, the Bébé Brunch menu (adults 220F, children 4-12 110F, under-4s free) is especially geared towards families. Set menu (buffet) 295F. ***Seats** 250. Meals 7am-10.30pm.*

Hotel de l'Orchidée 502F

Tel 43 22 70 50 **Fax 42 79 97 46** Map B1.18 **H**
65 rue de l'Ouest 75014 Mº Gaité

The reception area of this simply-appointed, family-owned hotel in the heart of Montparnasse has a small bar and lounge area with cane furniture, green plants and contemporary paintings and looks out on to an open terrace and garden. Basic comforts are provided in the bedrooms and all bathrooms have both tub and shower. Sauna and jacuzzi are available, like reception, 24 hours a day. Just one, reservable, parking place at 70F for 24 hours. ***Rooms** 40. Amex, Diners, Mastercard, Visa.*

ORLÉANS PALACE HOTEL — 550F

Tel 45 39 68 50 **Fax 45 43 65 64** Map C2.19 **H**
185-187 bd Brune 75014 Mº Porte d'Orléans

Virtually at Porte d'Orléans, the hotel has well-equipped bedrooms which are modern and functional (satellite TV, mini-bar, room safe, both tub and shower in the bathroom); about half overlook an interior garden. The piano bar serves light snacks and drinks until 1am. Two conference rooms, the larger holding up to 70 people theatre-style. ***Rooms*** *92. Amex, Diners, Mastercard, Visa.*

HOTEL DU PARC MONTSOURIS — 370F

Tel 45 89 09 72 **Fax 45 80 92 72** Map C2.20 **H**
4 rue du Parc Montsouris 75014 Mº Porte d'Orléans/Cité Universitaire

Close to the delightful Parc Montsouris with its lawns, trees, lake and flower-beds. There are seven apartments that sleep four (480F). Rooms are equipped with baths or showers and have satellite TV, desk and direct-dial telephone. The hotel's breakfast is a better bet than those at nearby cafés. There's limited street parking. ***Rooms*** *35. Amex, Mastercard, Visa.*

PAVILLON MONTSOURIS — 700F

Tel 45 88 38 52 **Fax 45 88 63 40** Map D2.21 **R**
20 rue Gazan 75014 Mº Cité Universitaire

The L-shaped restaurant in this delightful Belle Epoque house looking out over the charming Parc Montsouris provides an ideal setting for either a romantic dinner or a family occasion. In summer, seats on the outdoor terrace are sought after to enjoy the view while eating from one of the *carte-menus* compiled by chef Stéphane Ruel. The choice of his 'cuisine d'aujourd'hui' could include *fondant de pomme de terre au foie gras de canard,* ballotine of quail, roast monkfish with a juniper sauce, sweet and sour *lieu jaune* (a cod-like fish) with spinach pancakes, wild duck, roast saddle of lamb with a simple rosemary jus, *dome de café glacé* with chicory macaroon and *croustillant de figues aux épices.* Over 100 wines on an all-French list. Two private rooms (max 40). Set menus 199F & 265F. ***Seats*** *160 (+ 100 outside). L 12-2.30 D 7.30-10.30. Amex, Diners, Mastercard, Visa.*

15th Arrondissement
Places of Interest

Montparnasse, M° Montparnasse-Bienvenue
Tour Montparnasse (panoramic view from 56th & 59th storeys), 45 38 52 56, M° Montparnasse-Bienvenue
Héliport de Paris, 45 54 95 11, M° Balard
Parc A. Citroën (Futurist), M° Balard
Parc George Brassens, M° Convention
Porte de Versailles (Parc des Expositions de Paris), 43 95 37 00, M° Porte de Versailles
Musée de la Poste, 42 79 23 45, M° Montparnasse-Bienvenue

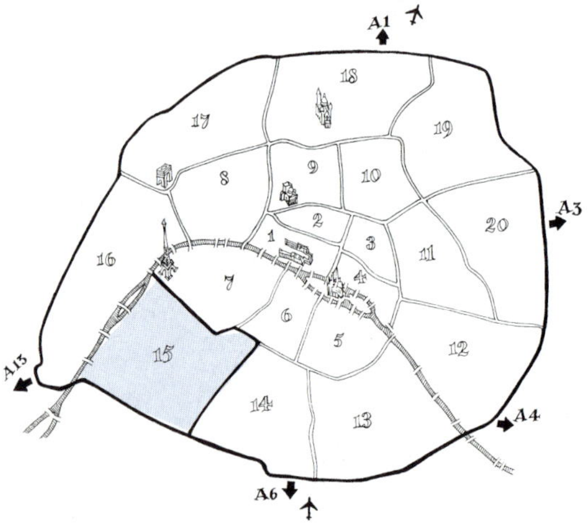

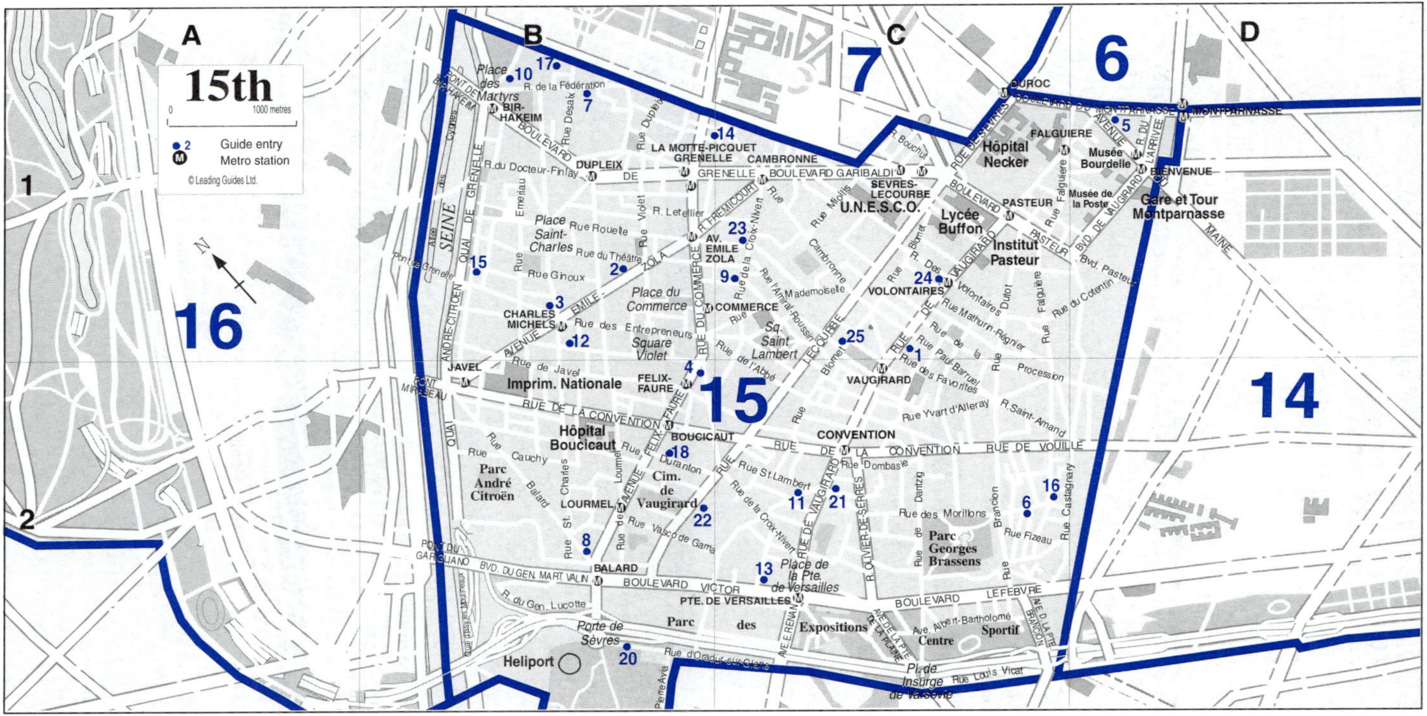
15th
0
1000 metres
Guide entry
Metro station
© Leading Guides Ltd.
A
B
C
D
1
2
16
7
6
14
15
Place des Martyrs
R. de la Fédération
BIR-HAKEIM
Rue Desaix
LA MOTTE-PICQUET GRENELLE
CAMBRONNE
DUPLEIX
R.du Docteur-Finlay
BOULEVARD GARIBALDI
SEVRES-LECOURBE
U.N.E.S.C.O.
Lycée Buffon
Hôpital Necker
FALGUIERE
Musée Bourdelle
BIENVENUE
Musée de la Poste
Gare et Tour Montparnasse
MONTPARNASSE
DUROC
PASTEUR
Institut Pasteur
Bvd. Pasteur
MAINE
SEINE
Place Saint-Charles
Rue Rouelle
Rue du Théâtre
Rue Ginoux
R. Letellier
AV. EMILE ZOLA
Place du Commerce
COMMERCE
CHARLES MICHELS
Rue des Entrepreneurs
Square Violet
Sq. Saint Lambert
VOLONTAIRES
VAUGIRARD
JAVEL
PONT MIRABEAU
Imprim. Nationale
FELIX-FAURE
RUE DE LA CONVENTION
Hôpital Boucicaut
BOUCICAUT
CONVENTION
RUE DE VOUILLE
Parc André Citroën
Cim. de Vaugirard
LOURMEL
BALARD
Rue des Morillons
Parc Georges Brassens
Place de la Pte. de Versailles
PTE. DE VERSAILLES
BOULEVARD VICTOR
BOULEVARD LEFEBVRE
Parc des Expositions
Centre Sportif
Porte de Sèvres
Heliport
Pl. de Insurgé de Varsovie
Rue Louis Vicat

ADAGIO — 895F

Tel 40 45 10 00 **Fax 40 45 10 10** Map C1.1 **H**
257/263 rue de Vaugirard 75015 M° Vaugirard

Built in 1990, the Adagio offers good standards of modern comfort ranging from airy public rooms and a bar with flower-filled terrace to neat, practical bedrooms, each of which has air-conditioning, double-glazing, satellite TV and mini-bar. There are hairdryers in the bathrooms. Conference facilities are versatile and most rooms have daylight. Good-value weekend breaks. Parking for 70 cars (70F for 24 hours). ***Rooms*** *187. Amex, Diners, Mastercard, Visa.*

ALIZÉ GRENELLE — 410F

Tel 45 78 08 22 **Fax 40 59 03 06** Map B1.2 **H**
87 ave Emile Zola 75015 M° Charles Michels

In the same ownership as the nearby *Beaugrenelle St Charles,* this is an inexpensive and pleasantly furnished hotel with double-glazed en suite bedrooms which are all equipped with hairdryer, trouser press, satellite TV, telephone, alarm clock and mini-bar. There is room service of breakfast, or it can be taken in your bedroom. ***Rooms*** *50. Amex, Diners, Mastercard, Visa.*

BEAUGRENELLE ST CHARLES — 400F

Tel 45 78 61 63 **Fax 45 79 04 38** Map B1.3 **H**
82 rue St Charles 75015 M° Charles Michels

Sister hotel to the *Alizé Grenelle* not far away, this is a modern hotel where the reception rooms have a distinctive art deco style and the bedrooms have bath or shower, toilet, satellite TV, direct-dial telephone, mini-bar, digital alarm, hairdryer and trouser press. A continuing programme of refurbishment means that this year 14 bedrooms were completely redecorated. Breakfast can be taken in your bedroom or in the pleasant ground-floor breakfast room. Meeting room (max 20). ***Rooms*** *51. Amex, Diners, Mastercard, Visa.*

BISTRO 121 — 600F

Tel 45 57 52 90 **Fax 45 57 14 69** Map B2.4 **R**
121 rue de la Convention 75015 M° Convention/Boucicaut

Jean Moussié greets customers in his 30-year-old bistro, whose Slavik-designed interior – mirrored ceiling and walls, pictures of life in Russia, claret-coloured carpet, maroon leather banquettes – seems to be from another era. The cuisine nevertheless keeps evolving, though fish predominates here and there's game like roast partridge and *lièvre à la royale* in season. The three-course menus (which include wine, coffee and service) are good value at 168F & 285F. House specialities include venison terrine, and orange sorbet with a rum punch. Other choices could be a fricassee of wild mushrooms with garlic, fried whitebait, braised bream with lemon and bay leaves, feuilleté of scallops with ginger, roast rack of lamb with a herb crust, duck breast with passion fruit, iced coffee parfait with a coffee sauce and pear crème brulée. Extensive wine list. ***Seats*** *80. L 12-3 D 7.30-12. Amex, Diners, Mastercard, Visa.*

CHEZ YVETTE — 350F

Tel 42 22 45 54 Map D1.5 **R**
1 rue d'Alencon/46bis bd du Montparnasse 75015 M° Montparnasse/Duroc

M Pineau prepares a selection of delicious seasonal fare at this very traditional Parisian restaurant which also enjoys a delightful family atmosphere. Rabbit terrine and foie gras are offered among the starters while main dishes could be trout in white wine, sole meunière or in champagne, or chateaubriand. There are excellent game dishes too, such as fillet of red deer with a game sauce and chestnuts, roast grouse and cock pheasant. Lovely desserts, too, such as *gateau aux noix, tartelettes aux poires ou quetsch* or *iles flottantes.* ***Seats*** *40. L 12-2 D 7-10.* ***Closed*** *Sat, Sun & Aug. Mastercard, Visa.*

Le Clos Morillons 600F

Tel 48 28 04 37 Fax 48 28 70 77 Map C2.6 **R**
50 rue des Morillons 75015 Mº Convention/Porte de Vanves

The menus here offer a short selection of dishes that combine unusual and exotic spicing with classic French cooking. The setting is very appropriate, being colonial in style with ceiling fans, wooden blinds, bamboo furniture and papyrus plants. It's owned and run by two brothers (one the chef, the other managing front of house), who together have created a very special place. Dishes on the carte are priced at 75F for starters and 125F for main courses, with one or two supplements. Begin with terrine of wild duck with green lentils and mace flowers, spiced calf's sweetbreads and aubergines wrapped in cabbage leaves, or fricassee of snails with ginger and celery. Main courses could be fricassee of guinea fowl with lime, masala and fettuccine, roast salt cod with potatoes and tonka beans or roast saddle of venison with spiced bread and puréed turnips. Desserts are equally innovative with crème brulée with caraway, or chocolate fondant with a jasmine-infused sauce. There's a good selection of cheeses (priced at 45F), and wines from the Loire take precedence. ***Seats** 30. L 12-2 D 8-10. **Closed** L Sat, all Sun & 2 weeks Aug & Public Holidays. Amex, Mastercard, Visa.*

Erawan 450F

Tel 47 83 55 67 Fax 47 34 85 98 Map B1.7 **R**
76 rue de la Fédération 75015 Mº La Motte Picquet Grenelle/Dupleix

A short stroll from the Champs du Mars, this friendly Thai restaurant offers a good selection of set menus (English versions of these and the carte are readily available). Traditional foods offered incude Thai rolls, shrimp cake fritters, fish steamed in a banana leaf, spicy chicken and bamboo shoots in Thai yellow curry and fried beef with green pepper and basil. French wine and Thai beer. Set menus 75F (L only, min 2 people), 116F, 142F, 152F, 175F. ***Seats** 80. L 12-2.30 D 7-10.30. **Closed** Sun, Aug, 25 Dec, 1 Jan & 1 May. Amex, Mastercard, Visa.*

La Farigoule 550F

Tel 45 54 35 41 Map B2.8 **R**
104 rue Balard 75015 Mº Balard

Behind a somewhat unprepossessing exterior, at the Balard metro end of the road, this is quite a smart little restaurant with panelled walls and large golden orange 'dish' lights lending a warm glow, matched by the friendly welcome. The cooking is firmly based in Provence; Jean Gras together with son Thierry hail from Toulon and offer a short menu of the specialities of that region beginning with marinated anchovies, stuffed sardines with virgin olive oil and rolled stuffed cabbage leaves with a filling of spinach, meat and lentils. Main dishes feature the well-known favourites of the area – *bouillabaisse du pecheur* and *bourride provençale*, both for a minimum of 2 diners, as well as *pieds et paquets marseillaise, daube provençale* and *aïoli du cabanon* – a cooked-to-order dish which includes salt cod, artichokes, cauliflower, beans, carrots and potatoes as well as mussels and whelks. Just a few desserts – *marquise au chocolat, oeufs à la neige*, pears poached in wine, sorbets and a feuilleté of apples with cinnamon, the last needing to be ordered at the beginning of the meal. ***Seats** 25. L 12-2 D 7.30-10. **Closed** D Mon, all Sun & last 2 weeks Aug. Amex, Mastercard, Visa.*

Fellini 460F

Tel 45 77 40 77 Map C1.9 **R**
58 rue de la Croix-Nivert 75015 Mº Commerce/Cambronne

Chef-patron Giuseppe Feleppa scours the markets daily for the ingredients for his daily-changing list of specials. This is the place to come for a wide selection of different home-made pastas, each accompanied by a well-made sauce. Tagliolini or fettuccine, for instance, could come with gorgonzola and spinach,

See over

porcini mushrooms or artichokes. Other starters could be stuffed squid, baked langoustines or clams. Main dishes include sea bass, red mullet and calf's liver, all prepared in the traditional Italian manner. Set L 130F. ***Seats*** *40. L 12-2.30 D 7-10.45.* ***Closed*** *L Sat, all Sun & Aug. Mastercard, Visa.*

Frantour Paris Suffren — 880F

Tel 45 78 50 00 **Fax 45 78 91 42** Map B1.10 **H**
20 rue Jean Rey 75015 Mº Bir Hakeim

A modern chain hotel that benefits from being just a three-minute walk from the Eiffel Tower, with most bedrooms also having a view of it. Rooms have satellite TV, mini-bar and a hairdryer in the bathrooms, which have both bath and shower facilities. The American-style bar Les Quatres Saisons is an impressive feature. There are also ten meeting rooms (max 170). ***Rooms*** *407. Amex, Diners, Mastercard, Visa.*

A glossary of French menu items starts on page 274

Le Gastroquet — 550F

Tel 48 28 60 91 Map C2.11 **R**
10 rue Desnouettes 75015 Mº Convention

Very much a neighbourhood restaurant, but chef-patron Dany Bulot's reputation (he was in charge of the kitchen at *Benoit (qv)* for 16 years) also brings customers from further afield to enjoy his robust, flavourful country cooking. *Saumon fumé mariné à l'ancienne, bouchées d'escargots avec un beurre à l'ail,* and *filets de rougets sur tartine de tapénade* feature among the delicious starters. Popular main courses are the *contrefilet à la confiture d'oignons,* confit of duck and *lièvre à la royale.* For an enjoyable dessert try *nougat glacé au miel* or *millefeuille à la crème pralinée.* Also look out for the daily specials like breaded veal escalope with curry sauce and rice. Madeleine Bulot organises the front of house offering a straightforward but professional service – staff never have to ask who is having what. Just down the road from the Parc des Expositions at Porte de Versailles, it sometimes opens on winter weekends when there is a major exhibition. Set L 105F Set L & D 149F. ***Seats*** *50. L 12-3 D 7-10.30.* ***Closed*** *Sat, Sun, Aug & most Public Holidays.*

Kim Anh — 600F

Tel 45 79 40 96 **Fax 40 59 49 78** Map B1.12 **R**
15 rue de l'Eglise 75015 Mº Charles Michels

A tiny, smartly decorated Vietnamese restaurant offering carefully prepared specialities from Saigon such as steamed ravioli filled with mushrooms, stuffed oven-baked crab, prawn curry with saffron rice and fish brochettes *à la tonkinoise.* The chef-proprietors are a charming husband and wife team, he looking after the front of house while she, single-handedly, cooks. Booking is essential. Set D 220F. ***Seats*** *30. D only 7.30-11.30. Amex, Diners, Mastercard, Visa.*

Mercure Paris-Vaugirard — 884F

Tel 44 19 03 03 **Fax 48 28 22 11** Map C2.13 **H**
69 bd Victor 75015 Mº Porte de Versailles

Across the boulevard from the Porte de Versailles exhibition centre, the hotel is popular with both exhibitors and visitors. Bedrooms are of a good size and have a good range of amenities including double-glazing, air-conditioning, cable TV and mini-bar. Smart bathrooms have marble floors and vanity units. Conference room (max 200). Private parking under the hotel (50F for 24 hours). ***Rooms*** *91. Amex, Diners, Mastercard, Visa.*

MOROT-GAUDRY ★ 900F

Tel 45 67 06 85 **Fax 45 67 55 72** Map B1.14 **R**
6 rue de la Cavalerie 75015 Mº La Motte Picquet Grenelle

The two greatest assets of this restaurant on the 8th floor of a 1930s building are the panoramic view of the Paris rooftops extending over to the Eiffel Tower and the fixed-price four-course lunch menu at 230F (wine and service included). Another set menu (390F) is also available to parties at both lunch and dinner; with a different glass of wine with each course it costs 550F. Book well in advance for a window table in the octagonal dining-room decorated with wood panelling and a large chandelier of Murano glass. Sample dishes from the à la carte menu are turbot with virgin olive oil and basil, *noix de St Jacques poelées avec crème de betteraves et flan de cresson, pièce de boeuf poelé au vieux Médoc* and, in season, breast of roast grouse with juniper and *lièvre à la royale à ma façon* (prepared to M Hamand's secret recipe), terrine of duck foie gras with Cadillac (a sweet white Bordeaux) or ravioli of *petits gris* with morels. After cheese comes the luxuriant decadence of *confidentiel pour chocophile*.
Set L 230F Set L & D 390F & 550F. ***Seats*** *70 (+ 26 outside). L 12-2 D 7.30-10.30.* ***Closed*** *Sat & Sun. Amex, Mastercard, Visa.*

HOTEL NIKKO DE PARIS 1690F

Tel 40 58 20 00 **Fax 45 75 42 35** Map B1.15 **HR**
61 quai de Grenelle 75015 Mº Bir Hakeim/Charles Michels

On the banks of the Seine between the Eiffel Tower and Mirabeau Bridge, the Nikko is a tall (31 floors), strikingly modern Japanese-owned hotel. Public areas are bright, cool, smart and spacious. La Seine Bar shows a more traditional side, with well-upholstered lightwood furniture, splendid Japanese murals and a nightly pianist. The majority of the bedrooms offer good views and are modern in style and design, each with cable TV, hairdryer and mini-bar among the up-to-date facilities provided. Executive rooms are on the top floor. There are 17 conference rooms, the largest with room for 900 theatre-style. Indoor swimming pool, gym, sauna. ***Rooms*** *764. Amex, Diners, Mastercard, Visa.*

Les Célébrités 1000F

Tel 40 58 21 29 Fax 40 58 16 03

A table by the window looking out over the Seine must be the best location to sit in this spacious, modern restaurant. As a starter you could choose pan-fried scallops with girolles, *escalope de foie gras poelé*, followed by *blanc de turbot à la tomate fraiche et au basilic, lièvre à la royale* or *cote de veau de lait avec pointes d'asperges*. If the excellent sweet trolley doesn't tempt you, try the *croustillant praliné au chocolat*. Open for breakfast 7-9.30am. Set menus 290F & 390F. ***Seats*** *70. L 12-2.30 D 7-10.* ***Closed*** *Aug.*

Benkay 1400F

Tel 40 58 21 26 Fax 40 58 21 30

Located on the 4th floor and with panoramic views, a Japanese restaurant with modern decor. On offer is a variety of set meals as well as a short but comprehensive *carte*. Even though there are 300F dinner and 520F tasting menus, lunchtime is best for lower-priced set menus (135F). The teppanyaki counter offers the opportunity for eating in a group and being entertained by the dexterity of the chef. ***Seats*** *120. L 12-2 D 6.30-10.*

L'OIE CENDRÉE 400F

Tel 45 31 91 91 Map C2.16 **R**
51 rue Labrouste 75015 Mº Plaisance

This is a neighbourhood restaurant with a rustic, provincial decor. Chef-patron Olivier Andreys prepares a selection of dishes from South-West France with duck and goose dominating a well-thought-out menu. Begin with *paté de foie gras*, scrambled eggs with wild mushrooms or *brik d'escargots*, a delicious variation, with snails and garlic butter, on the Tunisian *brik à l'oeuf*. Main dishes

See over

could be duck breast with a mustard sauce, aiguillettes of duck with a red wine sauce, cassoulet or veal kidneys with a garlic sauce. Round off an enjoyable meal with prunes in armagnac, chocolate charlotte with a mint sauce or *délice de chataignes*, a delicious chestnut confection. Set menu 138F. ***Seats*** *30. L 12-2 D 7.30-10.* ***Closed*** *L Sat, all Sun, 1st 2 weeks Aug, 25 Dec & 1 Jan. Mastercard, Visa.*

PARIS HILTON — 1590F

Tel 43 38 56 00 **Fax 44 38 56 10** Map B1.17 **H**
18 ave de Suffren 75015 M° Bir Hakeim

Close to the Eiffel Tower in the northernmost corner of the 15th arrondissement, the hotel enjoys splendid views over Gustave Eiffel's masterpiece, the Chaillot Palace and Trocadéro Gardens with their magnificent fountains and waterjets. Bedrooms are all equipped with air-conditioning, cable TV (18 channels) in stereo with remote control, radio, mini-bar and direct-dial telephone. Light meals are served in the Terrasse Restaurant 7am to 11pm while the Western Restaurant reflects the American South West in its choice of food. The Toit de Paris Bar on the 10th floor has a panoramic view. Conference centre and meeting rooms (max 800), valet parking. ***Rooms*** *462. Amex, Diners, Mastercard, Visa.*

PIERRE VEDEL — 600F

Tel 45 58 43 17 **Fax 45 58 42 65** Map B2.18 **R**
19 rue Duranton 75015 M° Boucicaut

A typical Parisian bistro with cream walls, plenty of mirrors, red leather bench seating, green plants and smart waiters. Owner Pierre Vedel buys his produce directly from the market and his wine from vineyards thus assuring fresh food and reasonably priced, personally chosen wines. Red mullet with saffron, saddle of hare with a celery purée and *grand veneur* sauce or *blanquette de veau à l'ancienne* could precede *oeuf poché avec brandade de morue en tapénade*, wild mushrooms sautéed with shallots, sardine fillets with sherry vinegar or artichokes with a salad of mussels and chives with a hint of curry. Foie gras is a speciality. From a choice of several desserts, choose a Catalan crème brulée or bitter chocolate charlotte with praline sauce. ***Seats*** *45. L 12-2 D 8-10.15.* ***Closed*** *Sat & Sun. Mastercard, Visa.*

LE RELAIS DE SÈVRES ★ — 800F

Tel 40 60 33 66 **Fax 45 57 04 22** Map B2.20 **R**
Hotel Sofitel 8-12 rue Louis-Armand 75015 M° Balard

A large hotel with a very elegant restaurant decorated in Louis XV style with a soft pastel decor, mirrors and paintings. In this setting Bruno Turbot creates his own version of haute cuisine, introducing subtle innovations to classic preparations. Choose from starters such as a salad of langoustines with a beetroot vinaigrette or smoked duck breast with Touraine goat's cheese and follow with a main course of great subtlety like braised pike steak with aged wine vinegar and shallots or small fillets of pork with ceps. Desserts could include a baked apple filled with spice ice cream surrounded by a cassis sauce. Menus change every Wednesday and the 320F *Menu Club* includes an aperitif, half a bottle of wine, mineral water and coffee. International wine list. Set menu 320F. ***Seats*** *45. L 12-2 D 7.30-10.* ***Closed*** *Sat, Sun, Aug, 1 week Christmas and Public Holidays.*

RÉSIDENCE SAINT-LAMBERT — 550F

Tel 48 28 63 14 **Fax 45 33 45 50** Map C2.21 **H**
5 rue Eugène-Gibez 75015 M° Convention

A neatly maintained and comfortable hotel which is approximately one kilometre north of the Porte de Versailles exhibition halls. All the bedrooms have satellite TV and mini-bars among a range of modern amenities. There is a small courtyard garden where breakfast can be taken in fine weather (breakfast can also be served in your room). ***Rooms*** *48. Amex, Diners, Mastercard, Visa.*

AUX SENTEURS DE PROVENCE 600F

Tel 45 57 11 98 **Fax 45 58 66 84** Map B2.22 **R**
295 rue Lecourbe 75015 Mº Lourmel

A very agreeable restaurant which specialises in the cooking of Provence, with dishes listed according to market availability. Popular items include starters such as fillets of red mullet with Mediterranean prawns and artichoke bottoms and ravioli of fresh salt cod with pistou. Main courses range from grilled sea bass with fennel and baby turbot grilled with a creamy fish sauce to *double d'agneau à la provençale* and a speciality of Marseilles, *pieds et paquets* – lamb tripe stuffed with savory, garlic and basil. To finish try the *marquise au chocolat à l'ancienne* or *nougat glacé* with acacia honey. Wines from the South-East predominate. Set menu 136F. ***Seats*** *40 (+ 10 outside). L 12.15-2 D 7.15-10.30.* ***Closed*** *L Sat, all Sun, 2 weeks Aug, 25 Dec & 1 Jan. Amex, Diners, Mastercard, Visa.*

WALLACE 650F

Tel 45 78 83 30 **Fax 40 58 19 43** Map C1.23 **H**
89 rue Fondary 75015 Mº Emile Zola/Cambronne/La Motte Picquet Grenelle

The short distance from three separate metro lines gives this neatly maintained hotel a good level of accessibility, while those arriving by car have the choice of 4 lock-up garages as well as 10 further spaces. Accommodation is cheerful in brightly decorated rooms which have modern facilities such as satellite TV, mini-bar, safe and a hairdryer in the bathroom. The courtyard has been glassed in and now offers a lovely setting for a buffet breakfast. ***Rooms*** *35. Amex, Diners, Mastercard, Visa.*

YLLEN 580F

Tel 45 67 67 67 **Fax 45 67 74 37** Map C1.24 **H**
196 rue de Vaugirard 75015 Mº Volontaires

The hotel stands directly across the road from the metro's only exit and is only a short distance from the Pasteur Institute. The neo-classical architecture of the building conceals a tastefully decorated modern interior with a marble entrance hall, leather chairs, oak panels and original paintings. Rooms, also with attractive paintings, are fully equipped, with marble bathroom, direct-dial telephone, satellite TV, mini-bar and individual electronic safe. Some have a hairdryer. Breakfast can be taken in the basement breakfast room or in your bedroom. ***Rooms*** *40. Amex, Diners, Mastercard, Visa.*

YVES QUINTARD 700F

Tel & Fax 42 50 22 27 Map C1.25 **R**
99 rue Blomet 75015 Mº Vaugirard

Yves Quintard's bright and colourful restaurant is a refreshing stop in rather austere residential surroundings. His lively and enthusiastic wife takes great care of her clientele, whether regulars or tourists. Equally colourful is the cooking, full of inventive and refreshing ideas like *saucisson de lièvre à la maison, salade d'endives aux noix* to begin, followed by fillets of baby red mullet with coriander, *parfait de ris de veau aux girolles, sauce Noilly, tarte fine de canard sauvage roti au miel et pommes de terres confites à la cive* or saddle of hare with a blackcurrant sauce. Desserts could include *beignets de figues, crème anglaise au Cointreau* or *crepes fourrées pralinées sauce vanille.* Set menus 175F & 280F. ***Seats*** *40. L 12.15-2.15 D 7.30-10.30.* ***Closed*** *L Sat, all Sun & 2 weeks Aug. Mastercard, Visa.*

16th Arrondissement

Places of Interest

Trocadéro
Palais de Chaillot, M° Trocadéro
Musée de la Marine, 45 53 31 70, M° Trocadéro
Musée du Cinéma, 45 53 74 39, M° Trocadéro
Palais de Tokyo (modern art), 47 23 61 27, M° Iéna
Parc des Princes, 42 88 02 76, M° Porte de Saint Cloud
Stade Roland Garros, 47 43 48 00, M° Porte d'Auteuil
Maison de Radio-France, 42 30 22 22, M° Ranelagh/Passy
Musée d'Ennery (China/Japan *objets d'art*), 45 53 57 96, M° Porte Dauphine
Musée Guimet (Asiatic art), 47 23 61 65, M° Boissière/Iéna
Maison Honoré de Balzac, 42 24 56 38, M° La Muette/Passy
Bois de Boulogne
Jardin d'Acclimatation
Musée National des Arts et Traditions Populaires, 44 17 60 00, M° Sablons
Hippodrome d'Auteuil (steeplechasing), M° Porte d'Auteuil
Hippodrome de Longchamp (flat racing)
Musée Dapper (pre-colonial Africa), 45 00 01 50, M° Victor Hugo
Musée des Monuments Français, 44 05 39 10, M° Trocadéro

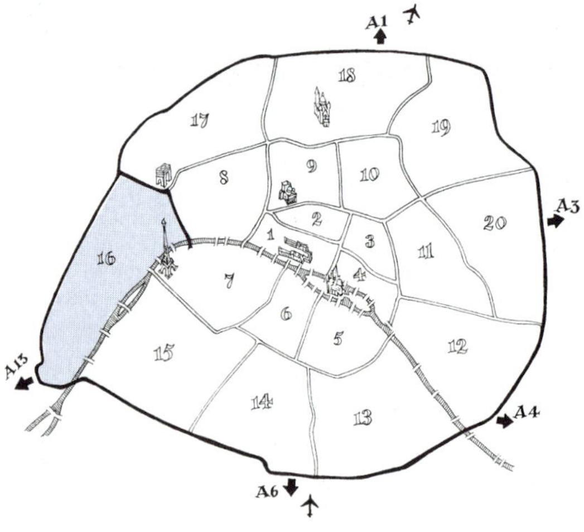

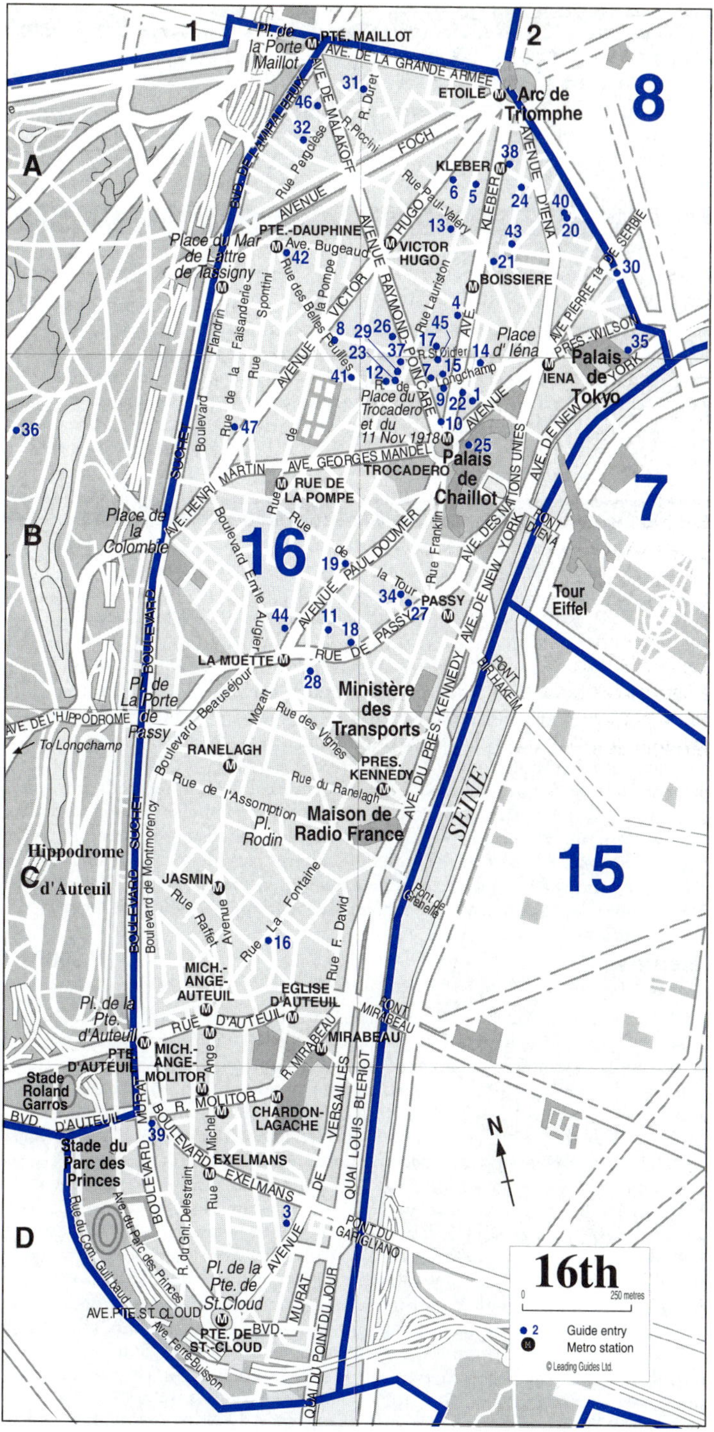
16th
0
250 metres
2 Guide entry
Metro station
© Leading Guides Ltd.
1
2
A
B
C
D
8
7
15
16
Pl. de la Porte Maillot
PTE. MAILLOT
AVE. DE LA GRANDE ARMEE
ETOILE
Arc de Triomphe
BVD. DE L'AMIRAL BRUIX
AVE. DE MALAKOFF
R. Duret
R. Piccini
Rue Pergolèse
AVENUE FOCH
KLEBER
AVENUE KLEBER
AVENUE D'IENA
Rue Paul-Valéry
AVE. HUGO
PTE.-DAUPHINE
Ave. Bugeaud
VICTOR HUGO
Place du Mar de Lattre de Tassigny
BOISSIERE
Rue Lauriston
AVENUE RAYMOND POINCARE
AVENUE VICTOR
Rue de la Pompe
Rue des Belles Feuilles
Spontini
Rue de la Faisanderie
Boulevard Flandrin
R. St Didier
Longchamp
Place d' Iéna
IENA
Palais de Tokyo
AVE. PIERRE 1er DE SERBIE
PRES.-WILSON
AVE. DE NEW YORK
Place du Trocadero et du 11 Nov 1918
Palais de Chaillot
TROCADERO
AVE. GEORGES MANDEL
AVE. HENRI MARTIN
RUE DE LA POMPE
AVE. DES NATIONS UNIES
PONT D'IENA
Tour Eiffel
Place de la Colombie
Boulevard Emile Augier
Rue de la Tour
AVENUE PAUL DOUMER
Rue Franklin
PASSY
RUE DE PASSY
LA MUETTE
PONT BIR-HAKEIM
Ministère des Transports
Pl. de La Porte de Passy
AVE. DE L'HIPPODROME
To Longchamp
Boulevard Beauséjour
Mozart
Rue des Vignes
RANELAGH
PRES. KENNEDY
Rue du Ranelagh
Rue de l'Assomption
AVE. DU PRES. KENNEDY
SEINE
Maison de Radio France
Pl. Rodin
Hippodrome d'Auteuil
BOULEVARD SUCHET
Boulevard de Montmorency
JASMIN
Rue Raffet
Avenue
Rue La Fontaine
Rue F. David
Pont de Grenelle
MICH.-ANGE-AUTEUIL
EGLISE D'AUTEUIL
Pl. de la Pte. d'Auteuil
RUE D'AUTEUIL
PONT MIRABEAU
MIRABEAU
R. MIRABEAU
PTE D'AUTEUIL
MICH.-ANGE-MOLITOR
Stade Roland Garros
R. MOLITOR
CHARDON-LAGACHE
AVE. DE VERSAILLES
QUAI LOUIS BLERIOT
BVD. D'AUTEUIL
BOULEVARD MURAT
Stade du Parc des Princes
EXELMANS
BOULEVARD EXELMANS
Rue Michel Ange
R. du Gnl. Delestraint
Rue du Com. Guilbaud
Ave. du Parc des Princes
PONT DU GARIGLIANO
Pl. de la Pte. de St.Cloud
AVENUE DE VERSAILLES
BVD. MURAT
QUAI DU POINT DU JOUR
AVE.PTE.ST.CLOUD
PTE. DE ST.-CLOUD
Ave. Ferré-Buisson
N

Al Mounia — 500F

Tel 47 27 57 28 Map B2.1 **R**
16 rue Magdebourg 75116 M° Trocadéro

Moorish decor – carved wood, mosaics, copper-topped tables – and a moreish menu of couscous, tagines and pastillas. The owners, who hail from Casablanca, have two other restaurants, one there and one in Madrid. ***Seats*** *60. L 12-1.30 D 8-10.30.* ***Closed*** *Sun & mid Jul-1 Sep. Amex, Mastercard, Visa.*

La Baie d'Ha Long — 400F

Tel 45 24 60 62 Fax 42 30 58 98 Map D1.3 **R**
164 ave de Versailles 75016 M° Porte St-Cloud

Roger Leroy's excellent little Vietnamese restaurant, whose decor includes ethnic *objets* and paintings and a number of aquaria, remains a popular haunt of showbiz folk. Nathalie Leroy is in charge in the kitchen, producing dishes to rouse and delight the palate: *lac xa* (soup with prawns and coconut milk), *ga gung* (chicken caramelised with ginger), *nuong nuong* (pork with lemon grass), *tom chien* (prawn fritters). Vietnamese fondue for two is a speciality as are various grills. Set L 99F. ***Seats*** *40 (+8 outside). L 12-2.30 D 7-10.* ***Closed*** *Sun, Aug, 24 Dec & 1 Jan. Amex, Mastercard, Visa.*

Baltimore — 1990F

Tel 44 34 54 54 Fax 44 34 54 44 Map A2.4 **HR**
88 bis ave Kléber 75116 M° Boissière

Gustave Eiffel is reputed to have been one of the designers of this hotel, built over 100 years ago, and recently renovated to its present luxury standard. It became a hotel in 1920 and took its name from one of its first and most famous clients, Lord Baltimore. It's an attractive corner building with green awnings and wrought-iron balustrades, in an enviable position between the Champs Elysées and Trocadéro. From the impressive marble-floored foyer with its sculptures on plinths to the elegant panelled library and intimate bar, the hotel oozes charm and elegance. There are some 700 works of contemporary art dotted around, making this a showcase for talented artists. Individually decorated bedrooms are air-conditioned, with deep-pile carpets, quality fabrics and cherrywood furniture, and offer as standard mini-bar, cable TV, bathrobes and decent toiletries in the smart bathrooms. In addition, 19 luxury bedrooms provide a safe, facilities for making tea and coffee, and a telephone extension in the bathroom. There's a non-smoking floor and cots are available. Valet parking. ***Rooms*** *105. Amex, Diners, Mastercard, Visa.*

Bertie's — 600F

Tel 44 34 54 34

Englishman Simon Gale has recently taken over in the kitchen of this most British of Parisian restaurants, but anglophile Albert Roux (of London's *Le Gavroche*) remains as a consultant and is the inspiration behind a menu (written in English with French translations) that takes diners on a culinary journey around the British Isles: Scottish oak-smoked salmon, Dublin Bay prawns 'Balmoral', celery and Stilton soup with a touch of port, traditional fish and chips, haddock wrapped in bacon, bubble and squeak with veal collops, steak and kidney pie, game (in season) roasted in the English fashion. Desserts include bread-and-butter pudding, Bramley apple crumble, hot chocolate fudge cake and Devon ices or there are British farmhouse cheeses, served with celery of course, and savouries like Welsh rarebit. There's a daily roast from the trolley for both lunch and dinner; always beef Wellington on Saturday and roast rib of Aberdeen Angus beef, complete with Yorkshire pudding and horseradish sauce, on Sunday. The decor follows the theme of the menu with black and white photos of British royals, past and present, around the cherrywood-panelled walls. Still just two English wines to leaven an otherwise all-French list, but to compensate there is an impressive list of single malt whiskies. Set menus 195F (Mon-Sat) & 250F (Sun, includes glass of pink champagne). ***Seats*** *60. L 12.30-2 D 7.30-10.30.*

LE BISTROT DE L'ETOILE 500F

Tel 40 67 11 16 **Fax 45 00 99 87** Map A2.5 **R**
19 rue Lauriston 75016 M° Kléber

One of Guy Savoy's 'other' restaurants: there are several, with the man himself at the one that carries his name in the 17th *(qv)*. Dark green outside and with foodie pictures decorating the interior, this little bistro offers a short *carte* (about six main dishes) plus daily specials that often change between lunch and dinner. Typical offerings might include carpaccio of duck with a citrus vinaigrette; brandade of haddock and marinated salmon with a warm salad of leeks, potatoes and aubergines; salmon steak cooked with a crispy skin and served with Puy lentils and mussel juice; *chartreuse de chou au lapereau confit, jus à l'estragon* and stuffed shank of veal simmered in cider and served with tagliatelle with mushrooms and parmesan. Finish with the likes of roast figs with cinnamon ice cream, warm apple tart or a spicy crème brulée. William Ledeuil cooks with invention that avoids gimmickry. Short, all-French wine list with three or four available by the glass. Pleasant service. ***Seats*** *52. L 12-2.30 D 7.30-12.* ***Closed*** *L Sat & all Sun. Amex, Mastercard, Visa.*

> The best way to get around Paris is by bus or metro –
> buy a book (carnet) of tickets at any metro station and save money

HOTEL DU BOIS 495F

Tel 45 00 31 96 **Fax 45 00 90 05** Map A2.6 **H**
11 rue du Dome 75116 M° Etoile

Small, neatly kept hotel on the corner of Rue du Dome and Avenue Victor Hugo, just a few steps away from the Arc de Triomphe. Bedrooms have a Laura Ashley look. The price quoted above is for a double with shower in low season but rates range up to 595F for a room with bath in high season. Continental breakfast is served in rooms or in a little lounge with 1930s-style leather chairs, opposite reception. No room service. Sister hotel to the *Queen Mary* in the 8th *(qv)*. ***Rooms*** *41. Amex, Mastercard, Visa.*

LA BUTTE CHAILLOT ★ 600F

Tel 47 27 88 88 **Fax 47 04 85 70** Map B2.9 **R**
112 ave Kléber 75116 M° Trocadéro

Owned by Guy Savoy, this fashionable restaurant is located on the ground floor and basement of a luxurious modern development in the 16th arrondissement. The decor makes effective use of iron girders and columns, and the turquoise of the seats matches the colour of the waiters' shirts. Provençal and Mediterranean influences are conspicuous on the short carte which includes *carpaccio de magret de canard au basilic, carré d'agneau au thym et à la tapénade* and simple desserts such as *tarte fine aux pommes*. Set menu 210F. ***Seats*** *90 (+ 40 outside). L 12-2.30 D 7-12. Amex, Diners, Mastercard, Visa.*

CARETTE

Tel 47 27 88 56 Map B2.10 **R**
4 place du Trocadéro 75116 M° Trocadéro

The redoubtable Mme Letard-Carette is the third generation to run this old-fashioned *salon de thé*/patisserie/restaurant established in 1927 and still a popular meeting place – bang on the Place Trocadéro, opposite the Parvis and Chaillot. It's open all day for coffee, tea, cakes and light savouries, and there are a few more substantial daily specials at lunchtime. Fresh seafood from the Rungis market – feuilleté of langoustines, fillet of hake *dieppoise* – is a speciality. There's also a busy take-away trade – all the patisserie is first-class, with macaroons a particular favourite. ***Open*** *8-6.45.* ***Closed*** *Tue. No credit cards.*

CHEZ GÉRAUD — 600F

Tel 45 20 33 00 Map B1.11 **R**
31 rue Vital 75016 M° La Muette

The carte changes with the seasons, the fixed-price menu daily according to the market, at this restaurant in a former bakery with marble floor, oak bar and an eye-catching faience fresco. Daniel Vacher's cooking is fairly traditional with the likes of baby leeks vinaigrette with shavings of foie gras, fricassee of wild mushrooms, tuna steak with green peppercorns, *carré de veau de lait roti*, entrecote steak either *persillée, nature* or with a wine sauce and game in season, notably hare *à la royale*, saddle of hare with sauce poivrade and roast partridge. Afters might include *Paris-Brest au café, crème caramel* and *nougat glacé*. About 100 entries on the all-French wine list – all their Beaujolais are bought in casks direct from the producer and bottled on the premises. Set menu 200F. *Seats 40. L 12-2 D 7.30-10.* ***Closed*** *L Sat, all Sun & Aug. Amex, Mastercard, Visa.*

CHEZ NGO — 400F

Tel & Fax 47 04 53 20 Map B2.12 **R**
70 rue de Longchamp 75116 M° Trocadéro

There are two styles of cooking here – Chinese and Thai. The specialities concern seafood, as in steamed bass with Chinese mushrooms and soya sauce, sautéed mussels with Thai basil leaves, or sautéed lobster with ginger and chives. Meat-eaters are not neglected, however, and may like to try the sautéed beef Peking-style. A ten-metre-long fresco of Chinese landscape and plenty of wood create a realistic old Chinese decor. Drink French wines or Oriental beers. Set L 97F & 98F (Mon-Fri including wine) Set L & D 398F (for two). ***Seats*** *90 L 12-3 D 7-11. Amex, Diners, Mastercard, Visa.*

CONTI ★ 750F

Tel 47 27 74 67 **Fax 47 27 37 66** Map A2.13 **R**
72 rue Lauriston 75116 M° Boissière

In intimate, quietly luxurious surroundings a civilised clientele enjoys the high-quality Italian cooking of Frenchman Michel Ranvier. The produce of both countries combines in a delightful menu that might include tomato and sardine tart, *carpaccio fondant de boeuf*, tagliatelle with ceps, ricotta ravioli with sage butter, potato gnocchi with gorgonzola, red mullet with caramelised onions and a balsamic vinegar jus, grilled langoustines *au pistou*, escalopes of duck with *mostarda di Cremona* and polenta, and *foie de veau au Moscato*. Desserts are equally tempting: *dolce aux fraises de bois*, bitter chocolate gateau, *panna à la vanille gousse caramel Marsala*. 300-strong wine list includes all areas of Italy and most of the 'grands vins' of France. Set L 198F. ***Seats*** *45. L 12-2.30 D 7.30-10.30.* ***Closed*** *Sat, Sun, 3 weeks Aug & Christmas-New Year. Amex, Diners, Mastercard, Visa.*

FAKHR EL DINE — 500F

Tel 47 27 90 00 **Fax 47 27 11 39** Map B2.14 **R**
30 rue de Longchamp 75016 M° Trocadéro

Good classic and modern Lebanese cuisine is guaranteed in the warm surroundings of two spacious dining-rooms decorated with large frescoes. Begin with *fatayers* (spinach rissoles) or *sojok* (spicy sausages flambéed with lemon juice) and move on to *chiche taouck* (chicken brochettes marinated in lemon, oil and garlic) or lamb cutlets, followed by one of a variety of sweet Lebanese desserts. Lebanese and French wines, the latter including a Beaujolais bought by the cask and bottled on the premises. Also at Rue Quentin Bauchart in the 8th (Tel 47 23 44 42) and the Institut du Monde Arabe in the 5th (Tel 46 33 47 70, closed Mon). Set menu 160F. ***Seats*** *110. Meals 12-12. Amex, Diners, Mastercard, Visa.*

FAUGERON ★★★ 1200F

Tel 47 04 24 53 **Fax 47 55 62 90** Map B2.15 **R**
52 rue de Longchamp 75116 M° Trocadéro

It was in 1972 that Henri Faugeron first put puréed truffles together with a simple soft-boiled hen's egg, added brioche 'soldiers', and created his now famous signature dish *oeufs coque Faugeron*; a dish as popular now as it was then. But there are many other wonderful dishes to be enjoyed here: tournedos of lobster with ravioli of ceps is stunning and a dish of fresh foie gras with figs and caramelised butter lacks only "the sound of trumpets" – both from the day's *Grand Menu Dégustation*. What you will not find here is asparagus in autumn or strawberries in winter as Henri is a stickler for using ingredients only in their natural season when they are at their very best. Game is a particular speciality in season – noisettes of venison with autumn fruits, *croustillant et salmis de faisan aux jus de truffes* – and amongst the desserts *mille-feuille 'Amadéus' en duo de chocolats*, the creation of Gerlindé Faugeron, who is the charming hostess overseeing the discreetly cosseting service. The immaculately hand-written wine list is outstanding and wine waiter Jean-Claude Jambon was voted the 'best sommelier in the world' a few years ago. Each month there is a selection of three or four wines by the glass, usually including a first-growth claret. Our Paris restaurant of the year in 1995. Set L 290F Set L & D 650F (*dégustation*) Set D 550F (with wine). Valet parking at lunchtime. ***Seats*** *50. L 12-2 D 7.30-10.* ***Closed*** *Sat (except D Oct-Apr), Sun, Aug & 23 Dec-2 Jan. Amex, Mastercard, Visa.*

LA FONTAINE D'AUTEUIL 700F

Tel 42 88 04 47 Map C1.16 **R**
35bis rue la Fontaine 75016 M° Jasmin

A former brasserie, with dark wood and lots of flowers, this high-class neighbourhood restaurant is situated near the Maison de la Radio. Xavier Grégoire's style is traditional, lightened for today's tastes, and many of his best dishes are based on fish and shellfish: warm lobster salad with Sauternes and ginger vinaigrette (a speciality), scallops simply sautéed with a balsamic vinegar dressing, *filet de rouget poelé à l'aïoli avec pommes roseval au jus de tapénade, pate choux de ris de veau champignons anis*, tournedos of salmon with bacon and green lentils. Other specialities include fillet of lamb with a rosemary jus and breast of pigeon marinated in soya and lemon and served with a herb salad and, among the desserts, millefeuille and *chiboust aux framboises beurre d'orange*. No wines by the glass are shown on the wine list but they will happily come up with something on request. Set L 170F Set L & D 350F (*dégustation*) Set D 230F. ***Seats*** *40. L 12-2.15 D 7.30-10.* ***Closed*** *L Sat, all Sun, 1 week Feb & 3 weeks Aug. Amex, Diners, Mastercard, Visa.*

See page 9 for a list of starred restaurants

GARDEN ELYSÉE 1450F

Tel 47 55 01 11 **Fax 47 27 79 24** Map A2.17 **H**
12 rue St Didier 75116 M° Boissière/Trocadéro

Spacious air-conditioned bedrooms with satellite TV, individual room-safe and bathrooms with both tub and shower in a modern, six-storey (with lifts) building set back from the street with gardens front and rear. Room service operates till 11pm and the bar stays open until midnight. Refurbishment of all rooms was planned to be complete by the end of 1995. Private parking for four cars (150F for 24 hours). ***Rooms*** *48. Amex, Diners, Mastercard, Visa.*

Hameau de Passy 560F

Tel 42 88 47 55 **Fax 42 30 83 72** Map B1.18 **H**
48 rue de Passy 75016 Mº Passy/La Muette

Glass-enclosed spiral staircases either side of the main entrance are an unusual feature at this peaceful hotel opposite a private garden in a cul de sac near Trocadéro. Bright, modern, straightforward accommodation (12 rooms have shower and WC only); pleasant staff. Room rates include breakfast, served in your room or in the lounge. Room service, provided from outside the hotel, is available between 5pm and 3am. ***Rooms*** *32. Amex, Diners, Mastercard, Visa.*

Jean-Claude Ferrero 850F

Tel 45 04 42 42 **Fax 45 04 67 71** Map B1.19 **R**
38 rue Vital 75016 Mº La Muette

In this grand Second Empire *hotel particulier* the grandest way to celebrate is to work through the seasonal truffle or mushroom menus. If those are earthier than your taste, try the *bouillabaisse raphaëloise*, herb-stuffed bass *en croute* (both for 2 persons), noisettes of venison with bilberries, the fish of the day with olive oil and a gratin of fennel or one of the traditional dishes like *brandade de morue salée* and *blanquette de veau à l'ancienne*. As we went to press, the restaurant was closed for renovation. Set L 200F Set L & D 280F & 350F. Three private rooms. ***Seats*** *50. L 12-2.30 D 6-10.30.* ***Closed*** *Sat, Sun (except D Nov-Feb) 1st 2 weeks May & last 3 weeks Aug. Amex, Mastercard, Visa.*

See page 9 for a list of starred restaurants

Joël Robuchon

Tel 47 27 12 27 **Fax 47 27 31 22** Map A2.26 **R**
59 ave Raymond Poincaré 75016 Mº Trocadéro

As we went to press, our information was that by publication date Joël Robuchon would have left the Paris restaurant scene. Acknowledged as one of *the* greatest chefs in the world, he made an enormous impact during his years in Paris, and a seat at one of his tables was always the result of booking months, not just weeks, ahead. Specialities such as *gelée de caviar à la crème de chou-fleur, tarte friande de truffes aux oignons et lard fumé* and *lièvre à la royale* earned superlatives in these and other pages, and in Robuchon's hands even the humble *pommes purée* was elevated to almost regal status. If he changes his mind, get on the phone now. ***Seats*** *45. L 12.15-2.15 D 7.30-10.15.* ***Closed*** *Sat, Sun & 4 weeks Jul/Aug. Access, Visa.*

Kambodgia 600F

Tel & Fax 47 23 31 80 Map A2.20 **R**
15 rue Bassano 75016 Mº George V

Oriental wood panelling and embroideries lend a clubby atmosphere to this intimate restaurant just off the Champs Elysées. There are some Thai and Vietnamese dishes but the cooking is mainly Cambodian: tropical fish soup, an assortment of hors d'oeuvre from Indo-China, *feuilleté* of curried chicken, prawns and squid sautéed with basil and pimentos, spicy beef with coconut milk, chicken with honey and lemon in a crisp pastry case. Steamed dishes include a 'ravioli' of prawns with bamboo shoots and from the rotisserie come grilled chicken with saté, pork with Thai herbs and fish wrapped in banana leaves with ginger. For afters there are exotic fruits and sorbets along with various fritters (apple with caramel, flambéed banana) and iced mango soup with coconut milk. Short list of French wines and a couple of beers, one Thai and one Chinese. Set L 170F. ***Seats*** *54. L 12-2.30 D 7-11.* ***Closed*** *L Sat & all Sun. Amex, Diners, Mastercard, Visa.*

L'Hotel Kléber — 740F

Tel 47 23 80 22 **Fax 49 52 07 20** Map A2.21 **H**
7 rue Belloy 75116 Mº Kléber/Boissière

A second Empire building between Etoile and Trocadéro in the business and embassy district. Small and comfortable with friendly staff and bedrooms that are well equipped with multi-channel TV, direct-dial phone and hairdryer. All bathrooms have both shower and tub. The bar, which also serves snacks, is open 24 hours a day. ***Rooms** 23. Amex, Diners, Mastercard, Visa.*

Kléber Palace — 1310F

Tel 44 05 75 00 **Fax 44 05 74 74** Map B2.22 **H**
81 ave Kléber 75016 Mº Trocadéro

Located in the 16th arrondissement, near the Palais de Chaillot, this plush, ultra-modern *résidence hotelière* opened in October 1993. All bedrooms are air-conditioned and have kitchenettes (sometimes only a sink and hob in a cabinet) and overlook either the hotel's plant-filled atrium or the street. Leisure facilities are good: the fitness centre in the basement has a mini-gym, sauna, Turkish bath, solarium and huge jacuzzi. Three conference rooms are available for hire. Limited room service. Private parking 60F. ***Rooms** 83. Amex, Diners, Mastercard, Visa.*

Hotel de Longchamp — 620F

Tel 47 27 13 48 **Fax 47 55 68 26** Map B2.23 **H**
68 rue de Longchamp 75116 Mº Trocadéro

Quiet, comfortable and welcoming hotel near Place de Mexico. Modernised behind its traditional facade, it offers all the necessities, including satellite TV and mini-bars, in bedrooms done out in pastel shades. The rate quoted above is the high season price for a room with shower and WC only, rooms with bath are 680F or 750F. Prices are reduced by 20% in July and August. Private parking 100F per day (reserve when booking room). ***Rooms** 23. Amex, Diners, Mastercard, Visa.*

Majestic — 1170F

Tel 45 00 83 70 **Fax 45 00 29 48** Map A2.24 **H**
29 rue Dumont-d'Urville 75116 Mº Kléber

Traditionally furnished bedrooms come with air-conditioning at this charming hotel not far from the Arc de Triomphe. Other modern amenities include satellite TV, mini-bar and room safe. Pick of the accommodation is the penthouse suite (1900F) with a flowery balcony. Double-glazing keeps things peaceful. Some of the atmosphere of old France remains in the civilised public areas. Sister hotel to the nearby *Raphael (qv)* and the *Regina (qv)* in the 1st. ***Rooms** 30. Amex, Diners, Mastercard, Visa.*

Les Monuments — 600F

Tel & Fax 44 05 90 00 **Map B2.25** **R**
1 place du Trocadéro Mº Trocadéro

Part of the main concourse of the Musée des Monuments Français at the Palais de Chaillot, Les Monuments has a big plus in the view of the Eiffel Tower, especially in summer when tables spill out on to the terrace. It is run by chocolatier/patissier Christian Constant (see entry in the 7th), so it is not surprising that desserts – *tarte fondante au chocolat, millefeuille aux poires* – are a highlight of a menu that might also include a salad of lobster and langoustines with lime and ginger, duck with mango and a ragout of veal sweetbreads. In the afternoon (4-6pm) the restaurant becomes a *salon de thé* with snacks like ham quiche and salad of white cabbage with Bayonne ham plus, of course, Monsieur Constant's patisserie and chocolate creations. At the time of going to press they were no longer opening for dinner. Set meal 180F. ***Seats** 40. **Open** 12-2.30 (lunch) & 4-6pm (salon de thé). **Closed** Tue. Mastercard, Visa.*

Le Parc 2300F

Tel 44 05 66 66 **Fax 44 05 66 00** Map A2.26 **HR**
55 ave Raymond Poincaré 75016 Mº Trocadéro

A discreet hotel, between the Place Victor Hugo and the Trocadéro, which aims to combine English refinement with French hospitality, and does so with great charm. The English 'country house' feel is achieved with wood panelling and brass chandeliers in the lobby and Nina Campbell interiors featuring her hallmark dark green and red plaid fabrics in the bar-lounge. Bedrooms, in five buildings set around a delightful courtyard full of trees and flowers, come in nine different colour schemes ranging from light and summery to rich and warm. Some beds are four-posters and many of the others canopied, and all have padded headboards that gain muslin anti-macassars in the evening when beds are turned down, lights lit and curtains drawn. Air-conditioning, two direct telephone lines, room safe, mini-bar and Bang & Olufsen cable TV are standard. 24-hour room service. One floor of rooms is designated non-smoking. Valet parking 150F a day. ***Rooms*** *120. Amex, Diners, Mastercard, Visa.*

Le Relais du Parc ★ 700F

Tel 44 05 66 10

Two rooms running by the side of a leafy courtyard, into which the tables spill out in summer, are decorated in a colonial style that includes old photographs of safaris. Redwood is used for the bar, the tables and the chairs, whose grey and white upholstery takes up the colour of the tiled floor. Managers are smart and soberly suited, and the waiters wear distinctive silk waistcoats. Chef Gilles Renault's menu has an immediate, straightforward appeal: hot mackerel tart; duck terrine flavoured with thyme; roast lobster with basil butter; black pudding with puréed potatoes; steak with shallots, lightly poached bone marrow and dauphinoise potatoes; breaded veal escalope with fresh tagliatelle and lemon grass. Desserts range from classics like café liégois and crème caramel *à la cassonade* to a peach and strawberry soup with hibiscus flowers or simple fresh fruit salad. Booking advisable. Set meal about 300F (no-choice, daily-changing). ***Seats*** *80 (+ 90 outside). L 12-2.30 D 7.30-10.30.*

Passy Eiffel 580F

Tel 45 25 55 66 **Fax 42 88 89 88** Map B2.27 **H**
10 rue de Passy 75016 Mº Passy

The rooms here are spread over five floors, and one or two are large enough for family occupation. Traditionally-styled bedrooms boast fresh-cut flowers and about half are air-conditioned. The price quoted above is for a room with shower and WC (there's a 70F supplement for a bathtub) in high season. No restaurant, but there's a conservatory breakfast room with a couple of tables out on a patio when the weather allows. The hotel is just across the river from the Eiffel Tower. ***Rooms*** *50. Amex, Diners, Mastercard, Visa.*

Passy Mandarin 500F

Tel 42 88 12 18 **Fax 42 60 33 92** Map B1.28 **R**
6 rue Bois le Vent 75016 Mº La Muette

Three handsomely appointed dining areas (one reserved for non-smokers), with walls and furniture in dark wood and Chinese artwork in traditional style, make up one of the capital's leading Chinese restaurants. Cooking is Cantonese, with a short list also of Vietnamese dishes and, new this year, a few spicy Thai dishes. Dim sum, available lunchtime and evening, are particularly good, and as well as the familiar varieties there are prawn-stuffed courgette rings, shark's fin ravioli and buns (*bau*) with a filling of curried chicken. Elsewhere, prawns, crab, monkfish, chicken, pork and beef are all well prepared in straightforward style, along with six ways with duck – lacquered is a speciality. A Chinese fondue for a minimum of two diners is for special occasions. Another branch, more sumptuously decorated, is in the 2nd arrondissement (*qv*). That one is closed on Sundays. Staff at both are friendly and attentive. Set menu 460F (for two, Peking duck). ***Seats*** *90. L 12-2.30 D 7-11. Amex, Mastercard, Visa.*

Paul Chene — 750F

Tel 47 27 63 17 Map B2.29 **R**
123 rue Lauriston 75116 M° Trocadéro

Classic dishes make up the majority of the menu at this elegantly appointed, formal restaurant just up from Trocadéro. *Terrine de canard*, fillets of sole *'tout Paris'*, whole baby turbot with hollandaise sauce, *daube de boeuf à l'ancienne* and *confit d'oie* will appeal to traditional tastes. A particular speciality in their season is fresh truffles, either with a simple salad or *en feuilleté* with a *sauce périgourdine*. Among desserts such as chocolate profiteroles and fresh pineapple with Kirsch look out, in winter, for their *croustillant de pommes* with vanilla ice cream. Along with this traditional style of cooking goes smart, correct and efficient service. It's a quiet, civilised place with a jolly maitre d'hotel who's a past master at filleting and presenting fish dishes. The wine list majors on Bordeaux, and there's a selection of grand and expensive digestifs. A Sauternes and a Muscadet are served by the glass and a champagne by the goblet. Set menus 200F & 250F. ***Seats*** *55. L 12.30-2.45 D 7.30-10.30.* ***Closed*** *L Sat, all Sun, 28 Jul-21 Aug & 22 Dec-2 Jan. Amex, Diners, Mastercard, Visa.*

> The best way to get around Paris is by bus or metro –
> buy a book (carnet) of tickets at any metro station and save money

Pavillon Noura — 500F

Tel 47 20 33 33 **Fax 47 20 60 31** Map A2.30 **R**
21 ave Marceau 75116 M° Alma-Marceau/George V

The Middle East, especially Lebanon, is very much in evidence on entering the large dining-room. Frescoes of Tyre and Sidon taken from 17th-century drawings cover two walls. The exotic interior of wood and ceramic surfaces, chandeliers and banquette seating sets the stage perfectly for some authentic Lebanese food. *Tabbouleh* (cracked wheat with parsley, mint, lemon, olive oil and onions) and *falafel* (bean croquettes with garlic, chick peas and sesame oil) are cold and hot starters respectively, which could be followed by charcoal-grilled skewered lamb or *kofta korfalyeh* (lamb meatballs with tomato). The Patisserie Noura a few doors up the road supplies the sweet pastries (also to take away) and the Noura Traiteur, on the opposite corner to the Patisserie, is a less formal, snackier version of the Pavillon. Set L 156F & 190F Set D 220F, 280F & 320F. ***Seats*** *105. L 12-2.30 D 8-12. Amex, Diners, Mastercard, Visa.*

Hotel Pergolèse — 960F

Tel 40 67 96 77 **Fax 45 00 12 11** Map A2.31 **H**
3 rue Pergolèse 75116 M° Argentine

Ultra-modern behind its fin-de-siècle facade, the Pergolèse offers comfort, service and a style all its own. Half the bedrooms are on the street side, the others over look the courtyard, and all feature ash bedheads. TVs and mini-bars are hidden away in the furniture; bathrooms gleam in glass, marble and chrome. The price above is for low season; in high season the rate rises to 1160F. Room service till 10pm. ***Rooms*** *40. Amex, Diners, Mastercard, Visa.*

Le Pergolèse — 700F

Tel 45 00 21 40 **Fax 45 00 81 31** Map A1.32 **R**
40 rue Pergolèse 75116 M° Porte Maillot

A pastel-pretty restaurant with some delightful paintings and flower displays. Chef-patron Albert Corre's style is classic, suitably lightened, and there are some

See over

interesting combinations on his menu: ravioli of langoustines with duxelles, scallops cooked in little jacket potatoes, red mullet with fresh pasta, olive oil and basil, magret of duck with a honey and vinegar sauce, veal kidneys with a violet mustard sauce. Desserts like *moelleux chocolat* with vanilla ice cream and a macaroon *surprise* with red berry coulis are equally appealing, and there's a good regional French wine list. Set menus 230F & 320F. ***Seats** 45. L 12.2.30 D 8-10.30.* ***Closed** Sat, Sun, 24, 25 Dec & Aug. Amex, Mastercard, Visa.*

La Petite Tour ★ 850F

Tel 45 20 09 31 Map B2.34 **R**
11 rue de la Tour 75116 Mº Passy

Christine Israël's flower displays are one delight at this friendly little restaurant with its rough-painted walls and red plush upholstery, but the main one is Freddy Israël's excellent cooking. A menu of classic dishes acknowledges the season but otherwise does not change much – quite deliberately: *bisque de homard*, brochette of scallops, hot duck foie gras with blueberries, *cassolette d'escargots aux aromates*, escalopes of salmon with sorrel, fillet of sole with orange, magret of duck with fresh ceps, veal kidneys with mustard sauce, *tete de veau sauce ravigote*, jugged hare with fresh pasta, venison with a Grand Veneur sauce, crème brulée, *vacherin glacé*, chocolate gateau, *ile flottante aux pralines*. Well-balanced, all-French wine list. ***Seats** 40. L 12-2.30 D 7.30-10.30.* ***Closed** Sun & 2 weeks mid-Aug. Amex, Diners, Mastercard, Visa.*

Port Alma 850F

Tel 47 23 75 11 Map A2.35 **R**
10 ave de New York 75116 Mº Alma-Marceau

A quayside seafood restaurant (air-conditioned in summer) which is more or less an enclosed terrace with large picture windows offering views across the Seine to the Eiffel Tower. Next door to the Musée de l'Art Moderne, it's decorated in blue and white, with well-spaced round tables and period-style chairs. The restaurant, run by a husband-and-wife team with Paul Canal in the kitchen and Sonia at front of house, is popular with the business community at lunchtime when booking is advisable. Changing daily, according to the market, a typical menu might include roast lobster with courgettes, feuilleté of scallops with wild mushrooms, warm oysters with chicory and squid *à l'encre* among the starters and the likes of sea bass cooked in salt, *croustillant de turbot avec flan de poireaux*, fricassee of sole with foie gras, and grilled lobster with tarragon in the main-course section. Short but well-balanced list of desserts such as *tarte aux pommes*, chocolate soufflé, ice cream and sorbets. Set L 200F. ***Seats** 50. L 12.30-2.30 D 7.30-10.30.* ***Closed** Sun, 24 Dec & Aug. Amex, Diners, Mastercard, Visa.*

Brasserie de la Poste 400F

Tel 47 55 01 31 **Fax 42 25 94 31** Map B2.7 **R**
54 rue de Longchamp 75016 Mº Trocadéro

Opposite a post office, hence the name and the logo (a franking mark) on the menu and on the paper table covers. This is an old-style neighbourhood brasserie both in looks – marbled paint in nicotine colour, ceiling fans, mirrors, a show or two of flowers – and in its menu of simple classics. Specialities include *choucroute, cassoulet, confit de canard* and pig's trotters. Other regulars include goose foie gras in a Riesling aspic, snails, marinated salmon, whole veal kidneys with an excellent *sauce béarnaise* and *tripes à la mode de Caen*. Daily specials widen the choice still further – *navarin d'agneau, coquilles St Jacques provençale* – or a long-simmered casserole of beef cheek with carrots. Honest, reliable cooking at reasonable prices, with affable, efficient service. Set menu 120F (including wine). ***Seats** 64. L 12-3 D 7-12. Amex, Mastercard, Visa.*

LE PRÉ CATELAN ★★ 1500F

Tel 45 24 55 58 **Fax 45 24 43 25** Map B1.36 **R**
route de Suresnes, Bois de Boulogne 75016 Mº Porte Dauphine (2km)

Enjoying a wonderful location in the Bois de Boulogne, this beautiful restaurant has been restored to its full 18th-century glory by Christian Benais. The grand dining-rooms and summer terraces are a fine setting for Roland Durand's superb cooking, which he describes as neo-classic with rustic tendencies and light touches of the Orient. Among the imaginative starters on his seasonal carte are *cervelle d'agneau en marinade citronée aux épices, tomate confite et coeur de laitue* (lamb's brains marinated in lemon and spices, served with tomato confit and lettuce hearts), and *soupe rafraichissante de carottes au parfum de cumin* (cold carrot soup perfumed with cumin). Main dishes are equally delicious: *risotto noir* of langoustines and Thai basil, and rack of lamb scented with rosemary and served with courgettes and stuffed aubergines. Nectarine crumble with a vanilla sabayon and pastis ice cream makes a fine end to a meal. The wine list includes some good Italian and Californian bottles. Set L 270F (weekdays) Set D 550F. Private parking. ***Seats** 80 (+ 80 outside). L 12-2.30 D 7.30-10.30.* ***Closed** D Sun, all Mon & 2 weeks in Feb. Amex, Diners, Mastercard, Visa.*

QUACH 500F

Tel 47 27 98 40 Map B2.37 **R**
47 ave Raymond Poincaré 75016 Mº Trocadéro

A comfortable room jutting out on to a broad pavement, exotic but sober in style, with large tropical fish in a couple of aquaria. Cantonese and Vietnamese dishes make up the bulk of the menu, which numbers grilled prawns with curry sauce, steamed dim sum, mussels with basil, lamb grilled with lemon grass and lacquered duck among its specialities. Some 20 French wines plus beer from Thailand, China and the Netherlands. Set menu 109F. ***Seats** 60. L 12-2.30 D 7-11. Amex, Diners, Mastercard, Visa.*

RAPHAEL 1970F

Tel 44 28 00 28 **Fax 45 01 21 50** Map A2.38 **H**
17 ave Kléber 75116 Mº Etoile/Kléber

Opened as a hotel in 1925, the Raphael has ever since that time been synonymous with opulence, elegance, calm and high levels of service. Luxury is all around, from Oriental rugs on marble floors to oak-panelled meeting rooms, gilt and elaborate marquetry in the salon bleu, treasured books and magical tapestries in the library and crimson plush and amberwood in the air-conditioned English Bar. Spacious bedrooms offer the highest levels of comfort, with rich, solid furnishings, mainly in rococo style, magnificent wardrobes and vast bathrooms, of which some 60% are now thoroughly modernised. Two-thirds of the bedrooms are now air-conditioned. Every possible accessory is included, and 24-hour room service is provided. Valet parking. ***Rooms** 90. Amex, Diners, Mastercard, Visa.*

RELAIS D'AUTEUIL ★ 1100F

Tel 46 51 09 54 **Fax 40 71 05 03** Map D1.39 **R**
31 bd Murat 75016 Mº Porte d'Auteuil

From the moment that a member of staff appears and parks the car for you, it is apparent that this is a 'serious' restaurant. Charismatic young chef Patrick Pignol is often on hand, dressed in his immaculate whites, first to welcome diners and then to explain the day's special dishes not on the printed menu. Recent refurbishment has taken the decor even more up-market but the covered terrace, impressionist paintings, expensive floral arrangements and beautiful Italian tableware remain as before. Smartly-dressed staff are extremely professional and provide an appropriately high level of service to complement some really splendid cooking. Specialities – some are seasonal – include grilled

See over

langoustines with coriander, *foie gras de canard et sa terrine, cote de veau de lait fermier*, young partridge *en cocotte* with sage, grouse cooked in the 'English style', *compote de lièvre en crépinette* with fresh pasta, scallops meunière *au sel de Guérande*, desserts like a bitter chocolate tart with Grand Marnier butter and *soufflé cacao et chicorée*. The wine cellar runs to about 1000 bins; almost all are French, but not all are expensive, as sommelier Frédéric Claude takes pride in being able to offer a range of interesting, quality wines at less than 250F a bottle. There are also a good number of halves and, unusually for a restaurant of this class, some are available by the glass. Fine coffee comes with both petits fours and chocolates. Set L 230F Set L & D 390F (6-course Classic) & 480F (*dégustation*). ***Seats*** *40. L 12.15-2.30 D 7.15-10.30.* ***Closed*** *L Sat, all Sun, 1 week Feb, 1st 3 weeks Aug & 3 days Christmas. Amex, Mastercard, Visa.*

La Résidence Bassano — 750F

Tel 47 23 78 23 **Fax 47 20 41 22** Map A2.40 **H**
15 rue Bassano 75016 M° Etoile/George V

The building is Haussmann vintage, but inside the decor is in clean-cut Swedish style. Bedrooms, all with marble-clad bathrooms boasting both tub and shower, include three suites, two of which have kitchenettes. As we went to press the bedrooms were being recarpeted and fitted with double-glazing. Mini-bar and cable TV are standard features. The hotel has two restaurants, one French, the other Vietnamese (see *Kambodgia*). ***Rooms*** *31. Amex, Diners, Mastercard, Visa.*

Hotel du Rond-Point de Longchamp — 1000F

Tel 45 05 13 63 **Fax 47 55 12 80** Map B1.41 **H**
86 rue de Longchamp 75116 M° Trocadéro

Double glazing keeps the traffic noise away from this comfortable hotel, whose other assets include air-conditioning, billiard room, bar and internal communication with a branch of the popular tea shop **Angelina**. Since last year all the bedrooms (which boast satellite TVs, room safes and mini-bars) have been completely refurbished. Just five bathrooms have shower and WC only, the others all having both tub and shower. ***Rooms*** *57. Amex, Diners, Mastercard, Visa.*

Saint James Paris — 1550F

Tel 44 05 81 81 **Fax 44 05 81 82** Map A1.42 **H**
5 place du Chancelier Adenauer, ave Bugeaud 75116 M° Porte Dauphine

Built in 1892 by a charitable foundation to house outstanding scholars studying in the capital, the Saint James has all the appearance of a country chateau (fronted by a fountain and complete with landscaped grounds) transplanted to this residential area of Paris near the Avenue Foch. Air-conditioned bedrooms, ten of which on the third floor open on to a winter garden, were originally designed by Andrée Putman in an uncluttered 1930s style but for more recently refurbished rooms a less austere 'English' style is being preferred. Day rooms include a well-stocked library bar where a pianist plays each evening except Friday, when it is the turn of a jazz trio. Other amenities include a health club and free secure parking. 24-hour room service. ***Rooms*** *48. Amex, Diners, Mastercard, Visa.*

Hotel de Sévigné — 700F

Tel 47 20 88 90 **Fax 40 70 98 73** Map A2.43 **H**
6 rue de Belloy 75116 M° Kléber/Boissière

The 30 rooms all have little lobbies, and some rooms interconnect for family use. Colour schemes vary from floor to floor, but fittings are standard, including 20-channel TVs, safes and telephone extensions in the bathrooms, all but five of which have both tub and shower. 24-hour room service of drinks and light snacks. There are five reservable parking spaces at 120F per day. ***Rooms*** *30. Amex, Diners, Mastercard, Visa.*

BRASSERIE STELLA 450F

Tel 47 27 60 54 Map A1.8 **R**
133 ave Victor Hugo 75016 Mº Victor Hugo

One of the most popular of neighbourhood brasseries, with a menu that runs from the everyday (egg mayonnaise) to the out-of-the-ordinary (sea urchins). *Fruits de mer* are a speciality (there's also a roaring take-away trade) and others include *andouillette*, tripe, *petit salé, choucroute* and the very popular steak tartare, the last deftly composed by the waiters in between their other duties. Daily dishes are also worth considering – *boeuf à la mode* on Monday, *blanquette de veau* and *faux-filet* on Tuesday, *pot-au-feu*, sauté of lamb and *coq au vin* on Wednesday, *tete de veau* and *boudin noir* on Thursday, *brandade de morue* and skate with capers on Friday, *gigot d'agneau, poule au riz* and cassoulet on Saturday and *gigot d'agneau* (again) and *canard aux petits pois* on Sunday. Book (but you might still have a wait at the bar) or arrive early, because it sometimes seems as though most of the 16th is in the queue. An all-French wine list with most wines also sold by the glass or 45cl carafe. ***Seats*** *120. Meals noon-1am.* ***Closed*** *about 1 week mid-Aug. Amex, Mastercard, Visa.*

LE TOIT DE PASSY ★ 1000F

Tel 45 24 55 37 **Fax 45 20 94 57** Map B1.44 **R**
94 ave Paul Doumer (6th floor) 75016 Mº La Muette

A rooftop restaurant filled with plants and with a terrace affording fine views of the city. Dedicated chef Yannick Jacquot's cooking is as elevated as his restaurant, with subtle combinations of flavours and textures evident in such specialities as foie gras – either hot with polenta, raisins, passion fruit and a sweet and sour sauce or cold in a light Graves and port jelly; grilled scallops with noodles, broccoli and a lemon thyme broth; fillets of red mullet and its liver with potato 'scales' and *sauce antiboise*; risotto of sweetbreads with ceps, wild duck roasted with figs and served on a galette of sweetcorn with a pepper sauce; and pigeon baked in salt and served with a garnish of cabbage and foie gras *en feuilletage*. Desserts include caramelised apple tart, roast figs with honey sorbet and dark chocolate soufflé perfumed with rum. The 510F menu is a *dégustation* of seven courses (served only to the whole table) with a choice only for the principal course. A predominantly French wine list majors in reds from Bordeaux and whites from Burgundy. Set L 200F & 300F Set D 395F & 510F. ***Seats*** *70 (+ 30 outside). L 12-2.30 D 7.30-10.30.* ***Closed*** *L Sat, all Sun, 3 days Easter & 3 days Christmas. Amex, Mastercard, Visa.*

See page 9 for a list of starred restaurants

TROCADÉRO 620F

Tel 45 53 01 82 **Fax 45 53 59 56** Map A2.45 **H**
21 rue St-Didier 75116 Mº Trocadéro/Boissière

A smiling welcome and all the usual comforts in a well-run hotel just north of Trocadéro. Bedrooms boast mini-bar, room safe and multi-channel TV. All but four rooms have both tub and shower in the bathroom. Children under 12 are accommodated free in their parents' room. Room service is limited to breakfast. ***Rooms*** *23. Amex, Diners, Mastercard, Visa.*

LA VILLA MAILLOT 1900F

Tel 45 01 25 22 **Fax 45 00 60 61** Map A1.46 **H**
143 ave de Malakoff 75116 Mº Trocadéro

This former embassy near Porte Maillot has been converted into a refreshingly understated and stylish art deco hotel. The striking public rooms include the lovely Le Jardin conservatory where a meal, snack or cocktail can be enjoyed while gazing at the lush trees and shrubs outside. The light and airy bedrooms

See over

are equipped with air-conditioning, soundproofing, satellite TV and mini-bar and have luxurious rose-coloured marble bathrooms. The hotel's three suites are named after Picasso, Chagall and Modigliani while a motoring theme runs through the Bugatti, Maserati and Ferrari rooms. Private parking 100F. ***Rooms*** *42. Amex, Diners, Mastercard, Visa.*

VIVAROIS ★ 1200F

Tel 45 04 04 31 **Fax 45 03 09 84** Map B1.47 **R**
192 ave Victor Hugo 75116 Mº Rue de la Pompe

Colourful fabric panels in abstract designs bring some warmth to this well-lit restaurant done out in grey marble with 60s-style moulded plastic chairs behind its plate glass windows on the ground floor of a modern block near the Place Tattegrain. Here since 1970, chef-patron Claude Peyrot presents a shortish handwritten menu that does not change much and is somewhat poetic in style so that some explanation from Claude's wife Jacqueline is often required. *Pourpre de turbot Sylvestre* for example is so called because tomato in the sauce tends to give a purple colour to the fish, and *soufflé de l'écureuil* is not squirrel soufflé but is made with nuts, the squirrel's favourite food. In addition to the written carte there are as many verbally described specials, based on the best of what the day's market has to offer; calf's sweetbreads with ceps, *crépinette* of skate stuffed with onions and mushrooms, jugged hare and stuffed partridge were all offered on an autumn day. Desserts might include apple cake, nut gateau, *mousse de cassis Cote de Nuits, parfait de marrons d'Ardèche* and Claude's renowned chocolate tart. There is also a fixed-price lunch (345F) that offers a choice at each stage and changes daily. ***Seats*** *50. L 12-2 D 8-10.* ***Closed*** *Sat, Sun, Aug & Bank Holidays. Amex, Diners, Mastercard, Visa.*

17th Arrondissement
Places of Interest

Arc de Triomphe, 43 80 31 31, M° Charles de Gaulle-Etoile
Palais des Congrès (Porte Maillot), 40 68 22 22, M° Porte Maillot
Place de Clichy
Parc Monceau, M° Monceau

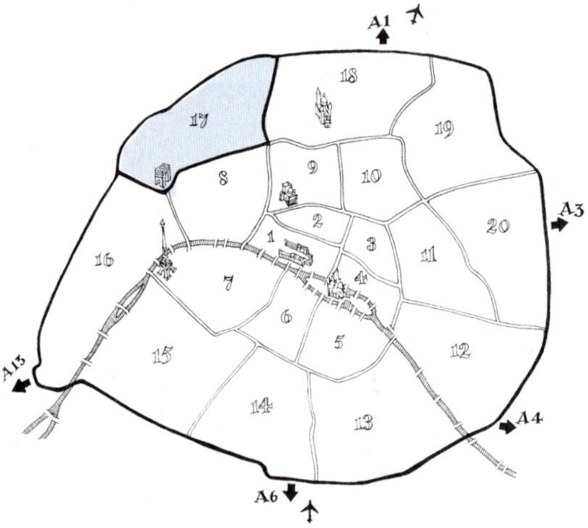

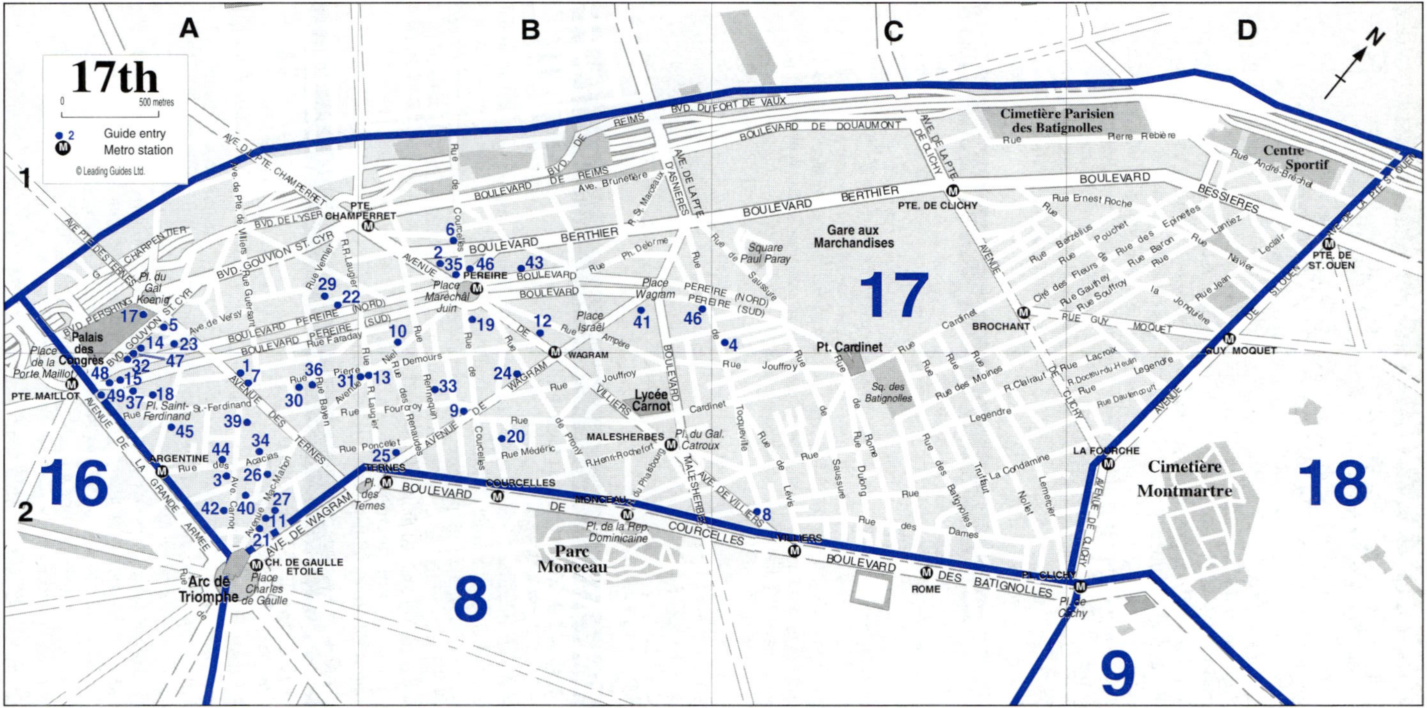

17th
0 500 metres
Guide entry
Metro station
© Leading Guides Ltd.
A
B
C
D
1
2
N
16
17
18
8
9
Cimetière Parisien des Batignolles
Centre Sportif
Gare aux Marchandises
Square de Paul Paray
Pt. Cardinet
Sq. des Batignolles
Lycée Carnot
Cimetière Montmartre
Parc Monceau
Palais des Congrès
Arc de Triomphe
Place Charles de Gaulle
Place de la Porte Maillot
Place Maréchal Juin
Place Wagram
Place Israël
Pl. du Gal. Catroux
Pl. de la Rep. Dominicaine
Pl. des Ternes
Pl. Saint-Ferdinand
Pl. du Gal Koenig
PTE. MAILLOT
ARGENTINE
CH. DE GAULLE ETOILE
TERNES
COURCELLES
MONCEAU
VILLIERS
ROME
PL. CLICHY
LA FOURCHE
GUY MOQUET
PTE. DE ST. OUEN
BROCHANT
PTE. DE CLICHY
WAGRAM
PEREIRE
MALESHERBES
PTE. CHAMPERRET
BOULEVARD BERTHIER
BOULEVARD DE DOUAUMONT
BVD. DUFORT DE VAUX
BOULEVARD BESSIERES
BOULEVARD DES BATIGNOLLES
BOULEVARD DE COURCELLES
BOULEVARD PEREIRE
BOULEVARD MALESHERBES
AVENUE DE WAGRAM
AVENUE DES TERNES
AVENUE DE LA GRANDE ARMEE
AVENUE DE CLICHY
AVENUE DE ST. OUEN
AVE. DE VILLIERS
AVE. DE LA PTE. D'ASNIERES
AVE. DE LA PTE. DE CLICHY
BVD. GOUVION ST. CYR
BVD. DE L'YSER

Amphyclès ★ 1500F

Tel 40 68 01 01 **Fax 40 68 91 88** Map A2.1 **R**
78 ave des Ternes 75017 Mº Porte Maillot

Chef-proprietor Philippe Groult's cooking is a marvellous mixture of traditional and modern, inventive and often light, with many dishes featuring subtle use of herbs and spices. Much of the menu involves intriguing combinations: brochette of partridge, wild duck and wild pigeon with truffled juices, grilled scallops and chestnuts with a salad flavoured with white Piedmont truffles, and slice of turbot with vanilla-flavoured *fleur de sel*. There are also some more familiar favourites (ox cheek with confit of carrots and fillet of Lozère lamb with a *persillade* of orange and lavender are specialities), plus fine cheeses and superb desserts – try the *tarte fine aux pommes, raisins et noix de pécan* or *crepes Suzette*, the latter served only to the whole table. Three fixed-price menus are available, also for everyone at a table – *'menu des nos terroirs'*, *'menu crustacés aux saveurs d'autrefois'* and *'menu prestige'*. Private rooms 5/20. Set L 260F Set L & D 580F, 680F & 920F. ***Seats*** *42. L 12-2.30 D 7-10.30.* ***Closed*** *L Sat, all Sun. Amex, Diners, Mastercard, Visa.*

Apicius ★★ 1400F

Tel 43 80 19 66 **Fax 44 40 09 57** Map B1.2 **R**
122 ave de Villiers 75017 Mº Péreire

A firm grounding in French culinary classics has given chef Jean-Paul Vigato a solid platform from which to experiment with more contemporary and individual ideas. His carte changes twice a year and includes dishes as varied as tempura-style langoustines, *foie gras de canard poelé en aigre doux aux radis noirs confits* (duck foie gras sautéed in a sweet and sour sauce with a confit of black radishes) and turbot cooked with thyme and rosemary and served with an *émulsion* of shellfish. Desserts are equally good, particularly those involving chocolate, such as *soufflé au chocolat noir, chantilly sans sucre et glace vanillée*. All the major French wine regions are represented on the 400-strong list, as well as some Spanish, Italian and American bottles. Set menus at 380F and 520F. ***Seats*** *60. L 12.30-2 D 7.30-10.15.* ***Closed*** *Sat, Sun & Aug. Valet parking. Amex, Diners, Mastercard, Visa.*

Astrid 425F

Tel 44 09 26 00 **Fax 44 09 26 01** Map A2.3 **H**
27 ave Carnot 75017 Mº Etoile

A couple of minutes' walk from the Arc de Triomphe, the Astrid is a charming traditional hotel run in a friendly and efficient manner by a long-standing team. Bedrooms, though simply furnished, are pleasantly comfortable, each with cable TV, a safe and hairdryer in the bathroom. Four rooms are triples/quadruples designated *chambres familiales*. A large underground car park is nearby. Breakfast is included in the room price; room service operates for breakfast only. ***Rooms*** *42. Amex, Diners, Mastercard, Visa.*

Augusta 850F

Tel 47 63 39 97 **Fax 42 27 21 71** Map C1.4 **R**
98 rue de Tocqueville 75017 Mº Villiers/Malesherbes

The blue of the dining-room is an appropriate colour for this restaurant, which specialises in the best varieties of seafood. The menu features fish from the Atlantic and from the Mediterranean with starters which include *soupière de poissons de roche, salade Augusta* (with fresh shellfish) and pan-fried Mediterranean prawns. As a main course you can choose between *St Jacques et endives croquants au vinaigre balsamique, fricassée de homard et de ceps à l'échalote* and *bouillabaisse aux pommes de terre* (for two). A couple of meat dishes are available, plus some tempting desserts like *truffe glacée au chocolat tiède* and *croustillant de poire au miel citronné*. Booking essential. ***Seats*** *40.* ***Closed*** *Sat, Sun (except D Oct-Apr), 2 weeks mid-Aug & 25 Dec. Mastercard, Visa.*

LE BALLON DES TERNES — 450F

Tel 45 74 17 98 **Fax 45 72 18 84** Map A1.5 **R**
103 ave des Ternes 75017 Mº Porte Maillot

This brasserie consists of two rooms decorated in late 19th-century style creating a traditional atmosphere. The menu is traditional, too, majoring on fish and shellfish, choucroute and grills. Oysters, fillet of fresh salt cod roasted with *verjus*, seafood pot-au-feu, sole meunière, monkfish provençale, steak tartare, *andouillette*, veal kidneys with Meaux mustard, *confit de canard* and fricassee of chicken with taglierini are among the favourite choices, with *millefeuille à la vanille* a popular dessert. Wines come direct from the owners and include a section of grands crus Beaujolais. ***Seats*** *120 (+ 24 outside). L 12-4 D 7-12.30.* ***Closed*** *1-20 Aug. Amex, Mastercard, Visa.*

HOTEL DE BANVILLE — 740F

Tel 42 67 70 16 **Fax 44 40 42 77** Map B1.6 **H**
166 bd Berthier 75017 Mº Porte de Champerret

A family-run hotel offering abundant charm and peace in its quiet location near Place Maréchal Juin (aka Place Péreire). Bedrooms differ in detail – some in country style, many with marble bathrooms – but all are cheerful and comfortable. A lift serves all but the top (8th) floor, whose little rooms have sloping ceilings and great views. Three or four bedrooms are renovated each year, so everything is in good order. Each room is provided with satellite TV and a safe. 24-hour room service includes snacks and light meals. Three kinds of breakfast are available – Continental, diet and English with eggs and sausages. No restaurant. ***Rooms*** *39. Amex, Mastercard, Visa.*

BAUMANN TERNES — 500F

Tel 45 74 16 66 **Fax 45 72 44 32** Map A2.7 **R**
64 ave des Ternes 75017 Mº Etoile/Porte Maillot/Ternes

The pavement terrace is the place to be in the summer, but inside, on two levels, is equally inviting, with handsome panelling, leather banquettes or wicker-backed chairs, and a large bar which dominates the ground floor. Choucroute is one of the main specialities of this Alsatian institution (seven versions include *aux poissons*, which Guy-Pierre Baumann created 20 years ago), Other popular choices take in shellfish, grills and steak tartare, the last available prepared 8 ways in the summer, 4 in the winter). Desserts are based on seasonal fruits. Pleasant staff are a bonus. A sister restaurant *L'Etage Baumann* is in the 8th (*qv*) and another 3 plus a hotel are in Strasbourg. Set menus 112F & 163F. ***Seats*** *125. L 12-2.30 D 7-12. Amex, Diners, Mastercard, Visa.*

LE BISTROT D'À COTÉ — 500F

Tel 47 63 25 61 Map C2.8 **R**
16 ave de Villiers 75017 Mº Villiers

Michel Rostang's brilliant restaurant in Rue Rennequin (see *Michel Rostang* in this arrondissement) has, in the current fashionable trend, spawned several less formal offspring, including this marvellous bistro at the eastern end of Avenue de Villiers. The cramped little tables fill up quickly at every session, and the reason is very evident. Not only is the food of very high quality, but the prices are reasonable and the place has a great bustle, assisted in no small measure by the attentive manager and his cheerful, hard-working staff. Everything on the 'menu carte' (142F for 2 courses, 189F for 3) is a model bistro dish – nothing too elaborate and everything extremely well prepared: salad of calf's head with dried apricots and hazelnuts, duck paté en croute, cream of pumpkin soup with smoked salmon, or ravioli of goat's cheese and squid with a fennel cream to start; cod with cabbage and *beurre blanc*, pan-fried bream *à la vierge* or lamb roasted with thyme for a main course; and to complete a memorable meal warm pancakes with bilberry conserve and double cream, baked apple with sultantas

See over

and spiced gingerbread ice cream or Valrhona bitter chocolate tart. Best value among the wines is the house selection – Cotes du Lubéron white and rosé, Cotes du Ventoux red – at 59F for a 46cl fillette. Set L 109F, Set L & D 142F & 189F. ***Seats** 65. L 12.30-2 D 7.30-11.* ***Closed** L Sat, all Sun. Amex, Mastercard, Visa.*

The Neuilly branch, at 4 rue Boutard 92200 Tel 47 45 34 55, has the same menu, while the other branch in the 17th (10 rue Gustave-Flaubert, Map B2.9 Tel 42 67 05 81) has an à la carte menu of similar inspiration.
See also entry in the 5th.

Le Bistrot de l'Etoile — 450F

Tel 42 27 88 44 **Fax 42 27 32 12** Map B1.10 **R**
75 ave Niel 75017 Mº Péreire

One of Guy Savoy's very successful restaurants serving a menu of modernised bistro dishes. Vincent Berthamaux is the chef at this one, an old 'bistro de l'époque' with attractive woodwork and mirrors. The main menu changes with the seasons, with additional *plats du jour* adding to the choice. Carpaccio of tuna with a shellfish vinaigrette, warm salad of snails and potato, chicken with preserved lemon, green olives and coriander, and entrecote with bone marrow and crispy polenta are typical choices, joined each day by *les bonnes habitudes du Bistrot* – veal kidneys with macaroni on Tuesday, roast chicken with savory and mashed potato on Thursday and brandade of salt cod on Friday. Set D (Sun only – 'retour de weekend') 180F. ***Seats** 70. L 12-2 D 7.30-12.* ***Closed** L Sun. Amex, Mastercard, Visa.*

A glossary of French menu items starts on page 274

Le Bistrot de l'Etoile — 450F

Tel 42 67 25 95 Map A2.11 **R**
13 rue Troyon 75017 Mº Etoile (Wagram exit)

Guy Savoy's first bistro, a tiny, cheerful little place with a huge mirror running along one wall. The same high-quality produce as at the Avenue Niel outlet is the basis of a different menu, the regular choice being supplemented by daily suggestions. Typically starters could be *poule au pot en terrine avec vinaigrette de légumes, saumon mariné à l'huile* or *nage de joue de boeuf au chèvre frais.* Main dishes range from haddock in Noilly and fillet of bream in red wine to *entrecote poelé* and *onglet de veau*, while desserts include perennial favourites such as crème brulée and *fondant au chocolat*. The third Bistrot de l'Etoile is in the 16th (see entry). ***Seats** 24. L 12.30-2 L 7.30-11.30.* ***Closed** Sat, Sun & Public Holidays. Amex, Mastercard, Visa.*

Bistro du 17e — 340F

Tel 47 63 32 77 Map B1.12 **R**
108 ave de Villiers 75017 Mº Péreire

A great formula – kir with sparkling wine, half a bottle of wine, three courses and coffee – keeps this roomy bistro at Place Péreire very busy for most of the time. The cooking is actually nothing out of the ordinary, but to walk into a restaurant knowing what the final bill will be is in itself a delight. The menu offers 10-12 choices at each stage, and the moderate price does not preclude some luxury items: smoked salmon, ravioli of langoustines with saffron sauce, *gratin de pommes de terre au foie gras sauce morilles*, blanquette of monkfish with baby onions, calf's liver with endive, roast best end of lamb with dauphinoise potatoes, profiteroles with hot chocolate sauce, *nougat glacé* with raspberry sauce and crème brulée show the range. Set menu 169F. ***Seats** 105. L 12-2.30 D 7.30-11. Amex, Mastercard, Visa.*

Bistrot Saint-Ferdinand — 340F

Tel 45 74 33 32 Map A2.48 **R**
275 bd Péreire 75017 M° Porte Maillot

Identical details to Bistrot du 17e in this arrondissement.

Caves Pétrissans — 450F

Tel 42 27 52 03 Fax 40 54 87 56 Map B2.13 **R**
30bis ave Niel 75017 M° Ternes/Péreire

For generations a gathering place for serious wine buffs, this classic wine bar with the look of the 30s was actually opened by the great-grandfather of the current owners. Its role as an emporium of fine wines has expanded to include a restaurant serving traditional French dishes. Simple classics are prepared with a sure touch by chef Jacques Bertrel: *terrine du cerf, lisette au vin blanc, tendron de veau à la campagnarde, pot-au-feu, tete de veau sauce ravigote, pruneaux à l'armagnac, nougat glacé* are all likely to appear on the set menus, while there are some slightly more elaborate dishes on the carte. The chef has a particularly good way with the less glamorous cuts of pork – *palette, travers, échine* served with cabbage. The splendid list of wines (all available in the shop) includes an inexpensive house selection of some 20, served in the restaurant by bottle or glass. You can still turn up just for a drink at the bar, where you will join half-a-dozen punters raising plenty of chat and a fair amount of smoke. Set menu 165F. ***Seats*** *40 (+ 30 outside). L 12-2.30 D 7.45-10.30.* ***Closed*** *Sat, Sun, 1st 3 weeks Aug & 1 week Christmas. Amex, Mastercard, Visa.*

Charly de Bab-el-Oued — 450F

Tel 45 74 34 62 Fax 45 74 35 36 Map A1.14 **R**
95 bd Gouvion Saint-Cyr 75017 M° Porte Maillot

In an exotic setting of palms and cedarwood and colourful tiles and fountains, diners feast on splendid, generously served dishes from North Africa. *Bestelles* and *briks*, sardines and *chakchouka* are among the starters, while the major main courses are couscous (8 varieties) and tagines. The nice but naughty way to end a meal is the *mosaïque de patisseries orientales* – a selection of 10 at 52F per person. A set menu (200F) is available for all at a table, otherwise it's à la carte. Note for kidney lovers: *rognons blancs* are testicles, not kidneys. All the pastry, bread and sorbets are made on the premises. Wines from France, Algeria and Morocco. Take-away and delivery service available. ***Seats*** *200. L 12-2.30 D 7-11. Amex, Diners, Mastercard, Visa.*

Chez Georges — 600F

Tel 45 74 31 00 Fax 45 74 02 56 Map A2.15 **R**
273 bd Péreire 75017 M° Porte Maillot

A classic bistro-brasserie with a large and loyal clientele. Lunchtime sees it at its busiest and most Parisian, with customers enjoying the comforting dishes which have made it so popular since its opening 70 years ago and the cooking remains very sound and reliable. Speedy, professional waiters bear the main meat dishes from the kitchen and carve them by the table: *petit salé* with cabbage or lentils, *gigot d'agneau* with flageolets and ribs of beef with excellent *gratin dauphinois* are the ever-present stars of the show, but salmon tartare and steak tartare play an increasingly important support role. Lyonnais sausage, *terrine de foies de volaille*, foie gras, *salade de museau de boeuf* and marinated herrings are popular starters, and giant éclairs make a splendid end to the meal. The speciality cheese is a very good Brie de Meaux, with which *crottins de chèvre* are offered.
An easy-drinking Brouilly is a favourite accompaniment to the consistently good food. ***Seats*** *130 (+ 30 outside). L 12-2.30 D 7-11.30.* ***Closed*** *Aug. Mastercard, Visa.*

CONCORDE LAFAYETTE 1450F

Tel 40 68 50 68 **Fax 40 68 50 43** Map A1.17 **HR**
3 place Général Koening 75107 M° Porte Maillot

The top six of the 34 floors of this building are called 'Le Top Club', where 157 executive bedrooms (supplement) have butler service and use of a business support centre as well as a health club located in the basement of the hotel (not part of the establishment). It has its own check-in area and private lounge. The hotel is part of the Palais des Congrès, where exhibitions, conventions, congresses, trade fairs and concerts are held, and where 80 shops and four cinemas are located. The conference room, divisible into smaller sections, has a capacity of 2000 (7000 in the Palais). The business centre is fully equipped and staffed, with translation and secretarial services available. The view across Paris from the standardised, comfortable and well-equipped bedrooms is exceptional. It can be even more appreciated from the panoramic bar Plein Ciel on the 34th floor. The coffee shop, Les Saisons, is open from 6am to midnight. ***Rooms** 970. Amex, Diners, Mastercard, Visa.*

Etoile d'Or 1000F

Tel 40 68 51 28

On the first floor of the hotel is a modern, comfortable restaurant with lightwood panelled walls and ceiling and claret-coloured carpet and chairs. Diners are serenaded by a harpist in the evenings while enjoying Jean-Claude Lhonneur's classic but inventive cuisine: sea urchin soup with fennel seeds, fried oysters with horseradish cream, spider crab cocktail with a crab vinaigrette, eel fillet in vermouth, scallops with endives, pot-au-feu of Challans duck, and beef fillet in a vegetable court bouillon. Hot soufflés, feuilleté of pineapple conserve with rum and baked spiced comice pear with caramel ice cream make fitting endings to an enjoyable meal. Set menu 270F. ***Seats** 80. L 12-2.30 D 7-10.30. **Closed** Sat, Sun, Aug & Public Holidays except 1 Jan.*

LE CONGRÈS MAILLOT 500F

Tel 45 74 17 24 **Fax 45 72 39 80** Map A2.49 **R**
80 ave de la Grande Armée 75017 M° Porte Maillot

The leading restaurant in the extensive Gérard Julie empire (6 other restaurants and 20+ Batifol bistros) is a giant brasserie at Porte Maillot, open 24 hours a day every day and specialising in seafood. The display of shellfish stretches round the corner from the main entrance on Avenue de la Grande Armée to Boulevard Péreire. *Fruits de mer* may be the most popular order, but there's plenty more besides, including some very good grilled fish (bass, turbot), skate with capers and meaty options. Our most recent meal included scrambled egg with crayfish and excellent lamb cutlets served with *gratin dauphinois*. Set menu 120F. ***Seats** 280. Meals 24 hours. Amex, Diners, Mastercard, Visa.*

LA COQUILLE 750F

Tel 45 74 25 95 Map A2.18 **R**
6 rue de Débarcadère 75017 M° Argentine/Porte Maillot

The scene was set many years ago and little has changed in the meantime. The well-maintained decor is an elegant mix of greens and orangey-pinks, creating a discreet and intimate ambience. For an aperitif try the house cocktail, champagne with a pineapple ring, and for a starter the *coquilles St Jacques au naturel* (available from October to April), very simply baked. *Foie gras* and *jambon persillé* are alternatives. For a main course the choice could include veal sweetbreads with Sancerre and morels, sole with noodles, black pudding with apples, chicken fricassee or chateaubriand with matchstick potatoes. The speciality dessert is hazelnut soufflé with Grand Marnier. Clément Lausecker is the chef, his wife the business-like, charming hostess. Set menu 230F. ***Seats** 45. L 12-2.30 D 7-10.30. **Closed** Sun, Mon, Aug & 10 days Christmas/New Year. Amex, Diners, Mastercard, Visa.*

COURCELLES 675F

Tel 47 63 65 30 **Fax 46 22 49 44**
184 rue de Courcelles 75017
Map B1.19
Mº Péreire
H

Just south-east of Place Péreire, this hotel offers pleasant, modern accommodation. Each room has a mini-bar and satellite TV, and there are both tubs and showers (also hairdryers) in the bathrooms. The ground floor houses an attractive bar-cum-breakfast room with an indoor garden theme. Continental breakfast is available from room service, which operates throughout the day. ***Rooms** 42. Amex, Diners, Mastercard, Visa.*

EBER MONCEAU 580F

Tel 46 22 60 70 **Fax 47 63 01 01**
18 rue Léon Jost 75017
Mº Courcelles
H

Jean-Marc Eber's little hotel in a quiet side street near the charming Parc Monceau has 13 rooms all with bath or shower and WC, and five apartments. All number a mini-bar and cable TV among their amenities. Day rooms include a bar and two small sitting-rooms. In summer breakfast can be served out on the patio. Car park (paying) 150m from the hotel. There is 24-hour room service even for breakfast. Meals can be delivered from a nearby restaurant. 24-hour reception. ***Rooms** 18. Amex, Diners, Mastercard, Visa.*

ETOILE PARK 613F

Tel 42 67 69 63 **Fax 43 80 18 99**
10 ave Macmahon 75017
Map A2.21
Mº Etoile
H

Double-glazed bedrooms are decorated and furnished in unfussy modern style, and each has its own bath or shower room with hairdryer, plus safe, mini-bar, direct-dial phone, radio and cable TV. There's room service of breakfast but the best deal is to be had in the breakfast room located in the basement where a quite extensive buffet is available. Reception has a small bar. ***Rooms** 28. **Closed** 1 week Christmas. Amex, Diners, Mastercard, Visa.*

ETOILE PÉREIRE 760F

Tel 42 67 60 00 **Fax 42 67 02 90**
146 bd Péreire 75017
Map A1.22
Mº Péreire
H

Run in friendly, cheerful style, the Etoile Péreire is on two levels within a quiet courtyard. Bedrooms have a contemporary elegance, with decor inspired by New York or Italy. All rooms have hairdryer, satellite TV and mini-bar. Room service (minimum 76F; hot dishes available) is offered from 10.30 to 2 and from 6.30 to 11. An attractive basement breakfast room decorated in white and grey with photographs of sailing boats is a pleasant place to start the day. The buffet includes a selection of 40 jams and honeys. Private parking is available 300m away at 100F for 24 hours. ***Rooms** 26. Amex, Diners, Mastercard, Visa.*

LA FAMIGLIA FULIGNA 600F

Tel 45 74 20 28
2 rue Waldeck-Rousseau 75017
Map A1.23
Mº Porte Maillot
R

The combined talents of the Fuligna family have made a considerable success of their comfortable Italian restaurant behind the Méridien Hotel at Porte Maillot. They specialise in the traditional cooking of Emilia Romagna with outstanding pasta, all prepared by hand. *Cappelletti al pasticcio, ravioli, fusilli in fungi freschi* and *gnochettini al ragu* are among those offered. Main courses include Venetian-style calf's liver, veal *ai tre gusti* with wild mushrooms, asparagus, prosciutto and mozzarella, grilled fresh scampi and a speciality of a platter of five different grilled fish. For dessert try the *dolce della famiglia* – three desserts on one plate: tiramisu, chocolate cake and warm apple tart. Mostly Italian wines, and a few French. ***Seats** 48 (+ 40 outside). L 12-3 D 7-11.30. **Closed** Sun, 25 Dec. Amex, Mastercard, Visa.*

FAUCHER ★ 800F

Tel 42 27 61 50 Fax 46 22 25 72 Map B2.24 **R**
123 ave de Wagram 75017 M° Ternes/Wagram

Nicole and Gérard Faucher's bright, elegant restaurant, with a terrace looking out on to a quiet street, lies in a pleasant residential quarter. With Monsieur in the kitchen and Madame at the front of house, this is very much a family-run operation – witness the fresh flower arrangements and choice of pictures on the walls. The cooking is in the modern fashion with a good à la carte choice: pickled leeks and calf's tongue with ravioli of beetroot with capers, risotto of langoustines and squid, salmon with lentils and a meat jus, roast saddle of spiced lamb with aubergines, shoulder of beef with herb vinaigrette, truffled jus and buttered cabbage. Finish with pineapple conserve with a Grand Marnier baba and coconut milk or raspberry tart. ***Seats*** *50 (+ 30 outside). L 12-2 D 8-10.* ***Closed*** *L Sat, all Sun & Public Holidays except 1 Jan. Amex, Mastercard, Visa.*

GOLDENBERG 400F

Tel 42 27 34 79 Fax 42 27 98 85 Map B2.25 **R**
69 ave de Wagram 75017 M° Ternes

Serving some of the best kosher food in Paris, Patrick Goldenberg's eponymous restaurant has long opening hours for classic middle European Jewish food every day of the year except Yom Kippur. Zakouski, blinis, stuffed poultry neck, gefilte fish, pojarski, Wiener schnitzel, salamis and pastramis are among the specialities. Grills include King David, with lamb chops, merguez and steak. Various set menus (98F for Russian, Yiddish, Romanian, Turkish, 150F 'formule schnaps'), 20 vodkas, kosher wines (and others). Popular at all times, including Saturday & Sunday brunch (120F, children 100F). Cold food is available outside meal times. ***Seats*** *45 (+ 50 outside). L 12-3 D 7-11. Mastercard, Visa.*

See page 9 for a list of starred restaurants

GRAINDORGE 500F

Tel 47 54 00 28 Fax 44 09 84 51 Map A2.26 **R**
15 rue de l'Arc de Triomphe 75017 M° Etoile

Two rooms in 30s style make up this appealing restaurant, whose name derives from a variety of beer (there's a very interesting list of beers). Before setting up on his own, Bernard Broux spent six years as chef at Alain Dutournier's *Au Trou Gascon*. Many of his dishes originate in his native Flanders, and the 230F menu is his Flanders speciality menu, with dishes such as *waterzooi*, or *hochepot d'épaule d'agneau*. Croustade of hen pheasant with cabbage and a wild mushroom sauce is typical of the seasonal game offerings. Eels in a herby green sauce remain a great favourite, and raspberry sabayon with a raspberry-flavoured beer or *pain perdu de brioche caramélisée à la cassonade* are desserts worth saving room for. Set L 150F & 165F Set D 188F & 230F. ***Seats*** *45. L 12-2.30 D 7.30-11.* ***Closed*** *L Sat, all Sun. Amex, Mastercard, Visa.*

GUY SAVOY ★★★ 1600F

Tel 43 80 40 61 Fax 46 22 43 09 Map A2.27 **R**
18 rue Troyon 75017 M° Etoile

Guy Savoy's air-conditioned restaurant, close to the Arc de Triomphe, is one of the gastronomic temples of Paris. The atmosphere is intimate and sophisticated, with pastel colours, bold wallpaper, modern paintings, exquisite china, copious flowers and lightwood screens sectioning off eating areas. Since the restaurant opened in 1986, Savoy has established an enviable reputation as one of the city's top chefs and the secret of his success lies in his refreshingly simple style. The pleasure he takes in his cooking is evident in every dish, from deceptively straightforward starters such as *supreme de volaille de Bresse, foie gras et artichauts* (breast of Bresse chicken with foie gras and artichokes), and *thon et petits pois marinés aux herbes* (tuna and peas marinated in herbs) to main courses like *Saint-Pierre roti, parmentier d'herbes à l'huile d'olive et roquette poelée* (pan-fried John Dory with a herb and olive oil parmentier and rocket) and pigeon *poché-grillé* with new vegetables and a giblet vinaigrette. Desserts are equally superb: *terrine de pamplemousse, sauce au thé* (grapefruit terrine with tea sauce) and *chaud-froid* of peach and blackcurrant, for example. Unusually, a reasonable selection of wines from Spain, Italy and California is available as well as some excellent French wines by the glass. The *menu dégustation* is 820F. ***Seats*** *100. L 12.30-2.30 D 7.30-11.30.* ***Closed*** *L Sat, all Sun. Valet parking. Amex, Mastercard, Visa.*

A glossary of French menu items starts on page 274

MAGELLAN 595F

Tel 45 72 44 51 Fax 40 68 90 36 Map A1.29 **H**
17 rue Jean-Baptiste Dumas 75017 Mº Péreire/Porte de Champerret

The garden has just been landscaped and public rooms have been very attractively refurbished in art deco style, thereby creating very favourable first impressions. Bedrooms are done out in a practical, contemporary style. Satellite TV, radios and hairdryers are standard, and the bathrooms all have baths, showers and bidets. There's a large bar in the lobby and in the summer guests can sit out in the garden for drinks or breakfast. Secure parking is available for 4 cars (85F per day). 24-hour reception. Room service offers a menu from an outside caterer. ***Rooms*** *75. Amex, Diners, Mastercard, Visa.*

LE MANOIR DE PARIS ★ 900F

Tel 45 72 25 25 Fax 45 74 80 98 Map B2.30 **R**
6 rue Pierre Demours 75017 Mº Ternes/Etoile

Carved wood, wall mirrors, pillars and abundant flowers and greenery make a splendid setting for the superb, sunny cooking of Gilles Méry. Dishes, often elaborate, many with a Mediterranean influence, are typified by *pastilla* of young rabbit rubbed with rosemary and accompanied by honeyed carrots and turnips, and ravioli of fresh goat's cheese and tomato with pistachio oil among the starters. Main dishes could include *rouget et pommes Charlotte au sucs de Modène, macis et parmesan*, or spiced breast fillet of duck with peaches and grapes. Equally appealing sweets such as *tarte fine au chocolat* and *millefeuille aux fruits de bois;* fine wines. Set menus 265F, 295F & 380F. ***Seats*** *70. L 12-2.30 D 7.30-10.30.* ***Closed*** *L Sat, all Sun & Public Holidays. Amex, Diners, Mastercard, Visa.*

LES MARINES DE PÉTRUS 500F

Tel 47 63 04 24 Fax 44 15 92 20 Map B2.31 **R**
27 ave Niel 75017 Mº Ternes

The name and the bright, nautical decor tell you that this is indeed a seafood restaurant: the menu is even posted outside on an old bathing hut. Small blackboards list the likes of *carpaccio de dorade, tartare aux trois poissons, mi-cuit de cabillaud* or *gazpacho de langoustines* to begin. As a main course there's peppered swordfish steak, salt cod with garlic mayonnaise, sea bream in a spiced honey crust, and *saumon à l'unilateral*. Just one or two meat dishes – fillet of beef *béarnaise* or pig's trotters. Madame Barrié also owns the more formal *Pétrus* (*qv*) just along the road at Place Péreire (aka Place Maréchal Juin). ***Seats*** *50. L 12-2.30 D 7-11.* ***Closed*** *25 Dec, 1 Jan & Aug. Amex, Diners, Mastercard, Visa.*

LE MÉRIDIEN ETOILE 1450F

Tel 40 68 34 34 **Fax 40 68 31 31** Map A2.32 **HR**
81 bd Gouvion Saint-Cyr 75017 Mº Porte Maillot

The city's largest hotel, opened in 1972, stands on nine floors at Porte Maillot and the Palais des Congrès, where the Air France shuttle bus leaves for Charles de Gaulle airport every 15 minutes. Day rooms are a hive of activity, from power breakfasts at 7.30 through Sunday jazz brunch to dinner in one of several restaurants then dancing till dawn at the Ecume des Nuits discothèque (membership required). There's also a most impressive conference centre with facilities for up to 1000 attendees. A multilingual secretarial service is offered 24 hours a day, as is room service for the bedrooms which, though not notable for their spaciousness, are quiet, comfortable and well equipped. There are 17 suites. Two floors of rooms offer the *Club Président* service, which includes speedy check-in and check-out, a lounge (complimentary breakfast in the morning and soft drinks throughout the day) with terrace, and priority booking in the restaurant and the Lionel Hampton Jazz Club. Private parking 90F for 24 hours. ***Rooms*** *1025. Amex, Diners, Mastercard, Visa.*

Le Clos Longchamp ★ 1200F

Tel 40 68 30 40 Fax 40 68 30 81

The hotel boasts a Japanese restaurant and the Café Arlequin, but gastronomic pride of place undoubtedly goes to the refined and elegant Clos Longchamp with its central garden. Chef Jean-Marie Meulien's seasonal menus add Mediterranean and Oriental influences to classic French cuisine, shown in such dishes as prawns with Thai herbs, tandoori navarin of lamb and fricassee of sole and artichokes with pine nut oil. *Marbré de foie de canard au Beaumes de Venise* is a home-grown speciality! Set L 270F Set D 340F & 470F (*dégustation*). ***Seats*** *60. L 12-2.30 D 7.30-10.30.* ***Closed*** *Sat, Sun & Aug.*

MICHEL ROSTANG ★★ 1600F

Tel 47 63 40 77 **Fax 47 63 82 75** Map B2.33 **R**
20 rue Rennequin 75017 Mº Ternes

Despite his far-flung culinary interests, Michel Rostang still cooks full time in his restaurant in north-west Paris. The striking interior has an almost Oriental atmosphere, with dark red lacquered woodwork, matching walls, carpets and chairs, and a cream and red ceiling. Michel's cooking is bursting with life and invention, although his classic dishes such as *soufflé de quenelle de brochet au homard* and *volaille de Bresse à la crème d'estragon* are admirably unfussy. The carte offers starters such as terrine of veal sweetbreads and duck foie gras with a compote of onions and raw wild mushroom salad. Tempting mains are pan-fried red mullet with a purée of peas and olive oil and a red mullet liver jus, and pigeon *en crapaudine* (spatchcocked) roasted in a garlic crust with beetroot juice and chards pan-fried with parmesan. The cheese selection is excellent and desserts include the intriguing *risotto de peches blanches aux aromes de vanille tuiles aux pralines* and a marvellous cold raspberry soufflé. Service is effortlessly efficient. Set menus 298F (lunch), 540F and 720F (lunch and dinner). Valet parking. ***Seats*** *65. L 12-2 D 8-10.15.* ***Closed*** *Sat (but open D Sat Jun-Sep), Sun & 1st 3 weeks Aug. Amex, Diners, Mastercard, Visa.*

L'OUSTALET 400F

Tel 43 80 82 65 Map B1.46 **R**
10 place du Maréchal Juin 75017 Mº Péreire

The menu at this long-established corner bar-restaurant is straight-down-the-line traditional, but the cooking always shows care, the place is particularly bright and clean, and the owners and staff are nothing if not friendly and courteous.

Jambon de pays, snails, oysters or herring with potatoes in oil could get your meal under way, followed perhaps by sole meunière, *petit salé aux lentilles*, veal escalope or a steak (excellent *frites*). Finish off with chocolate mousse or the day's tart or gateau. Short, everyday wine list, but plenty of halves and 25cl carafes. Set menu 120F. ***Seats** 60. L 12-3 D 7-10.30. **Closed** L Sat, all Sun. Mastercard, Visa.*

LE PETIT COLOMBIER ★ 950F

Tel 43 80 28 54 **Fax 44 40 04 29** Map A2.34 **R**
42 rue des Acacias 75017 M° Etoile

Just a short walk from the Arc de Triomphe, Bernard Fournier's provincial-style auberge has remained for 60 years a bastion of classic French cooking. Amid the woodwork and the flowers and the copper ornaments an appreciative clientele tucks into seasonal delights such as hare soup with wild mushrooms, pie of grouse and wild duck with a bordelaise sauce, pheasant ballotine with calf's sweetbreads, truffles and pistachios in a champagne-flavoured gelatine or a fricassee of pheasant with red and green cabbage. Other dishes, equally delicious, might include duck confit with potatoes sautéed in duck fat and tournedos Rossini with foie gras and Périgord truffles, or the day's superb roast, carved at the table. Bitter chocolate truffle with a coffee-flavoured crème brulée or a biscuit with caramelised lime and pear with a raspberry coulis are tempting desserts. There's a great cellar, with bottles selected from all round the world, and every month sees a special promotion, with a red and a white on offer by the glass. The 200F four-course *menu carte* offers remarkable value for money; the set dinner is 360F. ***Seats** 80. L 12.15-2.30 D 7.30-10.30. **Closed** L Sun, all Sat & 1st 2 weeks Aug. Amex, Mastercard, Visa.*

PÉTRUS 900F

Tel 43 80 15 95 **Fax 43 80 06 96** Map B1.35 **R**
12 place du Maréchal Juin 75017 M° Péreire

Smart, well-established seafood restaurant with a corner site on the Place du Maréchal Juin (sometimes known as Place Péreire): limed oak panelling, 1920s-style light fittings, mirrors painted with appropriately fishy motifs. Specialities 'Les Classiques Pétrus' include *tournedos de thon Rossini* (the tuna cooked pink, topped with fresh foie gras and served with a truffle sauce), a trio of bass, mullet and gambas grilled with pesto, Breton lobster baked with tarragon and John Dory steamed with seaweed and fennel. Just a couple of meat dishes for resolute carnivores. Shortish wine list with the emphasis on whites along with a good selection of champagnes. See also *Les Marines de Pétrus* above. Set menu 250F. ***Seats** 60. L 12-2.30 D 7-11. **Closed** Aug. Amex, Diners, Mastercard, Visa.*

QUALITY HOTEL 650F

Tel 44 01 04 90 **Fax 44 40 25 54** Map B1.46 **H**
51 bd Péreire 75017 M° Wagram

Modern accommodation in an old building on the south side of a boulevard which straddles RER line C. Satellite TV, mini-bar, hairdryer, safe, computer points in all bedrooms. Continental breakfast served in the rooms, buffet in the breakfast room. No restaurant. Overnight parking 100F. ***Rooms** 44. Amex, Diners, Mastercard, Visa.*

REGENT'S GARDEN 700F

Tel 45 74 07 30 **Fax 40 55 01 42** Map A2.36 **H**
6 rue Pierre Demours 75017 M° Etoile/Ternes

Built by Napoleon III for his private physician and since 1920 a hotel of abundant charm and personality with a delightfully peaceful garden at the back. Bedrooms are furnished in traditional style but offer cable TV and mini-bar.

See over

Modern bathrooms come with hairdryers and both shower and tub. The price above is for a standard room; ten particularly spacious rooms are priced at 940F. There's space for eight cars in the courtyard at the front of the hotel (first come, first served, 50F for 24 hours). 24-hour reception but room service only for breakfast. ***Rooms*** *39. Amex, Diners, Mastercard, Visa.*

LE RELAIS DE VENISE (L'ENTRECOTE) 320F

Tel 45 74 27 97
271 bd Péreire 75017

Map A2.37
M° Porte Maillot

R

A winning formula of dressed salad with walnuts followed by a nicely cooked entrecote and a bowlful of good *frites* is what keeps an almost permanent queue outside, while inside the closely-packed tables and loud chatter create a lively atmosphere. The only choices available are in the wines and at the end of your meal, in the selection of pastries. No bookings and no cheques. Set menu 109F. ***Seats*** *100. L 12-2.30 D 7-11.45.* ***Closed*** *Good Fri & all July. Mastercard, Visa.*

LA ROTISSERIE D'ARMAILLÉ 500F

Tel 42 27 19 20 Fax 40 55 00 93
6 rue d'Armaillé 75017

Map A2.39
M° Etoile/Ternes

R

Jacques Cagna's Rotisserie in a street of restaurants is a very handsome place with lightwood panelling, a spot-patterned green carpet, paintings and prints of food and animals, fuchsia for upholstery and green stripes in the banquettes. The menu is 155F for two courses, 198F for three and what you get is a good choice (plus daily specials) of classics and updated classics prepared by Lionel Delage and his team: *oeuf en cocotte aux crustacés avec fondue de courgettes, flan de cèpes au beurre d'ail citronnée* or pan-fried langoustines with cumin and a lentil purée are offered to begin. To follow, choose between such dishes as roast rack of lamb with cardamom and an almond crust, rib of milk-fed Quercy veal with a jus of onions and wild mushrooms, and pot-au-feu of lightly salted duck with a confit of the leg. In season game dishes are a speciality and include *lièvre à la royale* and *perdreau roti sur canapé*. Pride of place among the desserts must go to the delicious steamed chocolate sponge with melted chocolate at the heart, and the banana and chocolate marquise with a cinnamon sauce. Sister restaurant to *Rotisserie d'en Face (qv)* in the 6th and *Rotisserie Monsigny (qv)* in the 2nd. ***Seats*** *85. L 12.15-2.30 D 7.15-11.* ***Closed*** *L Sat, all Sun. Amex, Mastercard, Visa.*

SORMANI ★ 1000F

Tel 43 80 13 91
4 rue du Général-Lanrezac 75017

Map A2.40
M° Etoile

R

Situated a short distance north of the Arc de Triomphe, this establishment has all the trappings of a stylish and elegant restaurant. Chef-patron Jean-Pascal Faiget offers a very French-sounding menu but it is, in fact, a blend of modern and traditional Italian cooking. As a starter try the house speciality, the *grand hors d'oeuvre d'antipasi* or maybe lobster and puréed onion tart on a bed of rocket, deep-fried scampi and squid, Venetian-style beef carpaccio or grilled red mullet with an aubergine and courgette gratin. Fish main courses vary daily according to market availability while meat dishes could be *osso buco à la milanaise*, lamb medallions on polenta crostini with Tuscan beans, and veal stuffed with black truffles accompanied by ravioli *alfredo*. There's an excellent selection of desserts like *crepes soufflées* with pineapple and maraschino, peach soup with red fruits and vanilla ice cream and a duo of tiramisu with an apple compote. Wines are mainly from Italy, with a leaning to Tuscany and Piedmont. ***Seats*** *65 (+ 12 outside). L 12.30-2.30 D 7.30-10.30.* ***Closed*** *Sat, Sun, 1 week Easter, 3 weeks Aug & 1 week Christmas. Mastercard, Visa.*

LA SOUPIÈRE — 550F

Tel 42 27 00 73 **Fax 46 22 27 09** Map B1.41 **R**
154 ave de Wagram 75017 Mº Wagram

Trompe l'oeil decor, pink tablecloths, crystal glass and silver cutlery add up to a picture of elegance in Camille and Christian Thuillart's splendid little restaurant. Market-led menus show both classic and modern elements, and Christian's passion for mushrooms means that they have their very own menu at the appropriate time of year. A la carte suggestions could be crab charlotte wrapped in leeks, warm lobster salad with basil, terrine of duck foie gras or a fricassee of wild mushrooms to start, then maybe fillet of bass cooked on the skin side only with olive oil and Guérande salt or carpaccio of beef with basil, and finally coffee parfait, *diplomate* of cherries or millefeuille of red fruits. Set menus 138F, 165F & 240F. ***Seats*** *30 (+ 10 outside). L 12-2.30 D 7.30-10.30.* ***Closed*** *L Sat, all Sun, Public Holidays & 2 weeks mid-Aug. Amex, Mastercard, Visa.*

A glossary of French menu items starts on page 274

SPLENDID ETOILE — 1030F

Tel 45 72 72 00 **Fax 45 72 72 01** Map A2.42 **H**
1bis ave Carnot 75017 Mº Etoile (ave Carnot exit)

A solidly handsome building on the corner of Avenue Carnot and Rue de Tilsitt, just a few paces from the Arc de Triomphe. Bedrooms are comfortable and generally spacious, with Louis XV-style reproduction furniture, plus modern amenities inlcuding mini-bar, safe, satellite TV and both tub and shower in bathrooms. About two-thirds of the rooms have air-conditioning and those facing the road are double-glazed. Day rooms include an English-style bar and a small restaurant, the Pré Carré. There's also a 20-seat conference room. 24-hour reception and room service till 11pm. ***Rooms*** *57. Amex, Diners, Mastercard, Visa.*

LE SUD — 500F

Tel 45 74 02 77 Map A1.47 **R**
91 bd Gouvion-Saint-Cyr 75017 Mº Porte Maillot

Under the same ownership as the Moroccan Charly de Bab-el-Oued which is a few doors away down the street, but divided by the Mediterranean when it comes to the food. This restaurant specialises in the cooking of Provence and has a colourful Southern decor including a glass-roofed, plant-filled conservatory. Fish is delivered from the South of France and is used to make the *bouillabaisse* and *bourride*. Another dish to look out for is the confit of lamb, and don't miss the section *'il n'y en a pas toujours'* – a constantly changing choice that could include *filets de rougets à la niçoise*, daube of octopus in red Provence wine or grilled whole baby sea bass with olive oil or flamed in Pernod. ***Seats*** *130 (+ 50 outside). L 12-2.30 D 7-11.* ***Closed*** *Sun. Amex, Diners, Mastercard, Visa.*

LA TABLE DE PIERRE — 700F

Tel 43 80 88 68 Map B1.43 **R**
116 bd Péreire 75017 Mº Péreire

The kitchen and the front of house are both Basque-run, the furniture is Basque and the pictures on the walls of this cheerful, good-looking restaurant have a theme of the Basque country. So of course does the menu, with specialities such as Serrano ham, *pipérade, foie gras* with potatoes and cinnamon, calamares cooked in olive oil, pimentos stuffed with salt cod, *chipirons* (baby squid) in their ink, roast shoulder of baby lamb and a fine *gateau Basque de cerises* to round things off. Some dishes must be ordered 24 hours in advance, for a minimum of four diners: *ttoro* (a Basque soup), *paella Valenciana, cassoulet, poule au pot Henry IV.* ***Seats*** *45. L 12.30-2.45 D 7.30-10.45.* ***Closed*** *L Sat, all Sun. Amex, Mastercard, Visa.*

TAÏRA 650F

Tel 47 66 74 14 Map A2.44 **R**
10 rue des Acacias 75017 M° Argentine

Just north of the Avenue de la Grande Armée, this restaurant features walls hung with striking paintings by a modern Romanian artist. Chef Taïra Kurihara puts his personal stamp on classic French dishes offering a menu that is almost exclusively fish (one exception being the *foie gras de canard maison*) and includes starters such as sole fillets with fried onions, tuna carpaccio and scallops in the shell grilled with a tarragon sauce. For a main course try ravioli of turbot with Marennes oysters or bouillabaisse and finish with stuffed figs with vanilla ice. Fillet of bream grilled under a stout shell of sea salt is a speciality. The set menu (150F/170F) offers excellent value for money; there's also a *menu dégustation* at 320F. ***Seats*** *34. L 12-2.30 D 7.30-10.30.* ***Closed*** *L Sat & Public Holidays, all Sun. Amex, Diners, Mastercard, Visa.*

TIMGAD 700F

Tel 45 74 23 70 Fax 40 68 76 46 Map A2.45 **R**
21 rue Brunel 75017 M° Argentine

Long established and one of the best known Arab restaurants in France, Timgad offers a classic selection of North African specialities in very plush Moorish surroundings, including *harira*, a hearty and spicy Moroccan soup, merguez and various *briks* – thin, crispy pastry envelopes containing lamb, tuna, egg, brains, prawn or salmon. Hand-rolled couscous is served alongside a list of meats and vegetables and there are also many variations of lamb or chicken tagines, for instance with olives, prunes, almonds or artichokes and peas. Charcoal-grilled meats include pigeon and lamb kebabs. There are several 'party' dishes for 4 or more (lamb or chicken tagine with quinces, stuffed chicken, stuffed gigot, pastilla). Finish with a selection of choice Arab pastries and a delicious glass of mint tea (also available with pine nuts). Wines from Algeria, Morocco, Tunisia (all the same price) and France. ***Seats*** *70. L 12-2.30 D 7.30-11. Amex, Diners, Mastercard, Visa.*

18th Arrondissement

Places of Interest

Marché aux Puces (Porte de Clignancourt)
Montmartre
Basilique du Sacré Coeur, 42 51 17 02, M° Anvers
Cimitière de Montmartre (Stendhal, Berlioz, Nijinsky, Zola, Truffaut, Degas), 43 87 64 24, M° Blanche/Place de Clichy
Moulin Rouge, 46 06 00 19, M° Blanche
Espace Montmartre Salvador Dali, 42 64 40 10, M° Abbesses

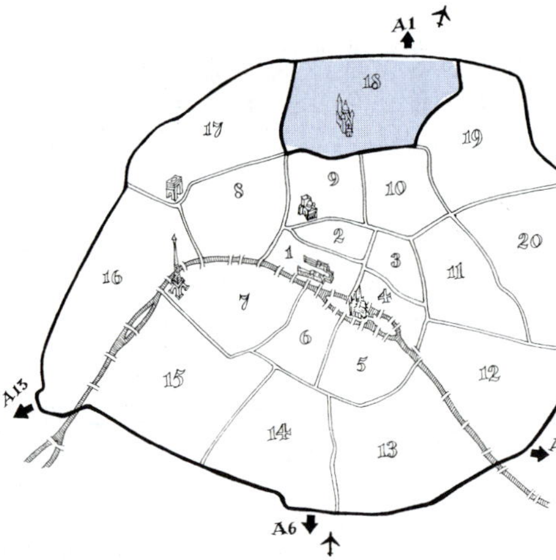

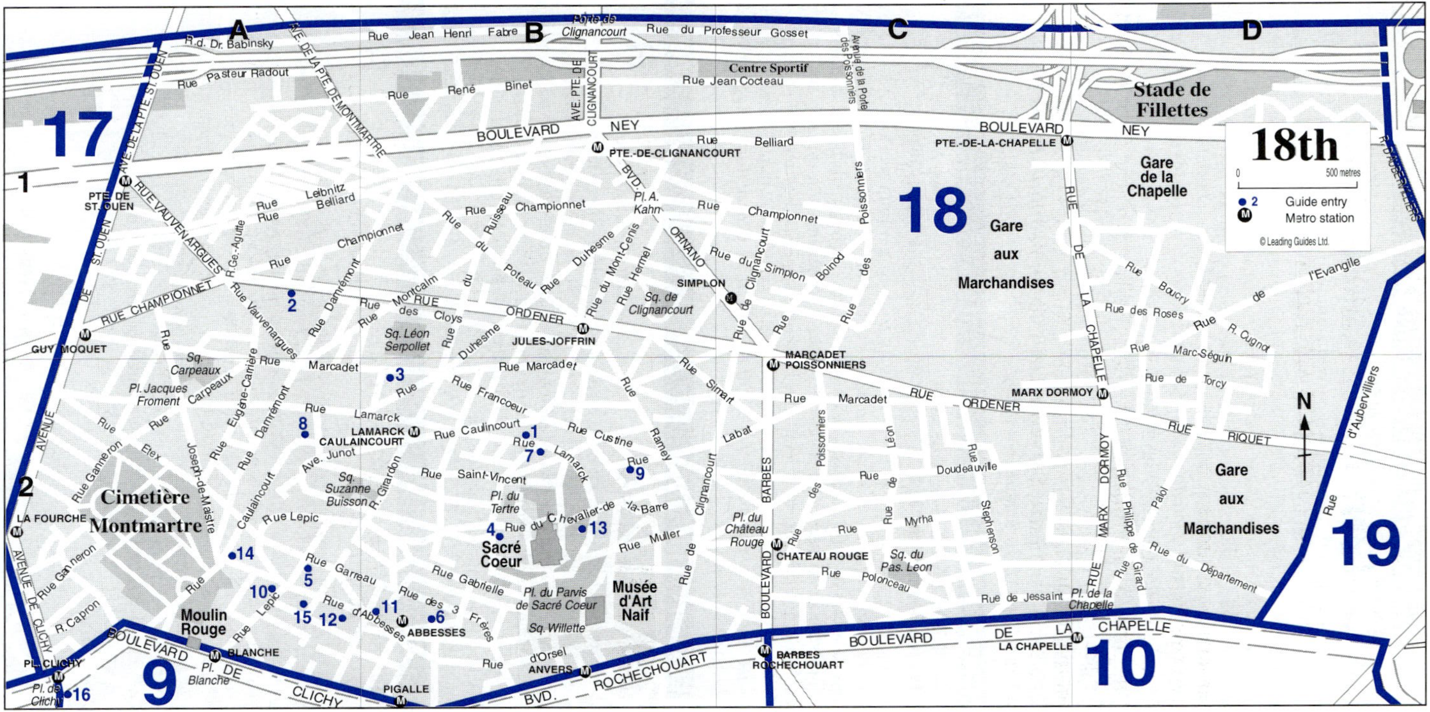
18th
0
500 metres
2 Guide entry
Metro station
© Leading Guides Ltd.
17
18
19
10
9
A
B
C
D
1
2
Stade de Fillettes
Centre Sportif
Gare de la Chapelle
Gare aux Marchandises
Gare aux Marchandises
Cimetière Montmartre
Moulin Rouge
Sacré Coeur
Musée d'Art Naif
Sq. Léon Serpollet
Sq. de Clignancourt
Sq. Carpeaux
Sq. Suzanne Buisson
Sq. du Pas. Leon
Sq. Willette
Pl. du Tertre
Pl. du Parvis de Sacré Coeur
Pl. du Château Rouge
Pl. Jacques Froment
Pl. A. Kahn
Pl. de la Chapelle
Pl. de Clichy
Pl. de Blanche
N
PTE DE ST. OUEN
GUY MOQUET
LA FOURCHE
PL. CLICHY
BLANCHE
PIGALLE
ABBESSES
ANVERS
LAMARCK CAULAINCOURT
JULES-JOFFRIN
SIMPLON
MARCADET POISSONNIERS
MARX DORMOY
CHATEAU ROUGE
BARBES ROCHECHOUART
LA CHAPELLE
PTE.-DE-CLIGNANCOURT
PTE.-DE-LA-CHAPELLE
BOULEVARD NEY
BOULEVARD DE LA CHAPELLE
BVD. ROCHECHOUART
BOULEVARD DE CLICHY
BOULEVARD BARBES
BVD. ORNANO
RUE ORDENER
RUE DE LA CHAPELLE
RUE MARX DORMOY
RUE RIQUET
RUE CHAMPIONNET
RUE VAUVENARGUES
AVENUE DE CLICHY
AVE. DE LA PTE. ST. OUEN
AVE. DE LA PTE. DE MONTMARTRE
AVE. PTE DE CLIGNANCOURT
Porte de Clignancourt
Avenue de la Porte des Poissonniers
R.d. Dr. Babinsky
Rue Jean Henri Fabre
Rue du Professeur Gosset
Rue Pasteur Radout
Rue René Binet
Rue Jean Cocteau
Rue Belliard
Rue Championnet
Rue Leibnitz
Rue Belliard
R.Ge.-Agutte
Rue Damrémont
Rue Montcalm
Rue des Cloys
Rue du Ruisseau
Rue du Poteau
Rue Duhesme
Rue du Mont-Cenis
Rue Hermel
Rue du Simplon
Rue de Clignancourt
Rue Boinod
Rue des Poissonniers
Rue Marcadet
Rue Eugene-Carrière
Rue Lamarck
Rue Caulaincourt
Rue Francoeur
Rue Custine
Rue Ramey
Rue Simart
Rue Labat
Ave. Junot
R. Girardon
Rue Saint-Vincent
Rue du Chevalier-de-la-Barre
Rue Muller
Rue Lepic
Rue Garreau
Rue d'Abbesses
Rue des 3 Frères
Rue Gabrielle
Rue d'Orsel
Rue Etex
Rue Joseph-de-Maistre
Rue Ganneron
R. Capron
Rue Léon
Rue Doudeauville
Rue Stephenson
Rue Myrha
Rue Polonceau
Rue de Jessaint
Rue Philippe de Girard
Rue Pajol
Rue du Département
Rue d'Aubervilliers
Rue Boucry
Rue des Roses
Rue de l'Evangile
R. Cugnot
Rue Marc-Séguin
Rue de Torcy
R. D'AUBERVILLIERS
1
2
3
4
5
6
7
8
9
10
11
12
13
14
15
16

A. Beauvilliers 1100F

Tel 42 54 54 42 Fax 42 62 70 30 Map B2.1 **R**
52 rue Lamarck 75018 Mº Lamarck Caulaincourt

Chef-patron Edouard Carlier has created a unique restaurant from this former bakery. The three dining-rooms are decked out in fine 19th-century style, each with enormous bouquets of flowers, gold-leafed framed mirrors, old furniture, portraits in oil, spectacular crystal chandeliers, elegant china and glass all set against a blue background. In summer, guests can sit out on the leafy terrace and savour such traditional specialities as *raviolis de fromage aux champignons, persillé de canard, pintade et lapin* and *millefeuille de langoustines aux feuilles de pommes de terre croustillantes et tomates confites* to begin. Main dishes include fillet of beef filled with smoked ham and mustard seeds, *timbale de macaroni au foie gras, ris de veau avec morilles lié à la crème fleurette et truffe* and *rognonnade de veau*. Desserts are excellent, *millefeuille au chocolat et glace pistaché, crème brulée* and *tarte tatin* being typical. Set L 185F & 300F (wine incl) Set D 400F. ***Seats*** *86 (+ 40 outside). L 12-2 D 7.30-10.45.* ***Closed*** *L Mon, all Sun. Amex, Diners, Mastercard, Visa.*

Chez Frézet 600F

Tel 46 06 64 20 Fax 46 06 10 79 Map A1.2 **R**
181 rue Ordener 75018 Mº Jules-Joffrin

Re-opening with new owners as we went to press but long-serving chef Robert Antoine remains with a menu that ranges from bouillabaisse, beef steak *béarnaise* and cassoulet to *selle d'agneau en croute*, magret of duck with honey and lime, *choucroute de la mer* and *marmite dieppoise*. Finish with home-made ices or patisserie. In summer, sit at a table in the covered plant-filled interior courtyard for a more tranquil meal away from the street noise. Set menus 165F & 180F. ***Seats*** *90 (+ 30 in courtyard). L 12-2.30 D 7.30-10.30.* ***Closed*** *Sun & Aug. Amex, Mastercard, Visa.*

Le Cottage Marcadet 700F

Tel 42 57 71 22 Map B2.3 **R**
151bis rue Marcadet 75018 Mº Lamarck Caulaincourt

A charming little restaurant decorated in pretty pastels where Jean-François Canot prepares imaginative French food of a high calibre. Starters could include *galette de ris de veau* or lobster ravioli with a light herb sauce followed by main dishes such as *dorade caramelisée aux épices et zestes de citron confits* and *civet de lièvre ravioles d'abats et poire aux épices*. To finish try the gratin of figs or blackberry parfait with blackberry sauce. Set L 120F Set L & D 210F (wine included). ***Seats*** *22. L 12-2.15 D 8-10.* ***Closed*** *Sun & Aug. Mastercard, Visa.*

La Crémaillère 1900 500F

Tel 46 06 58 59 Fax 42 64 08 57 Map B2.4 **R**
15 place du Tertre 75018 Mº Abbesses/Anvers

In a very Parisian square, a short distance from the Sacré Coeur basilica, the restaurant dates back to the 1900s and still retains the original decor including paintings by Mucha. Other attractive features include an internal courtyard garden and a terrace on the square. The comprehensive menu, served throughout the day, is of classic, familiar dishes, the simpler ones being best. Moules marinière, goujons of sea bass, duck confit with *gratin dauphinois* and grilled lamb cutlets as well as sole, salmon, prawns and sea bream grilled to order, are typical offerings. Knuckle of pork braised with beer is a special dish of chef Henri Boulard. This is a restaurant popular with group bookings. Set menus 68F, 89F, 148F, 185F & 245F. ***Seats*** *300.* ***Meals*** *11am-12.30am. Amex, Mastercard, Visa.*

See page 9 for a list of starred restaurants

La Galerie — 360F

Tel 42 59 25 76 Map A2.5 **R**
16 rue Tholozé 75018 Mº Abbesses/Blanche

On a steep street just away from the touristy part of Montmartre, this is a particularly cosy and inviting little restaurant, its walls a mini-gallery of artwork. At lunchtime, when the cheapest of the set menus offers quite remarkable value for money, it's generally quieter than in the evening, when locals and tourists dine by soft music and candle-light. Seafood is the favourite medium of chef-partner Eric Callait, who puts a personal stamp on dishes such as *feuilleté de camembert et d'andouille sauce au cidre, carpaccio de St Jacques au gingembre et au citron vert* and *terrine de foie gras aux épices et confiture d'oignons* among the starters, and mains ranging from monkfish or skate with curry and pistachios, to cabbage stuffed with pheasant and fricassee of veal and sweetbreads with sweet wine and girolles. Desserts include a simple but delicious crème caramel.
Set menus 75F (L only), 130F & 160F. ***Seats*** *28. L 12-2 D 7-10.30.* ***Closed*** *Sun, 1 week Feb (school holidays) & 1st 2 weeks Aug. Amex, Mastercard, Visa.*

Au Grain de Folie — 275F

Tel 42 58 15 57 Map B2.6 **R**
24 rue La Vieuville 75018 Mº Abbesses

A tiny, relaxed vegetarian restaurant with a particularly cheerful owner. Vegetable paté, soup of the day such as leek and potato, avocado with Roquefort sauce, houmus and taramasalata are simple starters, while composite main items include vegetable tart, baked goat's cheese with crudités, grains, lentils or beans and cooked vegetables. The most popular desserts are apple crumble and chocolate gateau. Set menus 65F, 80F & (with wine) 100F. ***Seats*** *20. L 12-2.30 D 7-11 (Sat & Sun all day). No credit cards.*

Langevin "Au Poulbot Gourmet" — 600F

Tel 46 06 86 00 Map B2.7 **R**
39 rue Lamarck 75018 Mº Lamarck Caulaincourt

Jean-Paul Langevin's little restaurant in Montmartre is decorated with painter Poulbot's pictures and there are also interesting scenes outside from the glass-enclosed terrace. Jean-Paul's creativity is noticeable not only in his food but also in its presentation. The *carte* changes two to three times a year and is always full of temptations: a summer menu could include *poelé de langoustines au beurre blanc, blanquette de filets de solette avec huitres tièdes* and *noisettes d'agneau au jus de thym* with *charlotte glacé aux deux chocolats, crème anglaise à la pistache* to finish. Winter sees game dishes such as *terrine de gibier* and *crépinette de faisan sur chou braisé* as well as *tete de veau avec sa langue et cervelles sauce ravigote*. A lovely iced chestnut charlotte will round off a meal admirably.
Set L 115F Set L & D 200F (incl. wine & aperitif). ***Seats*** *30. L 12-2 D 7.15-10.* ***Closed*** *Sun (except L Sun Oct-May). Mastercard, Visa.*

Le Maquis — 400F

Tel 42 59 76 07 Map A2.8 **R**
69 rue Caulaincourt 75018 Mº Lamarck Caulaincourt

A Montmartre bistro with a small pavement terrace which is delightful in summer. A varied choice of classic bistro-style dishes is offered: *tartine d'os à la moëlle avec gros sel* or duck terrine with green peppercorns to start, and *brandade de morue, magret de canard à l'aigre-doux* and *émincé de veau au basilic* are some examples. Finish with a delicious *charlotte au chocolat*.
Set L 63F (with wine) & 150F (Sun only, excl wine) Set L & D 159F (incl apéritif, wine, coffee). ***Seats*** *50 (+ 15 outside). L 12-2 D 7.30-10.30.* ***Closed*** *D Sun, all 25 Dec & 1 Jan. Mastercard, Visa.*

Aux Négociants 300F

Tel 46 06 15 11 Map B2.9 **R**
27 rue Lambert 75018 Mº Chateau Rouge

Begin the day in Montmartre by dropping by for a glass of wine at the Naviers' *bistro à vins* or linger longer to taste Jean's herring fillets with warm potatoes, rillettes or *paté de campagne*. The *plat du jour* could be *paté creusois* (potato and pork), *saucisse de Morteau, andouillettes* with a white wine sauce, *cassoulet* or *sauté d'agneau*. The Loire region is particularly well represented on the wine list. ***Seats*** *40. L 12-2.30 D 8-10.30.* ***Closed*** *D Mon & Fri, all Sat, Sun & Aug. No credit cards.*

Prima Lepic 380F

Tel 46 06 44 64 Fax 46 06 66 11 Map A2.10 **H**
29 rue Lepic 75018 Mº Blanche

The hotel is close to the Moulin Rouge and a short walk from Sacré Coeur, through the narrow streets of Montmartre. Inside, all is neatly maintained, with potted plants in the reception rooms and prettily decorated bedrooms, all of which have en suite bathroom and direct-dial telephone as well as TV and hairdryer. No restaurant, but there is an attractive ground-floor breakfast room. ***Rooms*** *38. Mastercard, Visa.*

Regyn's Montmartre 435F

Tel 42 54 45 21 Fax 42 23 76 69 Map B2.11 **H**
18 place des Abbesses 75018 Mº Abbesses

The church of Sacré Coeur is a short stroll away from this clean, friendly hotel. Bedrooms are modest but quite adequate, and those on the 4th and 5th floors enjoy excellent views over Paris. Continental breakfast is served all day in a pretty ground-floor room with a garden theme. Staff are most helpful and pleasant too – booking tables, obtaining tourist concessions and providing information packs, if required. ***Rooms*** *22. Amex, Mastercard, Visa.*

Le Restaurant 400F

Tel 42 23 06 22 Map A2.12 **R**
32 rue Verou 75018 Mº Blanche/Abbesses

A bright and modern restaurant with a short, imaginative carte and a choice of fixed-price menus. Typical dishes in Yves Pelado's repertoire include sauté of forest mushrooms with poached eggs, salad of grilled salmon with lentils, coconut milk and ginger or *papillote de chou farci à la moëlle* to begin. Follow with *gigot de marcassin en poivrade, agneau fondant en tagine aux aromes orientales* or honey-roast duck with coriander and fig compote. Delicious sweets too such as crème brulée with spiced vinegar or a bitter chocolate sablé. Several wines are available by the glass. Set L 70F Set L & D 120F. ***Seats*** *50. L 12-3 D 8-12.* ***Closed*** *L Sat, all Sun & Mon. Amex, Mastercard, Visa.*

Le Sagittaire 320F

Tel 42 55 17 40 Map B2.13 **R**
77 rue Lamarck 75018 Mº Lamarck Caulaincourt

This is a small, lived-in restaurant, about a ten-minute walk from Sacré Coeur, with a horseshoe bar and lacy tablecloths. The new owner has changed little, offering a largely familiar choice of mainstream dishes making up the 160F menu, which also includes an aperitif and half a bottle of wine. There is *craquelin d'escargots au Roquefort, émincé de foie gras, oeufs pochés en meurette* or *saumon cru mariné à l'aneth* to begin. For a main course the choice includes fillet of beef with a green peppercorn sauce, escalope of salmon *en habit vert, fricassée de volaille au fumet de cèpes* and *pièce de veau à la normande* (with cream and mushrooms). To follow comes a salad course with brie, and desserts include apricots in whisky, *crème renversée à l'ancienne*, chocolate charlotte and profiteroles. Set L 95F Mon-Sat Set L & D 160F. ***Seats*** *50. L 12-2.30 D 7-10.30.* ***Closed*** *Sun & Mon. Mastercard, Visa.*

Terrass 1085F

Tel 46 06 72 85 **Fax 42 52 29 11**
12-14 rue Joseph-de-Maistre 75018
Map A2.14
Mº Place de Clichy
H

The hotel is across from the cemetery at Montmartre and a short walk from the market along the Rue Lepic, and has a traditional ambience as well as offering good standards of accommodation. Each room has satellite TV, a hairdryer and mini-bar. Bathrooms are fitted with either a bath or shower. Front-facing rooms on the 4th, 5th and 6th floors have superb views across to the Eiffel Tower which they share with the delightful roof terrace. Room prices include a buffet breakfast. There's a private car park directly opposite the hotel (100F a day). Valet parking. Porter. Laundry service. ***Rooms** 101. Amex, Diners, Mastercard, Visa.*

Utrillo 400F

Tel 42 58 13 44 **Fax 42 23 93 88**
7 rue Aristide Bruant 75018
Map A2.15
Mº Abbesses
H

A good location in the heart of Montmartre, close to the market on Rue Lepic and a short distance from the area's major tourist sights, is one of the advantages of choosing to stay at the Utrillo. Walls are decorated with prints of the artist's work as well as paintings bought at local antiques markets by the owners, who maintain the hotel in tip-top order. Rooms are equipped with TV, phone, hairdryer and mini-bar. ***Rooms** 30. Amex, Diners, Mastercard, Visa.*

Wepler 475F

Tel 45 22 53 24 **Fax 44 70 07 50**
14 place de Clichy 75018
Map A2.16
Mº Place de Clichy
R

With a tradition and ambience that date back to the end of the last century, this brasserie stands on the busy Place Clichy. The menu is a classic and familiar one, majoring on *fruits de mer*, notably in the *plateau*. Scallops *à la provençale* and roast monkfish with figs are other fishy possibilities, while on the meaty side you'll find *pot de fromage de tete*, duck foie gras and *choucroute paysanne*. Well-known desserts too such as *crème brulée à la vanille* and chocolate profiteroles. Set menu 150F. ***Seats** 250 (+ 50 outside). Meals noon-1am. Amex, Diners, Mastercard, Visa.*

19th & 20th Arrondissements
Places of Interest

Parc de la Villette
Cité des Sciences et de l'Industrie – La Villette, 40 05 70 00, M° Porte de la Villette
Musée de la Musique, 44 84 46 46, M° Porte de Pantin
Parc des Buttes Chaumont (Haussmann-designed), M° Botzaris/Buttes Chaumont
Cimitière Père Lachaise (Héloise & Abelard, La Fontaine, Chopin, Molière, Dumas, Proust, Jim Morrison, Wilde, Piaf, Balzac) 43 70 70 33, M° Père Lachaise

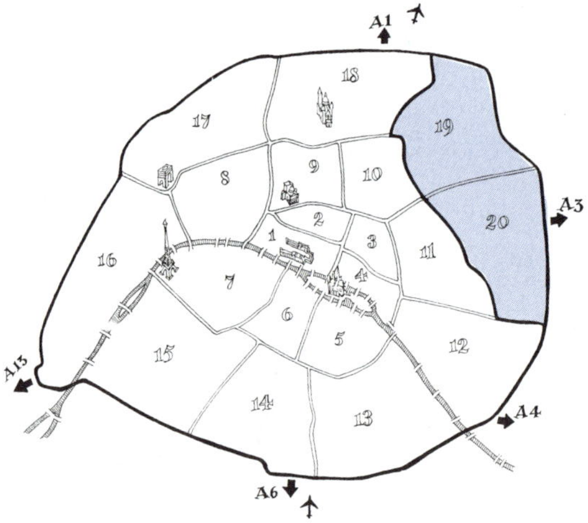

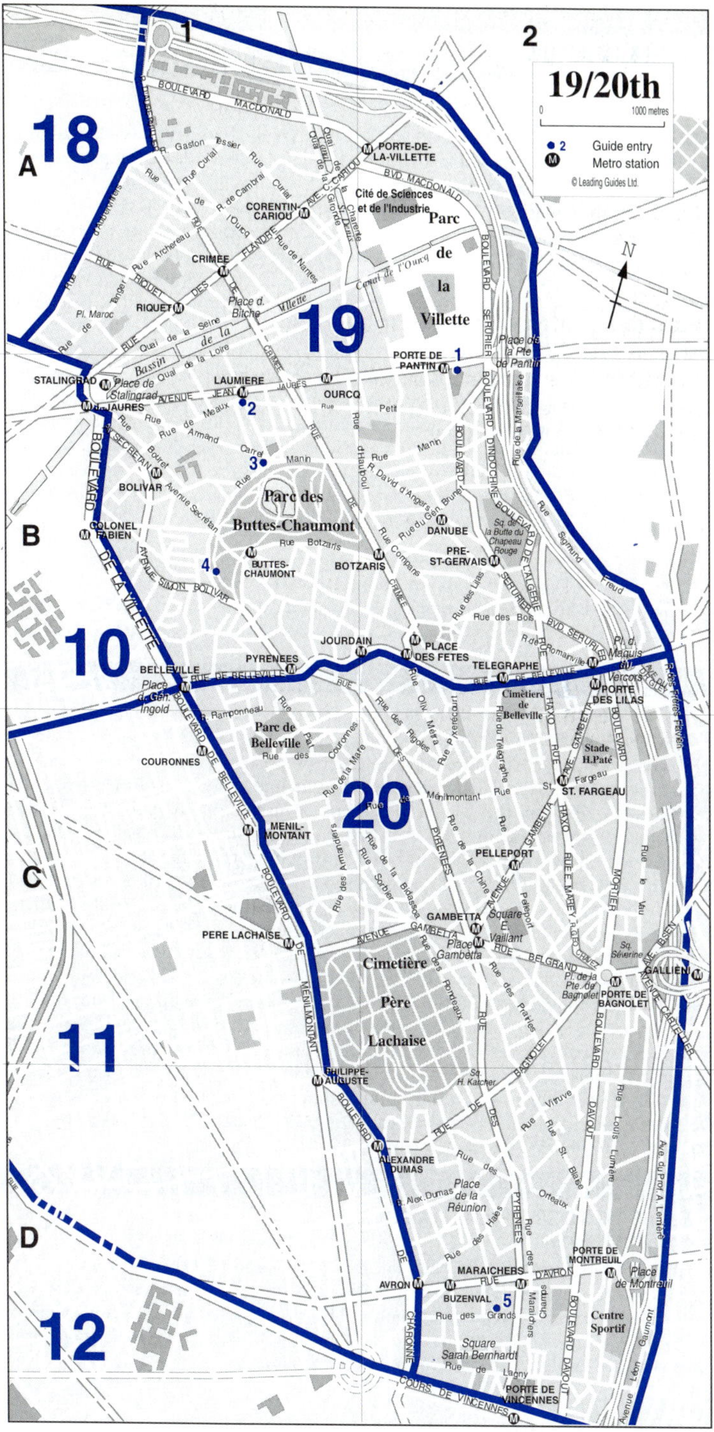

19/20th
0
1000 metres
2 Guide entry
Metro station
© Leading Guides Ltd.
18
19
20
10
11
12
A
B
C
D
1
2
N
Parc de la Villette
Cité de Sciences et de l'Industrie
Parc des Buttes-Chaumont
Parc de Belleville
Cimetière Père Lachaise
Cimetière de Belleville
Stade H.Paté
Centre Sportif
PORTE-DE-LA-VILLETTE
CORENTIN-CARIOU
CRIMEE
RIQUET
STALINGRAD
J. JAURES
LAUMIERE
OURCQ
PORTE DE PANTIN
BOLIVAR
COLONEL FABIEN
BUTTES-CHAUMONT
BOTZARIS
DANUBE
PRE-ST-GERVAIS
JOURDAIN
PLACE DES FETES
PYRENEES
BELLEVILLE
TELEGRAPHE
PORTE DES LILAS
COURONNES
ST. FARGEAU
MENIL-MONTANT
PELLEPORT
GAMBETTA
PERE LACHAISE
GALLIENI
PORTE DE BAGNOLET
PHILIPPE-AUGUSTE
ALEXANDRE DUMAS
AVRON
MARAICHERS
BUZENVAL
PORTE DE MONTREUIL
PORTE DE VINCENNES
Boulevard Macdonald
Bvd. Macdonald
Place de Stalingrad
Place de la Pte de Pantin
Place Gambetta
Place de la Réunion
Place de Montreuil
Square Sarah Bernhardt
Bassin de la Villette
Canal de l'Ourcq
Boulevard de la Villette
Boulevard de Belleville
Boulevard de Ménilmontant
Boulevard de Charonne
Cours de Vincennes
Boulevard Davout
Boulevard Mortier
Boulevard Sérurier
Rue de Belleville
Rue de Ménilmontant
Avenue Jean Jaurès
Avenue Secrétan
Avenue Simon Bolivar
Avenue Gambetta
Rue des Pyrénées
Rue de Crimée
Rue d'Avron
Rue de Bagnolet

LES ALLOBROGES ★ 600F

Tel 43 73 40 00 Map D2.5 **R**
71 rue des Grands-Champs 75020 M° Maraichers

The Pateyrons, he in the kitchen and his wife front of house, are well established at this most appealing restaurant with its 'modern country' look – light browns, greys and greens in the decor, wallpaper made to look like panelling, large poppies in the upholstery, rustic pictures (farm animals) on the walls, terracotta vases, wheatsheafs decorating the central bread table, spotless white linen, straw tying the napkins. Dishes marked by care without undue elaboration include *galette de foie gras* (a galette of potato, wrapped in bacon and topped with meltingly delicious foie gras – well worth the 20-minute wait), confit tomatoes with a cream of green olives, roast Bresse chicken, Barbary duck with spices and dried fruit with Madeira, roast tuna with cabbage and bacon, knuckle of lamb braised with a confit of garlic and a lobster and monkfish fricassee. *Marquise au chocolat* is all that it should be, or you might try a citrus fruit salad with caramel sauce. Les Allobroges is a real gem – a romantic little spot in the far-flung limits of the 20th arrondissement, not usually associated with excellent or fashionable eating. Well worth a detour – Cours de Vincennes is the nearest landmark, and the 26 bus almost passes the door. Set menus 89F & 159F (4 courses). ***Seats** 30. L 12-2 D 7.30-10. **Closed** Sun, Mon & Public Holidays. Mastercard, Visa.*

> The best way to get around Paris is by bus or metro –
> buy a book (carnet) of tickets at any metro station and save money

AU COCHON D'OR 800F

Tel 42 45 46 46 **Fax 42 40 43 90** Map B2.1 **R**
192 ave Jean-Jaurès 75019 M° Porte de Pantin

The old abattoirs of Villette are opposite this appropriately-named restaurant, which has a tradition of good-quality meat served in copious portions. In particular, try *tete de veau* with a mustard sauce, grilled black pudding with apple, pig's trotters with *sauce choron*, veal kidneys with *béarnaise* or *grillade de boeuf spéciale Cochon d'Or, pommes soufflés* (for two). Start with classics like duck foie gras with truffles, duck terrine with armagnac, bone marrow on toast and *escargots de Bourgogne;* finish with a *nougat glacé* or a speciality soufflé (Grand Marnier, chocolate, Rothschild, raspberry) for two, 30 minutes wait. Plenty of seafood options too from oysters, sea urchins and a *plateau de fruits de mer* (240F) to grilled salmon hollandaise and sole meunière. Dating from 1924 and barely altered since, the decor is typical of a bistro of that era with mirrors and some wood panelling. The restaurant is divided into several rooms. An impressive wine list, reds especially, is rather grandly priced – just one red burgundy under 300F! What was their fish restaurant, *La Mer,* next door, has now become **Le Bistro de Cochon d'Or** with a menu along similar lines to the restaurant and the same telephone number. Valet parking. Set menu 240F. ***Seats** 105. L 12.30-2.30 D 7.30-10.30. Amex, Diners, Mastercard, Visa.*

LE LAUMIÈRE 270F

Tel 42 06 10 77 **Fax 42 06 72 50** Map B1.2 **H**
4 rue Petit 75019 M° Laumière

A modern hotel built in 1968 and entirely renovated in 1991, offering inexpensive, simple accommodation with a courtyard garden overlooked by some bedrooms and the breakfast room. The price quoted above is for a room with shower and WC only; the rate for a room with bath is 350F. Parking for five cars (45F a night). ***Rooms** 54. Mastercard, Visa.*

Le Palais de l'Inde 500F

Tel 42 39 31 14 Map B1.3 **R**
65 rue Manin 75019 M° Laumière

An agreeably lit, intimate Indian restaurant specialising in tandoori dishes of chicken, giant prawns and quail plus lamb and chicken tikka served with vegetable beignets. Set menus 62F (L only), 125F (vegetarian) & 150F. ***Seats*** *64 (+ 30 outside). L 12-2.30 D 7-11.30. Amex, Mastercard, Visa.*

Le Pavillon Puebla 860F

Tel 42 08 92 62 Map B1.4 **R**
Parc Buttes-Chaumont 75019 M° Buttes-Chaumont/Pyrénées

To reach Le Pavillon Puebla, enter the Buttes-Chaumont park through the gate at the corner of Avenue Simon Bolivar and Rue Botzaris. Established a few years ago in an 1890s house, it has Napoleon III decor with an impressive chandelier in one of the dining-rooms and large bouquets of flowers everywhere. Three sides of the restaurant have plate-glass windows with floral drapes and in summer the outdoor terrace is set up with large parasols. Owner-chef Christian Vergès' Catalan origins are made evident in his cuisine in the way he adds spices and herbs to his light sauces. Carpaccio with seven peppers, terrine of rabbit with onion *marmelade* and sardines marinated in olive oil and lemon are typical starters, while prominent among the main courses are fish bouillabaisse-style, chicken thigh with snails and olives, and beef fillet grilled or peppered. Crown a splendid meal with a first-rate crème brulée or figs and pears in wine. Car parking is available in the Parc. Set menus 180F (Catalan speciality) & 230F. ***Seats*** *60. L 12-2.30 D 7.30-10.* ***Closed*** *Sun, Mon, 8 days Mar & 2 weeks mid-Aug. Amex, Mastercard, Visa.*

Around Paris

Places of Interest

La Défense: Grand Arche 49 07 27 57, M° Grande Arche de La Défense/RER A
Versailles (Chateau, musée), 30 84 74 00, RER C
Disneyland Paris, 64 74 30 00, Info Hotel 49 41 49 41, RER A Chessy-Marne-La-Vallée
Musée National de la Céramique Sèvres, 45 34 99 05, M° Pont de Sèvres
Fontainebleau (Chateau, musée), 64 22 27 40/64 22 34 39, SNCF from Gare de Lyon
Basilique St Denis (tombs of the kings of France), 48 09 83 54, M° St Denis-Basilique
Vincennes (Chateau), 43 28 15 48, M° Chateau de Vincennes, RER A
Musée des Transports Urbains, St Mandé (bus 46 passes entrance; open weekends pm), 43 28 37 12, M° Porte Dorée

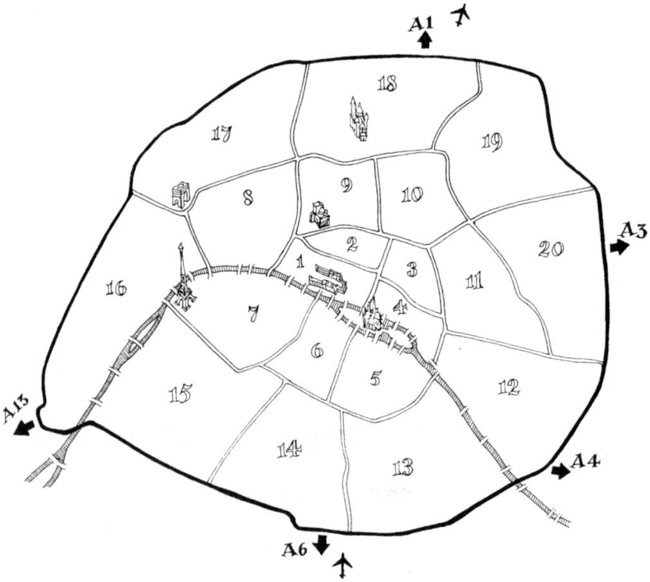

Le Bistrot d'à Coté

Tel 47 45 34 55
4 rue Boutard 92200 Neuilly M° Pont de Neuilly **R**

See 17th arrondissement Bistrot d'à Coté for details.

Ibis 450F

Tel 47 78 15 60 Fax 47 78 94 16
4 bd de Neuilly 92400 Courbevoie M° Esplanade de La Défense **H**

Sharing the same building as the *Novotel* (see below), the Ibis offers budget accommodation in the business district with excellent public transport connections to the rest of town. At weekends (Fri, Sat & Sun nights) the price drops to 390F per room. ***Rooms** 284. Amex, Diners, Mastercard, Visa.*

Novotel 790F

Tel 47 78 16 68 Fax 47 78 84 71
2 bd de Neuilly 92400 Courbevoie M° Esplanade de La Défense **H**

Mid-range chain hotel overlooking the Seine on the La Défense side of the Pont de Neuilly. All the bedrooms, which were being refurbished in the autumn of 1995, have air-conditioning, mini-bar and bathroom with separate loo. ***Rooms** 280. Amex, Diners, Mastercard, Visa.*

Sofitel CNIT 1400F

Tel 46 92 10 10 Fax 46 92 10 50
2 place de La Défense 92053 La Défense M° Grande Arche de La Défense **HR**

There are two Sofitel hotels at La Défense; this one is within the extraordinary CNIT building next to the even more striking Grande Arche. Practical bedrooms are notably spacious and have good bathrooms, all with both power and hand-held 'hair-washing' showers over tubs and polished, red-granite vanity units. A live pianist brings atmosphere to the modern open-plan bar each evening. 24-hour room service. Ample free parking nearby. ***Rooms** 147. Amex, Diners, Mastercard, Visa.*

Les Communautés 650F

Tel 46 92 10 30

The windows on one side of the fifth-floor restaurant look into the vast interior space of the CNIT building, while on the other the view is of Place de La Défense and Mitterrand's Grande Arche. The same menu is differently priced at lunch (295F for a four-course meal that includes the excellent cheese trolley) and dinner when starters are all 70F, mains 130F, cheese 40F and desserts 50F. There is also a short (two choices) 170F table d'hote dinner that is aimed at hotel guests but is available to all. Dishes have a modern slant and tend to feature bold flavours - charlotte of wild mushrooms with calf's sweetbreads and duck foie gras, oxtail ravioli with a fricassee of girolles, lettuce-wrapped fillet of brill with a wine sauce and strips of chicory, milk-fed veal with morels and a gratin of macaroni. Desserts might include *moelleux au chocolat* served warm with its sorbet and *tarte paysanne aux pommes tièdes* with a caramel sauce. It's a large room with well-spaced tables and plenty of bustling waiters, particularly at lunchtime when it is usually full of business folk. The wine list is not over-long but offers something to suit most pockets. Set L 295F Set D 170F. ***Seats** 110. L 12.15-2 D 7.30-10.30. **Closed** Sat, Sun, 25 Dec & Public Holidays.*

Sofitel 1300F

Tel 47 76 44 43 Fax 47 73 72 74
34 Cours Michelet 92060 La Défense M° Esplanade de La Défense **H**

The other Sofitel hotel at La Défense. Exceptionally good work space, with phone at the desk as well as at the bedside, and excellent bathrooms are features of comfortable if rather blandly decorated bedrooms. Room service is round the clock and all rooms have mini-bar and room safe. Private parking (75F for 24 hours). ***Rooms** 150. Amex, Diners, Mastercard, Visa.*

TRIANON PALACE 1914F

Tel 30 84 38 00 **Fax 39 49 00 77** **HR**
1 bd de la Reine 78000 Versailles RER Line C

Situated on the edge of the Royal Park, a short walk from the Palace of Versailles, and ten miles from the centre of Paris, the hotel has welcomed a long and distinguished line of guests. Monarchs and generals, oil magnates and film stars have walked the long, marble-columned corridors and stayed in the elegant, high-ceilinged bedrooms which are all furnished with antiques. The building dates from 1910 and was thoroughly renovated four years ago when it was bought by a Japanese company. Old-fashioned luxury is matched by the most up-to-date amenities, including an international conference centre in the neighbouring **Trianon Hotel** (linked by an underground corridor) with six conference and five committee rooms. Leisure facilities are equally splendid. In addition to a fully-equipped gym and health spa, guests can also swim, play tennis and relax in a traditional Moroccan hammam. 24-hour room service. Valet parking. ***Rooms*** *98. Amex, Diners, Mastercard, Visa.*

Les Trois Marches ★ 1400F

Tel 39 50 13 21 **Fax 30 21 01 25**

Chef Gérard Vié prides himself on the research and invention behind his cooking. Some of his dishes are fiendishly complicated, while others are nearer the peasant simplicity of the food of his youth. Examples are *galette de pommes de terre, lard et caviar* (potato, bacon and caviar pancake), *ragout d'abats caramélisés* (caramelised offal stew) and *langouste rose aux épices, figues, navets confits* (spiny lobster with spices, figs and turnip confit). Portions are not huge. A special dietetic menu is available. The excellent sommelier is particularly good at discovering petits vins from areas such as Languedoc/Roussillon. Set L 260F Set D 495F & 595F. ***Seats*** *60 (+ 60 outside). L 12-2 D 7.30-10.* ***Closed*** *Sun & Mon.*

LA TRUFFE NOIRE "JENNY JACQUET" 700F

Tel 46 24 94 14 **Fax 46 37 27 022** **R**
2 place Parmentier 92200 Neuilly M° Porte Maillot

Although just outside Paris in Neuilly, Jenny Jacquet's restaurant is only 150 metres from Porte Maillot metro station. Diners sit at widely-spaced tables in four small dining-rooms in a warm and comfortable atmosphere. Dishes change every two months with the three-course *menu-carte* (195F) providing the best value for money: terrine of smoked salmon with cucumber and horseradish, *rable et cuisse de lapin en vinaigrette chasseur*, fricassee of chicken with tarragon, *mousseline de sandre au beurre blanc* (a speciality). The main carte might include foie gras with spiced bread served on a salad, fillet of beef with bone marrow and autumn vegetables, wild duck sweet and sour, and, a speciality from the Loire, *beuchelle à la tourangelle* (calf's sweetbreads and kidneys and mushrooms with a white wine sauce). The *menu dégustation* varies with the seasons with three of the four courses based around a single main ingredient, langoustines in early autumn perhaps before the wild mushroom season begins, then comes game from mid-December to mid-February (till mid-March in a good year) it's always truffles that take pride of place. Set menus 185F & 250F (*dégustation* - the price of this menu rises during the truffle season). Valet parking. ***Seats*** *50. L 12.30-2 D 7.30-10.* ***Closed*** *Sat, Sun & 3 weeks Aug. Amex, Mastercard, Visa.*

> The best way to get around Paris is by bus or metro –
> buy a book (carnet) of tickets at any metro station and save money

Airports

Ibis 395F

Tel 49 19 19 19 **Fax 49 19 19 21** **H**
Roissypole, Aéroport Charles de Gaulle 95701 Roissy-en-France

Practical accommodation at a keen price just 200 metres from the airport's Terminal 9. No room service. Secure residents' parking (50F for 24 hours). ***Rooms*** *556. Amex, Diners, Mastercard, Visa.*

Maxim's 800F

Tel 48 62 16 16 **Fax 48 62 45 96** **R**
Aéroport Charles de Gaulle 95713 Roissy-en-France

The best of the airport eating is provided at this cool, elegant restaurant, where the skills of the chef are matched by service from a large and efficient team. Alain Bariteau, previously at the *Jules Verne* restaurant on the Eiffel Tower, presents an inviting menu: Vendée pigeon roasted with honey and spices, *feuillantine de coquilles St Jacques au curry*, hot honey soufflé with fruit, *tarte fine aux pommes* with vanilla ice cream. Fine wine list with plenty of half bottles. Set menus 220F & 290F. ***Seats*** *40. L 11.30-2.30 D 6.30-10.* ***Closed*** *Sat, Sun, 1 Jan & Aug. Amex, Diners, Mastercard, Visa.*

Sofitel 1050F

Tel 49 19 29 39 **Fax 49 19 29 00** **H**
Aéroport Charles de Gaulle 95713 Roissy-en-France

Handily situated right in the middle of the airport complex. All rooms have two phones plus mini-bar and multi-channel TV. Leisure facilities include an indoor swimming pool, sauna and tennis. Residents' parking 50F for 24 hours. ***Rooms*** *352. Amex, Diners, Mastercard, Visa.*

Orly Hilton 1100F

Tel 45 12 45 12 **Fax 45 12 45 00** **H**
Orly Sud 267 94544 Orly

Practical modern accommodation with the Hilton style, a short shuttle from Orly Sud and Orly Ouest, and half an hour from the city centre. The bedrooms are air-conditioned and double-glazed and come with all the usual modern comforts. There are rooms adapted for handicapped guests and some reserved for non-smokers. There are no fewer than 25 conference and function rooms, whose various configurations permit up to 500 to be seated together theatre-style. 24-hour reception and room service. New this year is a fitness room plus sauna. ***Rooms*** *359. Amex, Diners, Mastercard, Visa.*

Ibis 320F

Tel 46 87 22 45 **Fax 48 87 84 72** **H**
1 rue Mondétour 94656 Rungis

One of the Ibis budget chain. This one is in a complex of hotels, called the 'Delta Zone', about 10 minutes from Orly airport, halfway to the town of Rungis. No room service. Free secure parking. ***Rooms*** *119. Amex, Diners, Mastercard, Visa.*

Maxim's 700F

Tel 46 87 16 16 **Fax 46 87 05 39** **R**
94546 Aéroport d'Orly Ouest

Having extended in to what was previously the less formal **Grill**, there is now more room (and more space between the tables) here in which to enjoy chef Gil Jouanin's classically based cuisine. Terrine of duck foie gras with port; scallops and crayfish with lentils, ginger and coriander; monkfish roasted with paprika and black pepper with a caper and shallot sauce; grilled sea bass with fennel and

See over

an orange and cumin sauce; grilled Black Angus rump steak with *gratin dauphinois*; mallard duck roasted with fresh peaches and wild mushrooms; *tarte au chocolat* served warm with a mocha sauce and a gratin of pears flavoured with Gewurztraminer show the range of the regularly-changing carte. The restaurant is located on the second floor of the west terminal. The wine list is almost exclusively French. Set menu 230F. ***Seats*** *80. L 12-2.30 D 6.30-10.* ***Closed*** *Sat, Sun & Aug. Amex, Diners, Mastercard, Visa.*

Serviced Apartments

Paris is well supplied with serviced apartments which can offer over many advantages over hotels – privacy, security, freedom, cooking facilities, in short 'a place of your own' for individuals, pairs or even family groups. The apartments that are reviewed on the next few pages afford a wide choice of accommodation, from studios to grand penthouse suites, and the addresses vary from the fashionable heart of Paris to the quiet suburbs. Maid services are provided, and many boast well-equipped kitchens (all have at least rudimentary kitchenettes). Some apartments are effectively hotels, where guests have the choice of using the full hotel amenities or living an independent life. That choice naturally determines the level of service and the price (the latter is liable to vary greatly according to the season, the length of stay and of course the number of occupants in the apartment).

All the locations listed have been independently assessed by the Guide's inspectors, and all are highly recommendable.

Citadines Paris Austerlitz — 420F-920F

27 rue Esquirol 75013 — Mº Nationale/Campo Formio

The area is fairly modest, but the major asset of this particular Citadines is its quiet and peaceful location. Apartments range from little studettes to 2-room flats for 4. All have kitchenettes, multi-channel TVs and private telephone lines with alarm-call facilities; some rooms have their own tiny balconies. There's a laundrette in the basement, a car park and a breakfast cafeteria in operation from 8 till 11. Reception functions 8am-10pm. ***Apartments*** *49*.

Citadines Paris Opéra — 600F-1235F

18 rue Favart 75002 — Mº Richelieu-Drouot/Opéra

Citadines Paris Opéra, just off Boulevard des Italiens and handy for the Opéra and the Bourse, is part of a handsome redevelopment and opened its doors in June 1994. Accommodation comprises small studios (studettes), studio-flats and two-room apartments including some grand duplexes. Furnishings combine quiet good looks with solid practicality, and all rooms have air-conditioning, private telephone with message service, TV with Sky News, Eurosport and Canal+, a hob, oven, dishwasher and a full range of kitchen essentials. WCs are separate from bathrooms, which are provided with hairdryers. The résidence boasts a private underground car park, billiard room, keep-fit equipment, laundrette, American bar and a meeting room for 20. Entrance is through a peaceful courtyard into a large reception area manned from 6am to midnight. As with all Citadines, the room rate varies considerably according to the seasons (mid-July and August are the lowest) and to the length of stay. The rates quoted above are for stays of 1 to 6 nights at the lowest seasonal rate. ***Apartments*** *76*.

Citadines Paris Trocadéro — 490F-1420F

29bis rue Saint-Didier 75116 — Mº Trocadéro/Victor Hugo/Boissière

In a smart but not always very quiet part of town, this Citadines comprises 97 apartments including studettes, studios for 2 or 3 and 2- and 3-room flats with accommodation for 2, 4 and even 6. There's a private telephone line with alarm call facility, multi-channel TV and a well-equipped little kitchen in all apartments. The multi-lingual reception operates from 7.30am to 9.30pm and there's a breakfast salon for those who don't want to make their own. Private garage parking. The rates quoted above are for a short stay mid-July to 1st September – the cheapest period. ***Apartments*** *97*.

Kléber Palace — See entry in 16th arrondissement

RÉSIDENCE TIMES SQUARE ALMA MARCEAU 2000F-5500F

5-7 rue Jean-Giraudoux 75016 M° Alma-Marceau

Luxurious modern accommodation in a prestigious part of Paris, as quiet and private as you like, but also just a short walk from the bright lights and high life of the Champs Elysées. The Alma Marceau Residence offers all the essentials for comfortable, elegant living in apartments that range from 2-room (1-bedroom) to 6-room duplex flats. Furnishings in carved light wood are of a very high standard, beds large and comfortable, kitchens luxuriously equipped, videophone, private telephones, car parking and daily cleaning/caretaker services provided. The living and kitchen areas are particularly spacious, with plenty of standard lamps, parquet floors and mirrors fronting generous storage space. 22-channel TVs, one in the living area, one in the bedroom. ***Apartments** 10*.

There are three other Times Square Residences. On a similar level of luxury to Alma Marceau is Times Square St Honoré at 218 Rue du Faubourg St Honoré. All the apartments here overlook a courtyard, most have a private balcony or terrace and the full services of the adjacent hotel are available. Rates at St Honoré start at 2300F. Also on the premises is the marine centre Villa Thalgo with a seawater pool. On a more modest scale are Times Square Pascal at 71 Rue Pascal 75013, with 44 studio apartments, and Times Square Montparnasse at 121 Boulevard du Montparnasse 75006, with studios and duplexes. Prices at Pascal start at 590F per night, at Montparnasse 780F.

Bookings at the above serviced apartments may be made through the Apartment Service in London, freecall 0800 243 163.

Summary by Arrondissement

KEY

★ star(s) for cooking (see page 9)

B Champagne Bottle (see page 10)

L Last orders after 11pm

W Open Sat & Sun, lunch & dinner

A Open throughout August

1st Arrondissement

Establishment	Cat	Telephone No.	Star	B	L	W	A	Meal Price	Room Price
Agora	H	42 33 46 02							500F
L'Ami Léon	R	42 33 06 20		▲				350F	
Armand au Palais-Royal	R	42 60 05 11					▲	700F	
Brighton	H	47 03 61 61							600F
Britannique	H	42 33 74 59							720F
Cambon	H	42 60 38 09							1480F
Carré des Feuillants	R	42 86 82 82	★★	▲				1300F	
Les Cartes Postales	R	42 61 02 93					▲	750F	
Le Caveau du Palais	R	43 26 04 28					▲	500F	
Chez Clovis	R	42 33 97 07			▲		▲	450F	
Chez Elle	R	45 08 04 10					▲	450F	
Chez Pauline	R	42 96 20 70					▲	840F	
Chez Rosine	R	49 27 09 23					▲	400F	
Hotel du Continent	H	42 60 75 32							602F
Demeure Hotel Castille	H	44 58 44 58							1990F
Hotel des Ducs d'Anjou	H	42 36 92 24							592F
Duminy-Vendome	H	42 60 32 80							870F
Fellini	R	42 60 90 66			▲	▲	▲	550F	
La Fermette du Sud-Ouest	R	42 36 73 55						440F	
Gaya Rive Droite	R	42 60 43 03		▲				600F	

Gérard Besson	R	42 33 14 74	★★				▲	1200F	
Goumard-Prunier	R	42 60 36 07	★				▲	1350F	
Grand Hotel de Champagne	H	42 36 60 00							640F
Le Grand Véfour	R	42 96 56 27	★★					1400F	
A la Grille Saint-Honoré	R	42 61 00 93						550F	
Hotel Inter-Continental	HR	44 77 11 11							2900F
Terrasse Fleurie		44 77 10 44				▲	▲	1200F	
Joe Allen	R	42 36 70 13			▲	▲	▲	420F	
Juveniles	R	42 97 46 49		▲			▲		
Kinugawa	R	42 60 65 07					▲	800F	
Lescure	R	42 60 18 91						300F	
Lotti	H	42 60 37 34							2200F
Hotel du Louvre	H	44 58 38 38							1350F
Louvre Saint-Honoré	H	42 96 23 23							762F
Mayfair	H	42 60 38 14							1100F
Mercure Galant	R	42 96 98 89	★				▲	1100F	
Meurice	HR	44 58 10 10							3500F
Le Meurice			★			▲	▲	1100F	
Molière	H	42 96 22 01							592F
Montana-Tuileries	H	42 60 35 10							580F
Brasserie Munichoise	R	42 61 47 16			▲		▲	300F	
Normandy	H	42 60 30 21							1275F
Paolo Petrini	R	42 60 56 22		▲				650F	
La Passion	R	42 97 53 41					▲	350F	
Pharamond	R	42 33 06 72		▲			▲	750F	
Au Pied de Cochon	R	42 36 11 75			▲	▲	▲	520F	
Pierre au Palais-Royal	R	42 96 09 17						700F	

1st Arrondissement (cont)

Establishment	Cat	Telephone No.	Star	B	L	W	A	Meal Price	Room Price
Hotel de la Place du Louvre	H	42 33 78 68							682F
Le Poquelin	R	42 96 22 19						600F	
Regina Paris	H	42 60 31 10							1520F
Le Relais du Louvre	H	40 41 96 42							800F
Ritz	HR	43 16 33 33							3730F
L'Espadon			★			▲	▲	1500F	
Le Ruban Bleu	R	42 61 47 53						530F	
Saint-James et Albany	H	44 58 43 21							980F
Saint-Romain	H	42 60 31 70							692F
Tonic Hotel les Halles	H	42 33 00 71							590F
La Tour de Montlhéry	R	42 36 21 82			▲			450F	
Hotel des Tuileries	H	42 61 04 17							790F
Velloni	R	42 21 12 50						500F	
Willi's Wine Bar	R	42 61 05 09				▲	▲	450F	

2nd Arrondissement

Establishment	Cat	Telephone No.	Star	B	L	W	A	Meal Price	Room Price
Arco Tapas y Vinos	R	42 60 07 20			s		s	500F	
Auberge Perraudin	R	42 36 71 09						400F	
Chez Georges	R	42 60 07 11		▲				600F	
Country Life	R	42 97 48 51					▲	130F	
Coup de Coeur	R	47 03 45 70					▲	520F	
Aux Crus de Bourgogne	R	42 33 48 24						450F	
Drouant	R	42 65 15 16	★★			▲	▲	1600F	
Edouard VII	HR	42 61 56 90							1300F
Restaurant Delmonico		42 61 44 26						450F	
Favart	H	42 97 59 83							630F
Gallopin	R	42 36 45 38			▲		▲	460F	
Le Grand Colbert	R	42 86 87 88			▲	▲		500F	
L'Horset Opéra	H	44 71 87 00							1320F
Aux Lyonnais	R	42 96 65 04			▲		▲	425F	
Le Moï	R	47 03 92 05					▲	400F	
Les Noces de Jeannette	R	42 96 36 89		▲		▲	▲	320F	
Hotel de Noailles	H	47 42 92 90							780F
Passy Mandarin	R	42 61 25 50					▲	500F	
Pierre A la Fontaine Gaillon	R	42 65 87 04			▲			650F	
Pile ou Face	R	42 33 64 33	★					800F	
La Rotisserie Monsigny	R	42 96 16 61		▲	▲		▲	580F	

2nd Arrondissement (cont)

Establishment	Cat	Telephone No.	Star	B	L	W	A	Meal Price	Room Price
Café Runtz	R	42 96 69 86			▲			400F	
Le Saint Amour	R	47 42 63 82						750F	
Le Stendhal	H	44 58 52 52							1510F
Vaudeville	R	40 20 04 62			▲	▲	▲	550F	
Westminster	HR	42 61 57 46							1800F
Restaurant Le Celadon		47 03 40 42						1100F	

3rd Arrondissement

Establishment	Cat	Telephone No.	Star	B	L	W	A	Meal Price	Room Price
L'Alisier	R	42 72 31 04						400F	
Ambassade d'Auvergne	R	42 72 31 22				▲		500F	
Bar à Huitres	R	48 87 98 92		▲	▲	▲	▲	500F	
Bellevue/Chariot d'Or	H	48 87 45 60							390F
Hotel des Chevaliers	H	42 72 73 47							572F
Chez l'Ami Louis	R	48 87 77 48				▲	▲	1400F	
Chez Nénesse	R	42 78 46 49						450F	
La Guirlande de Julie	R	48 87 94 07			▲	▲	▲	350F	
Little Palace Hotel	H	42 72 08 15							590F
Hotel du Marais	H	48 87 78 27							390F
Meslay République	H	42 72 79 79							630F
Pavillon de la Reine	H	42 77 96 40							1700F
Hotel du Vieux Saule	H	42 72 01 14							460F

4th Arrondissement

Establishment	Cat	Telephone No.	Star	B	L	W	A	Meal Price	Room Price
L'Ambroisie	R	42 78 51 45	HH					1600F	
Axial Beaubourg	H	42 72 72 22							662F
Bastille Speria	H	42 72 04 01							622F
Benoit	R	42 72 25 76	★					1000F	
Le Bistrot du Dome	R	48 04 88 44	★	▲	▲	▲	▲	500F	
Bofinger	R	42 72 87 82			▲	▲	▲	550F	
Le Bistrot de Bofinger	R	42 72 05 23			▲	▲	▲	400F	
Hotel de la Bretonnerie	H	48 87 77 63							620F
Hotel Castex	H	42 72 31 52							340F
Coconnas	R	42 78 58 16				▲	▲	500F	
Le Coude Fou	R	42 77 15 16			▲		▲	450F	
Hotel des Deux-Iles	H	43 26 13 35							830F
Le Fond de Cour	R	42 74 71 52				▲	▲	500F	
Au Gourmet de l'Isle	R	43 26 79 27					▲	400F	
Le Grizzli	R	48 87 77 56					▲	400F	
A l'Impasse (Chez Robert)	R	42 72 08 45		▲				400F	
Jo Goldenberg	R	48 87 20 16		▲	▲	▲	▲	250F	
Hotel Malher	H	42 72 60 92							570F
Au Monde des Chimères	R	43 54 45 27					▲	500F	
Rivoli Notre Dame	H	42 78 47 39							630F

Hotel Saint-Louis-Marais	H	48 87 87 04						610F
Hotel du 7e Art	H	42 77 04 03						410F
Le Vieux Bistro	R	43 54 18 95			▲	▲	650F	
Woolloomooloo	R	42 72 32 11				▲	650F	

5th Arrondissement

Establishment	Cat	Telephone No.	Star	B	L	W	A	Meal Price	Room Price
Restaurant A	R	46 33 85 54				▲	▲	500F	
Agora St-Germain	H	46 34 13 00							750F
Hotel d'Albe	H	46 34 09 70							540F
Auberge des Deux Signes	R	43 25 46 56						900F	
Brasserie Balzar	R	43 54 13 67			▲	▲		400F	
Bar à Huitres	R	44 07 27 37		▲	▲	▲	▲	500F	
Le Bistro du Port	R	40 51 73 19				▲		400F	
Le Bistrot d'à Coté	R	43 54 59 10					▲	500F	
La Bucherie	R	43 54 78 06			▲	▲	▲	920F	
Chez Toutoune	R	43 26 56 81					▲	430F	
Chieng-Mai	R	43 25 45 45			▲			400F	
Hotel du Collège de France	H	43 26 78 36							500F
Le Départ de Saint-Michel	R	43 54 24 55			▲	▲	▲		
Dodin-Bouffant	R	43 25 25 14						800F	
E Marty	R	43 31 39 51				▲	▲	450F	
Elysa Luxembourg	H	43 25 31 74							720F
Familia	H	43 54 55 27							395F
Les Fontaines	R	43 26 42 80						500F	
La Gueuze	R	43 54 63 00			▲[1]		▲	300F	
Inajiku	R	43 54 70 07						500F	

Le Jardin de Cluny	H	43 54 22 66							775F
Le Jardin des Plantes	H	47 07 06 20							510F
Moissonnier	R	43 29 87 65						500F	
Hotel des Nations	H	43 26 45 24							600F
Hotel de Notre Dame	H	43 26 79 00							690F
Au Pactole	R	46 33 31 31					▲	750F	
Hotel du Panthéon	H	43 54 32 95							770F
Parc St-Séverin	H	43 54 32 17							600F
Hotel Résidence Henri IV	H	44 41 31 81							750F
Hotel Résidence Saint-Christophe	H	43 31 81 54							550F
La Rotisserie du Beaujolais	R	43 54 17 47				▲	▲	440F	
Select	H	46 34 14 80							650F
Hotel de la Sorbonne	H	43 54 58 08							410F
La Timonerie	R	43 25 44 42	★					800F	
La Tour d'Argent	R	43 54 23 31	★★★			▲	▲	2400F	
Hotel des Trois Collèges	H	43 54 67 30							450F

[1] Fri, Sat

6th Arrondissement

Establishment	Cat	Telephone No.	Star	B	L	W	A	Meal Price	Room Price
Hotel de l'Abbaye Saint-Germain	H	45 44 38 11							980F
Acacias Saint-Germain	H	45 48 97 38							750F
Allard	R	43 26 48 23					▲	650F	
Hotel d'Angleterre	H	42 60 34 72							800F
Aramis Saint-Germain	H	45 48 03 75							600F
L'Arbuci	R	44 41 14 14			▲	▲	▲	440F	
Atelier Montparnasse •	H	46 33 60 00							712F
Hotel de l'Avenir	H	45 48 84 54							450F
Belloy St-Germain	H	46 34 26 50							860F
Bistro de la Grille	R	43 54 16 87			▲	▲	▲	420F	
Le Bistrot d'Alex	R	43 54 09 53					▲	500F	
Les Bookinistes	R	43 25 54 94	★	▲	▲		▲	500F	
Hotel Buci-Latin	H	43 29 07 20							970F
Le Caméléon	R	43 20 63 43						450F	
Aux Charpentiers	R	43 26 30 05			▲	▲	▲	450F	
Le Chat Grippé	R	43 54 70 00	★	▲				800F	
Chez Maitre Paul	R	43 54 74 59					▲	450F	
Crystal Hotel	H	45 48 85 14							600F
Danemark	H	43 26 93 78							690F
Café des Deux Magots	R	45 48 55 25			▲	▲	▲		

Dominique	R	43 27 08 80						500F	
L'Ecaille de PCB	R	43 26 73 70					▲	600F	
L'Epi Dupin	R	42 22 64 56		▲			▲	410F	580F
Ferrandi	H	42 22 97 40							580F
Hotel de Fleurie	H	43 29 59 81							850F
Café de Flore	R	45 48 55 26			▲	▲	▲		
Grand Hotel Littré	H	45 44 38 68							815F
L'Heure Gourmande1	R	46 34 00 40				▲		260F	
L'Hotel	HR	43 25 27 22			▲				1000F
Le Belier					▲	▲	▲	500F	
Jacques Cagna	R	43 26 49 39						1200F	
Latitudes Saint-Germain	H	42 61 53 53							940F
Left Bank	H	43 54 01 70							990F
Brasserie Lipp	R	45 48 53 91		▲	▲	▲	▲	560F	
La Lozère	R	43 54 26 64						320F	
Hotel Lutétia	HR	49 54 46 46							1280F
Le Paris		49 54 46 90	★					1000F	
Luxembourg	H	43 25 35 90							755F
Hotel du Lys	H	43 26 97 57							460F
Madison	H	40 51 60 05							1012F
Mariage Frères1	R	40 51 82 50		▲		▲	▲		
La Marlotte	R	45 48 86 79						460F	
Hotel des Marronniers	H	43 25 30 60							700F
La Méditerranée	R	43 26 02 30				▲	▲	500F	
Hotel de l'Odéon	H	43 25 70 11							760F
La Palette	R	43 26 68 15			▲			200F	
Perreyve	H	45 48 35 01							450F

6th Arrondissement (cont)

Establishment	Cat	Telephone No.	Star	B	L	W	A	Meal Price	Room Price
Le Petit St Benoit	R	42 60 27 92						250F	
Le Petit Vatel	R	43 54 28 49			s		▲	200F	
La Petite Cour	R	43 26 52 26			▲	▲	▲	500F	
Au Plaisir des Pains [1]	R	45 48 40 45					▲[1]		
Polidor	R	43 26 95 34			▲	▲	▲	240F	
Le Procope	R	43 26 99 20			▲	▲	▲	500F	
Le Régent	H	46 34 59 80							750F
Relais Christine	H	43 26 71 80							1630F
Relais Hotel du Vieux Paris	H	43 54 41 66							990F
Relais Louis XIII	R	43 26 75 96	★					1000F	
Relais Médicis	H	43 26 00 60							995F
Relais St-Germain	H	43 29 12 05							1500F
La Rotisserie d'en Face	R	43 26 40 98					▲	520F	
Hotel de Saint-Germain	H	45 48 91 64							695F
Hotel Saint-Germain-des-Prés	H	43 26 00 19							950F
Saint-Grégoire	H	45 48 23 23							930F
Sainte-Beuve	H	45 48 20 07							700F
Hotel des Saints-Pères	H	45 44 50 00							720F
Hotel Sénateur	H	43 26 08 83							750F
Taverne Basque	R	42 22 51 07						450F	

Victoria Palace Hotel	H	45 44 38 16							940F
La Vigneraie	R	45 48 57 04			▲		▲	500F	
La Villa	H	43 26 60 00							800F
Villa des Artistes	H	43 26 60 86							650F

[1] Last orders 7pm

7th Arrondissement

Establishment	Cat	Telephone No.	Star	B	L	W	A	Meal Price	Room Price
Altitude 95	R	45 55 20 04				▲	▲	400F	
Antoine et Antoinette	R	45 51 75 61						450F	
L'Arpège	R	45 51 47 33	★					2400F	
Beaugency	H	47 05 01 63							660F
Le Bellecour	R	45 55 68 38	★					1000F	
Bersoly's Saint-Germain	H	42 60 73 79							580F
La Boule D'Or	R	47 05 50 18					▲	500F	
La Bourdonnais	HR	47 05 45 42							650F
La Cantine des Gourmets		47 05 47 96	★		▲	▲	▲	1000F	
Bourgogne et Montana	H	45 51 20 22							870F
Chez Françoise	R	47 05 49 03		▲	▲	▲	▲	500F	
Chez Marius	R	45 51 79 42						700F	
Chomel	H	45 48 55 52							550F
Christian Constant	R	47 03 30 00				▲[1]	▲[1]		

7th Arrondissement (cont)

Establishment	Cat	Telephone No.	Star	B	L	W	A	Meal Price	Room Price
Clémentine	R	45 51 41 16						420F	
Derby Eiffel	H	47 05 12 05							690F
Les Deux Abeilles [2]	R	45 55 64 04							
Le Divellec	R	45 51 91 96	★★				▲	1300F	
Duquesnoy	R	47 05 96 78	★★	▲				1200F	
Ecaille et Plume	R	45 55 06 72						500F	
Eiffel Park Hotel	H	45 55 10 01							835F
Elysées Maubourg	H	45 56 10 78							710F
La Ferme Saint-Simon	R	45 48 35 74	★					600F	
Foc-Ly [3]	R	47 83 27 12				▲	▲[3]	600F	
Gaya Rive Gauche	R	45 44 73 73						600F	
Grand Hotel de France	H	47 05 40 49							490F
Les Jardins d'Eiffel	H	47 05 46 21							860F
Jules Verne	R	45 55 61 44	★			▲	▲	1500F	
Hotel Lenox	H	42 96 10 95							590F
Londres	H	45 51 63 02							555F
Michel Courtalhac	R	45 55 15 35						500F	
Montalembert	HR	45 49 68 68							1625F
Restaurant						▲	▲	700F	
Paul Minchelli	R	47 05 89 86			▲			1000F	

Le Petit Laurent	R	45 48 79 64						700F	
Le Récamier	R	45 48 86 58	★	▲			▲	1000F	
Résidence Latour-Maubourg	H	47 05 16 16							670F
Saint-Germain	H	45 48 62 92							570F
Saxe-Résidence	H	47 83 98 28							638F
Solférino	H	47 05 85 54							532F
Splendid	H	45 51 24 77							780F
Hotel de Suède	H	47 05 00 08							652F
Tan Dinh	R	45 44 04 84						700F	
Thoumieux	R	47 05 49 75			▲	▲	▲	300F	
Le Tourville	H	47 05 62 62							690F
Hotel de l'Université	H	42 61 09 39							800F
Hotel de Varenne	H	45 51 45 55							550F
Vin Sur Vin	R	47 05 14 20						700F	

[1] Last orders 8pm [2] Last orders 7pm [3] Not Mon

8th Arrondissement

Establishment	Cat	Telephone No.	Star	B	L	W	A	Meal Price	Room Price
Al Ajami	R	43 59 55 37			s	s	s	550F	
Alison	H	42 65 54 00							690F
Aux Amis du Beaujolais	R	45 63 92 21						400F	
Androuët	R	48 74 26 93					▲	600F	
L'Appart	R	53 75 16 34			▲	▲	▲	500F	
Atala	H	45 62 01 62							950F
L'Avenue	R	40 70 14 91			▲	▲	▲	700F	
Balzac	H	45 35 18 00							1830F
Le Bistrot du Sommelier	R	42 65 24 85						800F	
Le Boeuf sur le Toit	R	43 59 83 80			▲	▲	▲	500F	
Le Bristol	HR	42 66 91 45							3600F
Restaurant						▲	▲	1600F	
Hotel California	H	43 59 93 00							1800F
Caviar Kaspia	R	42 65 33 32			▲		▲	800F	
Centre-Ville Matignan	H	42 25 73 01							890F
Le Cercle Ledoyen	R	47 42 76 02			▲		▲	600F	
Chez André	R	47 20 59 57			▲	▲	▲	500F	
Chez Edgard	R	47 20 51 15			▲		▲	520F	
Chez Francis	R	47 20 86 83			▲	▲	▲	600F	
Chiberta	R	45 63 77 90	★					650F	

Claridge-Bellman	H	47 23 54 42							1000F
Concorde Saint-Lazare	H	40 08 44 44							1160F
Copenhague	R	44 13 86 26						850F	
Le Crétois [1]	R	45 63 34 17					▲[1]	300F	
Hotel de Crillon	HR	44 71 15 00							3500F
Les Ambassadeurs		44 71 16 16	★★			▲	▲	1600F	
L'Obélisque						▲	▲	600F	
Daniel Météry	R	42 65 53 13					▲	700F	
Hotel de l'Elysées	H	42 65 29 25							600F
L'Etage Baumann	R	47 20 11 11			▲			500F	
Fakhr el Dine	R	47 23 44 42			▲	▲	▲	400F	
Fauchon-Le 30	R	47 42 56 58					▲	800F	
La Ferme St-Hubert	R	47 42 79 20					▲	400F	
La Fermette Marbeuf	R	53 23 08 00			▲	▲	▲	600F	
Hotel Folkestone	H	42 65 73 09							812F
Fouquet's	R	47 23 70 60			▲	▲	▲	800F	
George V	HR	47 23 54 00							3200F
Les Princes Restaurant			★			▲	▲	1000F	
Les Georgiques	R	40 70 10 49					▲	1000F	
Golden Tulip St-Honoré	HR	49 53 03 03							1700F
Le Relais Vermeer								700F	
Le Grenadin	R	45 63 28 92					▲	650F	
Hédiard	R	43 12 88 99					▲	550F	
Lancaster	H	40 76 40 76							2350F
Lasserre	R	43 59 53 43	★★					1600F	
Laurent	R	42 25 00 39	★★				▲	1800F	
Ledoyen	R	47 42 35 98	★★	▲				1200F	

8th Arrondissement (cont)

Establishment	Cat	Telephone No.	Star	B	L	W	A	Meal Price	Room Price
Lido	H	42 66 27 37							930F
Lucas Carton	R	42 65 22 90	★					2600F	
La Maison d'Alsace	R	43 59 44 24			▲	▲	▲	550F	
Maison Blanche	R	47 23 55 99						1100F	
La Maison du Valais	R	42 60 22 72			▲		▲	550F	
La Marée	R	43 80 20 00	★					1200F	
Le Marignan	H	40 76 34 56							1690F
Maxim's	R	42 65 27 94					▲	2000F	
Au Petit Montmorency	R	42 25 11 19						900F	
Le Pichet	R	43 59 50 34			▲			900F	
Plaza Athénée	HR	47 23 78 33							3010F
Le Régence						▲	▲	1050F	
Relais Plaza					▲	▲	▲	650F	
Prince de Galles	H	47 23 55 11							2250F
Hotel Queen Mary	H	42 66 40 50							810F
Résidence Maxim's de Paris	H	45 61 96 33							2250F
Royal Monceau	HR	42 99 88 00							2600F
Le Jardin		42 99 98 70					▲	1000F	
Il Carpaccio		42 99 98 90				▲		900F	
San Regis	HR	44 95 16 16							2100F
Restaurant						▲	▲	900F	

Le Sarladais	R	45 22 23 62						650F	
Les Saveurs	R	45 63 17 44						650F	
Taillevent	R	45 61 12 90	★★★	▲				1350F	
Hotel de la Trémoille	H	47 23 34 20							2240F
Le Val d'Or	R	43 59 95 81						500F	
Vancouver	R	42 56 77 77	★					900F	
Vernet	HR	44 31 98 00							1850F
Les Elysées du Vernet			★					1000F	
Virgin Café	R	42 89 46 81			▲	▲	▲		
Warwick	HR	45 63 14 11							2670F
La Couronne								750F	
Yvan	R	42 89 16 69			▲		▲	700F	

[1] Last orders 6.30pm

9th Arrondissement

Establishment	Cat	Telephone No.	Star	B	L	W	A	Meal Price	Room Price
Ambassador	HR	44 83 40 40							1520F
Venantius Restaurant		48 00 06 38						900F	
Auberge Landaise	R	48 78 74 40						480F	
Aurore Montmartre	H	48 74 85 56							420F
Bergère	H	47 70 34 34							550F
Le Bistrot Blanc	R	42 85 05 30						400F	
Le Bistro des Deux Théatres	R	45 26 41 43			▲	▲	▲	340F	
Le Bistrot Papillon	R	47 70 90 03						550F	
Blanche Fontaine	H	45 26 72 32							559F
Brébant	H	47 70 25 55							890F
Casa Olympe	R	42 85 26 01						500F	
La Champagne	R	48 74 44 78			▲	▲	▲	600F	
Charlot Roi des Coquillages	R	48 74 49 64			▲	▲	▲	600F	
Chartier	R	47 70 86 29		▲		▲	▲	170F	
Chez Clément Opéra	R	47 42 00 25			▲	▲	▲	320F	
Copthorne Commodore	H	42 46 72 82							1250F
Le Grand Café Capucines	R	47 42 19 00			▲	▲	▲		
Grand Hotel Inter-Continental	HR	40 07 32 32							3040F
Restaurant Opéra		40 07 30 10						800F	
Brasserie Café de la Paix		40 07 30 20			▲	▲	▲	400F	

Hotel du Léman	H	42 46 50 66							450F
Libertel Lafayette	H	42 85 05 44							885F
Libertel le Moulin	H	42 81 93 25							785F
L'Oenothèque	R	48 78 08 76						650F	
Opéra Cadet	H	48 24 05 26							780F
Au Petit Riche	R	47 70 68 68			▲		▲	490F	
Hotel du Pré	H	42 81 37 11							545F
Riboutté-Lafayette	H	47 70 62 36							450F
Le Royal Vignon									
Le Roi du Pot-au-Feu	R	47 42 37 10		▲			▲	300F	
Scribe	HR	44 71 24 24							2200F
Les Muses		44 71 24 26							700F
La Table d'Anvers	R	48 78 35 21	★		▲		▲	900F	
Wally le Saharien	R	42 85 51 90			▲		▲	600F	

10th Arrondissement

Establishment	Cat	Telephone No.	Star	B	L	W	A	Meal Price	Room Price
Au Chateaubriant	R	48 24 58 94						550F	
Aux Deux Canards	R	47 70 03 23		▲				410F	
Brasserie Flo	R	47 70 13 59			▲	▲	▲	450F	
Flora	H	48 24 84 84							595F
L'Horset Pavillon	H	42 46 92 75							930F
Julien	R	47 70 12 06			▲	▲	▲	450F	
Le P'tite Tonkinoise	R	42 46 85 98		▲				400F	
Terminus Nord	R	42 85 05 15		▲	▲	▲	▲	500F	

11th Arrondissement

Establishment	Cat	Telephone No.	Star	B	L	W	A	Meal Price	Room Price
L'Aiguière	R	43 72 42 32					▲	700F	
Les Amognes	R	43 72 73 05					▲	480F	
Anjou-Normandie	R	47 00 30 59						400F	
Astier	R	43 57 16 35		▲				380F	
Cartet	R	48 05 17 65						550F	
Chardenoux	R	43 71 49 52						500F	
Chez Fernand (Les Fernandises)	R	43 57 46 25			▲			420F	
Chez Léon de Bruxelles	R	43 38 28 69			▲	▲	▲	300F	
Chez Philippe	R	43 57 33 78						650F	
La Galoche d'Aurillac	R	47 00 77 15			▲			400F	
Hotel du Grand Prieuré	H	47 00 74 14							350F
Holiday Inn République	HR	43 55 44 34							1540F
La Belle Epoque						▲	▲	600F	
Jacques Mélac	R	43 70 59 27							
Méridional	H	48 05 75 00							600F
Le Passage	R	47 00 73 30			▲		▲		
Le Roudoulié	R	43 79 27 46					▲	450F	
A Sousceyrac	R	43 71 65 30	★					650F	
La Table Richelieu	R	43 72 31 23					▲	600F	
Thai Elephant	R	47 00 42 00			▲		▲	600F	
Le Villaret [1]	R	43 57 89 76		▲	▲			400F	

[1] Dinner only

12th Arrondissement

Establishment	Cat	Telephone No.	Star	B	L	W	A	Meal Price	Room Price
Batifol	R	40 19 02 05			▲	▲	▲	350F	
Belle Epoque	H	43 44 06 66							590F
La Cipale	R	43 75 54 53						500F	
Hotel Claret	H	46 28 41 31							450F
La Gourmandise	R	43 43 94 41						680F	
Les Grandes Marches	R	43 42 90 32			▲	▲		550F	
Ibis Paris-Bercy	H	43 42 91 91							460F
Novotel Paris-Bercy	H	43 42 30 00							760F
L'Oulette	R	40 02 02 12	★	▲			▲	600F	
Le Pavillon Bastille	H	43 43 65 65							955F
Au Pressoir	R	43 44 38 21	★					1100F	
Le Quincy	R	43 28 46 76						550F	
Le Relais de Lyon	H	43 44 22 50							530F
Sipario	R	43 45 70 26						400F	
La Sologne	R	43 07 68 97	★	▲			▲	480F	
Le Temps des Cerises	R	43 67 52 08				▲		600F	
Le Train Bleu	R	43 43 09 06				▲	▲	600F	
Au Trou Gascon	R	43 44 34 26	★					800F	

13th Arrondissement

Establishment	Cat	Telephone No.	Star	B	L	W	A	Meal Price	Room Price
Equinoxe	H	43 37 56 56							395F
Mercure Paris-Bercy	H	45 82 48 00							690F
Mercure Paris-Tolbiac	H	45 84 61 61							690F
Le Petit Marguery	R	43 31 58 59		▲				650F	
Pizza César	R	43 31 68 60			▲	▲	▲		
Résidence des Gobelins	H	47 07 26 90							400F
Le Rhone	R	47 07 33 57						300F	
Les Vieux Métiers de France	R	45 88 90 03					▲	700F	

14th Arrondissement

Establishment	Cat	Telephone No.	Star	B	L	W	A	Meal Price	Room Price
L'Amuse Bouche	R	43 35 31 61						550F	
Les Armes de Bretagne	R	43 20 29 50						800F	
Bar à Huitres	R	43 20 71 01		▲	▲	▲	▲	500F	
Le Bistrot du Dome	R	43 35 32 00		▲			▲[1]	500F	
La Cagouille	R	43 22 09 01	★			▲	▲	600F	
Le Caroubier	R	43 20 41 49						400F	
La Chaumière des Gourmets	R	43 21 22 59						700F	
La Coupole	R	43 20 14 20		▲	▲	▲	▲	450F	
Le Dome	R	43 35 25 81			▲	▲	▲[2]	700F	
Le Duc	R	43 22 59 59					▲	900F	
Friant	H	45 42 71 91							340F
Aux Iles Marquises	R	43 20 93 58			▲			640F	
Istria	H	43 20 91 82							530F
Hotel Lenox	H	43 35 34 50							590F
Lous Landès	R	45 43 08 04						650F	
Mercure Paris-Montparnasse	H	43 35 28 28							880F
Méridien Montparnasse	HR	44 36 44 36							1518F
Montparnasse 25		44 36 44 25						1000F	
Justine		44 36 44 00				▲	▲	700F	
Hotel de l'Orchidée	H	43 22 70 50							502F
Orléans Palace Hotel	H	45 39 68 50							550F
Hotel du Parc Montsouris	H	45 89 09 72							370F
Pavillon Montsouris	R	45 88 38 52				▲	▲	700F	

[1] Not Sun, Mon [2] Not Sun

15th Arrondissement

Establishment	Cat	Telephone No.	Star	B	L	W	A	Meal Price	Room Price
Adagio	H	40 45 10 00							895F
Alizé Grenelle	H	45 78 08 22							410F
Beaugrenelle St Charles	H	45 78 61 63							400F
Bistro 121	R	45 57 52 90			▲	▲	▲	600F	
Chez Yvette	R	42 22 45 54						350F	
Le Clos Morillons	R	48 28 04 37						600F	
Erawan	R	47 83 55 67						450F	
La Farigoule	R	45 54 35 41		▲				550F	
Fellini	R	45 77 40 77						460F	
Frantour Paris Suffren	H	45 78 50 00							880F
Le Gastroquet	R	48 28 60 91		▲				550F	
Kim Anh [1]	R	45 79 40 96			▲	▲	▲	600F	
Mercure Paris-Vaugirard	H	44 19 03 03							884F
Morot-Gaudry	R	45 67 06 85	★				▲	900F	
Hotel Nikko de Paris	HR	40 58 20 00							1690F
Les Célébrités		40 58 21 29				▲		1000F	
Benkay		40 58 21 26				▲	▲	1400F	
L'Oie Cendrée	R	45 31 91 91						400F	
Paris Hilton	H	43 38 56 00							1590F
Pierre Vedel	R	45 58 43 17					▲	600F	

15th Arrondissement (cont)

Establishment	Cat	Telephone No.	Star	B	L	W	A	Meal Price	Room Price
Le Relais de Sèvres	R	40 60 33 66	★					800F	
Résidence Saint-Lambert	H	48 28 63 14							550F
Aux Senteurs de Provence	R	45 57 11 98						600F	
Wallace	H	45 78 83 30							650F
Yllen	H	45 67 67 67							580F
Yves Quintard	R	42 50 22 27						700F	

[1] Dinner only

16th Arrondissement

Establishment	Cat	Telephone No.	Star	B	L	W	A	Meal Price	Room Price
Al Mounia	R	47 27 57 28						500F	
La Baie d'Ha Long	R	45 24 60 62						400F	
Baltimore	HR	44 34 54 54							1990F
Bertie's		44 34 54 34				▲	▲	600F	
Le Bistrot de l'Etoile	R	40 67 11 16			▲		▲	500F	
Hotel du Bois	H	45 00 31 96							495F
La Butte Chaillot	R	47 27 88 88	★	▲	▲	▲	▲	600F	
Carette [1]	R	47 27 88 56				▲	▲		
Chez Géraud	R	45 20 33 00						600F	
Chez Ngo	R	47 04 53 20			▲	▲	▲	400F	
Conti	R	47 27 74 67	★					750F	
Fakhr el Dine	R	47 27 90 00			▲	▲	▲	500F	
Faugeron	R	47 04 24 53	★★★	▲				1200F	
La Fontaine d'Auteuil	R	42 88 04 47						700F	
Garden Elysée	H	47 55 01 11							1450F
Hameau de Passy	H	42 88 47 55							560F
Jean-Claude Ferrero	R	45 04 42 42						850F	
Joël Robuchon	R	47 27 12 27							
Kambodgia	R	47 23 31 80					▲	600F	
L'Hotel Kléber	H	47 23 80 22							740F

16th Arrondissement (cont)

Establishment	Cat	Telephone No.	Star	B	L	W	A	Meal Price	Room Price
Kléber Palace	H	44 05 75 00							1310F
Hotel de Longchamp	H	47 27 13 48							620F
Majestic	H	45 00 83 70							1170F
Les Monuments [2]	R	44 05 90 00				▲	▲	600F	
Le Parc	HR	44 05 66 66							2300F
Le Relais du Parc		44 05 66 10	★	▲		▲	▲	700F	
Passy Eiffel	H	45 25 55 66							580F
Passy Mandarin	R	42 88 12 18				▲	▲	500F	
Paul Chene	R	47 27 63 17		▲				750F	
Pavillon Noura	R	47 20 33 33			▲	▲	▲	500F	
Hotel Pergolèse	H	40 67 96 77							960F
Le Pergolèse	R	45 00 21 40						700F	
La Petite Tour	R	45 20 09 31	★	▲				850F	
Port Alma	R	47 23 75 11						850F	
Brasserie de la Poste	R	47 55 01 31		▲	▲	▲	▲	400F	
Le Pré Catelan	R	45 24 55 58	★★				▲	1500F	
Quach	R	47 27 98 40				▲	▲	500F	
Raphael	H	44 28 00 28							1970F
Relais d'Auteuil	R	46 51 09 54	★	▲				1100F	
La Résidence Bassano	H	47 23 78 23							750F

Hotel du Rond-Point de Longchamp	H	45 05 13 63							1000F
Saint James Paris	H	44 05 81 81							1550F
Hotel de Sévigné	H	47 20 88 90							700F
Brasserie Stella	R	47 27 60 54		▲	▲	▲		450F	
Le Toit de Passy	R	45 24 55 37	★				▲	1000F	
Trocadéro	H	45 53 01 82							620F
La Villa Maillot	H	45 01 25 22							1900F
Vivarois	R	45 04 04 31	★					1200F	

[1] Last orders 6.45pm [2] Last orders 6pm

17th Arrondissement

Establishment	Cat	Telephone No.	Star	B	L	W	A	Meal Price	Room Price
Amphyclès	R	40 68 01 01	★				▲	1500F	
Apicius	R	43 80 19 66	★★					1400F	
Astrid	H	44 09 26 00							425F
Augusta	R	47 63 39 97						850F	
Le Ballon des Ternes	R	45 74 17 98			▲	▲		450F	
Hotel de Banville	H	42 67 70 16							740F
Baumann Ternes	R	45 74 16 66			▲	▲	▲	500F	
Le Bistrot d'à Coté	R	47 63 25 61		▲			▲	500F	
Le Bistrot de l'Etoile (Niel)	R	42 27 88 44		▲	▲		▲	450F	
Le Bistrot de l'Etoile (Troyon)	R	42 67 25 95			▲		▲	450F	
Bistro du 17e	R	47 63 32 77				▲	▲	340F	
Bistrot Saint-Ferdinand	R	45 74 33 32				▲	▲	340F	
Caves Pétrissans	R	42 27 52 03						450F	
Charly de Bab-el-Oued	R	45 74 34 62				▲	▲	450F	
Chez Georges	R	45 74 31 00		▲	▲	▲		600F	
Concorde Lafayette	HR	40 68 50 68							1450F
Etoile d'Or		40 68 51 28						1000F	
Le Congrès Maillot	R	45 74 17 24		▲	▲	▲	▲	500F	
La Coquille	R	45 74 25 95						750F	
Courcelles	H	47 63 65 30							675F

Eber Monceau	H	46 22 60 70							580F
Etoile Park	H	42 67 69 63							613F
Etoile Péreire	H	42 67 60 00							760F
La Famiglia Fuligna	R	45 74 20 28			▲		▲	600F	
Faucher	R	42 27 61 50	★				▲	800F	
Goldenberg	R	42 27 34 79		▲		▲	▲	400F	
Graindorge	R	47 54 00 28					▲	500F	
Guy Savoy	R	43 80 40 61	★★★		▲		▲	1600F	
Magellan	H	45 72 44 51							595F
Le Manoir de Paris	R	45 72 25 25	★				▲	900F	
Les Marines de Pétrus	R	47 63 04 24					▲	500F	
Le Méridien Etoile	HR	40 68 34 34							1450F
Le Clos Longchamp		40 68 30 40	★					1200F	
Michel Rostang	R	47 63 40 77	★★					1600F	
L'Oustalet	R	43 80 82 65					▲	400F	
Le Petit Colombier	R	43 80 28 54	★	▲				950F	
Pétrus	R	43 80 15 95		▲		▲		900F	
Quality Hotel	H	44 01 04 90							650F
Regent's Garden	H	45 74 07 30							700F
Le Relais de Venise	R	45 74 27 97		▲	▲	▲	▲	320F	
La Rotisserie d'Armaillé	R	42 27 19 20		▲			▲	500F	
Sormani	R	43 80 13 91	★					1000F	
La Soupière	R	42 27 00 73						550F	
Splendid Etoile	H	45 72 72 00							1030F
Le Sud	R	45 74 02 77					▲	500F	
La Table de Pierre	R	43 80 88 68					▲	700F	
Taïra	R	47 66 74 14					▲	650F	
Timgad	R	45 74 23 70				▲	▲	700F	

18th Arrondissement

Establishment	Cat	Telephone No.	Star	B	L	W	A	Meal Price	Room Price
A. Beauvilliers	R	42 54 54 42					▲	1100F	
Chez Frézet	R	46 06 64 20						600F	
Le Cottage Marcadet	R	42 57 71 22						700F	
La Crémaillère 1900	R	46 06 58 59			▲	▲	▲	500F	
La Galerie	R	42 59 25 76		▲				360F	
Au Grain de Folie	R	42 58 15 57				▲	▲	275F	
Langevin 'Au Poulbot Gourmet'	R	46 06 86 00					▲	600F	
Le Maquis	R	42 59 76 07					▲	400F	
Aux Négociants	R	46 06 15 11						300F	
Prima Lepic	H	46 06 44 64							380F
Regyn's Montmartre	H	42 54 45 21							435F
Le Restaurant	R	42 23 06 22			▲		▲	400F	
Le Sagittaire	R	42 55 17 40					▲	320F	
Terrass	H	46 06 72 85							1085F
Utrillo	H	42 58 13 44							400F
Wepler	R	45 22 53 24			▲	▲	▲	475F	

19th/20th Arrondissements

Establishment	Cat	Telephone No.	Star	B	L	W	A	Meal Price	Room Price
Les Allobroges	R	43 73 40 00	★	▲			▲	600F	
Au Cochon d'Or	R	42 45 46 46				▲	▲	800F	
Le Laumière	H	42 06 10 77							270F
Le Palais de l'Inde	R	42 39 31 14			▲	▲	▲	500F	
Le Pavillon Puebla	R	42 08 92 62						860F	

Around Paris

Establishment	Cat	Telephone No.	Star	B	L	W	A	Meal Price	Room Price
Le Bistrot d'à Coté	R	47 45 34 55					s		
Ibis	H	47 78 15 60							450F
Novotel	H	47 78 16 68							790F
Sofitel CNIT	HR	46 92 10 10							1400F
Les Communautés		46 92 10 30					▲	650F	
Sofitel	H	47 76 44 43							1300F
Trianon Palace	HR	30 84 38 00							1914F
Les Trois Marches		39 50 13 21	★					1400F	
La Truffe Noire "Jenny Jacquet"	R	46 24 94 14						700F	

Airports

Establishment	Cat	Telephone No.	Star	B	L	W	A	Meal Price	Room Price
Ibis (Charles de Gaulle)	H	49 19 19 19							395F
Maxim's (Charles de Gaulle)	R	48 62 16 16						800F	
Sofitel (Charles de Gaulle)	H	49 19 29 39							1050F
Orly Hilton (Orly)	H	45 12 45 12							1100F
Ibis (Orly)	H	46 87 22 45							320F
Maxim's (Orly)	R	46 87 16 16						700F	

MENU GLOSSARY

Words in italics also have their own entries

AAAAA – Association Amicale des Amateurs d'Andouillettes Authentiques
abatis – fowl giblets
abats – offal, including head meat, heart, liver, kidneys, tripe, feet
abricot – apricot
acajou – cashew nut, as in **noix d'acajou**
acidulé – sour, acidulated
affiné – refined, mature – a description used for cheeses
agneau – lamb (**agneau de lait** – milk-fed lamb)
agrume – citrus fruit
aiglefin – haddock (sometimes also **aigrefin** and **églefin**)
aigo – Provençal garlic soup
aigre – sour, bitter
aigre-doux – sweet-sour
aigrelette – lightly vinegared
aiguillette(s) – long, thin slices, usually duck breast. Also cut of beef from the sirloin
ail – garlic
aile – wing (as in chicken or skate)
aileron – fin of fish or wing of fowl
aïoli – garlic mayonnaise
airelle – **airelle myrtille** – bilberry
airelle rouge – cranberry
albertine – poached fish in white wine sauce with mushrooms, truffles and parsley
albigeoise – meat garnish of stuffed tomatoes, ham and potato croquettes. Also a rich meat soup
alcide – white wine sauce with chopped shallots and grated horseradish
algérienne – steak garnish of tomatoes and sweet peppers. Also with sweet potatoes
algues – seaweed
alicot/alicuit – duck or goose giblets and wings cooked with mushrooms
aligot – puréed potatoes with aligot cheese and garlic
allemande – *velouté* sauce blended with egg yolks. Also a beef *consommé* with red cabbage
allumettes – matchstick fried potatoes. Also sweet or savoury puff pastry sticks
alose – shad (herring-like fish)
aloyau – sirloin of beef
alsacienne – garnish of any combination of foie gras, truffles, sauerkraut and ham, sausage and potatoes
amande – almond
amande de mer – a small shellfish
amandine – almond-flavoured
ambassadeur – meat garnish of *duchesse* potatoes, artichoke hearts with mushrooms and horseradish. Also a chicken *consommé* with truffles and mushrooms
ambassadrice – sauce of pounded chicken and cream. Also a chicken *consommé* with truffles, chicken and mushrooms
amer/amère – bitter
américaine – also **armoricaine** – sauce of pounded lobster with truffles, chicken and mushrooms. Also a garnish of lobster tails and truffles (see *homard*)
amourettes – spinal marrow
amuse-gueule – complimentary pre-starter or appetiser, also **amuse-bouche**
ananas – pineapple
anchoïade, anchoyade – anchovy paste
anchois – anchovy
ancienne – traditional or old-fashioned, also a cream sauce with small onions and mushrooms
andalouse – garnish of mayonnaise with sweet peppers stuffed with rice and sautéed aubergines. Also a *consommé* with rice and ham

andouille, andouillette – sausage of chopped chitterling and stomach, see also *AAAAA*
aneth – dill
anglaise – usually of fish fried in egg and breadcrumbs. Also applied to simple boiling, poaching or steaming. See also *crème anglaise*
anguille – eel
animelles – lamb's testicles, also known as *rognons blancs*
anis – aniseed
anis étoilé – star anise
anna – as in **pommes anna**: cake of sliced potatoes cooked in butter
antiboise – with garlic, tomato, anchovy or sardine and often cheese
arachide – groundnut, peanut
araignée de mer – spider crab
ardoise – slate, blackboard
aretes – fish bones
argenteuil – dish or garnish with asparagus
aromates – *velouté* sauce of mixed herbs. Also the name given to distinctly flavoured herbs and roots
assaisonné – seasoned
assiette anglaise – plate of assorted cold meats
aubépine – hawthorn
aulx – plural of *ail* (garlic)
aumonière – 'purse' or 'money-bag' made of either pastry or a pancake
aurore – white sauce tinged with tomato
automne – autumn

baba – yeast cake usually flavoured with rum or kirsch
badiane – star anise
ballotine – meat, fowl, game or fish boned, stuffed and rolled, served either hot or cold. Similar to a *galantine*, which is always cold
bar – bass
barbe-à-papa – candy floss
barbue – brill
barigoule – mushroom found in the South of France. Also the name given to globe artichoke stuffed with *duxelles* mixture including pork and bacon
barquette – small, boat-shaped pastry shell filled with sweet or savoury mixture
basilic – basil
basquaise – usually *poulet* basquaise: cooked with tomatoes, onions and sweet peppers. Also a meat garnish of fried wild mushrooms and moulds of *pommes anna* or a beef *consommé* with tomato and sweet peppers
baudroie – monkfish, also *lotte*
bavarois – cold custard cream with gelatine and often flavoured and garnished with fruits, nuts or chocolate
bavaroise – hollandaise sauce flavoured with crayfish butter and chopped crayfish tails
baveuse – runny (especially of omelettes)
béarnaise – warm sauce of butter, egg yolks, shallots, wine vinegar, pepper, tarragon and chervil
béatilles – poultry offal
bécasse – woodcock
bécassine – snipe
béchamel – basic white sauce, made from a roux of flour and butter with milk added
beignet – sweet or savoury batter fritter
belle hélène – Pears poached in vanilla syrup and served with vanilla ice cream and hot chocolate sauce. Also a meat garnish of grilled mushrooms stuffed with tomato, peas or carrots
belons – flat oysters
bercy – *velouté* sauce with fish stock, white wine, shallots and butter. Also a meat sauce made with white wine, shallots and butter garnished with beef marrow and meat glaze

berlugan – speciality of Provence consisting of small balls of cabbage leaves stuffed with spinach, meat and herbs and then gratinated
betterave – beetroot
beurre – butter
beurre à l'anglaise – melted butter
beurre blanc – reduction of white wine vinegar and shallots beaten vigorously with butter until white
beurre colbert – *beurre maitre d'hotel* with added tarragon and meat glaze
beurre maitre d'hotel – butter mixed with chopped parsley, salt, pepper and lemon juice
beurre marchand de vin – reduction of shallots and red wine to which meat glaze, butter, parsley and lemon juice is added
beurre meunière – browned butter with lemon juice and parsley
beurre rouge – as *beurre blanc* but using red wine vinegar
biche – venison (the doe)
bière – beer, **bière blonde** – lager, **bière à la pression** (often just *pression*) – draught beer
bigarade – sauce of reduced duck gravy mixed with zest and juice of orange and lemon
bigorneaux – winkles
billy by – cream of mussel soup
bisque – creamy shellfish soup: usually *homard* (lobster), *crevettes* (shrimps) or *crabe* (crab)
blanc/blanche – white
blanchailles – whitebait
blanquette – white meats mixed with vegetables and served with button onions and mushrooms in a cream sauce
blé – corn, wheat, **blé noir** – buckwheat
blette – chard
bleu – used to describe very rare steak
au bleu – as in **truite au bleu** – trout plunged into a vinegar *court bouillon* immediately it has been killed and cleaned causing the skin to take on a bluish hue
blonde – sauce, as *allemande*
boeuf – beef
bois – wood
boisson – drink or beverage
bombe – shaped ice cream dessert
bonne femme – fillets of sole poached and served with a white wine sauce with mushrooms, parsley and shallots added. Also meat or poultry cooked in a casserole with button onions, mushrooms and ham
bordelaise – sauce of chopped shallots, thyme, bay leaves and red wine with meat glaze, garnished with bone marrow
bordure – in the form of a ring or crown
bouché(e) – 'mouthful', usually a delicate pastry or small vol-au-vent
bouchot – mussel bed
boudin blanc – white sausage of chicken, pork, veal and sometimes *foie gras* and truffles
boudin noir – black pudding but without the cereal content
bouillabaisse – Mediterranean fish stew with saffron, tomato, garlic and olive oil. For authenticity it should contain John Dory, *rascasse*, gurnard and eel as well as monkfish, red mullet, sea bass and various shellfish
bouillon – broth
boulangère – sliced potatoes and onions on which a joint, usually lamb, is baked
bouquet – prawn
bouquetière – meat garnish of potatoes and vegetables sometimes arranged in the shape of a bouquet
bourdaloue – *consommé* with garnish of tomato, asparagus or carrots. Also a pastry tart filled with almond custard and topped with poached pears
bourgeoise – meat garnish of carrot, onion and bacon. Also a beef *consommé* with diced root vegetables and chervil

bourguignon(ne) – Usually beef, braised with red burgundy wine, mushrooms, small onions and carrots. Also a sauce similar to *bordelaise*
bourride – similar to *bouillabaisse* but with no saffron and *aïoli* added instead
boutargue – dried salt mullet or tuna roe; also *poutargue*
brandade de morue – pounded salt cod, olive oil, milk and garlic; served warm
brebis – ewe's milk cheese, abbreviation of **fromage de brebis**
bretonne – onion, white wine, garlic and tomato sauce. Also of leeks, celery, onions and mushrooms served with fish *velouté*
brik – North African cooking – parcel of deep-fried, thin, crisp pastry – **brik à l'oeuf** contains a soft-cooked egg
Brillat-Savarin – a cheese, also the name given to several preparations. A garnish for game or a soufflé of snipe or woodcock and truffles. A garnish for *noisettes* of *duchesse* potatoes with *foie gras*, truffles and asparagus. Also two chicken *consommés*, one thickened with tapioca and with chicken breast, pieces of *crepe*, lettuce, sorrel and chervil, the other thickened with arrowroot and with mushrooms, truffles and carrots
brioche – light yeast dough made with eggs, milk and sugar. Both sweet and savoury uses
brochet – pike. **Quenelles de brochet** is a dish of poached pike mousseline
brochettes – skewered pieces of meat or fish which are grilled
brouillés – scrambled (eggs)
brulé(e) – burnt
brunoise – diced mixed vegetables for flavouring or garnish
bruxelloise – seasoned butter and lemon juice sauce with hard-boiled egg, for asparagus. Also a garnish of brussels sprouts, *fondant* potatoes and light gravy
buisson – heap, mound as in salad piled on a plate
bulots – whelks
byron – thickened red wine sauce garnished with truffles

cabillaud – fresh cod
cacahouette – peanut
cacao – cocoa
Cadillac – sweet white wine from Bordeaux
café complet – Continental breakfast
café de Paris – garnish for steak comprising butter, herbs and sometimes anchovies
cagouille – type of small snail
caille – quail
calamars/calmars – squid, also *encornets*; see also *chipirons*
calisson – iced almond paste petit four, a speciality of Aix-en-Provence
campagne – country, rustic
camus – type of artichoke
canard/caneton/canette – duck, duckling
cancalaise – oysters or shrimps in a cream and white wine sauce
cannelle – cinnamon
capucine – chicken *consommé* with shredded spinach and lettuce. Also a garnish of cabbage leaves, or mushrooms, stuffed with forcemeat and masked with a Madeira sauce
capucines, feuilles de – nasturtium leaves
capres – capers, **capres capucines** – pickled nasturtium seeds
carambole – star fruit
carbonnade – a rich stew, often including beer. **Carbonnade à la flamande** is a Belgian national dish of beef with beer
cardinal – preparations with lobster
Careme – chicken and veal *consommé* garnished with carrots, turnips, lettuce and asparagus. Also a fish garnish of fish *quenelles*, truffles, cream sauce and *fleurons* and a garnish (for *tournedos* and *noisettes*) of olives stuffed with ham forcemeat with a Madeira sauce and potato croquettes
carmélite – *Bourguignonne* sauce with ham and button onions. Also a thickened fish *consommé* garnished with rice and fish forcemeat balls
carré – rack from the best end of lamb, pork or veal neck cutlets
carrelet – plaice or flounder

carte des vins – wine list
carvi – caraway
cassis – blackcurrant, **crème de cassis** – blackcurrant liqueur (not to be confused with the red wine from the town of Cassis near Marseilles)
cassolette – small flameproof container for sweet or savoury dishes. Also a moulded fried batter case with a savoury filling
cassonade – soft brown sugar, Demerara sugar
cassoulet – traditional Languedoc long-cooked stew with haricot beans, goose (sometimes duck), pork, mutton, sausages, onions and garlic
caudière, caudrée – sea-fish soup/stew with onions and mussels
cave – wine cellar
céleri-rave – celeriac
cèpe – boletus mushroom
cerf – red deer
cerfeuil – chervil
cerise – cherry
cerneau – green (immature) walnut
cervelas – pork sausage
cervelles – brains
cervelles des canuts – not brains, but fromage frais, shallots, white wine herbs and vinegar
céteaux – tiny sole-like fish
champetre – country style
champignon – mushroom
chanterelle – also known as a *girolle* – a small, yellow, trumpet-shaped mushroom
chantilly – With a sweet course **chantilly** means whipped cream sweetened with vanilla sugar. Also a sauce of mayonnaise and cream or a hot sauce of *béchamel* with whipped cream added
chapelure – breadcrumbs
chapon – capon. Also another name for *rascasse* (scorpion fish). Also a piece of bread rubbed with garlic and oil and used in a *salade au chapon*
charbon de bois – wood charcoal
charlotte – filled moulded sponge dessert. **Charlotte russe** – *génoise*-lined mould filled with either *bavarois* or crème *chantilly*
chartreuse – name of a liqueur, a moulded dessert, and a dish of cabbage cooked with partridge. Also a beef *consommé* thickened with tapioca and garnished with ravioli stuffed separately with *foie gras*, spinach and mushrooms
chataigne – chestnut
chateau, pommes – potatoes cut into small barrel shapes and sautéed in butter
chateaubriand – large centre cut of beef fillet garnished with pommes *chateau* and **chateaubriand** sauce (quite usual now to serve this with *béarnaise* sauce and *allumettes* potatoes). **Chateaubriand** sauce is one of white wine, meat glaze with shallots, butter and tarragon with cayenne and lemon juice added
chatelaine – artichoke bottoms with either tomatoes, braised celery and *chateau* potatoes or *soubise*, chestnuts and *noisette* potatoes.
chaud – hot
chaud-froid – *velouté* sauce with aspic, cream and egg yolks
chaudrée – fish soup/stew, usually including eel
chausson – turnover filled with apples or fruit or savoury items
chemise – similar to *papillote*. To cook *en chemise* is to bake or roast in a case which can be greased paper, pastry, batter or a vegetable leaf, such as lettuce, spinach or cabbage. Also means unpeeled
cheval – horse. Steak or hamburger à cheval has a fried egg on top
chèvre – goat. **Fromage de chèvre** – goat's cheese
chevreuil – roe deer, venison. Also a reduced red wine sauce for venison
chiboust – choux pastry filled with *crème patissière* mixed with crème *chantilly* or Italian meringue flavoured with bitter almond liqueur or other flavourings
chicorée – curly endive lettuce
chiffonade – vinaigrette with parsley, hard-boiled egg and beetroot. Also strips of sorrel, lettuce or vegetables cooked in butter
chipirons – baby squid
chips – potato crisps

chivry – chicken *velouté* sauce with white wine, shallots, tarragon, chervil, chives and burnet
choron – *béarnaise* sauce blended with tomato juice
choucroute – sauerkraut. **Choucroute garnie** is with ham, bacon or pickled goose, frankfurter sausage and boiled potatoes first braised in white wine or wine vinegar
chou(x) – cabbage(s)
choux – type of pastry of butter, sugar, salt and water boiled in a pan before adding flour and when cool, eggs. Pastry used for éclairs, profiteroles, gateau *Saint Honoré*. Fillings can be sweet or savoury. Also a cabbage (plural **choux**)
chou-fleur – cauliflower
chou navet – swede
choux de bruxelles – brussels sprouts
christ-marine – samphire
ciboulette – chives
cigale – variety of flat lobster
citron – lemon
citron vert – lime
citronnelle – lemon-grass, also a lemon liqueur
cives – chives, normally called *ciboulette*
civet – red wine stew of game garnished with small onions, bacon and mushrooms, classically thickened with the blood of the animal. Hare is the most usual meat, as in **civet de lièvre**. In the Languedoc spiny lobster is used together with onions, garlic and white wine
clafoutis – thick, moist batter pudding with cherries. Sometimes other soft fruit is used
claire – *creuse*-type oyster with a green tinge
clapoton – lamb trotter
clouté – garnished by studding
clovisse – type of clam
cochon de lait – suckling pig
cochonailles – pork charcuterie, from **cochon** – pig
cocos – small white beans
cocotte – small round or oval ovenproof dish used for cooking and serving
coeur – heart
coing – quince
col vert – mallard, a wild duck
colbert – light chicken stock to which lemon juice and parsley are added. Also applies to fried fish coated in egg and breadcrumbs
colère – **merlan en colère** – whiting cooked with its tail in its mouth
colin – hake
colineau/colinot – codling
compote – slow-cooked stew, also stewed fruit
concassé – coarsely chopped
concombre – cucumber
condé – creamed rice, **poire condé** pear with creamed rice
confit – Game, pork or duck cooked and preserved in its own fat. Also fruit or vegetables preserved in sugar, vinegar or brandy
confiture – jam, **confiture d'oranges**, marmalade
contre-filet – see *faux-filet*
consommé – rich, concentrated clear soup served hot or cold
copeaux – shavings, usually of chocolate or parmesan
coq, coquelet – cockerel; **coq au vin** – stewed in red wine with mushrooms and onions
coque, à la – softly or lightly cooked, as in **oeuf à la coque** – soft boiled egg and **moëlle à la coque** – lightly cooked bone marrow
coques – cockles
coquillages – shellfish
coquilles St Jacques – scallops
cornichons – gherkins
cote – rib, chop
cote première – loin chop
cotelette – cutlet

cotriade – Breton fish soup
cou – neck
couennes – pork rind
coulibiac – puff pastry roll filled with salmon or occasionally chicken. Originally a Russian dish
coulis – liquid purées of fruit, vegetables and sometimes game, poultry and fish
courge – marrow, pumpkin
court bouillon – broth made with either wine, vinegar or milk in which fish or meat is cooked
couteaux – razor shells
crapaudine – spatchcocked ie split and flattened
craquelin – a light pastry, usually with an apple filling
crécy – puréed carrot soup and the name given to preparations with carrots
crémant – semi-sparkling
crème anglaise – custard
crème de cassis – see *cassis*
crème chantilly – see *chantilly*
crème épaisse – thick or double cream
crème fleurette – light or whipping cream
crème glacée – ice cream
crème patissière – confectioner's custard
crépine – cawl
crépinette – small, flat sausage
cresson – watercress
cressonette – cress
cretes de coq – cockscombs
creuse – long, rough-shelled oyster
crevettes – shrimps and prawns
crevettes grises – small shrimps
crevettes roses – prawns
cromesquis – croquettes of meat, fish, poultry or eggs bound in a thick cream sauce and fried in batter
croquant(e) – crunchy, crisp
croque-madame – as *croque-monsieur* (see below) but with the addition of a fried egg
croque-monsieur – the classic toasted cheese sandwich with ham
crosne – type of Jerusalem artichoke
crottins – small, round goat's cheese
croustade – hollowed-out loaf or any similar case filled with the same mixture as a vol-au-vent
croustillant(e) – very crisp pastry case
croute – crust, as in pastry, also a slice of bread
croutons – small dice of fried or toasted bread used to garnish soup
cru – raw (**mi cru-mi cuit** means half raw-half cooked)
crustacés – generic name for crabs, langoustines, lobsters, shrimps etc
cuisine du (de) terroir – rustic, country cooking
cuisse – leg (thigh)
cuit(e) – cooked
cul – rump
curcuma – turmeric

daim – fallow deer (venison)
dariole – small cylindrical mould and the name given to anything cooked or prepared in such a mould
darne – thick slice of fish, usually salmon
darphin – flat cake of grated potatoes
daube – meat, poultry or game braised in stock with wine and herbs
daube de boeuf – slow-cooked casserole of larded beef in red wine with salt pork, bacon, onions, carrots and herbs
dauphine – duchesse potatoes mixed with choux paste, shaped into small rounds and deep fried. Also sole fillets, stuffed, folded and poached and rolled in a *villeroy* sauce, egged and crumbed and deep-fried, served with a cream sauce

dauphinois(e) – thinly sliced potatoes baked with cream, gruyère cheese and a hint of garlic
daurade/dorade – sea bream
daurade royale – gilt-head bream
dégustation – sampling, tasting
délice – delight; name give to a dessert or ice cream, also to a fillet of fish folded over on itself wide end up
demi-deuil – poultry larded under the breast skin with truffles and poached in a cream sauce. Garnished with pastry cases of sweetbreads and mushrooms
demi-glace – basic brown sauce with meat stock added then reduced
demi-sel – lightly salted
demi-tasse – small cup, usually of coffee
demoiselle – very small lobster
dentelle – lace; name given to very fine pastry or pancake
désossé – boned
diable – devilled; sauce of shallots, white wine and wine vinegar reduced, with the addition of *demi-glace*, herbs and cayenne pepper
diane – method of preparing steak, usually at the table, by sautéeing it with the addition of Worcestershire sauce, cream and butter. Also a partridge *consommé* garnished with truffles, game *quenelles* and Madeira or a thickened sauce *poivrade* flavoured with game extract
dieppoise – fish garnish of shrimps, mussels and mushrooms simmered in stock or butter. Also a fish *velouté* blended with shrimp butter, or a dish of brill cooked in white wine, with the above garnish and masked with the thickened fish stock and cooked mussels
dinde, dindonneau – turkey
diplomate – classic cold pudding of liqueur-soaked sponge layered with *bavarois* and currants and sultanas soaked in warm syrup. Also a sauce made from sauce *normande* mixed with lobster and mushroom extract and garnished with truffles and lobster. Also a garnish of calf's sweetbreads, cockscombs and mushrooms bound in a Madeira sauce
dodine de canard – rich duck stew with onions, herbs and red wine. Also a duck *galantine*
dorade/daurade – sea bream
dorée – John Dory also called *St Pierre*. Also golden as in **pommes dorées** – potatoes cooked golden brown
doria – garnish of cucumber cooked slowly in butter. Also a chicken *consommé* garnished with chicken *quenelles*, cucumber, fried puff pastry cheese balls and chervil
doux/douce – mild, sweet
Dubarry – soup of cauliflower, stock and cream. Also a garnish of cauliflower with *mornay* sauce and grated cheese
dos – back; as in **dos de saumon** – middle cut salmon steak
duchesse, pommes – puréed potato blended with egg yolks, either piped as a border or made into various shapes as a garnish
dugléré – method of preparing fine white fish. It is poached in white wine and butter with shallots, parsley and seasoning with cream, tomatoes and lemon juice added
dur/dure – hard
duxelles – preparation of finely chopped mushrooms with shallots, parsley and butter. The sauce of the same name is a white wine, onion and shallot reduction to which *velouté* sauce is added and into this is blended some of the above

eau-de-vie – usually applies to a colourless fruit spirit
eau gazeuse – sparkling water, also eau pétillante
eau plate – still water
écailler – oyster seller. **Banc de l'écailler** – shellfish stall (such as those outside some Parisian brasseries)
échalote – shallot
échine – loin (usually pork)
Echiré – renowned butter from Echiré in Poitou

écossaise – *consommé* of mutton broth with pearl barley and a *brunoise* of carrot, celery and leek
écrasé(e) – crushed
écrevisse – freshwater crayfish
effeuillé(e) – flaked (eg of fish)
effilochées – long threads, especially of fish and vegetables
embeurré(e) – buttered
émietté(e) – crumbled
émincé – dish of leftover roast or braised meat slices heated in a sauce. Also applies to fruit or vegetables thinly sliced
encornets – squid
encre – ink, in cooking, the ink of octopus or squid
entier/entière – whole
entrecote – sirloin steak
entremets – desserts
épaule – shoulder
éperlan – smelt
épice – spice
épicé(e) – spicy, hot
épigramme – slice of breast or lamb chop breaded and fried
épinard – spinach
érable – maple
escabèche – fried small fish such as sardines, anchovy or mullet, marinated for 24 hours in olive oil, herbs and wine vinegar and served cold
escargot – snail
espadon – swordfish
espagnole – one of the basic sauces along with *velouté* (cream) and *béchamel* (white); this is a brown sauce. Also a garnish of sweet red peppers, tomatoes and garlic
estouffade – highly seasoned beef broth used as base for sauces, soups and casseroles. Also the name of a dish in which the ingredients are stewed slowly, as in **estouffade de haricots blancs** – white haricot beans with pork, tomatoes and garlic
estragon – tarragon
été – summer
étrille – small crab
étuvée – as *estouffade* but also a dish of meat, poultry or vegetables stewed slowly with little or no liquid except butter or oil
éventail – arranged in a fan-shape

façon – in the style of (as in **du chef** – of the chef)
faisan – pheasant
faisandé – well-hung, gamey
fallette – stuffed breast of lamb
farineux – farinaceous or starchy
farci(e) – stuffed
faséole – kidney bean
faubonne – thick soup based on *St Germain* soup with a *julienne* of sautéed vegetables and chervil. Also a pheasant purée garnished with pheasant strips and truffles
faux-filet – steak cut from the top of the sirloin
faverolles – name given to many kinds of haricot beans
favorite – garnish of *foie gras*, truffles and asparagus tips for *tournedos* and *noisettes*, or for meat slices one of artichoke bottoms with celery and small *anna* or *chateau* potatoes. Also a *consommé* thickened with tapioca garnished with artichoke bottoms and mushrooms, small potato balls and chervil
fenouil – fennel
ferme – farm, farm produced; **fermier/fermiére** – garnish for meats of carrots, turnips, onions, potatoes and celery; **poulet fermier** – free-range chicken
feuillantine – sweet puff pastry strips. Also larger rectangles of puff pastry split and filled with either savoury or sweet fillings
feuille – leaf; **feuilles de capucines** – nasturtium leaves; **feuilles de limetier** – lime leaves (Far Eastern cookery); **feuilles de vignes** – vine-leaves

feuilletage – puff pastry in general
feuilleté – flaky puff pastry used in the making of pies and tarts
feuilleton – thin slices of veal layered with various stuffings or *salpicons* and braised. Also a mixture of chopped pork, veal and herbs encased in flaky pastry
fèves – broad beans
ficelle – beef fillet tied in string, browned and cooked in *consommé*. Also a thin baguette
figue – fig
figue de mer – see *violet*
filet mignon – small fillet steak
fillette – bottle (usually of house wine)
financière – poultry and sweetbread garnish of chicken quenelles, cockscombs, cock's kidneys, truffles, mushrooms and olives. Also a brown sauce flavoured with truffles, mushrooms and Madeira
fine de claire – Marennes oyster see *claire*
fines herbes – mixture of herbs usually parsley, chives and tarragon
flamande – meat garnish of cabbage, carrots, turnips and bacon. Also a method of poaching fish with light beer or a butter sauce seasoned with French mustard, lemon juice and parsley. Can be a beef *consommé* with puréed brussels sprouts, peas and chervil – see also *carbonnade à la flamande*
flammekueche – pizza-like Alsatian bacon, cream and onion flan
flan – sweet or savoury egg and milk mixture similar to a custard
flétan – halibut
fleur de sel – highest quality sea salt
fleurons – small, usually crescent-shaped, puff pastry garnishes
florentine – garnish with spinach as a main constituent
foie – liver (**foie gras** – the term applied to fattened duck or goose liver)
fondant – icing for cakes and gateaux. Also to cook until meltingly tender, eg apples, goat's cheese and *pommes fondantes*
fondue – Swiss national dish, also vegetables cooked in butter or oil until softened to a purée
forestière – meat garnish of sautéed *cèpes* or morels with bacon and *noisette* potatoes. Also a *demi-glace* sauce flavoured with sherry with sautéed mushrooms added
fouetté(e) – whipped
four – oven, as in **au four** – baked
fraiche/frais – fresh
fraicheur – freshness, crispness, coolness. Also fresh summery ingredients
fraise – strawberry
fraise des bois – wild strawberry
fraise de veau – part of a calf's gut
framboise – raspberry
frangipane – moist mixture of butter, eggs and ground almonds used as a tart filling. Also a mixture of flour, butter, milk and egg used to bind forcemeat for stuffing
frémi(e) – simmered in water
friandises – sweetmeats. See *petits fours*
frisée – curly endive (often **frisée aux lardons** – a salad with bacon bits and sometimes a poached egg)
frivolités – mixed hors d'oeuvre of moulded creams, *barquettes*, tartlets
froid(e) – cold, chilled
fromage – cheese
fromage blanc – cream cheese
fromage de tete – similar to brawn, a cold dish of pig's head, simmered then baked with spices
frotté(e) – rubbed
fruits de mer – seafood
fumé – smoked
fumet – highly concentrated meat, fish or vegetable extract
galantine – similar to a *ballotine* but always served cold; the meat, poultry or fish is cooked, stuffed and set with jellied stock

galette – round flat pastry, pancake or cake, also roundels of potato
gambas – giant prawns
garbure – thick stew of cabbage, bacon, preserved goose and/or pork simmered for several hours
garenne – rabbit warren, also used for wild rabbit
garni – garnished
gaufre – sweet waffle
gaufrette – wafer, also lattice potato crisp
gelée – jelly, usually aspic
genevoise – sauce of white roux with fish stock, parsley, mushrooms, shallots and white wine
genièvre – juniper
génoise – classic sponge of equal measures of flour, sugar and butter with vanilla and eggs
germiny – creamy sorrel soup with egg yolks
gésiers – gizzards
gibier – game
gigot – leg of lamb or mutton
gigue – haunch of venison or other game animal
gingembre – ginger
girofles – cloves
girolle – see *chanterelle*
glacé(e) – ice or iced
gougère – large choux pastry filled with a cheese mixture, served hot or cold
gousse – clove, as in **gousse d'ail** – clove of garlic. Also a pod as in pea and vanilla
gout – taste
goyave – guava
graisse – fat, lard
graisse de rognon – suet
graisserons – large pork *rillettes*
grand-duc – a fish and fowl garnish of truffles and asparagus. For fish, crayfish is also used with a *mornay* sauce
grand'mère – old-fashioned, homely cooking
grand veneur – sauce *poivrade* to which has been added venison extract, redcurrant jelly and cream. Served only with venison and furred game
granité – coarse crystalline water ice
gras/grasse – fat, fatty
gras-double – stew of tripe with ham, garlic, vegetables and herbs
gratin – dish browned under a grill or in the oven often topped with cheese or breadcrumbs
grecque – mushrooms artichokes, etc, cooked with lemon or wine vinegar with olive oil, onion, fennel, celery, thyme and coriander. Served cold
grenadier – white river fish with delicate flesh
grenadine – pomegranate syrup
grenadins – small slices of braised meat
grenouille – frog (**cuisses de grenouilles** – frogs' legs)
gribiche – cold sauce of hard-boiled egg yolks blended with olive oil, wine vinegar, gherkins, capers, parsley, chervil and tarragon
griottes/griottines – variety of bitter cherry
grondin – gurnard
gros/grosse – large
gros sel – salt crystals
groseille – currant (white or red)
groseille à maquereau – gooseberry

haché, hachis – chopped
hachis parmentier – chopped cold meat, usually roast beef, mixed with *demi-glace* and potato; sometimes served in scooped-out baked potatoes. French version of shepherd's pie
hareng – herring
haricot beurre – butter bean. Also called **haricot jaune**

haricot blanc – white bean
haricot d'Espagne – runner bean
haricot rouge – red kidney bean
haricot vert – French bean
hiver – winter
homard – lobster
houblon – hops, **jets de houblon** – hop shoots
huile – oil
huitre – oyster: see also *belons*, *claires*, *Marennes*
hure – chopped meats in aspic, particularly brawn
hydromel – mead

ile flottante – floating island. Soft poached meringue 'floating' on custard
impératrice – sweet dishes and cakes with a rice base
impérial – garnish of *foie gras*, truffles, mushrooms and *quenelles* with a Madeira sauce
infusion – herbal tea
italienne – garnish of artichoke bottoms, mushrooms and macaroni croquettes. Also a sauce of mushrooms, parsley, shallots in white wine. There is a cold sauce too of mayonnaise with mixed herbs and puréed calf's brains

jalousies – small flaky pastry cakes covered with almond paste and apricot jam
jambon – ham
jambon cru – raw, cured ham
jambon persillé – chopped ham with parsley in aspic
jardinière – garnish as well as a sauce of mixed vegetables
jarret – shin or knuckle
jésus de Morteau – pork sausage from Franche-Comté
joinville – sauce *normande* with a *coulis* of crayfish and shrimps. Also a fish garnish of mushrooms, shrimps and truffles
joue – cheek
julienne – finely shredded vegetables
jus – meat juices, gravy (unthickened) also fruit or vegetable juice
jus lié – veal stock thickened with arrowroot

kaki – persimmon, a sweet fruit eaten when deep red, soft and almost translucent
koulibiac – see *coulibiac*
kir – aperitif of dry white wine flavoured, usually, with *crème de cassis*, **kir royale** – with champagne or sparkling wine
kugelhopf – Alsatian brioche with candied fruits (many other spellings e.g. kougelhopf)

lait – milk
laitance – soft roe
laitue – lettuce
langouste – crawfish or spiny lobster
langoustines – Dublin Bay prawn, large Mediterranean prawns, scampi
langue – tongue
languedocienne – dishes from the Languedoc region. Accompanying sauces are flavoured with garlic. Also a meat garnish of aubergines, *cèpes*, tomatoes and parsley
lapereau – young rabbit
lapin – rabbit
lard – bacon
lardons – pieces or strips of fried bacon
laurier – bay (leaf)
lavande – lavender
léger, légère – light
légume – vegetable
lentilles du Puy – tiny bluish-green lentils from Puy
lentins de chene – shiitake mushrooms

liégeois – **café liégeois** is a dessert of coffee, ice cream and whipped cream. Also cooking with juniper berries
lieu – fish of the cod family, **lieu jaune** – pollack, **lieu noir** – coley
lièvre – hare
limande – lemon sole, dab
limousine – red cabbage with bacon fat and chestnuts used as a garnish
lisette – small mackerel
longchamp – soup of shredded sorrel, vermicelli and peas
longe – loin
lotte – monkfish
loup de mer – sea bass
lyonnaise – name for specialities of the Lyons region – tripe, omelettes, sausages. A region also famed for its onions and potatoes. Methods of preparation with fried or braised onions the major constituent

macédoine – mixture of diced raw or cooked fruit or vegetables
mache – lamb's lettuce
macis – mace
maconnaise – meat dish flavoured with red wine
madeleine – small oval sponge cake with a fluted base. Also a garnish for meat of artichoke bottoms, sauce *soubise* and puréed white haricot beans, or a garnish for fish of cream sauce with crayfish butter and celeriac
Madère – Madeira
magret – breast fillet of duck
maigre – lean (of meat) or low fat (of cheese)
maintenon – sauce *soubise*, *béchamel*, egg yolks and mushrooms. Also a garnish of sliced mushrooms in a thick onion purée with cream and truffles
maïs – sweetcorn
maison – house, refers to home-made as in **de (la) maison** – of the house
maitre d'hotel – butter blended with parsley, lemon juice, salt and pepper
malakoff – an almond pastry
maltaise – name given to preparations using the juice of oranges, especially blood oranges
manche de gigot – knuckle of leg of lamb
mandarine – mandarin orange liqueur
mangue – mango
maquereau – mackerel, also *lisette* when small
maraichère – market-garden style. A garnish for roasted and braised meats of braised small onions, stuffed cucumber, salsify and artichokes. Also a dish of veal cutlets sautéed in butter served with salsify and brussels sprouts
marbré(e) – marbled
marc – strong spirit distilled from grape pips, skins etc
marcassin – young wild boar
marchand de vin – similar to *bordelaise* sauce. See also *beurre marchand de vin*
Marengo – veal or chicken stewed with tomato, olives, white wine and mushrooms
Marennes – oysters from the port of the same name
marguéry – hollandaise flavoured with a purée of oysters and fish extract
mariné – marinated
marinière – fish or shellfish, particularly mussels, cooked in white wine with shallots and parsley
marjolaine – marjoram. Also a multilayered chocolate and nut cake
marmelade – thick, sweetened fruit purée (or onion purée). Not to be confused with orange marmalade (*confiture d'oranges*)
marmite – metal or earthenware covered pot used for serving soups. Also, as in **petite marmite**, a clear, strong broth which should contain oxtail, poultry, root vegetables and bone marrow. Garnished with diced bread and grated cheese
marmite dieppoise – stew of fish and shellfish with wine, leeks and cream
marquise – a very rich chocolate mousse with or without a thin plain sponge casing, or a garnish of calf's marrow with asparagus, truffles and sauce *suprême*. Also a hollandaise with caviar added just before serving

marron – chestnut
marseillaise – mayonnaise mixed with sea-urchin purée. Also a meat garnish of olives, anchovy stuffed tomatoes, potato chips and *provençale* sauce
massepain – marzipan
matelote – a rich fish stew made with red or white wine. Freshwater fish is more usual although matelote à la *normande* uses sea fish with cider instead of wine. Not to be confused with a matelot!
méchoui – North African cooking – long-cooked roast lamb
médaillon – thin round of meat
mélange – mixture or blend
méli-mélo – jumble or mixture
menthe – mint
merguez – spicy lamb sausage
merlan – whiting
merle – blackbird
merlu/merluche – hake
merluchon – codling
mesclun – salad of many different salad leaves
meunière – fried in butter
meurette – **oeuf en m.**, a dish of eggs poached in red wine, garlic, onions and bacon bits served with fried bread
mi cru-mi cuit – half raw – half cooked
miel – honey
mignardise – *petit four*
mignonette – coarsely ground white pepper or a mixture of white and black pepper
mignons – small cuts from the ends of a fillet
mijoté – simmered
millefeuille – thousand leaves. Layers of puff pastry with sweet or savoury filling. Sometimes used to describe other multi-layered dishes
mirabelle – small, golden yellow plum used in cooking and the manufacture of an ***eau de vie***
mirepoix – very small dice of vegetables sometimes with ham or belly pork
mirliton – twirl
miroir – name given to dishes with a polished, mirror-like finish
mitonné – simmered under cover in an oven
mocha, moka – name given to any preparation flavoured with coffee
moëlle – bone marrow
moelleux – soft, creamy, similar to *fondant*
mollet – soft or soft-boiled eggs
mont blanc – rich puréed chestnut dessert with crème *chantilly*
morceau – small piece
morille – morel mushroom
mornay – *béchamel* sauce with cheese
morue – salt cod. See *brandade de morue*; **morue fraiche** – fresh cod
moruette – young cod
mouclade – mussels in a creamy white wine sauce with herbs
mouette – gull
moules – mussels
mousseline – preparations to which whipped cream has been added. The sauce comprises hollandaise mixed with an equal amount of stiffly whipped cream and warmed gently
mousseron – St George's agaric, a small field mushroom
mousseux – sparkling (as in wine) or a light and frothy sauce of butter, cream and egg yolks accompanying fish
moutarde – mustard
mouton – sheep
moyen – medium
mulet – grey mullet
mure – blackberry
muscade – nutmeg
museau – muzzle
myrtille – bilberry

nage – aromatic *court bouillon* with vegetables used for cooking fish or shellfish
nantaise – chicken sautéed with root vegetables and white wine served with onions, carrots, mushrooms, artichoke hearts and hollandaise sauce
nantua – cream sauce made with crayfish butter and tomato purée. Prawns sometimes substitute for crayfish
nappé – masked or covered
navarin – a mutton stew with onions and potatoes. With other root vegetables it is a *ragout à la printanière*. Also a soup of puréed peas with crayfish tails and parsley
navet – turnip
neige – snow, as in **oeufs à la neige**/*ile flottante* – soft poached meringue on custard
nem – small Vietnamese spring roll
nesselrode – name given to several preparations including fillets of fish stuffed with a pike and lobster forcemeat in puff pastry, served with a lobster sauce and oysters. Also a soup of puréed woodcock and chestnuts, garnished with woodcock quenelles and croutons. An iced pudding of maraschino-flavoured custard mixed with chestnut purée, candied peel, crystallised fruit soaked in Malaga wine frozen in a charlotte mould and served with *marrons glacés*
newburg – sliced cooked lobster or other seafood sautéed in butter with brandy or Madeira with paprika, cream and egg yolks added. Also a sauce for boiled, baked or grilled shellfish of butter, brandy and Marsala, cream and paprika with egg yolks added and a dice of lobster coral if served with lobster
niçoise – name for dishes which contain tomato and garlic, anchovies, capers and olives, soups being garnished with tomato, chervil and green beans
nid – nest
noisette – hazelnut or round slice of meat from the fillet or rib of lamb or other meat e.g. venison. Also applies to small rounded shapes. **Pommes noisette** – small potato balls fried in butter till golden brown
noix – nut or walnut
noix de coco – coconut
normande – meat or fish cooked with apple cider or calvados. Also a method of cooking partridge in a casserole on a bed of stewed apples
norvégienne – the name for several savoury preparations including a thick cream soup of puréed swedes garnished with a *julienne* of beetroot, and poached salmon garnished with prawns, cucumber *timbales* filled with smoked salmon purée, eggs stuffed with shrimp *mousseline* and served with Russian sauce. **Omelette à la norvégienne/omelette surprise** – baked Alaska
nouilles – noodles

oeuf – egg
oeuf à la coque – soft boiled egg in its shell
oeufs brouillés – scrambled eggs
oeuf dur – hard-boiled egg
oeuf en meurette – see *meurette*
oeuf mollet – soft-boiled egg with its shell removed
oeuf poché – poached egg
oeuf sur le plat – fried egg
offert – complimentary
oie – goose
omble chevalier – char, also known as **ombre chevalier**
onglet – cut of beef – the skirt, used primarily in *carbonnades*
oreille – ear
oreiller – pillow
orge perlé – pearl barley
ortolan – European bunting
os – bone, **sur** or **à l'os** – on the bone
oseille – sorrel
oursin – sea urchin

paillard – thin slice, usually applied to veal
paille – straw, as in **pommes paille** – deep-fried straw potatoes
paillettes – long, fine sticks of vegetables especially potatoes or flavoured pastry sticks
pain – bread
pain complet – wholemeal bread
pain d'épice – spiced bread
pain perdu – *brioche* or crustless slices of bread soaked in egg and milk and fried in butter
paleron – chuck (of beef)
palmier – sweet icing sugar-coated puff pastry, often heart-shaped
paloise – *béarnaise* sauce flavoured with mint instead of tarragon, or a mint-flavoured hollandaise
palombe – wild pigeon
palourde – type of clam
pamplemousse – grapefruit
pan bagna – bread soaked in olive oil and filled with a mixture of anchovies,
panaché – mixed or mixture, also shandy
panais – parsnip
olives, peppers and onions
pané – breaded
panier – basket
pannequet – pancake
papillote – en papillote – to cook in a paper bag or aluminium foil
Paques – Easter
parfait – used to describe a creamy savoury mousse. Also an iced sweet akin to ice cream and usually suffixed by **glacé**. They are of a single flavour only
Paris-Brest – ring-shaped choux pastry sprinkled with almonds and filled with praline cream
parisienne – small balls of potato tossed in dissolved meat jelly and sprinkled with parsley
parmentier – preparations with potato. **Pommes parmentier** are cubed potatoes cooked in butter. Also puréed potatoes, as in *hachis parmentier*. The name given to potatoes cooked with the meat with which they are served
parsemé(e) – sprinkled
passe-pierres – type of seaweed, often pickled
pastèque – water-melon
pastilla – Moroccan dish of layers of wafer-thin pastry and (usually) pigeon, with spices and sugar
pate – general term for pastry including pasta, as in pates fraiches (fresh pasta)
pate brisée – short-crust pastry
pate d'amandes – marzipan
pate feuilletée – flaky pastry
pate frolle – short crust pastry with almonds and egg used for flans and sweet pies
pate moulée – raised pie pastry
pate sucrée – sweet rich shortcrust pastry, made with sugar, eggs and vanilla
patelle – limpet
paupiette – thin slice of meat or fish (usually sole) rolled around a forcemeat or mousse and braised
pavé – flat cut of meat or fish. Also a cold pie or mousse set in a square or rectangular mould
pavot – poppy, **graines de pavot** – poppy seeds
paysanne – as *fermière*
peche – peach
perdreau – young partridge, **perdrix** – partridge
périgourdine – name given to dishes garnished with truffle and *foie gras*
périgueux – classic sauce with chopped truffles and Madeira
persil – parsley
persillade – mixture of parsley and other chopped herbs
persillé(e) – parsleyed

pétillante – slightly sparkling (of wine or water)
petit déjeuner – breakfast
petit gris – variety of snail, also a name for *chanterelle* mushrooms
petit salé – salt pork or bacon, usually served with lentils or cabbage
petits fours – general name given to the selection of tartlets and small pastries served at the end of a meal
pétoncle – small scallop
pholiottes – thick orange fungus found in the South of France
pichet – jug or pitcher
pied – trotter
pied de cheval – large oyster
pied de mouton – sheep's trotter, also a variety of wild mushroom
pignon – pine kernel
pilon – drumstick (of poultry)
pilpil – Basque dish of salt cod with garlic
piment – pimento, hot pepper, chili
pimenté(e) – hot, spicy
piment doux – sweet pepper
pintade – guinea fowl, **pintadeau** – a young bird
pipérade – Basque speciality of green peppers, onions, tomatoes, garlic and basil stewed in oil and thickened with beaten eggs
piquant(e) – spicy
piqué(e) – spiked
pissaladière – Provençal dish with a pizza-like base and a topping of onions, anchovies and olives
pissenlit – dandelion
pistache – pistachio nut
pistou – French version of Italian pesto used in **soupe au pistou**
pithiviers – rich puff pastry cake usually filled with almond paste but also can be of chocolate. Savoury versions also
plat du jour – dish of the day, **sur le plat** – cooked and served on a plate or in a shallow dish
plate – native European oyster with a flat, smooth, often round shell. Also still, of table water
plateau – large platter
plateau de fruits de mer – large platter of various shellfish
pleurote – oyster mushroom
plie – plaice, also a fold
poché(e) – poached
pochouse – freshwater fish stew
poelé – pan-fried
à point – medium-rare (steak)
pointe – tip (as in asparagus tip)
poire – pear
poireau – leek
pois – peas, also **petits pois** (garden peas) **pois gourmands** (snow peas)
pois-chiches – chick peas
poisson – fish
poitrine – breast (in lamb) or belly (in pork)
poivrade – richly-flavoured peppery sauce
poivre – pepper
poivré – peppered
poivron – sweet pepper
pomme – apple, sometimes **pomme fruit** to distinguish it from *pomme de terre* (potato)
pommes en l'air – fried apple-rings
pommes fondantes – potatoes baked in stock, the tops allowed to become golden brown
pommes frites – French fried potatoes
pomme de terre – potato, sometimes just **pommes**
Pont-Neuf – as in **pommes Pont-Neuf** – extra thick French fried potatoes

porcelet – suckling pig
potage – thick soup
pot-au-feu – dish of boiled meat and vegetables. When chicken is used it is known as *poule-au-pot*
potée – rich meat and vegetable stew usually made with pork and cabbage
potiron – pumpkin
pouce – thumb, **à prendre sur le pouce** – quick snack or bite to eat
poule-au-pot – chicken, usually stuffed, simmered in a pot with vegetables
poularde, poule, poulet – fattened hen or chicken, boiling fowl and spring chicken respectively
poulette – young chicken, also a *velouté sauce* with lemon juice, parsley and enriched with egg yolks; **moules poulette** – moules (mussels) *marinière* with the addition of cream
poulpe – octopus
pourpier – purslane (a salad herb)
pourpre/pourprion – octopus
poussin – very small chicken or spring chicken
poutargue – dried mullet or tuna roe, also *boutargue*
praire – clam
praline – crumbed or ground mixture of caramel and almonds
praliné(e) – praline or toasted almond-flavoured
pré-salé – name given to lamb reared on salt marshes
pression – as in **bière (à la) pression** – draught beer
princesse – asparagus tip garnish
printanière – usually a garnish of mixed young vegetables
printemps – spring
provençale – name given to certain dishes which include garlic and often tomatoes and olive oil
prune – plum
pruneau – prune

quasi – chump end of loin
quenelle – very light, poached mousse
quetsch – variety of plum, used as the base for an *eau-de-vie* as well as in tarts
queue – tail (**queue de boeuf** is oxtail)
quiche lorraine – savoury egg custard flan with onion and bacon

rable – saddle, as in **rable de lièvre** – saddle of hare
radis – radish
radis noir – black radish
rafraichi(e) – chilled, cool
ragout – stew
raie – skate, **raie au beure noir (noisette)** – poached skate served with black (browned) butter and capers
raifort – horseradish
raisin – grape
raisins de Corinthe – currants
raisins de Smyrne – sultanas
rapé(e) – grated
rascasse – scorpion or hog fish – a constituent of *bouillabaisse*
rave – turnip
ravigote – highly seasoned white sauce served hot or cold
rechauffé(e) – reheated, or a dish made with ready cooked ingredients
régence – sauce *normande* for fish prepared with white wine, mushrooms and truffles. For chicken a *supreme* sauce is used
réglisse – liquorice
reine-claude – greengage
reinette – variety of apple
reinette giroflée – clove (spice)
religieuse – cake made with choux pastry
rémoulade – mayonnaise with chopped chervil, tarragon, spring onions, gherkins, capers, parsley and sometimes anchovy essence if served with cold fish

renne – reindeer
rhum – rum
rillettes – potted meat or fish, served cold
rillons – well-browned pieces of pork breast
ripopée – slow-simmered dish of various beef cuts
ris – as in **ris de veau** – sweetbreads
rissolé(e) – fried or browned
riz – rice
robert – classic brown sauce
rognon – kidney
rognons blancs – lamb's testicles
rognons de coq – cockerel's gonads, sometimes also red kidney beans
Romanoff – usually applied to strawberries with *chantilly* cream and curaçao liqueur
romarin – rosemary
rosette – large pork sausage from the Lyons region
rossini – garnish for *tournedos* and *noisettes* of *foie gras*, truffles and *demi-glace* with truffle extract and Madeira
roti(e) – roast
rouelle – round slice
rouennaise – dish of roast duck stuffed with its liver, the sauce thickened with its blood. Also fried, stuffed sheep's trotters
rouget – red mullet, also called **rouget-barbet**
rouille – fiery sauce served with Mediterranean fish soup. It is an *aïoli* made with pounded chilis and lobster coral (though tomato is sometimes used to make it pink)
roulade – 'Swiss roll' with sweet or savoury filling
roulé(e) – rolled
roussette – rock salmon
royale – poultry or fish with a cream sauce and truffles. **Lièvre à la royale** – boned and stuffed hare braised in red wine and brandy
rubané(e) – ribboned, striped
rumsteak – rump steak

sabayon – thin custard made with white wine instead of milk, sweet and savoury uses
sablé – usually a thin, circular rich shortbread-like biscuit often layered with fresh fruit and *chantilly* cream. Savoury **sablés** are made with cheese
sabodet – pig's head sausage
safran – saffron
saignant – very rare, bloody (usually applies to steaks)
Saint Germain – thick soup made with fresh peas. Also the name of a garnish whose principal ingredient is fresh peas
Saint Honoré – choux pastry gateau filled with *crème patissière*
Saint Jacques – scallop – short for **coquille Saint-Jacques**
Saint Pierre – John Dory
saison – season, **saisonier/saisonière** seasonal
salé – salted
salicorne – marsh samphire, sea asparagus
salmigondis – ragout of reheated meats
salmis – a stew of poultry or game birds
salpicon – diced meat, fish, fruit or vegetables bound in a sauce
sandre – zander, pike-perch
sanglier – wild boar. See also *marcassin*
sarladaise – potatoes cooked in goose fat with garlic. Also a garnish for lamb of truffles and diced potatoes cooked with thick gravy
sarriette – summer savory, a herb
saucisse – sausage
saucisson sec – salami
sauge – sage
saumon – salmon

sauté – lightly browned or fried
saupiquet – piquant sauce
sauvage – wild
savarin – yeasted cake usually in the form of a ring, soaked in rum or kirsch-flavoured syrup. Larger version of a *baba*
savoyarde – as *dauphinoise* but with stock instead of milk or cream and no garlic
sec/sèche – dry
seiche – squid or cuttlefish
seigle – rye
sel – salt
selle – saddle (of lamb)
semoule – semolina
sérieuse – serious, large glass (of beer)
service compris – service included
sirop d' érable – maple syrup
soissons – large white haricot beans
soubise – name given to dishes including onions in their preparation. The sauce is an onion purée mixed with *béchamel*
souris – simmered very gently, also knuckle of lamb
spätzli – German noodles also **spätzel**
suppions – tiny squid
supreme – usually a breast (of poultry). Also a *velouté* sauce with cream and mushroom extract

tablier de sapeur – Lyonnais dish of tripe cooked in bouillon, then fried in egg and breadcrumbs
tagine – North African stew made in an earthenware dish of the same name
tapénade – Provençal purée of capers, black olives, anchovies and olive oil
tarbais – Tarbes haricot beans
tarte tartin – caramelised upside-down apple tart
tartine – slice of bread with various toppings
terroir – soil, **cuisine du terroir** – regional country cooking
tete de veau/porc – calf/pig's head, as in brawn
thé – tea
thermidor, homard – lobster dish with a *bercy* sauce mixed with English mustard and parmesan, served in the shell
thon – tuna
tian – typical *Niçois* dish: any mixture cooked in layers in a gratin dish
tiède – warm
tilleuil – lime tree, leaf and/or blossom
timbale – thimble-shaped mould usually of pasta, rice or vegetable purées; also a double container, for the dining table, the lower part containing hot water or ice to keep the contents of the upper part hot or cold respectively
tisane – herbal tea
topinambour – Jerusalem artichoke
torchon – cooking method (commonly for *foie gras*) involving wrapping in muslin and poaching in stock
tournedos – small round fillet steak
tourte – covered tart
tourteau – large crab
tout-épicé – all spice
tranche – slice
trevise – red chicory (radicchio)
tripes à la mode de Caen – tripe cooked with vegetables, cider and calvados
tripous – Auvergne dish of small, stuffed cushions of sheep's or calf's tripe, also stuffed sheep's trotters
tronçon – chunk, also a *darne*
truffe – truffle
truite – trout, **truite saumonée** – salmon trout
ttoro – fish stew of Basque provenance, with garlic, onion and tomato
tuile – very thin almond biscuit

turban – combination of ingredients cooked in a ring mould
unilatéral – method of sautéeing fish slices skin-side down only

vacherin – meringue ring filled with *chantilly* cream and fruit and/or ice cream
Vallée d'Auge – garnish of cooked apples with cream and calvados
vapeur – steam
VDQS – vin délimité de qualité supérieure
veau – veal
velouté – white sauce made with veal or chicken stock
venaison – venison
ventrèche – cured pork breast
vénus – type of clam
vergeoise – brown or coloured sugar
verjus – juice from unripe grapes
vermit – large clam
véronique – garnish of white grapes
vert/verte – green, also *sauce verte* – mayonnaise blended with pounded spinach, watercress and parsley
vert-pré – watercress garnish
verveine – verbena
vessie – **en vessie** is to cook in a bladder
viande – meat
vichy – garnish of glazed carrots
vichyssoise – creamy leek and potato soup garnished with chives, often served chilled
vierge – frothy blend of butter whipped with lemon juice, salt and pepper; virgin (olive oil)
vieux/vieille – old
vignot – winkle, periwinkle
villeroy – *velouté* sauce with truffle essence often used as a coating before deep-frying in egg and breadcrumbs
vinaigre – vinegar
vin jaune – yellow wine from the Jura, used in sauce-making and for cooking poultry and other light meats
violet – an almost inedible mollusc, also known as *figue de mer*
volaille – poultry or fowl
à volonté – ad lib (eat as much as you like)

walewska – garnish for poached fish of mornay sauce, lobster and truffles
waterzooi – Belgian speciality of chicken or fish simmered with vegetables and white wine
witloof – white Belgian chicory

xérès – sherry

yaourt – yoghurt

zéphir – any light or frothy dish, sometimes applied to light mousses or mousselines
zingara – garnish of ham, tongue, mushrooms and truffles in *demi-glace* flavoured with tomato and tarragon

Glossary compiled by Mario Wyn-Jones

Index

Readers' Comments

Please use this sheet, and the continuation overleaf, to recommend establishments of **really outstanding quality. Complaints** about any of the Guide's entries will be treated seriously and passed on to our inspectorate, but we would like to remind you always to take up your complaint with the management at the time. We regret that owing to the volume of readers' communications received each year we will be unable to acknowledge these forms, but your comments will certainly be considered.

Please post to: Egon Ronay's Guides, 35 Tadema Road, London SW10 0PZ.
Alternatively, send your comments by fax on 0171 376 5071 (ref. Paris 1996).
Please use an up-to-date Guide. We publish annually (Paris 1996).

Name and address of establishment	**Your recommendation or complaint**

Name and address of establishment	Your recommendation or complaint

Your name and address (BLOCK CAPITALS PLEASE)

Readers' Comments

Please use this sheet, and the continuation overleaf, to recommend establishments of **really outstanding quality. Complaints** about any of the Guide's entries will be treated seriously and passed on to our inspectorate, but we would like to remind you always to take up your complaint with the management at the time. We regret that owing to the volume of readers' communications received each year we will be unable to acknowledge these forms, but your comments will certainly be considered.

Please post to: Egon Ronay's Guides, 35 Tadema Road, London SW10 0PZ.
Alternatively, send your comments by fax on 0171 376 5071 (ref. Paris 1996).
Please use an up-to-date Guide. We publish annually

Name and address of establishment	**Your recommendation or complaint**

Name and address of establishment	Your recommendation or complaint

Your name and address (BLOCK CAPITALS PLEASE)

Readers' Comments

Please use this sheet, and the continuation overleaf, to recommend establishments of **really outstanding quality. Complaints** about any of the Guide's entries will be treated seriously and passed on to our inspectorate, but we would like to remind you always to take up your complaint with the management at the time. We regret that owing to the volume of readers' communications received each year we will be unable to acknowledge these forms, but your comments will certainly be considered.

Please post to: Egon Ronay's Guides, 35 Tadema Road, London SW10 0PZ.
Alternatively, send your comments by fax on 0171 376 5071 (ref. Paris 1996).
Please use an up-to-date Guide. We publish annually

Name and address of establishment	**Your recommendation or complaint**

Name and address of establishment

Your recommendation or complaint

Your name and address (BLOCK CAPITALS PLEASE)

Readers' Comments

Please use this sheet, and the continuation overleaf, to recommend establishments of **really outstanding quality. Complaints** about any of the Guide's entries will be treated seriously and passed on to our inspectorate, but we would like to remind you always to take up your complaint with the management at the time. We regret that owing to the volume of readers' communications received each year we will be unable to acknowledge these forms, but your comments will certainly be considered.

Please post to: Egon Ronay's Guides, 35 Tadema Road, London SW10 0PZ.
Alternatively, send your comments by fax on 0171 376 5071 (ref. Paris 1996).
Please use an up-to-date Guide. We publish annually

Name and address of establishment	**Your recommendation or complaint**

Name and address of establishment

Your recommendation or complaint

Your name and address (BLOCK CAPITALS PLEASE)

Readers' Comments

Please use this sheet, and the continuation overleaf, to recommend establishments of **really outstanding quality. Complaints** about any of the Guide's entries will be treated seriously and passed on to our inspectorate, but we would like to remind you always to take up your complaint with the management at the time. We regret that owing to the volume of readers' communications received each year we will be unable to acknowledge these forms, but your comments will certainly be considered.

Please post to: Egon Ronay's Guides, 35 Tadema Road, London SW10 0PZ.
Alternatively, send your comments by fax on 0171 376 5071 (ref. Paris 1996).
Please use an up-to-date Guide. We publish annually

Name and address of establishment	**Your recommendation or complaint**

Name and address of establishment	Your recommendation or complaint

Your name and address (BLOCK CAPITALS PLEASE)

Readers' Comments

Please use this sheet, and the continuation overleaf, to recommend establishments of **really outstanding quality. Complaints** about any of the Guide's entries will be treated seriously and passed on to our inspectorate, but we would like to remind you always to take up your complaint with the management at the time. We regret that owing to the volume of readers' communications received each year we will be unable to acknowledge these forms, but your comments will certainly be considered.

Please post to: Egon Ronay's Guides, 35 Tadema Road, London SW10 0PZ.
Alternatively, send your comments by fax on 0171 376 5071 (ref. Paris 1996).
Please use an up-to-date Guide. We publish annually

Name and address of establishment	**Your recommendation or complaint**

Name and address of establishment	Your recommendation or complaint

Your name and address (BLOCK CAPITALS PLEASE)

READERS' COMMENTS

Please use this sheet, and the continuation overleaf, to recommend establishments of **really outstanding quality. Complaints** about any of the Guide's entries will be treated seriously and passed on to our inspectorate, but we would like to remind you always to take up your complaint with the management at the time. We regret that owing to the volume of readers' communications received each year we will be unable to acknowledge these forms, but your comments will certainly be considered.

Please post to: Egon Ronay's Guides, 35 Tadema Road, London SW10 0PZ.
Alternatively, send your comments by fax on 0171 376 5071 (ref. Paris 1996).
Please use an up-to-date Guide. We publish annually

Name and address of establishment	**Your recommendation or complaint**

Name and address of establishment	Your recommendation or complaint

Your name and address (BLOCK CAPITALS PLEASE)

Readers' Comments

Please use this sheet, and the continuation overleaf, to recommend establishments of **really outstanding quality. Complaints** about any of the Guide's entries will be treated seriously and passed on to our inspectorate, but we would like to remind you always to take up your complaint with the management at the time. We regret that owing to the volume of readers' communications received each year we will be unable to acknowledge these forms, but your comments will certainly be considered.

Please post to: Egon Ronay's Guides, 35 Tadema Road, London SW10 0PZ.
Alternatively, send your comments by fax on 0171 376 5071 (ref. Paris 1996).
Please use an up-to-date Guide. We publish annually

Name and address of establishment	**Your recommendation or complaint**

Name and address of establishment	Your recommendation or complaint

Your name and address (BLOCK CAPITALS PLEASE)

Readers' Comments

Please use this sheet, and the continuation overleaf, to recommend establishments of **really outstanding quality. Complaints** about any of the Guide's entries will be treated seriously and passed on to our inspectorate, but we would like to remind you always to take up your complaint with the management at the time. We regret that owing to the volume of readers' communications received each year we will be unable to acknowledge these forms, but your comments will certainly be considered.

Please post to: Egon Ronay's Guides, 35 Tadema Road, London SW10 0PZ.
Alternatively, send your comments by fax on 0171 376 5071 (ref. Paris 1996).
Please use an up-to-date Guide. We publish annually

Name and address of establishment	**Your recommendation or complaint**

Name and address of establishment

Your recommendation or complaint

Your name and address (BLOCK CAPITALS PLEASE)

READERS' COMMENTS

Please use this sheet, and the continuation overleaf, to recommend establishments of **really outstanding quality. Complaints** about any of the Guide's entries will be treated seriously and passed on to our inspectorate, but we would like to remind you always to take up your complaint with the management at the time. We regret that owing to the volume of readers' communications received each year we will be unable to acknowledge these forms, but your comments will certainly be considered.

Please post to: Egon Ronay's Guides, 35 Tadema Road, London SW10 0PZ.
Alternatively, send your comments by fax on 0171 376 5071 (ref. Paris 1996).
Please use an up-to-date Guide. We publish annually

Name and address of establishment	**Your recommendation or complaint**

Name and address of establishment

Your recommendation or complaint

Your name and address (BLOCK CAPITALS PLEASE)